Beginning DB2

From Novice to Professional

Grant Allen

Apress®

Beginning DB2: From Novice to Professional

Copyright © 2008 by Grant Allen

Softcover re-print of the Hardcover 1st edition 2008

ISBN-13: 978-1-4842-2041-2

ISBN-10: 1-4842-2041-2

ISBN-13 (electronic): 978-1-4302-0548-7

ISBN-10 (electronic): 1-4302-0548-2

DOI 10.1007/978-1-4302-0548-7

Lead Editor: Jonathan Gennick
Technical Reviewer: Fred Sobotka
Editorial Board: Clay Andres, Steve Anglin, Ewan Buckingham, Tony Campbell, Gary Cornell, Jonathan Gennick, Matthew Moodie, Joseph Ottinger, Jeffrey Pepper, Frank Pohlmann, Ben Renow-Clarke, Dominic Shakeshaft, Matt Wade, Tom Welsh
Project Manager: Kylie Johnston
Copy Editor: Nancy Sixsmith, ConText Editorial Services, Inc.
Associate Production Director: Kari Brooks-Copony
Production Editor: Kelly Winquist
Compositor: Diana Van Winkle
Proofreader: Linda Seifert
Indexer: Becky Hornyak
Artist: Diana Van Winkle
Cover Designer: Kurt Krames
Manufacturing Director: Tom Debolski

Distributed to the book trade worldwide by Springer-Verlag New York, Inc., 233 Spring Street, 6th Floor, New York, NY 10013. Phone 1-800-SPRINGER, fax 201-348-4505, e-mail orders-ny@springer-sbm.com, or visit http://www.springeronline.com.

For information on translations, please contact Apress directly at 2855 Telegraph Avenue, Suite 600, Berkeley, CA 94705. Phone 510-549-5930, fax 510-549-5939, e-mail info@apress.com, or visit http://www.apress.com.

Apress and friends of ED books may be purchased in bulk for academic, corporate, or promotional use. eBook versions and licenses are also available for most titles. For more information, reference our Special Bulk Sales—eBook Licensing web page at http://www.apress.com/info/bulksales.

The source code for this book is available to readers at http://www.apress.com.

For Lindsay, who laughed at all the right times.

Contents at a Glance

PART 1 ■■■ Getting Started

PART 2 ■■■ Beginning Administration with DB2 Express Edition

PART 3 ■■■ Database Fundamentals with DB2 Express Edition

PART 4 ▪▪▪ Programming with DB2 Express Edition

PART 5 ▪▪▪ Ongoing Database Administration with DB2

Contents

PART 1 ■■■ Getting Started

PART 2 ■ ■ ■ Beginning Administration with DB2 Express Edition

PART 3 ▪▪▪ Database Fundamentals with DB2 Express Edition

PART 4 ▪▪▪ Programming with DB2 Express Edition

PART 5 ■■■ Ongoing Database Administration with DB2

About the Author

GRANT ALLEN has worked in the IT field for nearly 20 years, most recently as Chief Technology Officer for a leading Australian software vendor, before taking on his current role at Google. His work has involved private enterprise, academia, and government around the world—consulting on large-scale systems design, development, performance, data warehousing, content management, and collaboration. Grant is a frequent speaker at conferences and industry events on topics such as data mining, compliance, relational databases, collaboration technologies, the business of technology, and more. He is now a team leader at Google, using database technologies to tackle problems of Google-scale and beyond.

About the Technical Reviewer

 **FRED SOBOTKA** is a database consultant with FRS Consulting. He began his software industry career in 1990 and started using DB2 in 1996. Fred helps businesses get the most out of DB2 for Linux, UNIX, and Windows. He is an award-winning IDUG speaker and the leader of NODE, a regional DB2 users group. Fred has written about DB2 for the *IDUG Solutions Journal* and *DB2 Magazine*, and regularly updates a DB2 blog he started in 2004. He enjoys the local coffee and bicycle paths of Portland, Oregon, where he lives with his wife, Allison, and their houseplant, Hector. Fred can be reached at fred@frsconsulting.com.

Acknowledgments

Thanks to all my family and friends who supported me along the way, and kept the humor up when it was most needed. Thanks to the members of the IBM team, who have just chalked up 25 years and make DB2 the awesome database technology it is today. Amazing!

Introduction

Welcome to *Beginning DB2: From Novice to Professional*. This book—which is all about the DB2 relational database management system for Linux, UNIX, and Windows—is designed to get anyone started on the road to mastering DB2. *Beginning DB2* is not designed to be a complete reference library for DB2; DB2 is far too large a piece of software for any one book to cover every advanced feature and option. But *Beginning DB2* is designed to capture the state of the art in DB2 capabilities and technology, presenting a comprehensive set of introductory and gradually more advanced material to allow anyone to be up and working with DB2 in no time.

Who This Book Is For

This book is for everyone. No, really! I'll even be sending a copy to my mother. Instead of writing a book just for database administrators, or database developers, or even developers of web and desktop systems that want to use a database, I wrote *Beginning DB2* to capture what you need to work DB2 into any environment or development project. Whether you're a web developer, project manager, avid blogger, or podcasting star, *Beginning DB2* will help you take your database work to the next level.

How This Book Is Structured

This book is split into five parts, each designed to help you master certain aspects of DB2:

- **Part 1** deals with DB2's heritage and shows you how to acquire and install your own copy of DB2.

- **Part 2** discusses the great tools that come with DB2 out of the box.

- **Part 3** leaps into the wide world of Structured Query Language (SQL) and treats you to the depth and breadth of DB2's SQL capabilities.

- **Part 4** takes a tour of the fantastic developer options IBM adds to DB2 for languages such as Ruby, PHP, Java, C#, Python, and more.

- **Part 5** covers the all-important administrative details that will make you a database administrator "par excellence" with DB2.

Conventions

I tried to keep the conventions in this book very simple. Where a piece of code is used, it is presented in fixed-width Courier font, such as this (working) example:

```
select * from sysibm.sysdummy1
```

For syntax descriptions and other technical elements, I use the same font for clarity, but have endeavored to use a conversational style to discuss the meaning and use of commands and technology. This helps you reach a better understanding in a shorter period of time. More importantly, it also saves trees because you don't need to buy a book that repeats the great reference material for DB2 that you can find online.

Prerequisites

There are very few prerequisites you'll need to get the most out of this book. In fact, there's nothing stopping you from reading the book without installing DB2 and trying the examples. But I'll take a wild guess that you *want* to do that, so you'll need a computer with a supported Linux distribution, such as CentOS, OpenSuSE, or the like; or Microsoft Windows XP or Vista. Exact versions and instructions on downloading the edition of DB2 suitable for you are in Chapter 1 and Chapter 2.

Downloading the Code

Examples and code snippets used in the book will be available in zip file format in the Downloads section of the Apress website (www.apress.com). The author has also set up the site www.beginningdb2.com, where the examples can also be obtained.

Contacting the Author

Any questions, comments, or errata can be sent to the author at grantondata@gmail.com, or visit the book's website at www.beginningdb2.com or the author's website at www.grantondata.com.

PART 1

###

Getting Started

CHAPTER 1

■ ■ ■

What Is DB2 and Where Can I Get It?

If you've ever wondered how easy it would be to learn DB2, one of the world's most mature and powerful relational databases, the answer is this: very easy! *Beginning DB2: From Novice to Professional* covers every aspect of the fundamentals of DB2 for Linux, UNIX, and Windows. The book will help you to quickly move from beginner to confident professional in using the power of DB2 to develop desktop and web applications, manage and administer DB2 databases, and take charge of your data as never before. It quickly builds your expertise so you can tackle new and existing software projects with the backing of IBM's leading database technology. In no time you'll power ahead, realizing your dreams of the next MySpace, YouTube, or Flickr.

Who Should Read This Book?

Everyone! Well, nearly everyone. This book is not designed to be a boring technical dissertation on the internal design of DB2, the minutiae of Structured Query Language (SQL) syntax, or the elegance of relational set theory.

This book will teach you the essentials of DB2, using DB2 as the storage and processing foundation for a range of applications that should get you thinking about what it can do for you. You'll learn the practical side of managing DB2 and the data it hosts, you'll feel comfortable and confident with database administration tasks, and you'll know when to relax and let the DB2 automated features do the heavy lifting for you. This book also shows how easy it is to build desktop and web-based applications such as blog hosting services, video catalogs, discussion forums, and social networking sites.

So if you're a PHP developer, a Ruby magician, keen on project management, a fabulous graphic designer, or a budding blogger, this book will give you just the right amount of DB2 to match your requirements.

After reading this book, you'll be able to do the following:

- Install and manage DB2 on Linux and Windows

- Easily control DB2 and its various features using the IBM-provided tools

- Quickly write useful SQL and SQL/PL commands to manage your data

- Simultaneously handle structured and unstructured data such as video, pictures, documents, and XML

3

- Combine DB2 databases with your web and desktop applications in languages such as Python, Ruby, C#, and others

- Use the added features of DB2 to manage backups, performance, and troubleshooting

- Comfortably handle the most complex data storage and manipulation requirements with the power of DB2

- Look forward to future developments in database capabilities with a strong grounding in DB2

Why Choose DB2?

You might have a pressing need to store vast quantities of data. You might have heard about the amazing features in the latest release of DB2. Perhaps you've used other databases in the past and are interested in expanding your exposure to different relational database management systems. Or maybe you just like the name! Whatever the motivation, there are excellent reasons to choose DB2 for your next project or application.

DB2 Has History on Its Side

The year was 1970. A brilliant man named E. F. "Ted" Codd wrote a seminal paper while working at the IBM research lab in San Jose, California. The paper, which was titled "A Relational Model of Data for Large Shared Data Banks," triggered a revolution in how people thought about data, its storage, its use, and its management.

You don't need to read that paper to benefit from Codd's ideas because IBM realized it had a winner on its hands. Other members of the IBM research team—Ray Boyce and Don Chamberlin—added to Codd's work in the following years, developing "SEQUEL," a language for structured English queries. This evolved into the "SQL" that is now the lingua franca used with most databases today.

DB2 Is at the Forefront of Database Technology Today

With the latest release of DB2, IBM is taking DB2 into new technological territory—to the benefit of all its users. You'll learn about all the fantastic features that DB2 9.5 offers as you read this book, but the most prominent technology to find its way into DB2 is the IBM "pureXML" hybrid storage technology. With pureXML, DB2 can store, manage, and leverage information in native XML form, right beside information stored in relational form. If you've ever had to wrestle with breaking down and rebuilding XML just to store it for later reference, or struggled with not having the tools you want to manage XML and relational data on an equal footing, DB2 9.5 and pureXML are a boon. (We'll let the section on pureXML speak for itself so you won't think that this topic is just a marketing exercise to promote DB2.)

DB2 Will Be Even Bigger in the Future

If you have ever started working with a new piece of technology and wondered whether there was any mileage left in it after you invested all your time and effort, you can rest easy about devoting your attention to DB2. Not only does IBM release new features and versions of DB2 at a regular steady pace; IBM has been doing that for more than 20 years and has already given a sneak preview of enhancements and new technologies it will make available in the forthcoming releases after DB2 9.5.

Choosing the Right DB2 Edition For You

IBM has always made sure that an edition of DB2 exists that is tailored to match any operating environment you can imagine. And that's true more than ever with the range of DB2 version 9.5 editions now available. Currently, you can choose from the following editions:

- *DB2 Express-C*: A fully functional version of DB2 for Microsoft Windows and Linux that is both free to download and free to distribute with your applications! That's right—free. IBM also has the most generous limits of any "express" edition of a commercial enterprise database. You can even buy an IBM-backed support service, just like all the other editions. The *C* in Express-C stands for *community*, and it is the community to which IBM contributes not just the amazing features and power of DB2 but also dedicated support staff on Express-C forums and input from numerous independent experts. Express-C is amazingly full-powered and brimming with features—you'll be surprised by how far it can take your database!

- *DB2 Express edition*: Like its cousin, Express-C, this version is targeted for quick installation and use. It is ideal for hybrid applications that make use of relational and XML features. DB2 Express supports up to 2 CPUs and 4GB of RAM. Platforms supported include Linux, Windows, and Solaris x86.

- *DB2 Personal edition*: A DB2 edition optimized for single-user operation, this edition can be frugal with memory and other resources while providing almost all the firepower present in multiuser DB2 versions.

- *DB2 Everyplace 9*: Take DB2 with you everywhere! On your land line, PDA, cell phone, or embedded device. Perfect for distributed applications, this edition includes synchronization tools to keep your data in step across your applications and across the world.

- *DB2 Workgroup edition*: This edition raises the bar again, allowing up to 4 CPUs and 16GB of RAM, and shares all the management and development tools of the DB2 range. Platform availability also expands from the DB2 Express edition to include AIX, HP/UX, and Solaris on UltraSPARC.

- *DB2 Enterprise edition*: DB2 with no limits! Serious horsepower to match the most demanding of applications. Advanced technology bundled with the Enterprise edition include high-availability technology for maximum up time, multinode clustering, specialized spatial data support, and more.

- *DB2 Enterprise Developer edition*: Because even the best features should be available to everyone to test and develop, IBM makes the Developer edition available so that you can make the most sophisticated applications with the minimum of fuss.

- *DB2 Data Warehouse edition*: DB2 with special features to manage truly gargantuan data warehouses. Special features include data partitioning, multidimensional clustering, and query materialization technology.

- *Other members of the DB2 family*: IBM is also famous for scaling DB2 all the way up to the mainframe, giving you unlimited potential when it comes to powering your applications. Related products in the DB2 family include DB2 for iSeries and DB2 for z/OS. All members of the DB2 family share a great deal of functionality and capability in common. DB2 for iSeries and DB2 for z/OS versions do take advantage of some of the unique properties of their respective platforms, and there are probably few readers who have such a system readily at hand. As such, I'll highlight in passing any important topics that relate to these two platforms, such as connectivity tools, but won't delve deeply into their inner workings.

This book focuses on the most common editions of DB2 so you become familiar with as much of the DB2 world as possible as quickly as possible. I'll start with DB2 Express-C and show you all its power, flexibility, and capability. In the latter chapters, I'll discuss the differences you'll find in the Workgroup and Enterprise editions, and also show you how easy it is to move quickly and easily between versions when required.

Obtaining DB2: A World of Choice

It should come as no surprise that as well as making available free editions of DB2, IBM also makes it incredibly easy to obtain DB2 to install and use. There is no surer way to date a book than to include in the text a reference to a specific website. You might think that other than http://www.ibm.com/, IBM must regularly change the content and layout of its website as its products, services and related information evolve. And you'd be right. But IBM doesn't just make one of the best database management tools available today; IBM actually understands at a deeper level the importance of managing fluctuating data such as URLs. That's a long-winded way of saying that http://www.ibm.com/db2 has consistently redirected to the current DB2 home page for the last decade or more!

As Figure 1-1 shows, the home page is constantly kept up to date with the latest information on DB2. So no matter when you find yourself reading this section, you can reliably enter that address into your web browser and be faithfully taken to IBM's DB2 offerings almost instantaneously. (Now that I have made such a bold statement, IBM will no doubt decide to add masses of video, audio, and as-yet-unthought-of bandwidth-hungry content to that site, and I'll be forced to eat my words on the "instantaneous" claim.)

The DB2 home page always includes a link for the DB2 download page, so you don't have to go digging to find the software you want. Point your browser at the DB2 home page, follow the link to the download page, and you'll see quite a few options that cover Windows, Linux, and other operating systems in both 32-bit and 64-bit forms. Depending on your platform, you'll need between 258MB to 365MB for the download. I'll cover more about the installation steps in Chapter 2, so for now, if downloading DB2 is your preferred option, go ahead and select the package that matches your operating system and start your download.

If you are a fan of virtual machines and the flexibility they provide, you'll see that IBM has partnered with Novell to make available a ready-made VMware SUSE Linux package with DB2 Express-C already installed, configured, and ready for use. The download package for the virtual machine weighs in at a hefty 1.1GB, but it can be a great kick start to using DB2 in a Linux environment. If you choose this option, you can skip Chapter 2, but you'll find the chapter a useful reference if you ever find yourself with questions about how your virtual machine was put together for you.

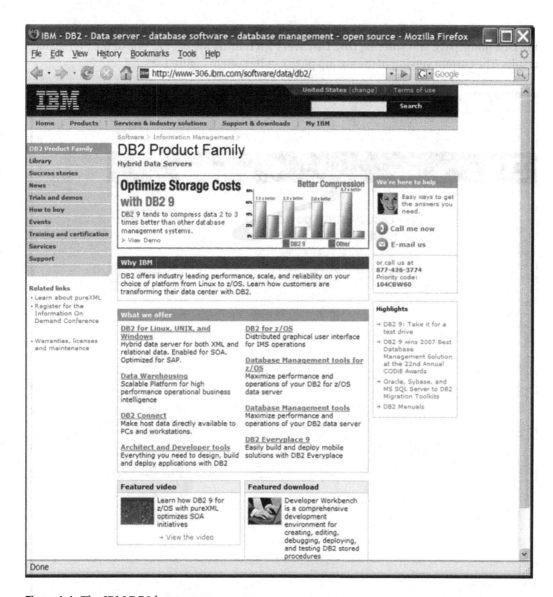

Figure 1-1. *The IBM DB2 home page*

If you can't use the offerings on the download page for whatever reason, there are other readily available ways to obtain DB2. For some years, IBM has made available at no charge its software Discovery Kit, a collection of its leading middleware products that lets anyone try out products such as DB2 at no charge. This is a great way to grab a diverse set of tools, information, and the DB2 software itself, all in one convenient package. It's also very useful if you find yourself at the end of an Internet connection with limited bandwidth or face steep excess usage fees from your ISP for the available downloads on the IBM DB2 home page.

The DB2 Discovery Kit is available by registering at this URL on the DB2 home page:
`http://www-304.ibm.com/jct03002c/software/data/info/expresscd/`.

Because this URL is likely to change over time, using the built-in search functionality on the DB2 home page and entering **DB2 Discovery Kit** returns the page as one of the first search results. The current version of the signup page can be seen in Figure 1-2.

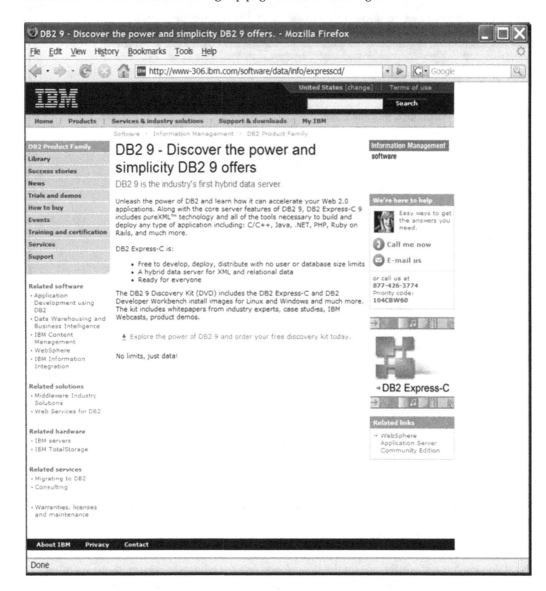

Figure 1-2. *Ordering the DB2 Discovery Kit*

IBM has even thought of those of you who can't get to their website to obtain DB2. You can e-mail or telephone IBM's DB2 team to arrange to have the Discovery Kit shipped to you.

NAMING CURRENT AND FUTURE VERSIONS OF DB2

IBM's current release of DB2 for Linux, UNIX, and Windows is DB2 9.5. You might also hear about DB2 Viper and wonder how it is related. DB2 *Viper* was the code name that IBM used during the development phase for DB2 9, and *DB2 Viper 2* was the code name that IBM used for DB2 9.5. So essentially, they are the same product—one is the beta form; the other is the final released form.

This style of code name has been used previously with DB2. DB2 version 8.2 was code named Stinger, and I'm sure IBM will use the same nomenclature for the next release of DB2 10 and later versions in the future.

The content presented in this book is designed to be applicable for current and future versions of DB2, so the fundamentals presented here will equip you to work with it, no matter whether you're reading this book now or sometime in the future when DB2 10, or an even later version has been released.

Summary

You now know all about the background of DB2, its history, and its tailor-made editions that are available to you to suit every conceivable data management requirement. If you haven't already got your hands on a copy of DB2 Express-C, jump to the website, telephone, or even use good old snail mail to get your copy now. The next chapter launches you right in to installing and using DB2.

CHAPTER 2

■■■

Installing DB2 for Linux and Windows

As you'd expect from a sophisticated product such as DB2, there are a wealth of options available during installation from which to choose. Although you're often well served by the default selection, if you're like me you always want to know what you might be missing. In this chapter, you'll step through the process of installing DB2 on both Microsoft Windows and Linux, and examine the options presented along the way.

Installing on Windows

I chose Windows XP with Service Pack 2 (SP2) for the Windows example because it will be very familiar to many readers. However, IBM supports DB2 on many Windows variants:

- Windows 2000

- Windows XP Professional, SP1 or later

- Windows Server 2003, SP1 or later

- Windows Vista

At the time of writing, Windows Vista (in its many editions) has just been released to market. IBM has moved quickly to support Windows Vista with the release of DB2 9 Fix Pack 2. This release allows the DB2 server components and most of the graphical tools to operate normally under Windows Vista. A few items, such as the DB2 Developer Workbench, do not operate under Windows Vista at this time. To check on the current state of Windows Vista support, refer to the DB2 Information Center on the DB2 homepage at http://www.ibm.com/db2.

Notice that Windows 2000 in the list of supported Windows versions. Although IBM does support DB2 9 installations on Windows 2000, upgrading to a later version of Windows is suggested to ensure that your operating system is supported by Microsoft.

Installing on Linux

The wealth of options offered by Linux distributions leaves you spoiled with choices in selecting the operating system for your DB2 environment. There are numerous excellent distributions from which to choose, and if you're anything like me, you'll have more than one favorite.

To put your mind at ease, IBM lists the following distributions as being supported:

- Novell Open Enterprise Server 9

- Red Hat Enterprise Linux (RHEL) 4

- RHEL 5

- SUSE Linux Enterprise Server (SLES) 9

- SLES 10

- Ubuntu 6.06 LTS

- Xandros 2.0

Because this list is subject to change, refer to the DB2 home page and search for "Recommended and Validated Environments for DB2 9" to see the latest compilation of supported Linux distributions. You'll also see the underlying architectures supported, including x86, x86_64, IA64, PPC, and so on.

For the exercises and examples in this book, I'll be using CentOS 4.5 on x86 hardware, which is the equivalent to RHEL 4. I'll also refer to examples using the SUSE 10.2 virtual machine mentioned in Chapter 1 to reassure you that no matter the distribution, DB2 usually behaves the same way.

Unpacking Installation Downloads

If you elected to download your installation source from the IBM DB2 download website, you'll have one (or both) of the following files:

- For Windows, you'll have the file db2exc_95_WIN_x86.zip. This is a zip file, and you can use Windows' built-in capabilities to extract its contents or you can use an unzip utility such as 7-Zip.

- For Linux, you'll have the file db2exc_95_LNX_x86.tar.gz. This is a tar archive compressed with gzip, and you can pipeline the necessary unpacking commands to extract its contents. Here's an example:

```
$ gunzip db2exc_95_LNX_x86.tar.gz | tar xpvf -
```

The unpacked installer for Windows requires approximately 395MB of disk space, and the space required to unpack the installer for Linux is about 322MB. Don't forget to allow approximately twice that much space for unpacking the archive; you'll have both the downloaded file and its contents on disk at once.

Using the DB2 9 Discovery Kit DVD

The DB2 Discovery Kit includes versions of DB2 for both Microsoft Windows and Linux in both 32-bit and 64-bit forms. Everything you need in one package! Pop the DVD into your computer; the Getting Started web page will open with a wealth of information about external resources, partnering with IBM, downloading FAQs and examples, and more.

One of the best additions to the Discovery Kit is the inclusion of a video demonstration of an install. The good editors here at Apress have promised me that in the future they'll have "video on paper" technology available, but for this edition of *Beginning DB2* we'll press ahead with a more traditional walkthrough of the task. I recommend that you watch the demonstration video if you have time because it's a great tool to use to double-check your options when performing an installation.

After you've reviewed the great material on the DVD, you'll find the installers available in the following directories:

- `D:\run\install\windows_x86` for the Microsoft Windows installer (assuming that `D:\` is your DVD drive)

- `/mount/cdrom/run/install/linux_x86` or `/mount/cdrom/run/install/linux_x86_64` for the Linux 32-bit and 64-bit installers, respectively (assuming that `/mount/cdrom/` is the mount point for your DVD device)

Note that the Linux installers are also gzip tar archives, so see the previous steps noted in "Unpacking Installation Downloads" from the DB2 download website to unpack these files to use for installation. You'll require approximately the same available disk space for both: 322MB.

Checking Preinstallation Requirements

One of the best features of modern databases, including DB2, is their capability to make complete use of all the hardware resources you have available. This also means that there are some minimum requirements below which things will generally still technically operate, but they might leave you tapping your fingers because of slow operation. There are also other requirements and options that are worth covering before you proceed because they might affect your choices for the security and configuration of the system.

Memory

IBM recommends that you have a minimum of 256MB of RAM available—and 512MB if you will run the graphical tools and utilities on the same machine. Of course, the more memory the better is the usual mantra with databases, and 1GB of RAM or more will be put to good use if you have it. DB2 includes automatic memory-tuning capabilities that will be discussed in later chapters; the good news for you now is that you don't have to set any unfamiliar configuration parameters during installation. Just having the memory present in your computer is all you need to worry about.

Disk

The DB2 software and its associated utilities, documentation, and support files can consume from 200MB to 800MB of space, depending on the installation choices you make. That should fit comfortably on modern hard drives, but if you are space-constrained in any way, I'll point out the compact installation options as you step through this chapter, helping you keep your DB2 installation trim, taut, and terrific.

The one big thing to keep in mind is that the 200MB–800MB range *does not* include your actual databases. Don't panic! The examples in the following chapters will use databases that are quite small, mostly under 100MB. Again, that should fit comfortably on almost any hard drive you have available. By the end of this book, you'll also be comfortable with how easy it is to keep tabs on the size of your databases, and you'll be able to deal with storage growth and other related tasks.

Users and Groups

When it comes to accessing DB2, connecting to a database to work with data relies on operating system users and their associated security privileges and permissions. That makes DB2 a little different from some other database systems that might allow the database itself to create its own little world of users.

In other respects, DB2 behaves exactly as any other piece of software under modern operating systems. DB2 processes or services will run under the operating system account of a nominated user, and that account will require particular privileges for normal operation.

This is important for the purposes of installation because you will want to know which users and groups the DB2 installer might create automatically, and you can plan ahead and create these users and groups prior to installation.

Users and Groups Under Windows

Under Windows, a user runs the DB2 services and also links to external functions in some circumstances (they are known as "fenced" functions, and we'll discuss them in later sections). By default, the installer uses the name db2admin and prompts you to enter a password. (You can choose any name you like instead of db2admin, but I'll use that name for the examples that follow.) The db2admin user, which can be a local or domain user, also operates under any password complexity rules you have in place.

You also have the option under Windows of configuring operating system group-related privileges at the time of installation. The installer will offer the option of creating two groups—DB2ADMNS and DB2USERS—which will be used later to separate some privileges. You can go ahead and create these groups now and choose any name you like, or you can let the installer do that for you in the later steps in this chapter. You can also control whether local or domain groups are used. All these group settings can be modified after installation, so if you prefer to not worry about these options now, let the installer follow the default options, and we'll return to these settings later.

Users and Groups Under Linux

Under Linux, three logins are created automatically by the installer if the default installation is used. These are the user db2usr1, to own and operate the DAS administration instance with a corresponding group called dasadm1; the user db2inst1, to own and operate the default database instance with the corresponding group called db2grp1; and db2fenc1, to own and operate "fenced" functions outside the default database instance with a corresponding group called db2fgrp1. Again, you can choose any names you want to override those defaults, but I'll stick with these names for the later examples in the book.

More Advanced User and Group Management

DB2 offers several advanced features for user and permissions management, including support for third-party LDAP servers, prepackaged LDAP schema extensions, NIS support, and more. These options are beyond the scope of this text, but you can find out more about these options in the DB2 documentation, and the "Getting Started" guide available from the DB2 website.

Other Configuration Prerequisites

Thankfully, there are very few (if any) other configuration options you need to be concerned about before diving in to the installation itself. A few of the obvious and not-so-obvious extras that you might want or need are the following:

- A browser, such as Internet Explorer 6.0 or higher, Mozilla 1.4 or higher, Firefox 1.0 or higher, or Netscape 7.0 or higher. The DB2 First Steps utility will require a browser if you intend to use it.

- An ssh server and client, such as OpenSSH, if you want to securely manage remote connections to your host server. You can use rsh or similar tools if unsecured connections are acceptable in your environment.

- Under Linux, if you later plan to use database-partitioning features (discussed later in this book), the pdksh Korn Shell package will be required.

- Under Linux, an X server is required to run the graphical installer and any of the graphical management tools.

Proceeding with the Installation

You're now ready to start the installation. I'll cover first the installation for Windows and Linux using the graphical installer and then the installation for Linux using the text-only option. Feel free to skip the section for the option you're *not* using, but you might find it useful to compare the two installations so you can see how similar they are and also learn the few nuances that do differ between the Linux and Windows installations.

Graphical Installation Under Windows and Linux

From the directory in which you unzipped your download, find and run the relevant setup file. For Windows, this is the `setup.exe` file. Double-click the executable, or from a command line run the file as follows:

```
C:\<path to your unzipped files>\setup.exe
```

For Linux, the `db2setup` script will launch the installer. Either run this directly or run from a shell as follows:

```
$ <path to your unpacked files>/db2setup &
```

This will start the DB2 Launchpad facility, as shown in Figure 2-1, which acts like a home page for installations, prerequisite checks, and starter information for your installation.

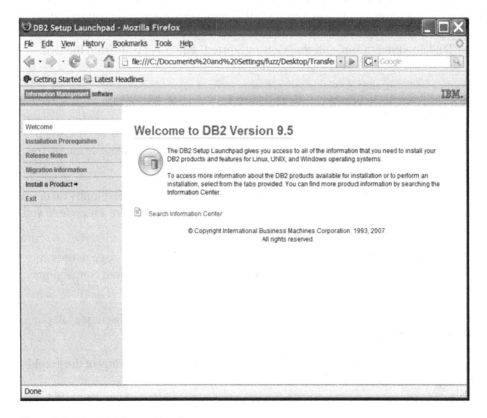

Figure 2-1. *The DB2 Launchpad*

From the DB2 Launchpad you have access to documentation on the prerequisites mentioned previously, but more importantly, any last-minute release notes are available directly from the Launchpad page. IBM sometimes releases later fix packs that are incorporated into the main installer, which might in turn alter the requirements for installation. They are generally well flagged, but the release notes are a handy way of seeing whether any recent changes have occurred in the prerequisites or system requirements.

You can launch the install process directly from the DB2 Launchpad. By choosing Install A Product from the left menu, the Launchpad will take you to the control page for all products that can be installed from your distribution package. An example of the Install A Product launch screen is shown in Figure 2-2.

The current DB2 9.5 Express-C download package includes the DB2 Express-C installer, and also packages an installer for the IBM Database Addins for Visual Studio 2005. We'll return to the Addins for Visual Studio 2005 in Chapter 15, so for now choose the DB2 Express-C installer and continue to the Installation Welcome screen shown in Figure 2-3.

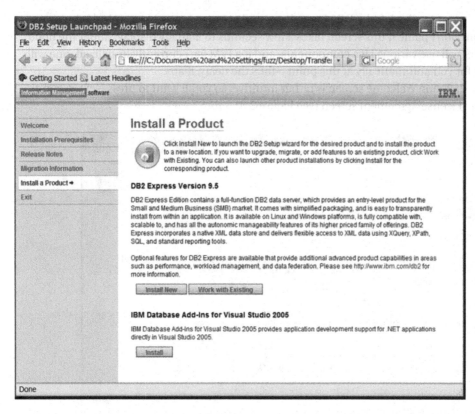

Figure 2-2. *Selecting the product to install from your distribution package*

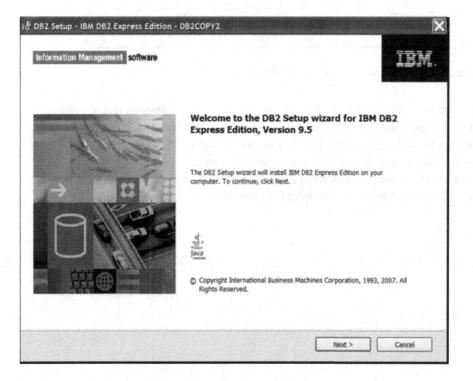

Figure 2-3. *The Installation Welcome screen*

At this point, you've left the DB2 Launchpad and are now executing a typical Windows installation. Don't panic if this screen takes a few seconds to actually display; under the hood, the installer will use various Java components, and if a JVM isn't currently initialized, one will be started for you automatically at this point—thus the delay, if any.

The Installation Welcome screen is rather intuitive, so you'll want to press Next to continue to the License Agreement screen (see Figure 2-4).

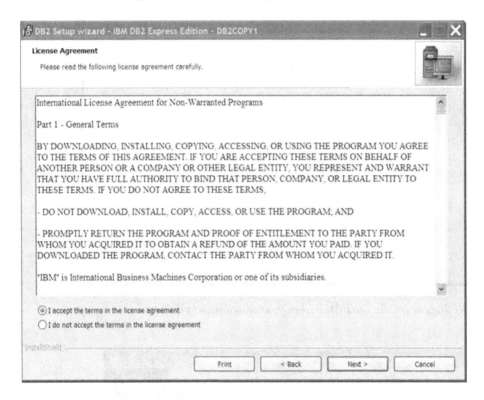

Figure 2-4. *The DB2 Express Edition License Agreement screen*

If you're an observant installer of software, you'll notice a few things on this installation screen. Apart from the ubiquitous license text and the necessary Accept and Decline options, you'll notice the title of the screen incorporates the term DB2COPY1. This name relates to the name of this installation of DB2, and its purpose becomes clear in just a few screens' time. This also means that it would be feasible to have different licensing agreements for different installations of DB2, but that's not something I've seen IBM exercise just yet.

Agreeing to the license allows you to progress to the screen shown in Figure 2-5, which allows you to select the type of installation you prefer. Your options are Typical, Compact, and Custom.

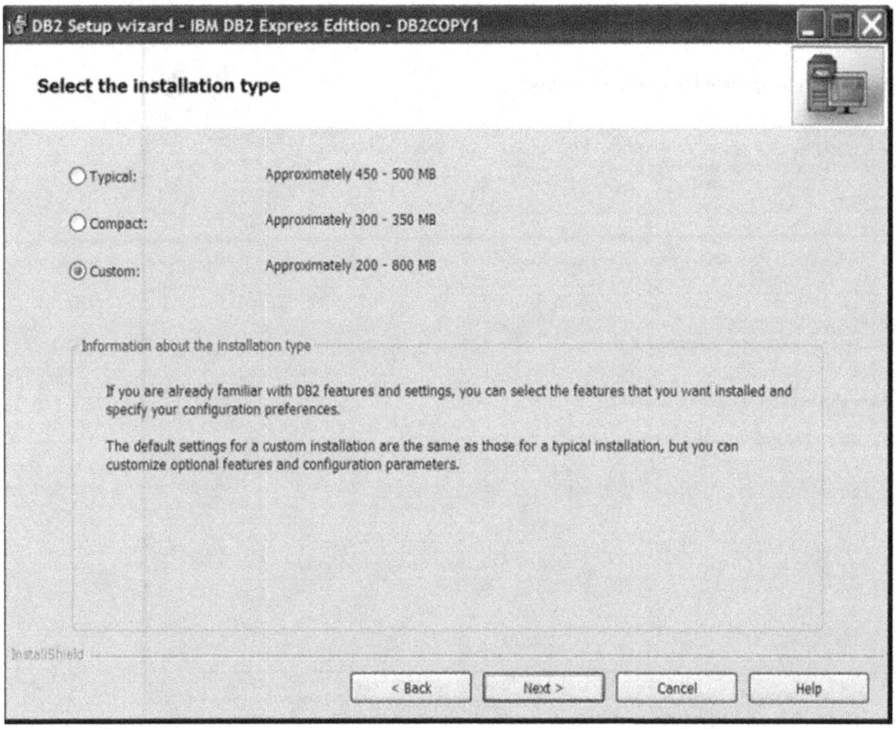

Figure 2-5. *Selecting the install type for your DB2 installation*

A Typical installation takes a number of sensible defaults, such as the user and group names mentioned previously, and assumes that you want the language packs installed to match your current locale, plus English. It creates the default instance called DB2 and configures it for normal network access over TCP/IP.

The Compact option strips out most of the supporting documentation, doesn't create any default databases, and installs support just for English.

The Custom installation option gives you full control over every aspect of the installation, from networking, to initial instances and databases, and through to language support. You'll work with this option so you'll be familiar with all the features available at install time. You can always revisit your installation at a later point and choose Typical or Compact.

If you choose Typical or Compact, many of the subsequent installation screens won't display. Choosing the Custom option and pressing Next brings you to the install and response file selection screen seen in Figure 2-6.

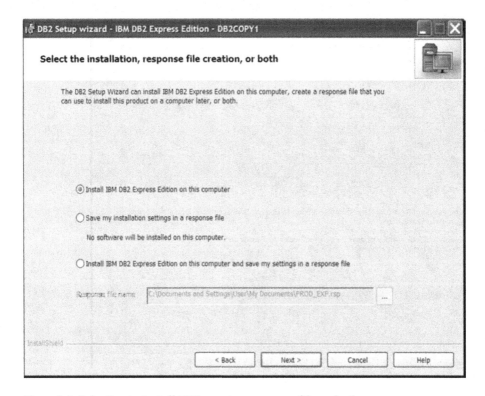

Figure 2-6. *Selecting to install DB2, create a response file, or both*

The first response to pop into your mind at the sight of this screen might be "Why *wouldn't* I want to install the software? I am running an *installer* after all." Bear with me. Your other option on this screen is to ask the installer to create a response file, which is a text file composed of simple shorthand notation that a subsequent invocation of the installer can use as answers to all the questions it needs to ask. In effect, this allows you to create your own custom installation scripts for DB2. Even better, they can be used in conjunction with the silent installation option to have DB2 installed exactly to your specification without lifting a finger! Think of it as automating your way to a well-earned coffee.

RESPONSE FILES, SILENT INSTALLATION, AND PACKAGING FOR REDEPLOYMENT

Response files are a great way of packaging the DB2 installer with your chosen set of options to provide for a repeatable, automated way of installing. This has big benefits if you decide, for instance, to bundle DB2 Express-C with a software application that you want to distribute. By using a response file, you can spare your audience the need to master the techniques for installation.

A response file is simply a text file in a special format that the DB2 installer understands; it has answers to all the questions it requires to successfully perform an installation. Here's a snippet of a response file:

```
PROD=EXPRESS_EDITION
INSTALL_OPTION=SINGLE_PARTITION
LIC_AGREEMENT=ACCEPT
FILE=C:\Program Files\IBM\SQLLIB\
INSTALL_TYPE=TYPICAL

LANG=EN
DAS_CONTACT_LIST=LOCAL

INSTANCE=DB2

TOOLS_DB.INSTANCE=DB2
TOOLS_DB.LOCATION=LOCAL
DB2.NAME=DB2
DEFAULT_INSTANCE=DB2
...
```

With such a response file, it is then easy to invoke the installer in silent mode to do its work. It's as simple as passing the name of the response file to the setup utility with the –u parameter. Here's an example:

```
setup.exe -u DB2_v9_InstallResponseFile.rsp
```

Response files usually have the extension .rsp, although any name is allowable.

Choose the Install DB2 Express Edition On This Computer option and click Next to bring up the feature selection screen shown in Figure 2-7.

Take the time to browse through each of the components the installer has listed. Even if you change nothing, you'll get an idea of how comprehensive the DB2 package is. You can deselect any item in which you genuinely have no interest. At the bottom of the dialog box you'll see the default installation directory. Feel free to change this to any directory you desire, either by typing the name directly or invoking the directory browser by clicking the Change button.

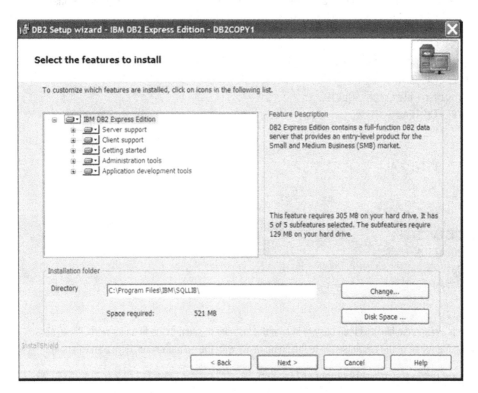

Figure 2-7. *Feature selection for your installation of DB2*

Once you're happy with your selected options and installation location, click Next to move on to the language selection screen, as shown in Figure 2-8.

Probably the most important thing to know about the language selection screen is that it does not determine which languages you can store in your database. Like most modern relational databases, DB2 supports the capability to store information in multiple character sets and Unicode, regardless of the language used by your operating system.

The language selection screen allows you to tell the installer which languages you want supported in the installed graphical tools, help message text, and so forth. In effect, you are selecting the textual information for the various DB2 tools and utilities *outside* any DB2 database.

Once again you can specify an installation directory, which doesn't affect your previous choice of directory for the core DB2 components. Instead you can specify the directory for the language support files separately so you can, for instance, place them in a common location with language support files for other applications or software you might also be using in a multilingual environment.

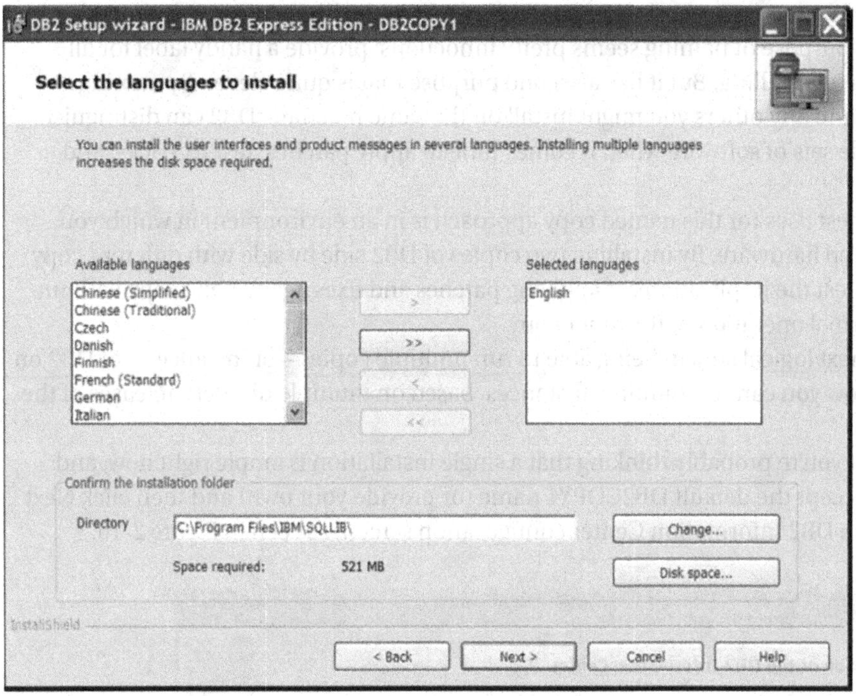

Figure 2-8. *Selecting language support for DB2 tools and interfaces*

Choose as few or as many language packs as you want and then proceed to the DB2 copy naming screen, as shown in Figure 2-9.

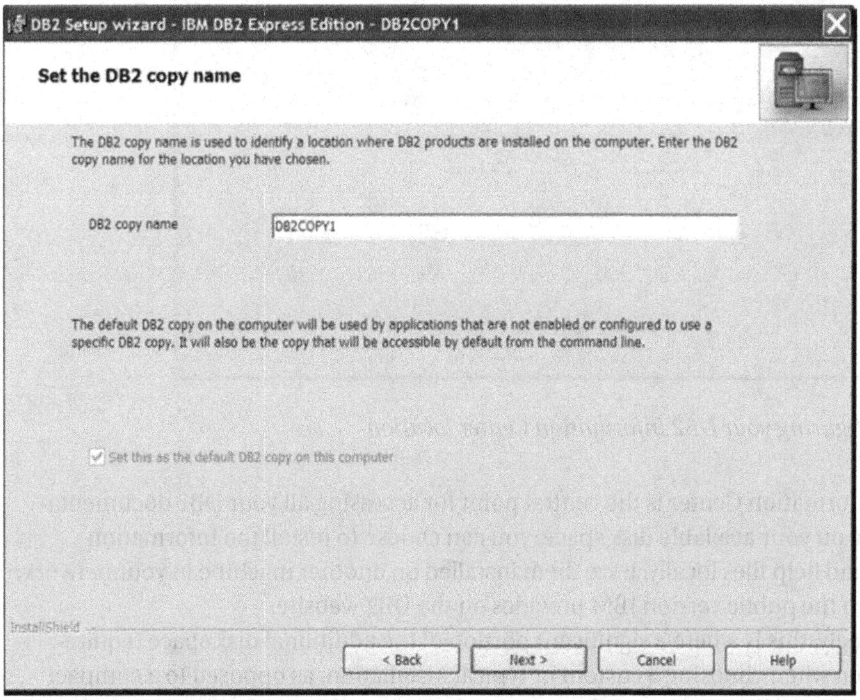

Figure 2-9. *Name your DB2 installation*

You knew this screen was coming! After alluding to it in the licensing description, it's finally here. The purpose of naming seems pretty innocuous; provide a handy label for all the software you're installing. But it has a second purpose that is quite clever. By naming this installation and any others you might install on the same machine, DB2 can distinguish between multiple sets of software when it comes time to apply patches, test fix packs, and so forth.

One of the best uses for this named copy approach is in an environment in which you might have limited hardware. By installing two copies of DB2 side by side with different copy names, you can test the implications of applying patches and fixes against one copy without affecting the normal operation of the other copy.

This is the next logical step in being able to run multiple copies—or instances—of DB2 on one machine. Now you can run multiple instances, based on multiple different releases of the software.

At this point you're probably thinking that a single installation is ample right now, and you'd be right. Accept the default DB2COPY1 name (or provide your own) and then click Next to move on to the DB2 Information Center configuration screen, as seen in Figure 2-10.

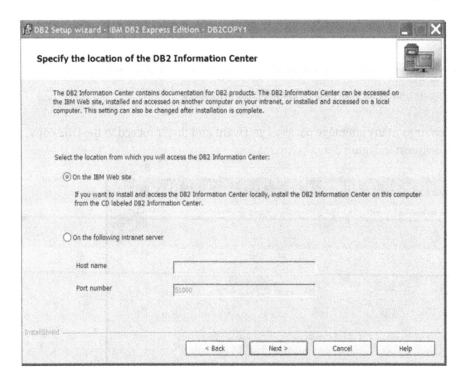

Figure 2-10. *Configuring your DB2 Information Center location*

The DB2 Information Center is the central point for accessing all your DB2 documentation. Depending on your available disk space, you can choose to install the Information Center service and help files locally, have them installed on another machine in your network, or simply refer to the public version IBM provides on the DB2 website.

Unsurprisingly, this is where a significant portion of the additional disk space requirement comes from when choosing a custom or typical installation, as opposed to a compact one. I recommend installing the DB2 Information Center on your machine because that way you'll have constant access to the Information Center documentation, even when you're not connected to a network or don't have your copy of *Beginning DB2* handy! You can always remove the Information Center at a later date.

Choose if and where you want to install the DB2 Information Center and then click Next to move on to the Administration Server user configuration screen shown in Figure 2-11.

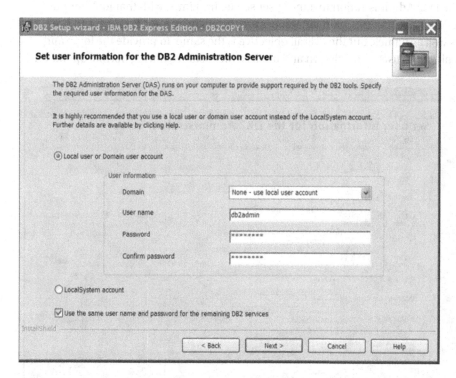

Figure 2-11. *User nomination for the DB2 Administration Instance and other instances under Windows*

The different kinds of DB2 Instances will be covered in more detail in Chapter 3, but the DB2 Administration Instance configuration screen gives you some idea about their purpose. On this dialog box, you nominate the user that will own and run the DB2 Administration Instance (known as DAS) on your machine. Depending on your platform, the installer will suggest the name db2admin (for Windows) or dasusr1 (for Linux). If you previously created user logins as part of your prerequisite checks, make sure that the name shown in the dialog box matches the login name you created. The DAS will use TCP port 523 for communication, and you should quickly check that this is free by using netstat or a similar networking tool. Normally it is free because IBM has received Well Known Port status from IANA for this port, but other applications you run might have been configured to use it.

If you plan to let the installer create the relevant user accounts for you, make sure that you specify a user name and password that meet any network restrictions that might be in place. For instance, if you use a Windows domain account and have a password policy in place that dictates minimum length, number of punctuation characters, and so on, you'll need to meet those same requirements because the users created by the DB2 installer are genuine operating system users.

Under Windows, using the same user for the DB2 Administration Instance and the first (and any subsequent) DB2 Instances is perfectly normal. Under Linux, ownership and operation of the DB2 Administration Instance and the first and later DB2 Instances is usually split between different users. You can choose any names you want at this point, but I'll use the default values of db2das, db2inst1, and db2fenc1 for the following examples. Compare Figure 2-12, the DB2 Administration Instance user screen for Linux, with that for Windows in Figure 2-11. You'll see that the main differences are the ability to specify group and user id numbers as well as names, but the overall objective is the same: to provide the login and password details of the user that will own and operate the Instance during normal operations.

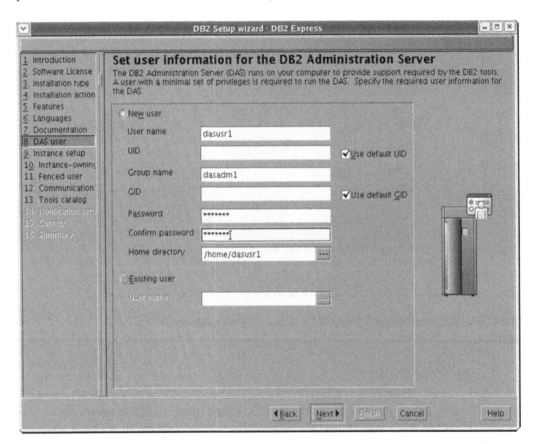

Figure 2-12. *User nomination for the DB2 Administration Instance under Linux*

At this point, you'll notice the one moderate difference between the installers for Windows and Linux. Other than the small cosmetic difference in rendering styles, you'll notice that the Windows installer allows you to select the option Use The Same User Name And Password For The Remaining DB2 Services, whereas the Linux installer explicitly walks you through two more identical dialog boxes to specify the DB2 Instance owner, and the DB2 fenced user.

After specifying the user name(s) and password(s), you can click Next to move on to the instance communication and startup screen shown in Figure 2-13.

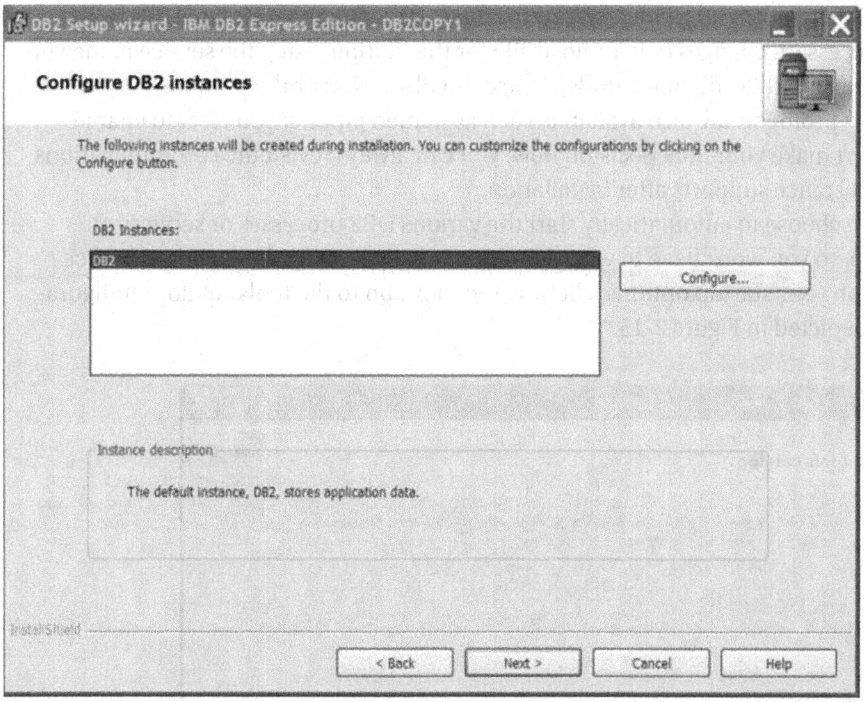

Figure 2-13. *Configuring your instance communication and startup options*

Under Windows, you actually have to click the Configure button to see the communication and startup options for your DB2 Instance. These then appear as shown in Figure 2-14.

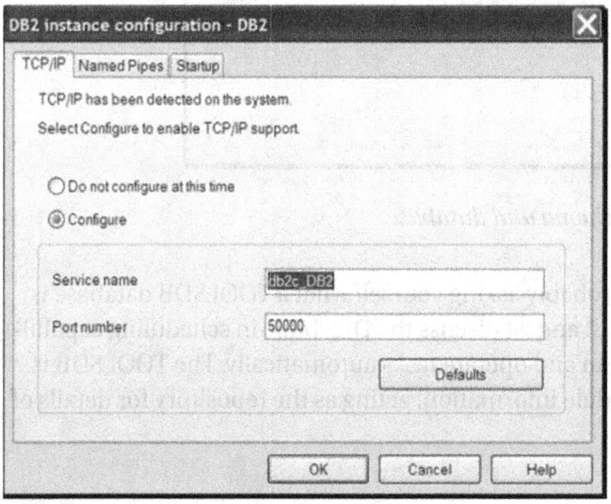

Figure 2-14. *Configuring your instance communication and startup options under Windows*

The Linux installer presents these options on the original screen, without needing to call up another dialog box. In either installer, the goals are the same. First, ensure that the DB2 Instance is listening on a TCP port with which you are happy. By default, the installer will choose port 50000 if not already allocated (for instance, for an older version of DB2) and it will make the necessary changes to your hosts file for this setting, using the service name you choose (or the default db2c_db2inst1 under Linux and db2c_DB2 under Windows). Other communications protocols are also available, such as named pipes, if you elect to enable them. You needn't make your final decision now; you can always revisit the communications protocols your instance supports after installation.

You can also choose to automatically start the various DB2 processes or services at machine startup, so you won't have to worry about manually starting them yourself. Once you've decided on your startup options, click next to move on to the tools catalog configuration screen, as depicted in Figure 2-15.

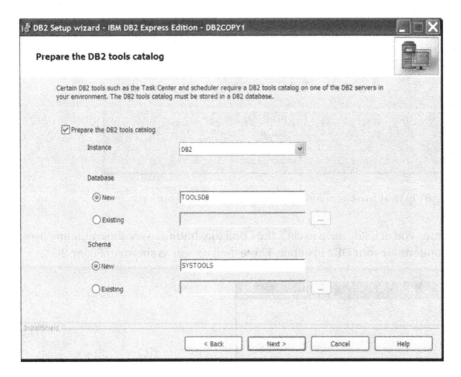

Figure 2-15. *Configuring your DB2 tools schema and database*

If you're new to DB2, you are now probably asking yourself what a TOOLSDB database is and why you might want one. Chapters 18 and 24 discuss the DB2 built-in scheduling capabilities and how to use its Task Center to plan and operate tasks automatically. The TOOLSDB is used by DB2 to store your task and schedule information, acting as the repository for details of what needs to be done—and when.

The TOOLSDB occupies about 60MB of disk space initially and then grows as new tasks and schedules are added. You can use any name you choose for the TOOLSDB, as well as nominate a new database or an existing database in which to house it. You can also decide that this is a topic you want to refer to later and add the TOOLSDB to your system after installation is complete.

Once you've decided on your initial TOOLSDB configuration, click Next to proceed to the notifications configuration screen, as shown in Figure 2-16.

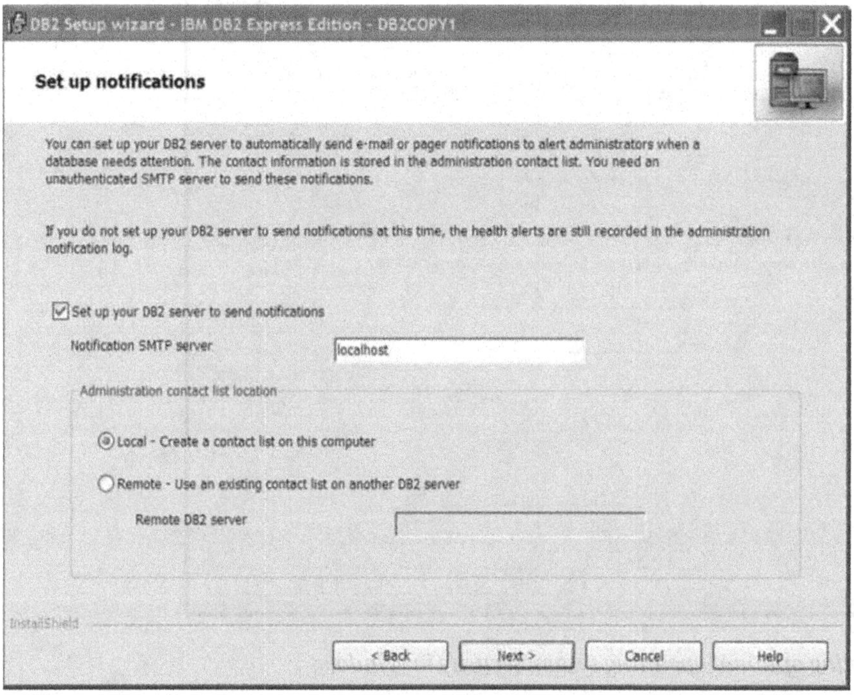

Figure 2-16. *Choosing notification options for your new DB2 environment*

During operation, DB2 will log any warnings, alerts, or "health issues" to its administration notification log, so that you can investigate and analyze any problems. You also have the option of enabling the notification system, so an e-mail or pager alert can be issued with alert details.

Even better, if you have multiple DB2 installations and multiple servers you have the option of configuring each server separately or pointing the servers to a common central notification service for maximum efficiency.

To enable notifications, simply click the check box and enter the name of the server running the SMTP mail service. As with many of the other configuration options, you can revisit this configuration after installation if you prefer not to nominate a notification server now. Once you've made you desired settings, click Next to move on.

If you are installing under Windows, you now see the optional operating system security for DB2 objects screen, as shown in Figure 2-17. Because operating system–level object security is a native attribute of Linux, you won't see this screen in the Linux installer. Instead, the permissions will be set according to the users you nominated earlier in the instance owner user name configuration screen.

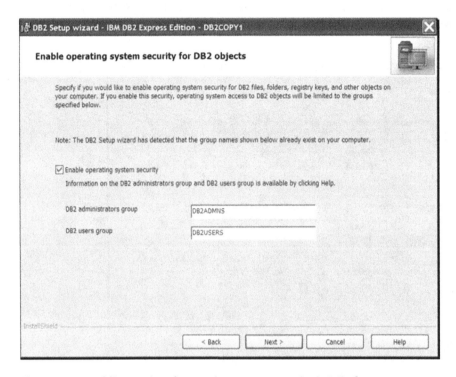

Figure 2-17. *Enabling optional operating system security in Windows*

The purpose of the operating system security settings is to provide security over the installation files, directories, and registry settings of your installation. In effect, they provide an additional layer of security to prevent unintended actions such as unauthorized changes to configuration or accidental deletion of your database directories! It certainly doesn't hurt to have it in place, so I recommend that you take the suggested group names and click the Enable Operating System Security option.

Once you're done, click Next to move on to the final installation screen, the confirmation dialog box shown in Figure 2-18.

You've now mastered every option available for the graphical DB2 installer. Review the choices you made. If you're happy and don't want to go back to make any last-minute alterations, click the Install button under Windows or the Finish button under Linux, and the copying process will begin. The process will take approximately 10 minutes to copy all the chosen files to the relevant destinations, start the database instances for the first time, and install your optional configuration selections such as the TOOLSDB.

Upon completion, the installer will notify you of its success (or failure if there has been a problem). The installer then automatically starts the DB2 First Steps Wizard, which is covered in detail in Chapter 3.

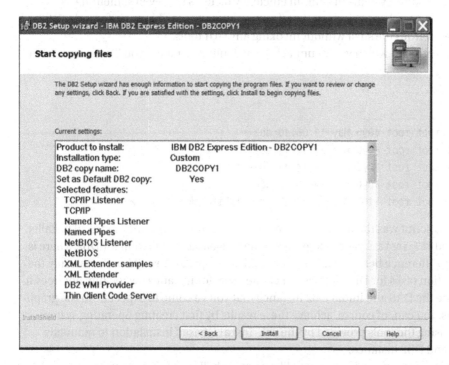

Figure 2-18. *Confirm your installation options and begin copying files.*

At this point, congratulations are in order because (assuming all has gone smoothly) you just completed your first successful installation of DB2.

MORE INFORMATION ON INSTALLATION TOPICS

There is a wealth of information available on the different options, approaches, and configuration choices for DB2 installation. IBM has a useful quick-reference document available from the DB2 documentation collection called "Getting Started with DB2 Installation and Administration on Linux and Windows," which is available as a PDF file named db2xpe90.pdf. Search for it on the DB2 website.

Whether you chose to install it or used IBM's hosted version, you have available the DB2 Information Center, which includes a complete section on basic and advanced installation topics.

Command-Line Installation Under Linux

Having a graphical user interface (GUI) wizard step you through the installation process is a great help, but on some systems maximum efficiency dictates that even something as innocuous as an X server has to give way. For these systems it's possible to perform the DB2 installation directly from the shell without invoking any GUI tools.

From the directory in which you've unpacked the Linux download, you'll see several shell scripts:

```
$ ls -l
total 52
drwxr-xr-x   6 root root 4096 May 19 06:10 db2
-r-xr-xr-x   1 root root 5090 Apr 27 14:43 db2_install
-r-xr-xr-x   1 root root 5078 Apr 27 14:43 db2setup
drwxr-xr-x  15 root root 4096 May 19 06:10 doc
-r-xr-xr-x   1 root root 5102 Apr 27 14:43 installFixPack
```

The db2setup script was the file used in the previous section to run the graphical installer. The script named db2_install is used to perform the text-based installation for DB2. There is one overarching difference between db2_install and dbsetup: db2_install performs only the software installation tasks for DB2. It does not create users for instance ownership, nor does it proceed to create the DAS and initial DB2 instance that you've come to expect from the graphical installations. You can, of course, achieve these results by first creating operating system users and then using the tools provided by the db2_install-based installation to manually create the DAS and DB2 instance.

The db2_install script can be executed like normal shell script. For example:

```
$ ./db2_install
```

The text-based installation assumes that a great many of the options should be configured per the defaults for the DB2 installation, so you need to answer only two questions. After the installer starts, it will prompt for an installation directory (and suggest the default /opt/ibm/db2/V9.5):

```
Default directory for installation of products - /opt/ibm/db2/V9.5

***********************************************************
Do you want to choose a different directory to install [yes/no]?
```

I'm intrinsically lazy, so I actually made a change to the installation path (you can, of course, choose any path you like). I reverted to a lowercase *v* for my version marker—no point in pressing Shift in the future if I don't have to:

```
yes
Enter full path name for the install directory -

-------------------------------------------------
/opt/ibm/db2/v9.5
```

Having made that subtle tweak (or indeed selected whatever directory you saw fit to choose), the installer then prompts you to select from the products included in the installation package. Because this package is sourced from the DB2 Express-C download on the DB2 website, the only option is for that version.

```
Specify one or more of the following keywords,
separated by spaces, to install DB2 products.

  EXP

Enter "help" to redisplay product names.

Enter "quit" to exit.

*************************************************************
```

I entered EXP, and installation begins immediately! Status information is printed to the console session as each step of the installation completes. For example:

```
DB2 installation is being initialized.

Total number of tasks to be performed: 44
Total estimated time for all tasks to be performed: 803

Task #1 start
Description: Checking license agreement acceptance
Estimated time 1 second(s)
Task #1 end

Task #2 start
Description: GSKit support
Estimated time 19 second(s)
Task #2 end
...
```

This continues for a few minutes until all 44 tasks are complete:

```
Task #43 start
Description: Initializing instance list
Estimated time 5 second(s)
Task #43 end

Task #44 start
Description: Updating global profile registry
Estimated time 3 second(s)
Task #44 end

The execution completed successfully.

For more information see the DB2 installation log at
"/tmp/db2_install.log.6794".
```

If you're particularly interested in the minutiae of the installation process, feel free to read the noted installation log file. It does have its uses if anything goes wrong during the installation process, so I should perhaps save my wit for another time.

You've now successfully installed DB2 using the text-based installer. You'll examine the results of your installation in Chapter 3.

Note Those of you who are familiar with early versions of DB2 under Linux or other UNIX-style operating systems will remember the installer's use of ksh scripts and its consequential requirement for Korn shell availability or its public-domain equivalent: pdksh. The good news is that unless you're planning an advanced multinode installation of DB2 with the Enterprise or Warehouse edition, you won't need Korn shell to install or use your DB2 software under Linux.

Uninstalling DB2

After reading that heading, I can imagine many of you saying, "What? I've only just installed it!" I feel that no chapter on installing software is complete without a matching briefing on how to remove it if you want to repeat the installation process or simply no longer have a use for the software on your machine.

The good news is that uninstallation is incredibly easy, both under Linux and Windows. For Windows environments, DB2 registers itself as an installed application and places the relevant uninstall option in the Windows Control Panel Add/Remove Programs utility. Simply select your DB2 installation from the list and follow the prompts to remove DB2. Note that removing the DB2 software does not delete your databases, so if you also want to remove them you have to delete the associated directories that house your data.

Under Linux, uninstalling DB2 is as simple as removing the directories specified for installation. By default, this will be /opt/ibm/db2/V9.5, although you might have changed it to a directory of your choice.

You might want to consult Chapter 19 on DB2 backups before removing anything from your system.

Reviewing Your DB2 Installation

After using the graphical installation tools, the command-line installer, and possibly perform-ing multiple installations and deinstallations, you might feel you need to take stock of your current DB2 landscape to examine what has survived. A useful utility to help investigate your current DB2 installation is the db2licm utility, the licensing manager for DB2. It has a number of command-line options, but the only one you'll need to know about at this stage is the -l option, which instructs it to list all known products installed on the computer and their associated license details:

```
C:\ > db2licm -l
Product name:              "DB2 Express-C"
License type:              "Trial"
Expiry date:               "08/31/2008"
Product identifier:        "db2expc"
Version information:       "9.5"
Max number of CPUs:        "2"
```

As you can see, it is unambiguous about providing exact details. It is especially handy if you ever find yourself confused over whether you've installed DB2 Express-C; the totally free DB2 edition; or DB2 Express, the edition with identical technical capabilities but somewhat different licensing rules.

Summary

You have now experienced the variety of methods by which DB2 can be installed. More importantly, you are now familiar with the nuances and options that are available to you and have some inkling of how they will be used in the coming chapters. DB2 is very mature soft-ware, and the installation is similarly well polished and can handle almost any scenario you throw at it. With the confidence you now have, you should be ready to install, reinstall, and uninstall DB2 at will.

PART 2

■■■

Beginning Administration with DB2 Express Edition

You've conquered the installation for DB2 in no time. Now, in less time than it takes to make your second cup of coffee, you'll take control of your new DB2 world with its bundled administration and development tools.

CHAPTER 3

■ ■ ■

DB2 Wizards: The Fast Path to Working with Your New Database

One of the big factors that led to database administration being considered as some form of arcane magic was the historic lack of tools that existed to help normal people, like you and me, do the kinds of work that we wanted to do with a database without having to learn inscrutable or cryptic commands.

Thanks to fierce competition in the database market, there has been an explosion in graphical tools, wizards, and guides that help you get the job done. Even better, many of these tools now provide you the option of telling them *what you want done* ("give me more room to store my data" or "make this task run when things are quiet") instead of having to guess all the various commands and tasks that would be needed to describe *how to get something done*.

IBM has been refining its set of tools for many years, and there's now a tool for every occasion. More importantly, there is also a core set of tools with a rich set of functionality, meaning you can spend much less time managing your database and more time investing in the higher levels of programs and applications that build on that database. Let's take a look at what's available.

DB2 First Steps

Taking control of your new DB2 installation starts happening literally during the installation process itself. Apart from the steps I've already covered—selecting user names, defining instances, and so forth—the installation process rounds itself out by launching the first tool with which you'll want to become familiar as the last step of the installation.

The tool is *DB2 First Steps*, and as the name suggests, it's designed to help you take your first tentative toe-pokes into your freshly installed DB2 realm. Before you dive into its capabilities, let's cover how you can invoke DB2 First Steps at any point, so that if you don't see it after installation or if you choose to exit First Steps and return to it at a later stage, you can find and launch it easily.

Launching DB2 First Steps Under Windows

Your new installation of DB2 naturally includes a software folder found under the Start menu. Open All Programs and you'll see a newly created program folder named IBM DB2. Navigate into this folder and you'll see a subfolder named according to the copy name you chose for your installation. If you went with the default value, it will be DB2COPY1 (Default). The *(Default)* portion is telling you that this is the current default installation on this machine. Navigate still lower, and you'll see a set of program folders, as shown in Figure 3-1. You'll want to navigate into the Set-up Tools program folder, in which you'll see a number of things, including the First Steps program, complete with a staircase icon for easy recognition.

Figure 3-1. *Launching DB2 First Steps from the Start menu*

If you examine the properties for this shortcut, you'll see that it points to the First Steps executable, and directly executing this file is another way to launch First Steps. For a default installation, such as the one covered in Chapter 2, the First Steps executable can be found here:

```
"C:\Program Files\IBM\SQLLIB\BIN\db2fs.exe"
```

This means that you can start First Steps by entering that line at the Run command (or from a command window), as shown in Figure 3-2. Even better, because the DB2 Installer is designed to add the path C:\Program Files\IBM\SQLLIB\BIN\ to your environment's path variable, you don't need to remember that long directory hierarchy. You can just execute the command directly.

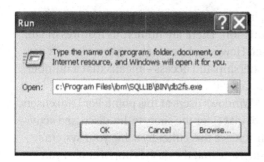

Figure 3-2. *Launch DB2 First Steps directly from the Run dialog box.*

At this stage, you are gaining some benefit from the default installation settings for DB2, which I'll discuss in later chapters. Under Windows, a user who is an administrator of the local machine can exercise some rights within DB2 First Steps that are normally the reserve of the instance owner. You should seriously consider getting into the habit of logging in as your (new) instance owner to perform the administrative tasks I'll cover shortly (at least until you get to the later chapters, in which authentication and authorization are discussed).

Launching DB2 First Steps Under Linux

First Steps under Linux is designed in a similar fashion to its cousin under Windows. It provides a browser interface to quickly access most of the standard tools for your DB2 installation and (more importantly) it provides all the help, information, and jump-off points a new DB2 user like you wants and needs.

Note A "gotcha" on some Linux installations is the security provided by the X server. Depending on your X server security, users and hosts (including you on your own machine) might be prevented from invoking First Steps and having its browser user interface (UI) presented by your X server. This is normal security on many systems, including those with SELinux features enabled. To ensure that you aren't caught out by this, use the xhost command to add your machine to the list of servers from which your X server will accept connections; for example:

```
xhost +servername
```

You'll notice pretty quickly if X Server security is blocking you. Upon issuing the db2fs command, a few seconds will pass and you'll then receive an error like this:

```
Xlib: connection to ":0.0" refused by server
```

This error will be followed by a Java exception dump.

To begin working under Linux, you could log in as a normal user—it's not necessary to log in as any of the special logins created during installation. There are numerous features of DB2 First Steps that you can explore as an ordinary user. However, Linux's strong security—in particular surrounding file, directory, and process ownership and access—means that a number of the more powerful tasks will succeed only if they are run by the instance owner.

I will go even further than my strong advice for Windows users at this point. For Linux users, you must log in as your new instance owner (e.g., db2inst1) for the soon-to-be-discussed activities, such as database creation, to succeed. You can achieve this either by using your system's graphical login screen or by using the su - command. Note that the dash is important so you inherit the instance owner's rights.

Open a shell window, such as Bash. To save yourself a bunch of typing and facilitate normal operation, you need to invoke the db2profile script, which will add the necessary directories to your $PATH and set other relevant environment variables to make life simple for your use of DB2. This is normally automatically added to your instance owner's shell startup script by the installer, but it doesn't hurt to know exactly how it's done so other user logins can benefit.

The db2profile script is normally located in the sqllib directory of the home directory of the instance owner. To illustrate, if you've taken the default name for your DB2 instance owner, db2inst1, the file is here:

```
/home/db2inst1/sqllib/db2profile
```

You can run it from your shell like this:

```
$ source /home/db2inst1/sqllib/db2profile
```

You can see its effect by examining some of the new environment variables it has configured:

```
$ set | grep DB2
DB2DIR=/opt/ibm/db2/v9.1
DB2INSTANCE=db2inst1
```

Clearly, having to manually set the db2profile every time you want to work with DB2 will become tedious very quickly. A good approach now is to edit your .profile, .bashrc, or equivalent file for your favorite shell to ensure that the db2profile is set permanently. In Bourne, Bash, Korn, or similar shells, add this line to the relevant file:

```
source /home/db2inst1/sqllib/db2profile
```

With the db2profile now set, you're ready to invoke First Steps. One important point to check at this stage is that your DB2 instance is actually running. There are several possible problems that might have prevented this, such as installing on an unsupported Linux distribution that lacks the necessary c libraries to enable successful installation and/or execution. Another possibility is that the automatic launching infrastructure for DB2 (which is discussed in the next chapter) might have been altered to prevent its start. To see if the DB2 instance is running, look for a process called db2sysc in the process list:

```
$ ps lax | grep db2sysc | grep -v grep
5  510  3059  3058  16  0 157016 29736 msgrcv S pts/1    0:00 db2sysc
```

If DB2 isn't running for any reason, jump ahead to Chapter 4 to see how to take control of starting and stopping DB2.

First Steps is launched under Linux by a script called db2fs. With your profile set, you can simply issue the command or run it from the Run dialog box:

```
$ db2fs
```

If you ever need to invoke First Steps using the full path, it can be found in both the instance owner's sqllib directory (e.g., /home/db2inst1/sqllib/) and in the installation's bin directory (e.g., /opt/ibm/db2/v9.1/bin).

Working with DB2 First Steps

Whichever way you decide to start First Steps, on its first invocation it will prompt you to choose between creating a browser profile specifically for First Steps or allow First Steps to share an existing browser profile, as seen in Figure 3-3.

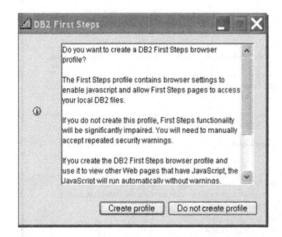

Figure 3-3. *DB2 First Steps browser profile selection*

This should provoke the obvious question in your mind, "Which option should I choose and why?" The reason for the profile option existence is to cater to First Steps' need to run JavaScript and perform operations that interact with your local machine—such as opening, reading, and writing files; and running executables from the browser. These actions might conflict with your desired security settings for your normal browser behavior, and in such circumstances it makes sense to quarantine these types of actions into a profile just for First Steps.

On the other hand, if you're happy with these types of actions being performed by your browser—and many people are—then it's safe to elect to not create a dedicated profile for First Steps and allow it to share your existing profile.

With that selection made, First Steps now launches. It's purposefully designed to be an intuitive browser interface (as can be seen in Figure 3-4), covering a wealth of tasks you might like or need to perform after installation.

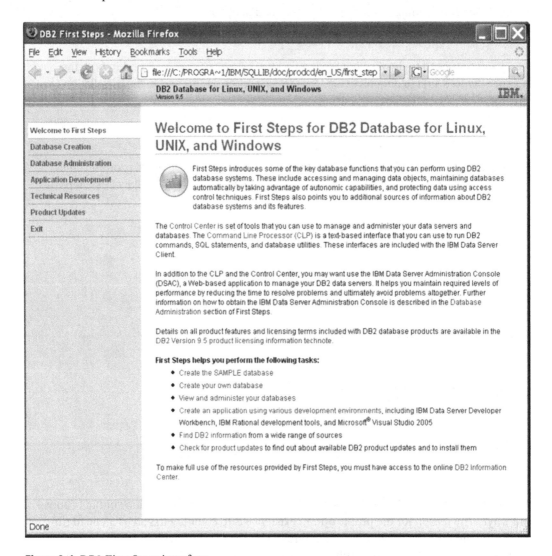

Figure 3-4. *DB2 First Steps interface*

The whole idea of First Steps is that it is a familiar GUI browser interface that even the freshest of DB2 recruits should feel comfortable exploring and using. So I'll spare you a page-by-page account of all the options that are included. Instead, I encourage you to follow every link to see what's included. You should find a taste of pretty much every topic you'll encounter throughout the rest of this book: database creation, database administration, developing with a variety of different languages, reference material on SQL and other topics, and more.

You'll use First Steps to do a number of things. First, you'll use it to create the SAMPLE database. Then you'll see how easy administration is made with the DB2 Control Center—you'll launch it from First Steps and explore the wizards it offers.

Creating the SAMPLE Database

You'll use the SAMPLE database as the basis for a host of examples throughout the following chapters, so now is a great time to create it and get a feel for what First Steps can do for you at the same time.

From the left menu of the First Steps home page, choose Database Creation. You'll be presented with a typical First Steps option screen (see Figure 3-5). It includes links to overview documentation on the DB2 Information Center, buttons to immediately invoke the Creation Wizard for normal (empty) databases, the SAMPLE database, and additional tools and information.

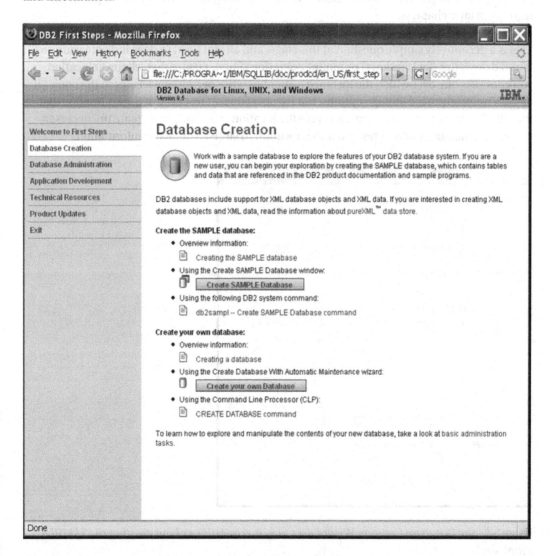

Figure 3-5. *Using DB2 First Steps to create the SAMPLE database*

If you feel that some additional reading is required, follow the link to the SAMPLE database creation overview. If you're ready to proceed (or after you finish reading the overview), go ahead and click the Create SAMPLE Database button.

You'll now see the wizard (see Figure 3-6) that asks you the only two questions you'll need to answer to create your sample database. That's right; two questions! (And you thought there'd be a dozen or more screens after your experience with the Installation Wizard.)

Your first option is a functional one. Do you want your SAMPLE database to be enabled for just SQL data and objects or do you want to include support for the new pureXML features of DB2 9 as well? It won't surprise you that my recommendation is to take the second option (XML And SQL Objects And Data) because you'll be making extensive use of the pureXML features in later chapters.

The second option is purely a storage question. Where do you want your data stored? This is a deceptively simple question at this stage, and all you need to do is indicate your preferred drive letter (for Windows) or mount point (for Linux). Ensure that whatever location you choose is one over which the instance owner has write permissions. Later in the book I'll discuss more advanced storage options, but for now you can rest easy in the knowledge that the DB2 Database Creation Wizard will take the location you give it and create the necessary storage and database structures under that location to store all database information.

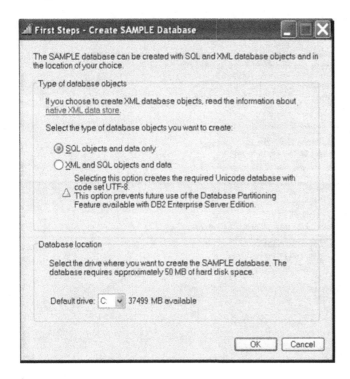

Figure 3-6. *The Database Creation Wizard asks only two questions about creating the SAMPLE database.*

Click OK when you're ready to start the wizard, and you'll see the progress dialog box spring to life, as shown in Figure 3-7.

Figure 3-7. *The Database Creation Wizard progress dialog box*

You might be tempted to think this: "Excellent, database creation is one of those complex things that will take ages. I've got time to make a cup of coffee." But you'd be wrong. The wizard will typically complete its job in under a minute! You don't want to be out of the room at the moment when your first successful job as a database administrator completes, do you?

Now your DB2 software is installed and you've created a database. You're no doubt thinking there's probably more to databases than that—and you're so right!

The DB2 Control Center

Any large organization or system is typically very chaotic until some bright spark realizes that a central point of control (a headquarters for all decision making) that has visibility over all that's going on tends to make processes go much more smoothly.

It was this kind of idea that led IBM to develop the DB2 Control Center. It's literally the central point of command and control for any number of DB2 systems. You'll explore it in terms of what it offers you to help manage and use your new installation, but everything you touch is available from one Central Control center for as many DB2 instances and host servers as you care to imagine.

Starting the DB2 Control Center from First Steps

You can jump straight to the DB2 Control Center from within the First Steps browser page. If you still have First Steps open after creating your SAMPLE database, simply choose the Database Administration heading in the left menu and under it select Basic Administration Tasks. You'll be taken to the launch page for DB2 Control Center, as shown in Figure 3-8.

You'll see a host of other options available from the launch page, most of which provide some background on how to do common tasks such as creating tables and inserting data. You'll take a look at these wizards from within the Control Center. Read them now if you want; after you finish, kick off the DB2 Control Center by clicking the Start DB2 Control Center button.

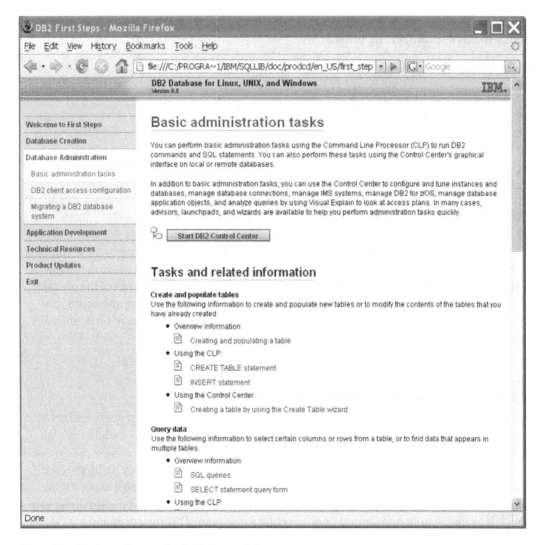

Figure 3-8. *The launch page for DB2 Control Center*

Starting the DB2 Control Center in Other Ways

If you closed First Steps or are returning to do regular work within the Control Center, you
will probably want to start the Control Center immediately instead of indirectly via navigating
through the First Steps browser. And you've no doubt guessed that typical shortcut approaches
exist.

An installation under Windows provides an IBM DB2 folder from the Start menu's All
Programs list. Assuming that you retained the default DB2 Copy name of DB2COPY1, navigate
through the menus DB2COPY1 (Default) ➤ General Administration Tools ➤ Control Center to
launch the Control Center.

Under both Linux and Windows, you can power up your DB2 Control Center session by running the db2cc command from a shell or command prompt; for example:

```
C:\db2cc
```

Note that under Linux if you're not the instance owner, you'll want to enable the db2profile, as described previously.

Selecting Your Preferred DB2 Control Center View

When the Control Center starts for the first time (and, optionally, every time), it prompts you to select how much detail you want to see in the GUI. You'll be presented with a dialog box (see Figure 3-9) containing Basic, Advanced, or Custom layout options.

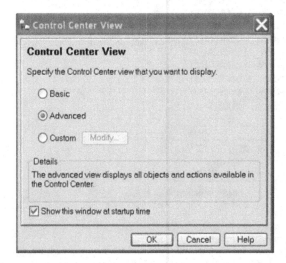

Figure 3-9. *Selecting the level of detail shown in the GUI for the DB2 Control Center*

The difference in settings between Basic and Advanced can best be thought of as one of visibility. In Basic mode, you see only your current DB2 instance and have access to the most common subset of objects and tasks. In Advanced mode, you see all registered instances and every object type within the databases hosted by those instances, and every function and wizard will be available.

There are two ways to get a feel for how the two differ. The obvious approach is to first run the Control Center in Basic mode and then run another copy in Advanced mode. You can compare the differences side by side; Figure 3-10 shows you how the advanced view for Control Center will appear, and you can open the basic view on you own computer for comparison.

The other approach to understanding the differences (and tweaking things to suit yourself) is to choose the Custom option and then step through the hundreds—yes, hundreds!—of visual elements you can turn on and off. Go mad and enjoy the personalization to its fullest! You can always go back to one of the stock display modes, Basic or Advanced.

I'll continue with some examples and exercises using the Advanced interface, but you can choose either one and follow along.

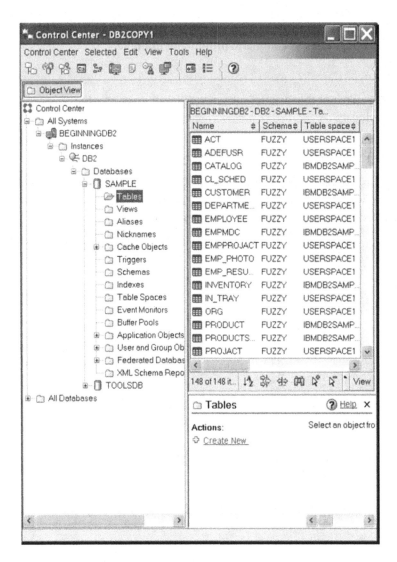

Figure 3-10. *Side-by-side comparison of Basic and Advanced interfaces for the DB2 Control Center*

Browsing the DB2 Control Center Object Views

I think I'd rapidly put you to sleep if I started a click-by-click walk through of every option within the Control Center. So instead I'll start with the Advanced side of the picture shown in Figure 3-10 and assume that you can get your Control Center to a similar point.

Tip I just expanded the tree until all database-level entries were visible and then expanded the SAMPLE database tree level to show the first-class object categories.

The first interesting thing to note as you browse around is that almost all the menu options within the Control Center are quite short and static (with the exception of the Selected menu—more on that shortly). The Control Center, Edit, View, and Help menus are pretty self-explanatory, letting you close the Control Center, tweak the layout to your liking, and call up the DB2 Information Center. The Tools menu is basically a shortcut for launching many of the graphical tools that complement the Control Center. The Command Editor works with SQL, the Task Center manages job scheduling and execution, the Health Center monitors the behavior and well-being of your DB2 environment, and more. (Many of these menus are discussed in more detail in Chapters 4 and 18.)

The Selected menu changes its contents based on the current item selected in the Control Center (you could probably guess that from its name). What might not be immediately obvious is that it changes to be an exact copy of the right mouse button context menu for the selected item in the object (tree) view. When you open the Control Center, it's usually the Control Center object that's selected in the object view; unsurprisingly this has very little to show in its menu. Click the instance entry DB2 and see how things change. By choosing the context menu with your right mouse button or pulling down the Selected menu, you now see a set of options concerned with managing the instance itself, as illustrated in Figure 3-11.

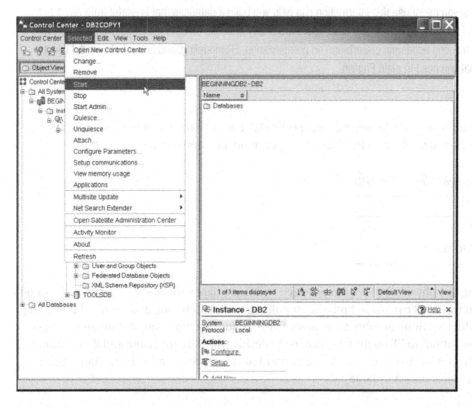

Figure 3-11. *The changing behavior of the Selected menu, equivalent to the context menu for your selected object view item*

To show just how much power is available from the context menu or the Selected menu, highlight your SAMPLE database under the databases object and you'll see a veritable laundry list of capabilities! This begs the question, though: how easy are these options to use? It's all well and good to have such easy access to all this power, but if the options themselves are overly complex they might leave you feeling a little jaded. So let's try one.

Invoking the Create Table Control Center Wizard

Databases are all about storing and using data (I hope I haven't surprised anyone with that statement), and the basic logical unit of storage is a table. The SAMPLE database has a handful of tables for a common employee/department/project example organization. One thing it doesn't have is a list of skills with which employees can associate themselves—something that is seen more and more in contemporary intranets and social networking sites. So let's add one with the Create Table Wizard.

Note Before you dive in and create a table, a little work understanding the actors (entities), their attributes, and how you might use this information can help you build a database that is useful from day 1 but also suitable for changing needs over time. There are plenty of books on data modeling available, so I won't bore you with a long academic dissertation on normalization, ER modeling, and so forth. Instead, I'll just describe what you need in plain English.

I want a simple, well-known name for each skill I want to track—as well as a description of what characterizes the skill itself. So my logical model is shown in Table 3-1.

Table 3-1. *Logical Model for Skills*

Skill
SKILLNAME
SKILLDESCRIPTION

Moving to a physical model, I might need to differentiate various skills that have the same name. That way, CPR can mean both Cardiopulmonary Resuscitation and Certified Practicing Rower. Adding a unique number as an identifier is a common modeling technique to achieve this differentiation, so I'll do that. I also need to decide what size my name and description will be (I suggest 50 characters for the name and 1000 characters for the description). So my physical model is shown in Table 3-2.

Table 3-2. *Physical Model for Skills*

Skill	
SKILLNO	(unique integer)
SKILLNAME	(up to 50 characters)
SKILLDESCRIPTION	(up to 1000 characters)

I'm sure many of you can work on this example to come up with far more elaborate and arguably better models, but let's charge ahead with this example. To start the Create Table Wizard, first highlight the Tables folder within the SAMPLE database in the Control Center object view. Your context menu and Selected menu now have the options Create and Create From Import. Choose the Create option; the wizard will start and present step 1 of the 7 available steps, as shown in Figure 3-12.

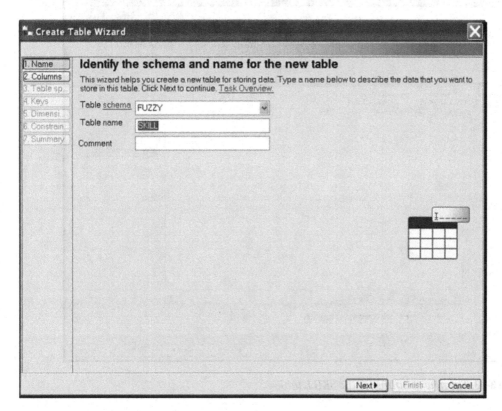

Figure 3-12. *Step 1 of the Create Table Wizard*

The first page of the wizard asks you for a schema, table name, and optionally a comment. For the table name use the name SKILL; for the comment you can enter anything you like. But what is a schema and what value should you use?

A *schema* in DB2 is very much like a namespace in programming terms in that it allows for multiple things such as tables to have the same name as long as they are in different schemas (namespaces). But schemas also act as a form of ownership "container," and if you place a table such as SKILL in a given schema, certain implicit privileges and qualities are inherited from that schema. (I'll talk more about them in Chapter 6.) For now, you see that the wizard has defaulted to using your login name as the schema, and that's fine. Click Next to move on to the second page of the wizard.

The second wizard page is where you enter the details you decided upon in your modeling of the SKILL table. The wizard makes it very easy to add your attributes as columns for the table, so instead of walking you through click by click, go ahead and add columns yourself. You'll see that it's very easy to end up with the arrangement shown in Figure 3-13.

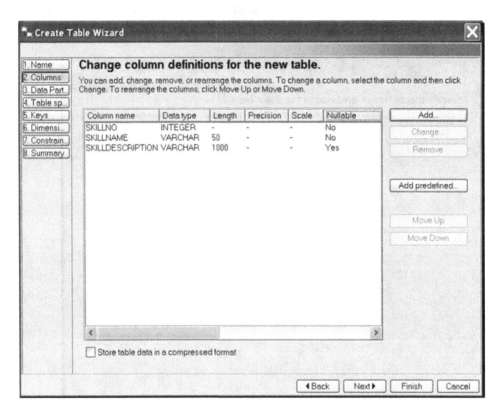

Figure 3-13. *The new columns for the SKILL table*

I'll talk more about the data types chosen (Integer, Varchar), and properties such as Nullability in Chapter 7, so don't worry if this topic seems to have taken a sharp turn into the realms of esoteric database internals. I'll head back on topic now!

Now is the time to notice that you're on page 2 of a 7-page wizard, but the Finish button is now active and available for clicking. That's right—you don't need to go any further if you don't want or need to. The DB2 Create Table Wizard can and will take sensible defaults for everything else to create your new table. Storage, compression options, and more can simply be left for later or remain with their defaults. You'll revisit the SKILL table later to add indexes, ensure that your identifier is unique, and do other interesting things, but for now you can just click Finish! The wizard will execute the command and present you with a summary that gives you both the SQL equivalent commands and the results of those commands, like this:

```
Commands Attempted:
CONNECT TO SAMPLE;
CREATE TABLE FUZZY.SKILL ( SKILLNO INTEGER  NOT NULL , SKILLNAME VARCHAR (50)
  NOT NULL , SKILLDESCRIPTION VARCHAR (1000)   ) ;
COMMENT ON TABLE FUZZY.SKILL IS 'Skills for Employees';
CONNECT RESET;

The  command completed successfully.

Explanation:

No errors were encountered during the execution of this command.

User Response:

No action required.
```

Close this message and you'll see your SKILL table appear in your tree view of tables in the Control Center. You might need to refresh your screen by clicking Refresh on the context or Select menu.

RESERVED WORDS

Astute readers will notice that my schema name in the preceding example is Fuzzy and might wonder where that name came from. It's the user name I used to install my DB2 Express-C software and with which I created the examples. Even more astute readers will notice that this is not my real name (it happens to be Grant). The most astute of all will realize the grand irony in that name. The word *grant* is a reserved word in DB2, meaning that it is part of the vocabulary that is predefined for DB2 commands and can't be used for object names such as tables and schemas.

More information on all the reserved words in DB2 can be found in the Information Center, and I'll talk more about them when I discuss DB2's particular dialect of SQL in Chapter 6.

Using the DB2 Command Editor

You mastered DB2 First Steps, started exploring the DB2 Control Center, and already created databases and tables for your nascent database. Let's round out the introduction to the graphical tools by working at the data level to see what the DB2 Command Editor has to offer.

The Command Editor can be launched from the General Administration Tools subfolder in the Windows Start menu, from the Tools menu in the Control Center on any operating system, or from the command line/shell by issuing the db2ce command.

Pick your favorite method and start the Command Editor now. You'll be presented with the main working screen for the Command Editor—one with which you'll probably become very familiar—as shown in Figure 3-14.

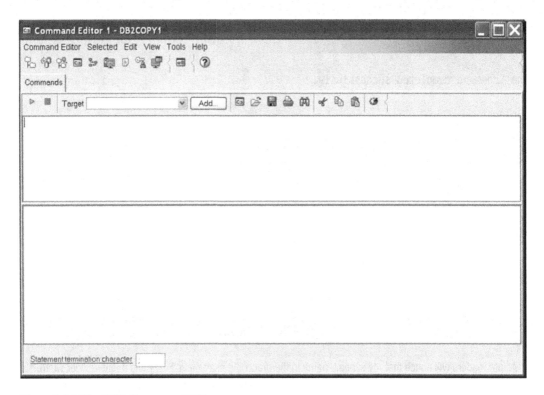

Figure 3-14. *The DB2 Command Editor*

Entire sections of your local library are probably dedicated to manuals on SQL, how it is written, its uses in business, and possibly even the added options that DB2 provides. And you're probably feeling comfortable now with browsing through a DB2 graphical tool yourself and don't need me to add 50 pages to this book of pretty screenshots. However, there's one great feature of the Command Editor that you should know about straight away, so let's take a look at it.

The Command Editor includes a wizard to help you build all manner of SQL statements: SQL Assist. To start it, ensure that you have the Commands tab selected, and then choose SQL Assist from the Selected menu.

SQL Assist helps you build just about every type of SQL statement imaginable; guides you through filtering, grouping, sorting; and more. It checks your syntax and gives suggestions for corrections. It also presents a similar tree view of tables and views as seen in the Control Center, improving it slightly by helpfully grouping objects into their governing schemas.

To see how easy it is to use, follow these steps to run a query against the EMPLOYEE table in your SAMPLE database.

1. For the statement type, choose SELECT.

2. For the FROM (Source Tables) option, navigate to your schema and choose the EMPLOYEE table.

3. For the SELECT (Result Columns) option, choose the EMPID, FIRSTNME, LASTNAME, and SALARY columns, using the arrow button to mark them as selected on the right side.

4. For the WHERE (Row Filter) option, choose SALARY less than 100000 as your formula and then use the arrow button to move it to the right side.

5. For the ORDER BY (Sort Criteria) option, choose SALARY again and select the added option DESC to sort in descending order

Your SQL Assist Wizard will look something like Figure 3-15.

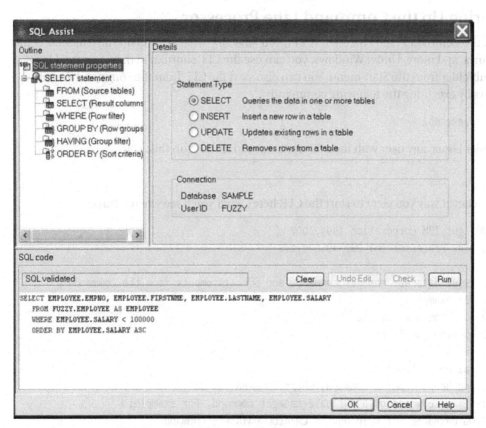

Figure 3-15. *A sample query constructed with SQL Assist*

You can click OK in SQL Assist, and the text of the SQL statement you've just constructed will be copied to the Command Editor, ready for running. Better still, you can click the Run button in SQL Assist and see your results right away. The Check button allows you to have your SQL examined for syntactic correctness, which usually isn't a problem if you've built the query graphically, but can help if you edit the text.

Command-Line Control of Your DB2 Environment

Graphical tools can be a great way to learn the capabilities and features of a product like DB2. But if you're like me, you want to know how to take complete control of your software from the command line as well. Believe me, it's not just because I'm some kind of dinosaur (Archaeopteryx, if you must ask). Instead, there are situations in which command-line control is very useful, including remote administration where the DB2 DAS instance is unavailable for some reason, and in commands and controls in scripts and batch jobs.

Powering Up the Command Line Processor

To start the Command Line Processor (CLP), you have the usual array of options: menus, command lines, and more. Under Windows, you can use the CLP shortcut in the Command Line Tools subfolder from the Start menu. You can also start the CLP from the command line on Windows by executing the following command:

```
C:\db2cmd.exe db2
```

Under Linux, any user with the db2profile set can simply run this:

```
$db2
```

Whichever way you elect to start the CLP, here's what you'll see when it runs:

```
(c) Copyright IBM Corporation 1993,2002
Command Line Processor for DB2 ADCL 9.1.2

You can issue database manager commands and SQL statements from the command
prompt. For example:
    db2 => connect to sample
    db2 => bind sample.bnd

For general help, type: ?.
For command help, type: ? command, where command can be
the first few keywords of a database manager command. For example:
 ? CATALOG DATABASE for help on the CATALOG DATABASE command
 ? CATALOG          for help on all of the CATALOG commands.

To exit db2 interactive mode, type QUIT at the command prompt. Outside
interactive mode, all commands must be prefixed with 'db2'.
To list the current command option settings, type LIST COMMAND OPTIONS.

For more detailed help, refer to the Online Reference Manual.

db2 =>
```

That's a lot of boilerplate text, but it actually contains some very useful hints. First, let's look at what you ended up with. By launching the CLP your shell has had numerous additional environment variables set, and the CLP interpreter has launched in interactive mode, providing you with the prompt db2 =>. From this prompt, you can now issue all manner of DB2 commands.

Learning About the Commands

But wait just a minute! You don't necessarily know any DB2 commands. Good point, so let's start by finding out what commands there are. Would you believe that the CLP has a sort of wizard to help you out? Well, okay, it's not a wizard in the traditional sense, but it does provide a way of finding the command you're looking for in a self-exploratory way.

The CLP supports a general-purpose help command, ? (the question mark), so entering ? and clicking Enter will present you with the full list of known CLP commands:

```
db2 => ?
```

ACTIVATE DATABASE	GET CONTACTS	RECOVER
ADD CONTACT	GET/UPDATE DB CFG	REDISTRIBUTE DB PARTITION
ADD CONTACTGROUP	GET/UPDATE DBM CFG	REFRESH LDAP
ADD DATALINKS MANAGER	GET DBM MONITOR SWITCHES	REGISTER LDAP
ADD DBPARTITIONNUM	GET DESCRIPTION FOR HEALTH	REGISTER XMLSCHEMA
ADD XMLSCHEMA	GET NOTIFICATION LIST	REGISTER XSROBJECT
ARCHIVE LOG	GET HEALTH SNAPSHOT	REORG INDEXES/TABLE
ATTACH	GET INSTANCE	REORGCHK
AUTOCONFIGURE	GET MONITOR SWITCHES	RESET ADMIN CFG
BACKUP DATABASE	GET RECOMMENDATIONS	RESET ALERT CFG
BIND	GET ROUTINE	RESET DB CFG
CATALOG APPC NODE	GET SNAPSHOT	RESET DBM CFG
CATALOG APPN NODE	HELP	RESET MONITOR
CATALOG DATABASE	HISTORY	RESTART DATABASE
CATALOG DCS DATABASE	IMPORT	RESTORE DATABASE
CATALOG LDAP DATABASE	INITIALIZE TAPE	REWIND TAPE
CATALOG LDAP NODE	INSPECT	ROLLFORWARD DATABASE
CATALOG LOCAL NODE	LIST ACTIVE DATABASES	RUNCMD
CATALOG NPIPE NODE	LIST APPLICATIONS	RUNSTATS
CATALOG NETBIOS NODE	LIST COMMAND OPTIONS	SET CLIENT
CATALOG ODBC DATA SOURCE	LIST DATABASE DIRECTORY	SET RUNTIME DEGREE
CATALOG TCPIP NODE	LIST DB PARTITION GROUPS	SET TABLESPACE CONTAINERS
CHANGE DATABASE COMMENT	LIST DATALINKS MANAGERS	SET TAPE POSITION
CHANGE ISOLATION LEVEL	LIST DBPARTITIONNUMS	SET UTIL_IMPACT_PRIORITY
COMPLETE XMLSCHEMA	LIST DCS APPLICATIONS	SET WRITE
CREATE DATABASE	LIST DCS DIRECTORY	START DATABASE MANAGER
CREATE TOOLS CATALOG	LIST DRDA INDOUBT	START HADR
DEACTIVATE DATABASE	LIST HISTORY	STOP DATABASE MANAGER
DECOMPOSE XML DOCUMENT	LIST INDOUBT TRANSACTIONS	STOP HADR
DEREGISTER	LIST NODE DIRECTORY	TAKEOVER
DESCRIBE	LIST ODBC DATA SOURCES	TERMINATE
DETACH	LIST PACKAGES/TABLES	UNCATALOG DATABASE
DROP CONTACT	LIST TABLESPACE CONTAINERS	UNCATALOG DCS DATABASE
DROP CONTACTGROUP	LIST TABLESPACES	UNCATALOG LDAP DATABASE
DROP DATABASE	LIST UTILITIES	UNCATALOG LDAP NODE
DROP DATALINKS MANAGER	LOAD	UNCATALOG NODE
DROP DBPARTITIONNUM	LOAD QUERY	UNCATALOG ODBC DATA
DROP TOOLS CATALOG	MIGRATE DATABASE	UNQUIESCE DATABASE

ECHO	PING	UNQUIESCE INSTANCE
EDIT	PREP/PRECOMPILE	UPDATE ALERT CFG
EXPORT	PRUNE HISTORY/LOGFILE	UPDATE COMMAND OPTIONS
FORCE APPLICATION	PUT ROUTINE	UPDATE CONTACT
GET/UPDATE ADMIN CFG	QUERY CLIENT	UPDATE CONTACTGROUP
GET ALERT CFG	QUIESCE DATABASE	UPDATE NOTIFICATION LIST
GET AUTHORIZATIONS	QUIESCE INSTANCE	UPDATE HISTORY
GET/UPDATE CLI CFG	QUIESCE TABLESPACES	UPDATE LDAP NODE
GET CONNECTION STATE	QUIT	UPDATE MONITOR SWITCHES
GET CONTACTGROUP	REBIND	XQUERY
GET CONTACTGROUPS	RECONCILE	

Note: Some commands are operating system specific and may not be available.

For further help:

```
              ? db2-command   - help for specified command
              ? OPTIONS       - help for all command options
              ? HELP          - help for reading help screens
The preceding three options can be run as db2 <option> from an OS prompt.


              !db2ic          - DB2 Information Center (Windows only)
This command can also be run as db2ic from an OS prompt.
```

You now know all these commands and are ready for an exam, right? Just kidding! I've been working with DB2 for nearly 20 years, and I still have to remind myself what some of those commands do.

Tip A little secret between you and me. Sometimes IBM forgets to include commands in that list because it considers them not strictly CLP commands. It probably has a point because including all the CLP commands, DB2 commands, SQL options, and more would run for dozens, if not hundreds, of pages.

Connecting and Disconnecting

Missing from the ? command's output are two of the most rudimentary commands: connect and disconnect. But now that you know they exist, how do you find out how to use them? The easiest way (described toward the bottom of that output) is to use the ? help feature in conjunction with the command stub in which you're interested. The CLP has this to say about the connect command:

```
db2 => ? connect
CONNECT [USER username [{USING password
[NEW new-password CONFIRM confirm-password] |
CHANGE PASSWORD}]]

CONNECT RESET
```

```
CONNECT TO database-alias
[IN {SHARE MODE | EXCLUSIVE MODE [ON SINGLE DBPARTITIONNUM]}]
[USER username [{USING password
[NEW new-password CONFIRM confirm-password] |
CHANGE PASSWORD}]]
```

So now you know that there are three different usage patterns. If you want to connect to the SAMPLE database, you can use the third option and skip all the other options:

```
db2 => connect to sample

   Database Connection Information

 Database server        = DB2/NT 9.1.2
 SQL authorization ID   = FUZZY
 Local database alias   = SAMPLE
```

I'm connected! Try it in your environment to make sure you can connect as well. The CLP also acts as a complete SQL interpreter and interface, so you can issue SQL commands just like those we used in the Command Editor example:

```
db2 => select firstnme, lastname from fuzzy.employee where empno = '000030'

FIRSTNME     LASTNAME
------------ ---------------
SALLY        KWAN

  1 record(s) selected.
```

One last command that is useful for you to know at this stage is the terminate command, which you use to exit out of the CLP. Use the terminate command to close any connections and exit the CLP.

```
db2 => terminate
DB20000I  The TERMINATE command completed successfully.
```

You'll learn more about the CLP and its many other capabilities in Chapter 4.

Summary

In this chapter, you've taken a whirlwind tour of the most important tools that come packaged with your DB2 software. There are many more graphical and command-line tools that will be covered in later chapters, and you'll also examine specific capabilities of the Control Center, Command Editor, and Command Line Processor in upcoming chapters.

CHAPTER 4

■ ■ ■

Controlling Your Environment with DB2 Control Center and Command-Line Tools

The first computer I used was a TRS80, and believe it or not the first program I used on that computer was a graphical game that involved spaceships, aliens, and numerous other things that could be rendered with little white squares on a black background. The one concrete thing I loved about the TRS80 was that when I started the tape drive to load a game, it was obvious when it had completed loading and the program started. Equally important, when I finished, it was obvious the game had exited.

What on earth does that have to do with managing DB2? Well, think for a moment about all the software you've ever installed and used in your life—whether databases, web servers, operating systems, utilities, or word processors. Have you ever asked these questions after installing an application?

Is it really installed?

Is it running?

Why is it still running? I thought I stopped it.

How do I stop this thing? It's eating all my CPU cycles!

Where is this stupid thing hiding its configuration options?

I know all those thoughts (and some that the kind editors at Apress wouldn't let me put in print) have occurred to me. So knowing how to really control your DB2 environment will help you feel confident and in complete control. Sometimes there's no better feeling than simply shutting everything down to prove to yourself that you're still the master of the machine!

Getting Started as the Right User

Security in DB2 is a topic in its own right, and we face a Catch-22 situation. Some of the nuances of tools and the required permissions to use them require a full understanding of authentication, privileges, and so on. But if we cover those topics first, you'll be left wondering when the *real* discussion of DB2 will start, with table and data and all that you'd expect from a database. To shortcut this process, you'll explore the tools and utilities in this chapter while logged in to the operating system as the instance owner. (The user chosen for installation under Windows is db2admin by default; under Linux, the user is db2inst1.)

Sometimes another user (such as root or administrator) is required, but I'll note that accordingly. With appropriate settings in place, any of the tools covered can be used by users other than the instance owner. (You'll learn more in Chapters 9 and 10, in which authentication, authorization, privileges, and security are discussed.)

Starting and Stopping DB2 Processes

Nothing puts you in more control of your software than the power to stop it in its tracks and start it on a whim. You'll probably be a little less neurotic than me when it comes to this, but even the most level-headed of you will want the know-how to do everything from move servers to apply patches. Before diving in to the nitty-gritty of individual processes and commands, it can be useful to picture the whole DB2 environment to get an appreciation for what components exist, how they fit together, and how you'll affect them with what you're about to learn. Figure 4-1 gives you a high-level view of the major components of the DB2 environment.

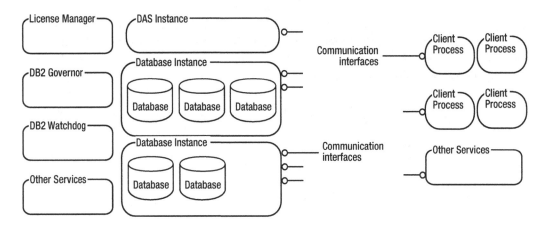

Figure 4-1. *A birds-eye view of the DB2 environment*

From the Control Center

Among the many talents of the DB2 Control Center includes its capability to control the state of DB2 instances. More specifically, the DB2 Control Center allows you to start and stop an instance, and thereby take its related databases offline or bring them online. To perform an instance startup or shutdown, simply highlight the instance in the Control Center, as shown in Figure 4-2, and right-click or use the Selected menu to bring up the list of options.

Start and Stop are pretty self-explanatory. When you stop an instance, you see a confirmation dialog box, as shown in Figure 4-3, which includes a useful option to disconnect any existing connections. Under the hood, this causes the Stop operation to invoke the force applications function of DB2, which forcibly disconnects any application that currently might be using one of the instance's databases.

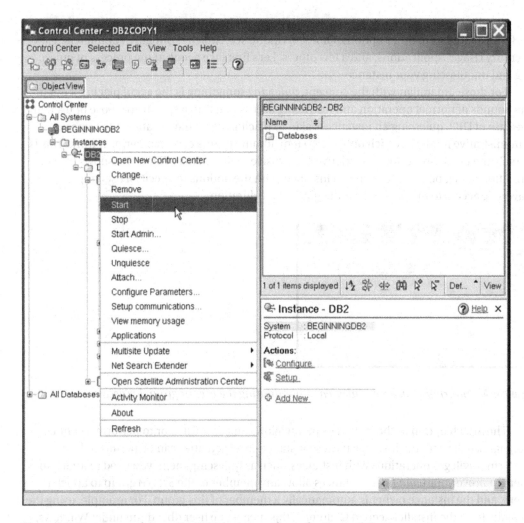

Figure 4-2. *Starting and stopping DB2 instances from the Control Center*

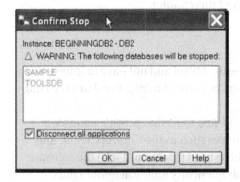

Figure 4-3. *Confirming instance shutdown with the option of disconnecting applications*

Besides starting and stopping instances, the menu for the instance in Control Center includes a number of other options: Quiesce, Unquiesce, Attach, Configure Parameters, View Memory Usage, Applications, and a few others. Let's first take a look at the process of quiescing and unquiescing your instance.

For those unfamiliar with the concept, *quiescing* something is the act of placing it out of the bounds of normal operation and restricting access or use to a specific purpose or user. In the case of DB2, quiescing an instance is akin to placing the whole instance into a special administrative mode, in which only the system administrators can then perform work. This is usually the precursor to some restrictive or intrusive maintenance. Figure 4-4 shows the confirmation dialog box for quiescing an instance, with the options to specify a user or group to have sole access to the instance for the quiescence duration.

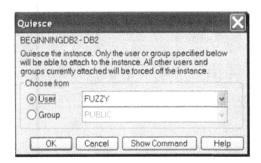

Figure 4-4. *Confirming instance quiescence, nominating the user or group for access*

The Attach option in the instance's menu allows an administrator to perform a connection handshake with the instance itself so instance-level activities can be performed. To perform privileges operations with instances, such as quiescing them, you need to attach to them to prove your *bona fides*. Instances allow any member of the SYSADM group to attach to them, and the instance owner is automatically a member of this group. For example, using the defaults from the installer seen in Chapter 2, this means the user db2admin under Windows, and db2inst1 under Linux.

The other options will be covered in the latter half of this chapter.

From the Command Line

Have you ever wanted to really, truly, and absolutely be in control and not have to interpret a pretty graphic to get a job done? Well, call me cranky (go on, I won't mind), but that's the kind of control I want from all my software, including DB2.

Fortunately, DB2 ships with a plethora of command-line tools that provide equivalent and/or complementary features to the graphical interfaces such as the Control Center. And there's no more important command-line tool than those used to start and stop the software.

First, the good news. The DB2 command-line tools are nearly identical under Linux, UNIX, and Windows, so you're already diversifying your skills. And the tools make use of environment variables that are also usually identical, so some of the advanced features operate in very similar ways under all of those platforms.

KILLING DB2 PROCESSES

Any discussion about process control usually ends up at this topic: What are the right way and wrong way to stop processes? The wrong way includes such extreme actions as killing processes with the kill, killall, or taskkill commands, or by powering off the host machine in an abrupt fashion.

In a word, don't! DB2 is an extremely robust system that is perfectly capable of recovering from accidental or deliberate process termination, but why take any chances? In most cases, DB2 will be the guardian of your precious data, so don't take unnecessary risks with that data if you don't have to.

Starting and Stopping the DAS Instance

You'll recall that the DB2 Administration Server (DAS) is a special "lightweight" instance of DB2 that doesn't actually directly manage any databases. Instead, its job is to allow various tasks such as remote administration. There's a Catch-22 that can occur when trying to work with a remote server: for many of the graphical tools to work remotely, you need to ensure that the DAS instance is running. But how can you use a remote tool to check that the DAS instance is running if it needs to be running before it can answer a remote tool. Chicken, meet egg; egg, meet chicken.

The db2admin command-line tool allows you to start and stop a local DAS instance, and by using ssh (or rsh or telnet if you are not concerned with security) you can connect to the host operating system and then use db2admin to control the DAS instance.

It's as simple as running db2admin with a command-line parameter of start or stop. Those of you familiar with init.d scripts and similar service controls under Linux will find this reassuringly consistent.

```
$ db2admin start
SQL4406W  The DB2 Administration Server was started successfully
```

Other than the confirmation message, a cryptic code has been returned along with the successful start of the DAS instance. This is a return message with a SQLCODE included for the command you just ran, and every DB2 and SQL command you issue can include such a code.

WHERE CAN I FIND OUT MORE ABOUT SQL CODES AND SQL STATES?

You won't always see SQLCODE values as you work with DB2 because they depend on the tools you are using. For instance, the graphical tools don't nag you with repeated dialog boxes that just contain eight-character codes. In other circumstances, you might see additional information included in a return message, reading something like this: SQL0104N An unexpected token ... SQLSTATE=42601. This is a SQLSTATE reference that is often used to report finer-grained details of a particular outcome.

For the moment, you can interpret any code as follows: A SQLCODE that ends in the letter *I* (Informative) is for information purposes only and is usually an indication of normal operation. A SQLCODE that ends in the letter *W* (Warning) is a warning of some kind that is worth reading but usually doesn't need remedial action. A SQLCODE that ends in the letter *N* (Negative) means an error of some kind has occurred, and you might then need to investigate that problem in more detail.

> SQLSTATEs take many forms, and you can ask DB2 for help about their meaning from the command line by simply typing ? nnnnn for the SQLSTATE number in question. You can also use ? SQLnnnnx to look up SQLCODE details.
>
> More about SQLSTATEs, error codes, and troubleshooting will be found in later chapters. More details on the error codes produced by all the DB2 applications can be found in the DB2 Information Center—either online or on your machine if you installed it as part of your environment.
>
> Given that I'm talking about command-line tools, here's a trick for jumping to the Information Center. Just type db2ic and it will launch! If you elected not to install the Information Center, fear not. IBM keeps an up-to-date, complete set of documentation available online at this URL: http://publib.boulder.ibm.com/ infocenter/db2luw/v9r5/. This is a great resource, and you should bookmark it now.

You can even call up the detailed help information for db2admin by running the command with the /h parameter:

```
C:\db2admin /h

SQL4413W Usage: DB2ADMIN creates, drops, starts, or stops the
          DB2 Administration Server.

Explanation:

The DB2ADMIN command syntax is:


   DB2ADMIN CREATE [
              /USER:<username>
              /PASSWORD:<password>
              ]
          DROP
          START
          STOP [/FORCE]
          SETID <username>
               <password>
          SETSCHEDID <username> <password>
          /h


 The command options are:
 ...
```

Take a look at what else is possible. For instance, if you decide to install the DB2 software under Windows but not have the Installation Wizard create the administration instance, you can simply invoke db2admin with the CREATE option to go ahead and create the DAS instance at your convenience. DB2 under Linux is stricter in this regard—you'll need to be logged in as root, or use su or sudo, to have the necessary permissions to run this command.

Under Linux, you can also use the dascrt command (as root) to perform DAS instance creation. You can also change the account used to operate the DAS instance, the account used to schedule tasks (I'll talk about that in a following chapter), and more.

Speaking of accounts, under Linux you'll generally find the db2admin tool in the ./bin directory of the nominated user for the administration instance. So for example, if you followed the defaults during installation, your administration instance user is called dasusr1, and you'll find db2admin under /home/dasusr1/das/bin.

One more useful feature is the ability to run db2admin with no parameters. This simply returns the name of the DAS instance and can be very useful for later use in scripts, batch jobs, and so on. It's also useful if you have multiple copies of DB2 installed on your server and need to remember at any point with which environment you're working. In such circumstances, only one DAS instance can ever be running because of port restrictions, but you might find yourself working in an environment like this and need to determine the current settings. Here's an example:

```
C:\db2admin
DB2DAS00
```

Starting and Stopping Database Instances

The job of running and stopping your regular DB2 instance is done very easily from the command line with the db2start and db2stop commands. All that you need to know about these commands are their names! It's as simple as that. Examples of what you'll see in action follow.

Under Windows:

```
C:\db2stop
SQL1064N  DB2STOP processing was successful.
```

Under Linux:

```
$ db2start
SQL1063N  DB2START processing was successful.
```

So simple! You might wonder how the db2start and db2stop commands know which instance to control. The value is sourced from the current DB2INSTANCE environment variable. So if you eventually decide to create more than one database instance, keep in mind that you'll need to set the DB2INSTANCE accordingly because the db2start and db2stop command-line tools take no parameters. More formally, you might like to source the db2profile script for the instance as a whole because it will set all the relevant environment parameters for you in one swoop and avoid slipups where you think you're working with one instance but are actually pointing to another. You can try to pass the db2start and db2stop command parameters—such as your instance name—but you'll be disappointed that it returns an error and leaves the instance state unchanged:

```
$ db2start db2inst1
SQL2032N  The "db2inst1" parameter is not valid.
```

So remember, if in doubt, passing parameters won't help. Instead, check the DB2INSTANCE value.

Under Windows, you can also use the general net start and net stop commands to control the relevant services for the DAS and regular instances, as well as the other services that are present. The only disadvantage of this approach is that you lose control of the additional options, such as /FORCE, which the native DB2 utilities provide for those circumstances in which evicting existing connections cleanly is desired.

Server Components

The DAS instance, and the regular instances of DB2 that host databases, run as part of normal DB2 operation. But they don't act alone. To interact with the operating system's security infrastructure, manage networking, and handle the sanity checks and monitoring that form part of DB2's advanced self-management capabilities, a range of processes act in unison to present the databases for you to work with.

DB2 Instances and the DAS Instance

Under Windows, the various DB2 services are registered with self-explanatory names. Based on a default installation, you'll see the service DB2—DB2COPY1—DB2, which represents the regular instance that will be hosting databases, such as the SAMPLE and TOOLSDB databases. If you happen to install the DB2 Enterprise edition, this service takes on a slightly different name to reflect the node number associated with your instance. For example, the first node will be called DB2—DB2COPY1—DB2-0. The *-0* indicates that this is node 0 (the first node).

Under Linux, your regular DB2 instance uses a multiprocess architecture to operate. This means that instead of a single monolithic process doing everything, some key components are broken out into their own child processes. The principle process is db2sysc, which is the engine that actually performs the core database functionality. Teaming up with this process are the following:

- db2acd: The "autonomic computing daemon" that's responsible for the automated health monitor and diagnosis features of DB2

- db2ckpw: The authentication facility for server-side credential checks

- db2gds: The global daemon spawner that acts as the catalyst for creating child processes

- db2ipccm: The IPC communications manager that acts as the listener for local connection requests that will use interprocess communication as their communications mechanism

- db2resyn: The resync manager that supports transactions that are involved in a two-phase commit

- db2tcpcm: The TCP communications manager that acts as the listener for remote requests that will use TCP as their communications mechanism

- db2wdog: The watchdog process that works in tandem with the db2gds process to monitor all DB2 processes and is the parent process for the instance as a whole

The db2start and db2stop commands take all the hard work out of managing these processes under Linux and UNIX. You'll also see db2agent processes spawned by the communications managers (db2ipcm, db2tcpcm, and so on) ready to manage work on behalf of clients. I'll talk more about db2agent and related processes when we discuss DB2 clients in Chapter 20.

The DAS has a service under Windows named DB2DAS—DB2DAS00 (using the installation defaults). Its counterpart under Linux is the process db2dasrrm. If you elected to install the TOOLSDB database, you'll also have a counterpart process named db2dasstm.

The DB2 Governor

The DB2 Governor is a bit like having Arnold Schwarzenegger as *The Terminator* look after your databases. It does not stop in its quest to hunt down rogue activities that breach rules you set on acceptable resource consumption, such as CPU time, memory use, and so on.

Under Windows, this is installed as the DB2 Governor (DB2COPY1) service—the copy name will reflect your choice if you used something other than DB2COPY1. Under Linux it is configured, started, and stopped using the db2govd command. Run it with no parameters to get the basic help instructions, like this:

```
$ db2govd

Usage: db2govd start    <Database> <NodeNum> <ConfigFile> <LogFile>
       db2govd stop     <Database> <NodeNum>
       db2govd validate <Database> <ConfigFile>
```

Use of the DB2 Governor is definitely part of advanced administration, so I won't talk any more about it. The DB2 Information Center has an entire section dedicated to its configuration and use, and it is sure to whet your appetite if you want to know more.

The DB2 License Server

I'm sure you've already guessed the purpose of the DB2 License Server from its name. It checks what license, if any, is present for your DB2 software at the time instances are started. It is installed once for each instance, and under Windows you'll see the service DB2 License Server (DB2COPY1). Under Linux, it runs as the process db2licm.

Using the DB2 Express-C edition pretty much frees you from worrying too much about the intricacies of license management. You'll also find that by default the License Server isn't running, so for now you won't need to know the mechanics of loading and using license files.

The DB2 Management Service

The DB2 Management Service is seen only under Windows. It acts to manage multiple sets of registry entries for multiple DB2 copies, given that the Windows registry is limited in allowing multiple identical configurations to exist simultaneously.

If you have two or more copies of DB2 installed on Windows, you'll actually see multiple DB2 Management Services, but only one will ever be (and should ever be) active. The DB2 Management Service for a given copy of DB2 will restore the Windows registry to the required state for that instance and stores away the required information so that it can this independently of other DB2 copies (and their respective Management Services) that might operate on the machine.

The DB2 Remote Command Server

So if the DAS supports remote management features, why is there another seemingly redundant facility such as the Remote Command Server? The answer lies in the capability of DB2 to operate a multinode environment in more advanced configurations, in which data is partitioned among multiple DB2 instances and databases. The Remote Command Server is the facility used by these multiple partitions for communication between themselves. This is not normally something you'll invoke and use directly, under either Linux or Windows, so there are no commands with which you'll need to be familiar.

The DB2 Security Server

The DB2 Security Server process exists to manage authentication when DB2 is configured for CLIENT authentication. I'll cover more about the different modes of authentication in Chapter 6. For now, you can file this away as one of the normal processes that should be running and think no more about it.

The DB2 Fault Monitor Coordinator

Some DB2 components operate as independent processes under Linux and UNIX environments, not as separate threads under the central DAS instance or normal instances. The normal process you'll see in operation in these environments is the DB2 Fault Monitor Coordinator. Its job is to act as the central coordinator to ensure that any DB2 instances configured to auto-start are always running. It does this by controlling one Fault Monitor for each regular instance. These in turn are responsible for ensuring that their respective instances are running.

If the Fault Monitor finds that the monitored instances aren't running, it has a configurable window of time in which to restart them, together with other options that govern restart attempts and related details. Normally, you don't have to be concerned with its operation—it is even clever enough that when used in conjunction with FixPacks for your DB2 software, it knows when to (and when *not* to) restart instances during patching. It is normally started automatically in a default configuration from an entry in the /etc/inittab file like this:

```
fmc:2345:respawn:/opt/ibm/db2/V9.5/db2fmcd #DB2 Fault Monitor Coordinator
```

To confirm that the Fault Monitor Coordinator and its dependent processes are running in your environment, you can examine your current process list and look for the process names db2fmcd (Fault Monitor Coordinator) and db2fmd (Fault Monitor Daemon). For example:

```
$ ps lax | grep db2fm | grep -v grep | awk '{print $13}'
/opt/ibm/db2/V9.5/bin/db2fmcd
/opt/ibm/db2/V9.5/das/bin/db2fmd
```

But there's a dedicated command-line tool just for such management, as you've come to expect. The db2fmcu utility can report on the process's status by invoking it with no parameters:

```
$ /opt/ibm/db2/V9.5/bin/db2fmcu
FMC: up: PID = 3705
```

So the Fault Monitor Coordinator is alive with PID 3705. If for any reason you want or need to stop the Fault Monitor processes from running in the future, the db2fmcu tool can be used to remove the relevant entry from /etc/inittab. You'll need to run this as a user with permissions to edit this file—usually that means root.

```
$ /opt/ibm/db2/V9.5/bin/db2fmcu -d
```

To restore the Fault Monitor Coordinator at any time, the db2fmcu tool can be used to restore the /etc/inittab entry as follows:

```
$ /opt/ibm/db2/V9.5/bin/db2fmcu -u -p /opt/ibm/db2/V9.5/bin/db2fmcd
```

That covers nearly all the usage scenarios for controlling the Fault Monitor Coordinator. If you invoke it with any unknown parameter (or an incomplete one), you'll get the usage details:

```
$ /opt/ibm/db2/V9.5/bin/db2fmcu -h
/opt/ibm/db2/V9.5/bin/db2fmcu - invalid option -h
usage: db2fmcu [-u -p <db2fmcd path>|-d] [-f <inittab>]
```

The only new option you'll notice there is the -f parameter. Use this option if you have a nonstandard location for your inittab file.

Configuring and Changing Your DB2 Instances and Databases

There are times when you need a little more finesse than simply starting and stopping the processes you now recognize as part of DB2. Whether it's for reasons of growth, performance, or a change in operating requirements, changing the parameters and settings that govern DB2's behavior is an integral part of administering databases.

At the suggestion of having to wrestle with dozens or hundreds of dials and levers to manage a database, many people groan inwardly and quickly move on to thinking about learning some other piece of software. IBM recognized that the continuously increasing complication of managing numerous parameters was a problem and set about making the job far easier in two ways.

First, IBM placed the parameters and the tools needed to work with them directly into the DB2 Control Center so that you didn't need yet another program or utility to look after them. It also introduced *autonomic* database management into DB2 several versions back, which in effect uses health monitoring, diagnostics, and feedback to automate much of the configuration work that has historically been performed manually by database administrators and users. I'll cover these autonomics in later chapters, so for now I'll concentrate on changes you might want to make and how they're made.

Two Different Levels of Configuration

Before examining the actual settings, a key concept for DB2 is the grouping of controlling parameters into those that work at the instance level and those that apply at the individual database level. The instance-level configuration is formally known as the Database Manager Configuration (DBM), and the database-level for each database is known as the Database Configuration (DB).

The kinds of parameters set at the instance level are those in which a consistent setting is needed for logical operation across all databases. Table 4-1 illustrates some sample parameters for instances.

Table 4-1. *Sample Instance-Level Parameters*

Parameter Name	Parameter Abbreviation	Example Value
Default database path	DFTDBPATH	c:
Java Virtual Machine heap size (4KB)	JAVA_HEAP_SZ	512
Size of instance shared memory (4KB)	INSTANCE_MEMORY	AUTOMATIC
TCP/IP Service name	SVCENAME	db2c_DB2
Discovery mode	DISCOVER	SEARCH
Discover server instance	DISCOVER_INST	ENABLE

Database-level parameters, as you have guessed, affect only their respective databases and allow different databases under the same instance to differ in behavior. Table 4-2 highlights a few of the many database parameters.

Table 4-2. *Sample Database-Level Parameters*

Parameter Name	Parameter Abbreviation	Example Value
Database code set		UTF-8
Self tuning memory	SELF_TUNING_MEM	ON
Log buffer size (4KB)	LOGBUFSZ	98
SQL statement heap (4KB)	STMTHEAP	2048
Interval for checking deadlock (ms)	DLCHKTIME	10000

Neither of these tables has an exhaustive list, but read on for a tip on how to quickly understand all the exposed parameters. Chapters 18 and 24 will cover the key parameters you'll want to know about in detail and will discuss their effects and interrelationships.

Configuring Your DB2 Instances from the Control Center

As described previously, the Control Center is your one-stop-shop for accessing the instance-level parameters. The context menu or Selected menu for your DB2 instance has numerous options that present themselves, as you can see in Figure 4-5. Buried about halfway down the list is the option Configure Parameters, which is thankfully exactly what it suggests: the option to choose when you want to configure parameters.

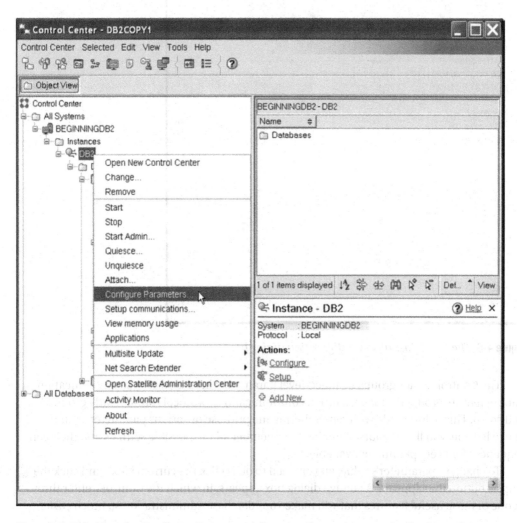

Figure 4-5. *Selecting the Configure Parameters function for an instance in the Control Center*

Choose it; a few seconds will pass if an attachment to the instance has to be made (you might see the generic Control Center progress dialog box), and you'll then be presented with the DBM Configuration dialog box shown in Figure 4-6, which covers every parameter available for your instance.

Figure 4-6. *The DBM (Instance) Configuration dialog box*

The Control Center groups instance-level parameters in related sets, so authentication parameters are grouped with each other, communications protocols are similarly grouped, and so on. This helps a little with remembering the purpose of various parameters, but if you're like me, you'll find yourself unable to remember all the possible settings and their consequences for every parameter available.

To change a parameter's value, all you need to do is click the current value and click the ellipsis button that appears. A change dialog box appears, in which the Control Center throws in one of those useful features that will make your database administration so much easier.

The change dialog box is customized for each parameter, so if you choose a parameter that uses a continuous range of numeric values, you provide an edit field that takes digits only. But choose a parameter that takes a defined set of keyword values, and the Control Center will render a dialog box that lets you choose these values only using radio-button controls. An example is shown in Figure 4-7 for the AUTHENTICATION parameter.

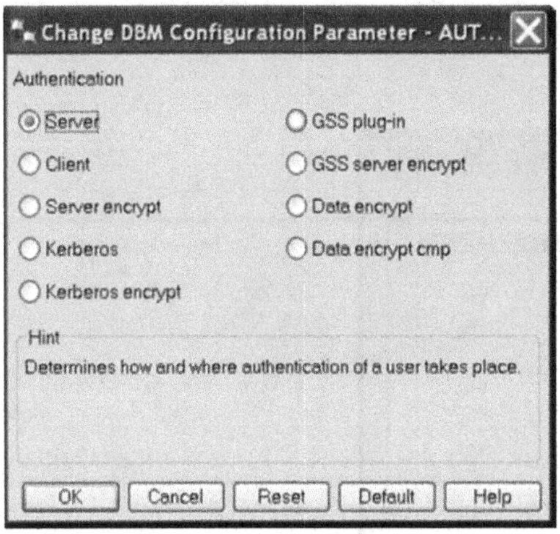

Figure 4-7. *Each parameter has a custom change dialog box.*

No chance to make a typo here (or accidentally choose a number that falls outside an allowed range). The custom dialog boxes are a nice feature and have saved my bacon a few times.

Tip When it comes to remembering each parameter's purpose, there is ample documentation available in the DB2 Information Center, various websites, and so forth. There is also the fantastic feature of parameter changing through the Control Center, which you can see in Figure 4-6 in the lower half of the dialog box. Each parameter includes a short synopsis of its purpose and range of values, which can trigger your memory in those moments when you're left wondering, "Is it TRUST_ALLCLNTS or TRUST_CLNTAUTH I need right now?" Shorter versions of these helpful descriptions are also shown in the main configuration dialog box when you highlight a parameter.

Configuring a DB2 Database from the Control Center

The mechanics of changing parameters for a database via the Control Center are analogous to those described previously for instance-level parameters. Using the context menu for your database or the Selected menu when your database is highlighted, you can display the Database Configuration dialog box for your database. This dialog box, shown in Figure 4-8, has the same structure as the one you've seen for instances, with its contents being the database-level parameters.

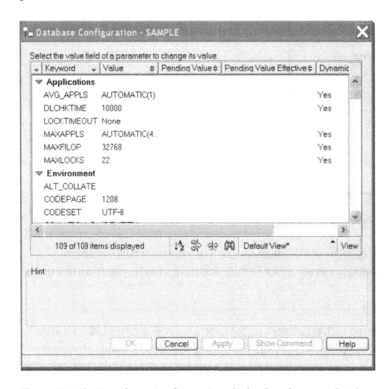

Figure 4-8. *The Database Configuration dialog box for your database*

Selecting a parameter for change (with the benefit of the custom change dialog boxes), works in the same fashion for databases as it does for instances. One of the extra features that you haven't yet explored is the ability to have the Control Center show you the equivalent textual command for the operation you're performing in the graphical user interface (GUI).

Choose the Interval for Deadlocks Check parameter (DLCHKTIME). Click the Show Command button, and you'll be presented with the equivalent DB2 commands to achieve the same change:

```
CONNECT TO SAMPLE;
UPDATE DATABASE CONFIGURATION USING DLCHKTIME 5000 IMMEDIATE;
CONNECT RESET;
```

Configuring and Changing Your DB2 Instances from the CLP

If the GUI tools make changing instance and database parameters so easy, you might be left wondering why you would want to bother with typing commands to achieve the same thing from the command line (other than as a relic of history). If that sounds rhetorical, I'm glad you spotted it. There are numerous reasons, including wanting to incorporate parameter changes into larger scripts or performing settings changes remotely from a system that has no GUI. Imagine being able to change your database configuration using a few short commands from your pager!

The mechanics of making any desired change are as simple with the Command Line Processor (CLP) as they are from Control Center. First, attach to your instance; second, update the configuration to reflect your required values.

Attaching to a DB2 Instance

When I first encountered the term *attaching* in the context of DB2, I wondered whether it was just a synonym for *connecting*. I was both right and wrong. It is synonymous with connecting, but it's the end-point of that connection where the subtlety lies. The act of attaching is always performed against an instance, so that when *attached* you are communicating with the instance itself, not any of the databases it controls. That sounds pedantic, I know, but the one thing to remember is that you attach to instances and connect to databases. You'll probably save hours of confusion and misdirection in the future if you can remember that simple distinction.

From the CLP prompt, the syntax in its simplest form is the following:

```
db2 => attach to db2

   Instance Attachment Information

 Instance server        = DB2/NT 9.5.0
 Authorization ID       = FUZZY
 Local instance alias   = DB2
```

You'll see that a few things have happened automatically. The attachment occurred under the auspices of my operating system login name, Fuzzy. I'll talk more about how authentication works in Chapter 9, but for now it's useful to know that you can also explicitly state whom you want to attach as. DB2 also makes life easy under Linux if you are working directly on the server itself. If you source the `db2profile` file, part of that process includes an implicit attachment to the related instance, so you don't actually need to explicitly use the attach command at all in that case.

First, I'll detach from the instance:

```
db2 => detach
DB20000I  The DETACH command completed successfully.
```

Now I'll explicitly tell the instance about who I am when attaching:

```
db2 => attach to db2 user fuzzy
Enter current password for fuzzy:
```

```
Instance Attachment Information

Instance server       = DB2/NT 9.5.0
Authorization ID      = FUZZY
Local instance alias  = DB2
```

Note that explicitly stating your credentials works only for users who have passwords. Most of you will be horrified at the thought of any userid not having a password, but it is possible under almost any operating system, including all the ones supported by DB2. Assuming that you have a reason for not having a password (and I don't have the space for a wide-ranging discussion on the topic here), remember to use the first method shown.

Note also that you can be attached to only one instance at a time from a given CLP session.

Issuing the Commands to Change Instance Parameters

Actually issuing the commands is straightforward—the thoughts and decisions about what to change will probably occupy your time. The good news is that the defaults for DB2 9 are very sensible, and you will probably have no need to change any instance parameters for some time.

The format of the command is always the same:

```
UPDATE DATABASE MANAGER CONFIGURATION USING {YOUR PARAMETER YOUR DESIRED VALUE}
[IMMEDIATE | DEFERRED]
```

You can also abbreviate the command as follows:

```
UPDATE DBM CFG USING {YOUR PARAMETER YOUR DESIRED VALUE}
[IMMEDIATE | DEFERRED]
```

The options provided of IMMEDIATE and DEFERRED reflect the capability of DB2 to make many parameter changes on the fly and don't need an instance restart to take effect. You can specify IMMEDIATE to have the change take effect right away and you can use DEFERRED to have the change wait for an instance restart, even if the parameter supports immediate change. You might want to do this, for instance, to allow a change to happen in conjunction with some alteration in the external environment. To speed up the process of setting or changing many values, you can specify multiple parameters and associated values in one command.

A useful parameter to work with as an example is the diagnostic reporting level, DIA-GLEVEL, of the instance. This parameter controls how much information is tracked in the diagnostic log and for what classes of issues when events happen to the server. You can choose from tracking nothing at all, just errors, errors and warnings, or errors plus warnings plus informational messages in increasing levels of detail. Reflecting those levels, the possible values are 0 to 4. Here's the command to set the diagnostic level to 4, the level that tracks everything:

```
db2 => UPDATE DBM CFG USING DIAGLEVEL 4 IMMEDIATE
DB20000I  The UPDATE DATABASE MANAGER CONFIGURATION command completed successfully.
```

Try some of the other levels yourself; when you're done, return the DIAGLEVEL to 3, which is the default.

Configuring and Changing a DB2 Database from the CLP

The approach to using the CLP to change database parameters is very similar to that used in the example covering instance-level changes: connect to the desired database and then issue the command to change the database configuration.

Connecting to a DB2 Database

I've touched on the differences in connecting to databases and attaching to instances. Suppose that you want to connect to the SAMPLE database. The command is the following:

```
db2 => connect to sample

   Database Connection Information

Database server       = DB2/NT 9.5.0
SQL authorization ID  = FUZZY
Local database alias  = SAMPLE
```

Simple, isn't it? Naturally, there are options to explicitly provide a user name and some to cover more advanced scenarios.

Issuing the Commands to Change Database Parameters

The command syntax is again very similar, but the key difference is that you're updating the database configuration, not the database manager configuration (i.e., instance configuration).

The format of the command is always the same:

```
UPDATE DATABASE CONFIGURATION USING {YOUR PARAMETER YOUR DESIRED VALUE}
[IMMEDIATE | DEFERRED]
```

As you'd expect, there's an equivalent abbreviated form:

```
UPDATE DB CFG USING {YOUR PARAMETER YOUR DESIRED VALUE} [IMMEDIATE | DEFERRED]
```

You might think that with only one letter difference, you might accidentally change instance parameters when meaning to change database parameters, or vice versa. Trust me, you won't. The parameter names are defined so that instance and database parameters never share the same name. So if you try something out of whack, you'll get a gentle error message and not totally unpredictable instance and/or database behavior:

```
db2 => UPDATE DBM CFG USING DIAGLEVEL 4 IMMEDIATE
SQL0104N  An unexpected token " DIAGLEVEL" was found following "USING".
Expected tokens may include:  "ADSM_MGMTCLASS".  SQLSTATE=42601
```

A real database-level parameter you can work with is the deadlock check time, DLCHKTIME. As you saw in the Control Center example, this parameter controls the window of time between deadlock checks, measured in milliseconds. Here again, the CLP helps where it can so that out-of-bounds values are prevented:

```
db2 => UPDATE DB CFG USING DLCHKTIME 5000000 IMMEDIATE
SQL5130N  The value specified for the configuration parameter "dlchktime" is
not in the valid range of "1000" to "600000".
```

Use a more realistic (and allowed) value and you'll have no problems:

```
db2 => UPDATE DB CFG USING DLCHKTIME 5000 IMMEDIATE;
DB20000I  The UPDATE DATABASE CONFIGURATION command completed successfully.
```

More GUI Tools to Help You Manage DB2

If you're operating DB2 under Windows, you have access to an additional GUI helper tool. The DB2 System Tray Tool, which plugs in to the system tray in Windows, is located in the Windows System Tray (see Figure 4-9) and looks like a little green database "cylinder" patiently waiting for you to call upon it.

Figure 4-9. *The DB2 System Tray Tool under Windows*

Click the tool and you'll be presented with handy shortcuts, as you can see in Figure 4-10, enabling you to start and stop your current instance, open the Control Center, and configure a handful of launch properties.

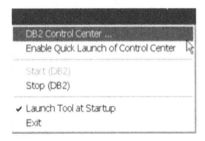

Figure 4-10. *Options provided by the DB2 System Tray Tool*

A very handy tool to which you'll quickly become addicted!

More Tools Available from the Command Line

There are extra tools available for command-line users, too (in fact, the number of these continues to grow with new releases of DB2). A full list would take many chapters to discuss, but here are some highlights.

The Version Information Utility: DB2LEVEL

DB2LEVEL is a very straightforward utility that can help you keep track of which version and FixPack of DB2 you have installed. It also comes in handy if you ever need to perform diagnostics on your system for any reason.

Simply execute the command from a shell or command prompt, and you'll see results like these:

```
$ db2level
DB21085I  Instance "db2inst1" uses "32" bits and DB2 code release "SQL09012"
 with level identifier "01030107".
Informational tokens are "DB2 v9.5.0.1", "special_17369", "MI00183_17369",
 and Fix Pack "2".
Product is installed at "/opt/ibm/db2/V9.5"
```

This utility can be really handy for finding DB2 installations that aren't in the default location.

The DB2 Registry Utility: DB2SET

Although you have dealt with instance-level and database-level parameters already, there's also a small set of parameters that covers the total machine environment for DB2, including all instances and databases. Although you very rarely need to work with these parameters, the tool you can use is DB2SET. This utility controls entries in what's known as the DB2 Registry, which shouldn't be confused with the Windows registry. Any DB2 server has a DB2 Registry, not just Windows servers.

You can see which values are currently in place by running the tool with no parameters from the command line:

```
C:\> db2set
DB2INSTPROF=C:\Program Files\IBM\SQLLIB
DB2COMM=TCPIP
```

If you're curious about further capabilities, try running db2set -? to see the extensive help.

The Instance Listing Utilities: DB2ILIST and DASLIST

I've covered in some detail the support DB2 has for multiple instances for managing your databases. It can be useful to quickly determine which database instances are actually active on a given host. For instance, if you're thrown into the deep end and asked to administer a server that was set up by someone else, you might have to find your own way. Two useful utilities exist to report the known instances on a given machine. The first, DB2ILIST, reports the known database instances and is invoked without parameters:

```
$ db2ilist
db2inst1
```

If you create more instances, they appear in that list.

A similar tool, DASLIST, exists to report the DAS instance. This tool is not in the normal bin directory—look in the ./instance directory to find DASLIST.

```
$ daslist
dasusr1
```

DASLIST takes no parameters and simply ignores anything you try to pass.

The DB2 Problem Determination Tool: DB2PD

The problem determination tool, DB2PD, is designed to be the Swiss army knife of technical diagnosis tools. It is unbelievably comprehensive and (even better) it's designed to do its work in a nonintrusive way.

First, what does it do? It can gather information about every aspect of DB2 and the platform on which it's running. Want to know what pages of data are in memory? DB2PD can do that. Want to examine operating system details that affect DB2? DB2PD can do that, too.

The way it achieves its goals is equally clever. Older tools for DB2 and other databases traditionally gathered information like this by either querying the database (and thus potentially adding load or confusing noise to a problem) or by having to invoke other tools to do the work in secret. DB2PD does its work by directly attaching to your DB2 instance's memory structures and processes. It then "x-rays" the system while the system goes about its normal work, oblivious to such scrutiny.

I think a whole book could probably be written on this tool alone, but to get you started, try invoking it from the command line as follows:

```
C:\ db2pd
db2pd> You are running db2pd in interactive mode.
db2pd> If you want command line mode, rerun db2pd with valid options.
db2pd> Type -h or -help for help.
db2pd> Type q to quit.
db2pd>
```

You're now at the prompt for the problem determination tool and can issue its commands interactively from there. The boilerplate text is helpful in that it leads you to look at the much larger help material that's available. Run help or -h from the tool (or run db2pd -h from the command line) and you'll see pages of information on the possibilities. Another command that's useful to know is quit, which exits the tool's interactive mode. Let's look at just one option of DB2PD to see what happens (this case uses the operating system information option, osinfo):

```
C:\ > db2pd -osinfo

Operating System Information:

OSName:   WIN32_NT
NodeName: BEGINNINGDB2
Version:  5.1
Release:  Service Pack 2
Machine:  x86 Family 6, model 14, stepping 8

CPU Information:
TotalCPU   OnlineCPU   ConfigCPU   Speed(MHz)   HMTDegree
1          1           1           2160         1            2

Physical Memory and Swap (Megabytes):
TotalMem   FreeMem     AvailMem    TotalSwap    FreeSwap
256        36          36          362          187
```

```
Virtual Memory (Megabytes):
Total      Reserved    Available    Free
618        n/a         n/a          223
```

A very tidy summary of your hardware, OS, and current resource state is presented. I'll leave the description there, but I encourage you to try a few other options to see how much detail this little tool can gather for you.

Summary

This chapter probably felt like an episode from the DIY channel, displaying tool after tool and showing you what's now at your disposal. By now you should feel comfortable taking control of every process and component of your new DB2 environment. You can bring databases up, take them down, and make them dance at every point in between.

I'll return to a few of the concepts discussed here in later chapters, so you'll get a second point of view on some of these topics to help broaden your understanding.

PART 3

■■■

Database Fundamentals with DB2 Express Edition

CHAPTER 5

∎ ∎ ∎

IBM Data Studio

Planning the design of a new system, whether it be a nascent social networking site or a mammoth enterprise resource planning (ERP) system, extends far beyond the realm of data modelling. There are interfaces to put on canvas, business decisions to make, and logic to capture. When it comes to ensuring that the application logic complements the data model you strived to create, DB2 provides equally capable tools to help you with the task. With DB2 9, IBM remodeled and relaunched its set of developer tools for DB2, first renaming it *Developer Workbench* and then (with the release of DB2 9.5) settling on the name *Data Studio*.

IBM Data Studio is tailored development environment for DB2 9.5 built on the Eclipse platform, providing you with a consistent integrated development environment (IDE) regardless of the operating system on which you develop: Linux or Windows. Its main game is to promote rapid design and development, enabling you to build business logic for your new DB2 applications quickly.

In this chapter, you'll take a crash course in the installation options provided and walk through some real-world scenarios that will show you the power of Data Studio for tasks such as connection management, working with SQL scripts and stored procedures, and adding business logic to the SAMPLE database.

Sourcing the Data Studio

IBM provides Data Studio as a separate download, primarily to prevent file sizes blowing out to several gigabytes if all the DB2 add-ons and samples were bundled together.

The Data Studio is also a new product for DB2 9.5, replacing the equivalent for DB2 v8: the DB2 Development Center. At the time of writing, the freely available software toolkits, DVDs, and sample CDs from IBM don't yet include the new Data Studio. Thankfully, the web comes to the rescue, as you can see in Figure 5-1.

Figure 5-1. *The download and information page for IBM Data Studio*

The DB2 website discussed in Chapter 1 is the place to go to source your copy of Data Studio: http://www.ibm.com/db2. This URL reliably redirects you to the DB2 home page, and from there a search for Data Studio will bring up the page dedicated to it, usually as the first search hit. A recent incarnation is shown in Figure 5-1—you can see more of its highlights mentioned and the link from which to download the Data Studio installation package.

The download is approximately 280MB for the Windows version and 240MB for the Linux version. IBM has stormed ahead with its development, making sure that as new releases of DB2 9 are made available, IBM Data Studio is similarly updated to support new database features, as well as adding new functions to the Data Studio itself. The "Viper 2" refresh of DB2 9 included a refresh of Data Studio released simultaneously, so it will pay to watch for associated releases of Data Studio as you see future DB2 releases made.

Installation Highlights

By now, you've enjoyed the pleasure of several different kinds of installation processes for DB2 components, so a detailed walkthrough isn't needed for Data Studio. There are some quirks involved in the installation process; I'll highlight them so you'll be prepared regardless of the system on which you plan to install. Unzip the installer to your desired temporary location and get ready for some seriously cool developer tools.

Multiple Installers for Data Studio

Start your installation under Linux by running the setup shell script installerImage_linux.bin and under Windows by running the setup.exe file.

Note At the time of writing, the latest version of Data Studio for Linux was the "Viper 2" DB2 9.5 release. The zip file unpacks to provide a disk1 directory; within it is the shell script mentioned: installerImage_ linux.bin. In the latest release, this file doesn't have the executable bit set. A quick chmod u+x on that file sorts it out.

You'll be presented with the installation dialog box shown in Figure 5-2. After you read its text, you'll probably start questioning your sanity, your vision, or IBM's capability to package software.

Figure 5-2. *An installation identity crisis: is this the installer for Data Studio, or not?*

The issue is this: you just executed the installer for the Data Studio, only to be staring at an install dialog box that promises to install the IBM Installation Manager. What's going on? Thankfully there is a reasonably sensible explanation.

By building Data Studio on the Eclipse framework, IBM has imbued it with the customary flexibility for which Eclipse is renowned. Controlling that flexibility and ensuring that installing the Data Studio is successful are the key reasons for interposing the IBM Installation Manager at this point. Its job is to deal with the enormous variety of existing Eclipse versions that might (or might not) be on your target machine, together with Java JDK/JRE versions, other IBM tools also build on Eclipse, and so on. It then ensures that you can either install Data Studio deep into the existing products it finds or wall it off into its own dedicated Eclipse, Java, and related environment.

The Power of Eclipse-Based IDE Installations

You should now proceed and allow the fresh install of IBM Installation Manager to complete. It automatically and seamlessly launches the *real* installer for Data Studio. You can confirm that the switchover in installers has happened by the text presented at the various points of installation as well as the distinct look and feel the IBM Installation Manager window takes on when installing Data Studio. Figure 5-3 shows the point at which the Installation Manager itself has been installed and subsequently invoked to walk you through the Data Studio installation.

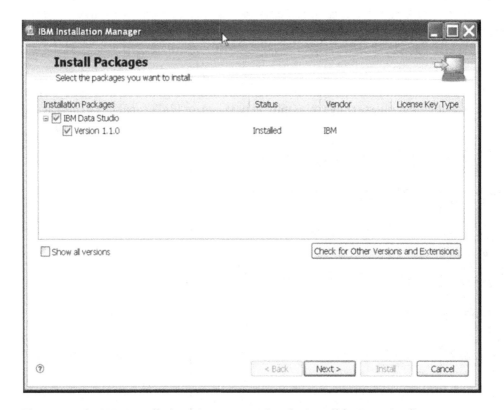

Figure 5-3. *The IBM Installation Manager starting the install for Data Studio*

Most of the dialog boxes you'll see throughout the Data Studio installation are largely self-explanatory: they control directories, licensing, languages, optional extras, and so forth. Of the dozen or so dialog boxes you'll see, two deserve some attention at this point to allow you to best decide how to efficiently install Data Studio in your environment.

Figure 5-4 shows the first of the two dialog boxes that control where Data Studio will be installed. IBM has modularized many of its Eclipsed-based tools using a standard packaging approach, called *package groups*, which helps enable multiple products to share one instance of the Eclipse IDE. One Eclipse instance can include products such as Data Studio, many of the Rational tools, the WebSphere modelling tools, and so on. As you can see, on a machine with no other components previously installed, you only have one option: to create a new package group. This makes sense because no package group exists that can be used.

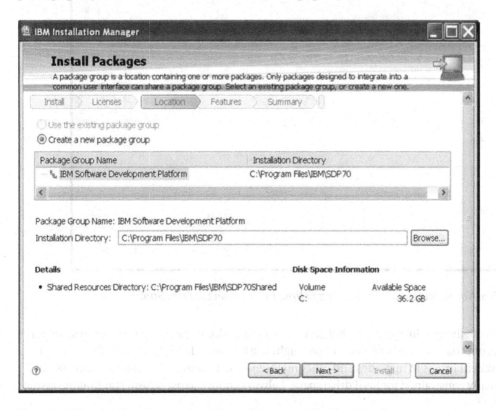

Figure 5-4. *Nominating the creation of a package group for Data Studio*

You can always change the location if you prefer your software to be installed into a custom directory on disk, but it won't change the functionality or other behaviors after it is installed.

Following package selection and the associated directory on disk, the second placement option is presented. Figure 5-5 shows the installer that prompts you to choose between the options of creating a new copy of Eclipse dedicated to Data Studio and nominating an existing installation, and a location for the Java JVM to be extended to include the Data Studio.

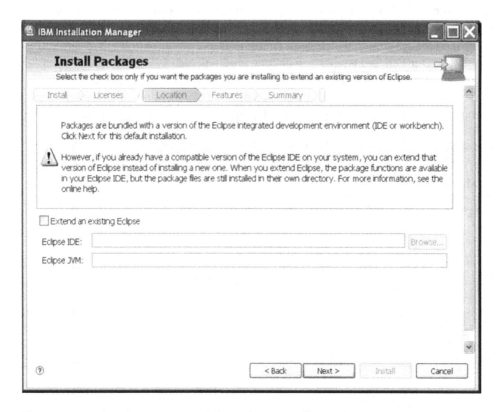

Figure 5-5. *Nominating a new or existing Eclipse installation for Data Studio*

You are the best judge of whether you want a stand-alone Eclipse instance or to share an existing one, based on other software you might use and the added complexity that a shared environment brings to upgrades and other maintenance. I'll admit right now that unless I'm particularly constrained for hard drive space, I always choose to use a fresh stand-alone install of Eclipse.

Running Data Studio

With installation out of the way, you're ready to dive straight in to using Data Studio to bring your data model to life. Under Windows, you should see a new program folder called IBM Software Development Platform. Within it, there is a subfolder named IBM Data Server Data Studio V9.5, and nested within that folder is the icon to launch the actual Data Studio.

After launching Data Studio for the first time, you'll see a typical Eclipse-style welcome dialog box (see Figure 5-6). If you've used Eclipse or any derivative based on it in the past, you'll know that this is its standard way of offering help, tutorial, overview, and other useful starting topics in one easy page. As you move through working with Data Studio, keep in mind that you can always return to this initial welcome dialog box at any time by choosing Welcome from the Help menu.

Note The installer creates a program folder and icon called IBM Data Server Data Studio V9.5 instead of Data Studio. The more generic name is due to IBM's actual and planned support for its other databases, such as Informix and Cloudscape, within the same Data Studio product.

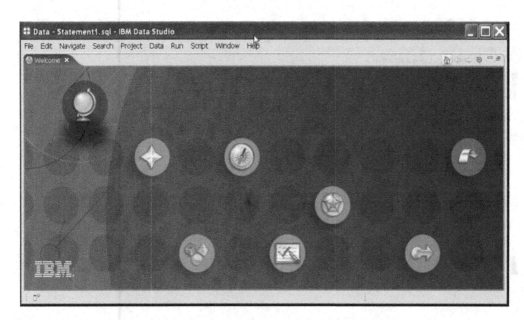

Figure 5-6. *The Data Studio welcome dialog box*

To get started, go straight to the normal interface by clicking the arrow icon on the far right. You can also click the close "cross" on the Welcome tab. You'll be presented with an empty project area split into all the usual Eclipse regions for files, code, debug messages, and so on. Don't panic because they are blank right now; they'll soon fill with more content than you can track.

Starting a New Data Project

The work you'll undertake in Data Studio will be managed as a collection under the auspices of an Eclipse project. This is very common terminology for most IDEs, but if you've never used an IDE such as Eclipse you can think of a *project* as a gathering into one set of all the files and settings for a group of work.

Data Studio leverages the simple wizard technology available from the Eclipse framework for project creation. The fastest way to create a new project is to open the File menu and choose Data Development Project from within the New submenu. The wizard starts, and the first dialog box prompts you for a project name (see Figure 5-7). I suggest EmpOfTheYear because you'll extend the SAMPLE database to provide structure and logic to allow employees to vote for their winning colleague. The other options presented might not be so obvious.

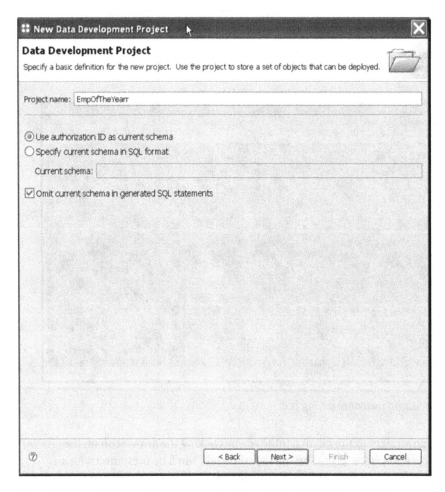

Figure 5-7. *Specifying project name and schema behavior in Data Studio*

The first option is to indicate whether to use the auth ID of the user who will eventually make the connection to the database as the current schema or nominate another ID to impersonate. This type of decision comes into play in many systems because it fundamentally affects things such as security and traceability. If a nominated ID is used to own all objects and perform all queries, stored procedure execution, and so on, it eases the modelling and maintenance to a degree but can cloud the issue of traceability—determining who did what—after the fact.

The alternative is to use the credentials that will be supplied with the connection at run time. This choice isn't necessarily better or worse than the first option; it's just different. Some design decisions need to take credential management into consideration—for instance, you can't just assume that everyone has privileges on everything because you might not be connecting as the auth ID that maps to the schema you plan to use. But it can also help you after your database code is deployed because you know by default that permissions need to be granted to allow access instead of worrying about a free-for-all. You'll use the auth ID as the current schema because the system is very straightforward.

The remaining choice is whether to omit the current schema in generated SQL statements. What this really means is this: would you prefer fully qualified object names such as FUZZY.EMPLOYEE or somewhat more readable object names with the schema omitted such as EMPLOYEE? Again, it's a flexibility-versus-security kind of issue. Omitting the schema means that your code is a little more readable and is easily moved around environments and schemas. But there's a risk that you might accidentally run test code against a production schema in an environment with development, test, and production schemas. Most database administrators avoid this issue by not using schemas for this segregation at all, but if you decide to use schemas for this purpose, you now know some of the pitfalls. I'll opt for schema name omission to keep the code more readable.

New Project Connection Management

The next decision is more straightforward: opting between defining a new connection to the database or selecting from an existing defined connection (see Figure 5-8). Because this is the first time you run Data Studio, only the sample Derby database connection exists, which is a totally different database from DB2. You need to create a new connection definition for use with this and other projects.

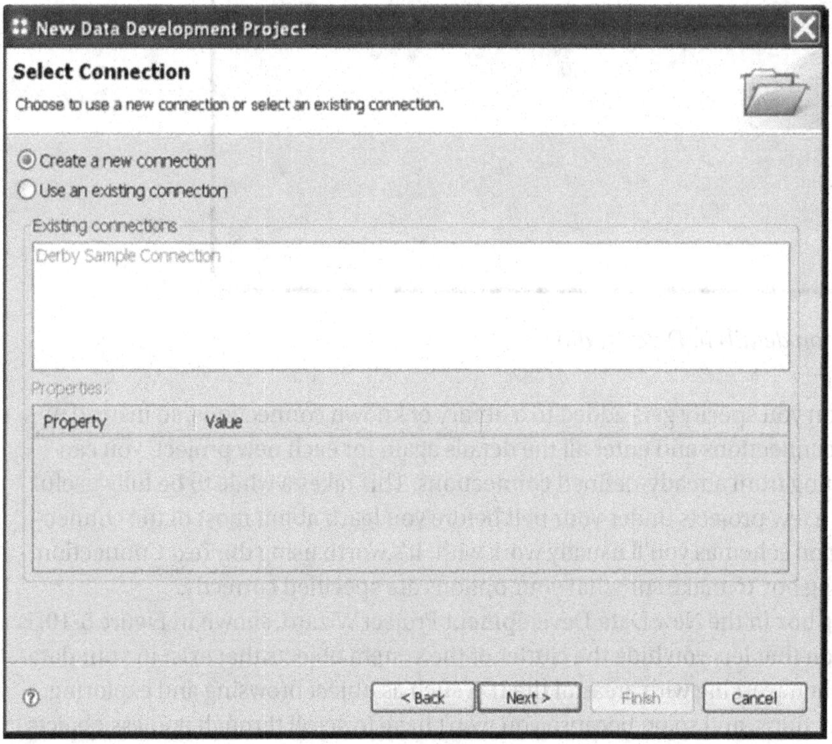

Figure 5-8. *Project connection specification in Data Studio*

Fortunately you are now in very familiar territory. The tour of connections, authentication, and related topics in earlier chapters should mean that the next step in the wizard is perfectly understandable. Your only challenge is to navigate the connection specification dialog box shown in Figure 5-9, which has to be one of the busiest dialog boxes I've ever seen.

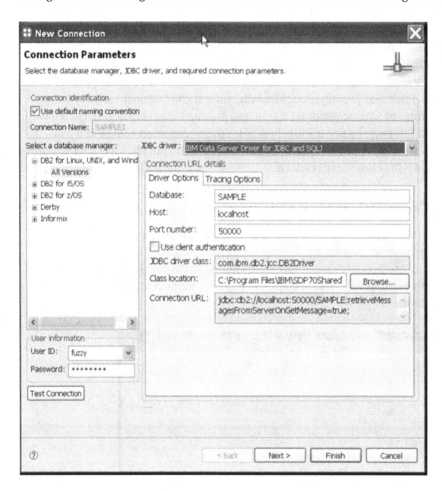

Figure 5-9. *Connection details in Data Studio*

The connection you specify gets added to a library of known connections, so instead of having to rebuild connections and enter all the details again for each new project, you can instead start selecting from already-defined connections. This takes a while to be fully useful because you need a few projects under your belt before you learn about most of the connection styles, users, and schemas you'll usually work with. It's worth using the Text Connection button on the dialog box to make sure that your options are specified correctly.

The last dialog box in the New Data Development Project Wizard, shown in Figure 5-10, is a handy filter option that lets you hide the clutter of the system objects that exist in your database. This helps when working with areas of the IDE such as object browsing and exploring, auto-complete functions, and so on because you won't have to scroll through endless objects called SYSIBM.SYSSOMETHING. There are times when this will be useful, and other times when you'll prefer to see these system objects. You can adjust your connection definition at any time or add different connection definitions to your library to handle the different scenarios; the choice is yours. For these purposes, you can accept the default value.

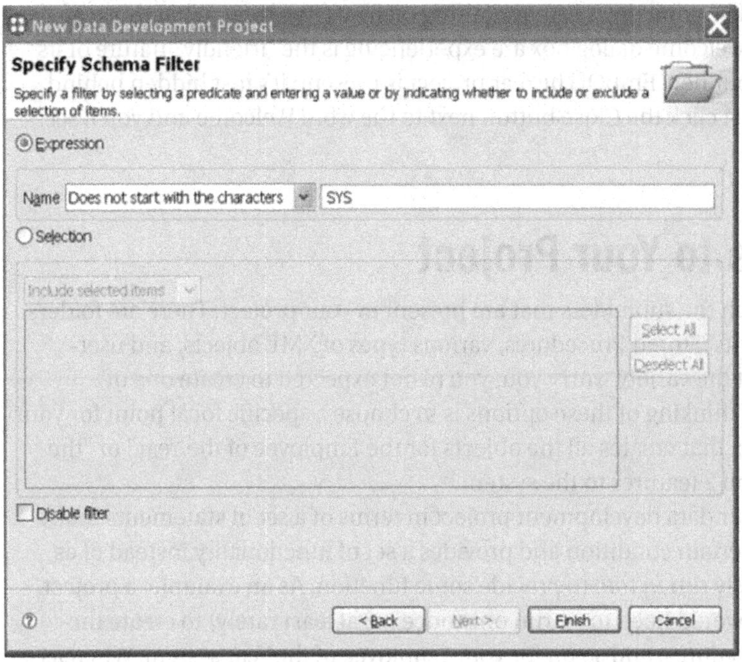

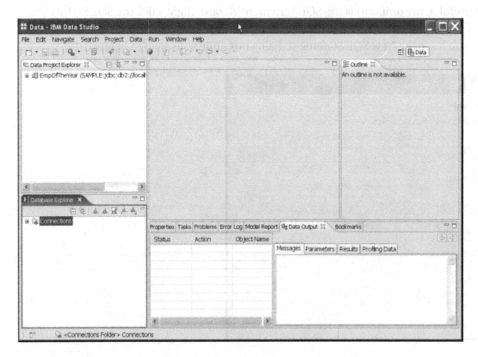

Figure 5-10. *Filter details in Data Studio*

After clicking the Finish button you can sit back; within seconds you'll be presented with the blank canvas for your Employee of the Year project (see Figure 5-11). However, I'm guessing that maybe 20 percent or more of my readership is now looking at the original welcome dialog box shown in Figure 5-6 instead.

Figure 5-11. *The completed project shell, ready for development*

So what went wrong? The good news is that nothing really went wrong. What those of you who are staring at the welcome dialog box are experiencing is the "friendly" nature of its always-on-top behavior. Your new EmpOfTheYear project is present; it's just hidden behind the welcome dialog box. Just click the Close button next to the word Welcome and you'll see your project.

Adding Objects to Your Project

Take a quick browse through the subfolders that are present in your project. There are folders to categorize SQL Statements, Stored Procedures, various types of XML objects, and user-defined functions. Don't let the variety worry you; you're not expected to create one of everything. A better way of thinking of these options is to choose a specific focal point for your project, such as "the project that creates all the objects for the Employee of the Year" or "the project that adds the version 2 features to the system."

In essence, think of your data development project in terms of a set of statements that places your database in a certain condition and provides a set of functionality instead of as code you might continuously run *in toto* to provide some function. As an example, a project that creates all the objects would need to be run only once (or at least rarely) to create the tables, indexes, stored procedures, and so on for your Employee of the Year system. Whereas a project that includes object creation scripts, data manipulation code, and so on might have its components run individually, but not often executed as one combined set of code.

New SQL Statement Wizard

By now, you've guessed that one of the bonus features of Data Studio is the additional set of wizards that streamline code creation to complement your projects. The first of the wizards (and most useful in my opinion) is the SQL Statement Wizard. Right-click the SQL Scripts folder within your project and choose the New ➤ SQL or XQuery Script menu option to launch the wizard. You'll see the New SQL Statement dialog box appear, as seen in Figure 5-12.

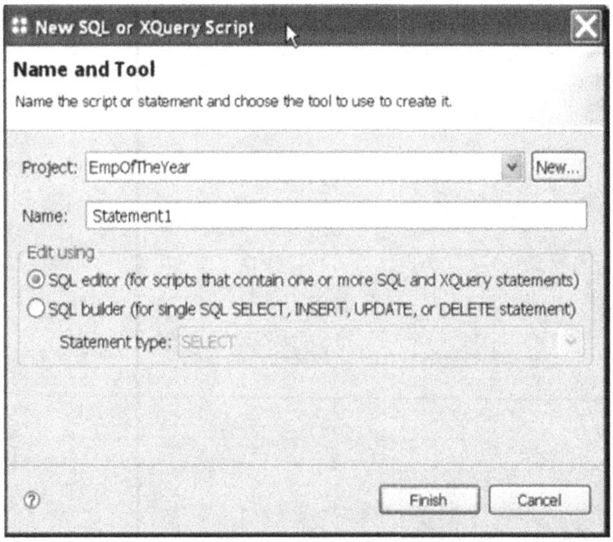

Figure 5-12. *The New SQL Statement Wizard*

This is the only dialog box for this wizard, with the actual logic of the code completed once the setup work has been done. As you'd expect from any IDE, it asks you to nominate the project to which the statement(s) belong. You're required to give this statement (or set of statements) a file name and you need to choose a statement template, which is the boilerplate text that's required as the "syntactic scaffolding" for a given kind of statement. So if you opt for a SELECT statement template, you'll later be presented with this default text from which to work:

```
Select *
  from
```

As you can see, it is very minimalist, in that it provides only the minimal SQL structure on which to then construct your real statement. It really doesn't matter what template you choose. If you decide to pick an INSERT template, but then decide you really meant to write an UPDATE statement, the wizard doesn't care. It's simply a case of overwriting the boilerplate text in the code window after the wizard has placed it there. The last options in the wizard (Edit Using SQL Builder or Edit Using SQL Editor) govern whether you'll be provided with a statement building assistant (akin to what you saw in the SQL Assist feature for the Command Editor) or whether you'll just be given a text stub to work with on your own. The SQL Editor provides two extra templates not present in the former: the Sample Statements template, which includes the syntactic stubs for a whole range of object-creation and data-manipulation statements; and no template (listed as None). Again, any of them can be used as a starting point because you'll just be editing text in the end.

To carry on with the example of a system for Employee of the Year, I'll build the first script as the CreateNominationTable script by choosing the SQL Editor option with None as a template and I'll include the code shown in Figure 5-13 to do the job of actually creating the Nomination table.

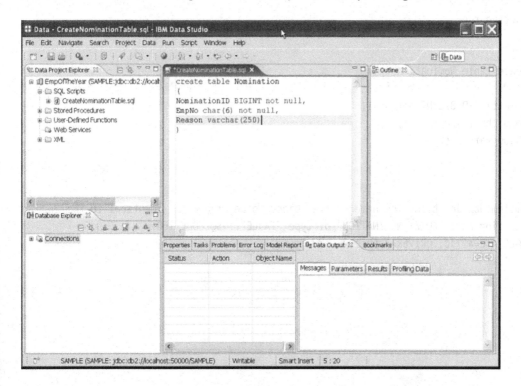

Figure 5-13. *The Nomination Table SQL Script in the Data Development Project*

Save this file and you now have built your first project component! Of course, my previous comment about Data Development Projects being slightly different from normal code development still stands. You won't execute or debug this 45 times because after the table is created additional attempts to create a table of the same name will result in an error. But the first time you run it, the statement should perform exactly as you intended. You can run it either by choosing Run SQL from the Run menu or by right-clicking the `CreateNominationTable.sql` file in your project list and choosing Run SQL. Go ahead and run one of those options now. In fact, run both, just so you see what an error looks like if you attempt to run a duplicate Create Table statement.

The first time you run the script, you should see this text appear in the Message tab in the lower-right corner of the dialog box:

```
Starting run

create table Nomination
(
NominationID BIGINT not null,
EmpNo char(6) not null,
Reason varchar(250)
)


Run successful
```

The Run successful message indicates all is well. If you run it again via any of the previous methods, the message should change to read as follows:

```
Starting run


create table Nomination
(
NominationID BIGINT not null,
EmpNo char(6) not null,
Reason varchar(250)
)


com.ibm.db2.jcc.b.lm: The name of the object to be created is identical to the
  existing name "FUZZY.NOMINATION" of type "TABLE".. SQLCODE=-601,
  SQLSTATE=42710, DRIVER=3.50.109
```

The text is quite understandable, and you are already familiar with SQLCODES and SQLSTATES from earlier chapters. If you want to deal with more complex environments, you can add more statements to your script to determine whether the table already exists and whether it exists with contents (i.e., rows of data) and then to change behavior accordingly. I'll cover some of those options in forthcoming chapters.

Another option at this point is to build a complementary script that drops the Nomination table. This might be useful as part of a development cycle, especially if you suspect that refactoring or a redesign of the table might be necessary. Create a new SQL script called DropNominationTable and give it the following code:

```
Drop table Nomination
```

Simple and useful. Naturally, you'd think twice about running this code against your finished system or a production environment. Both of your script files are currently unsaved, so you should probably invoke the Save All command from the File menu at this point. Together with the DB2 CLP, the Command Editor, and the Control Center, you now know four different tools to use to create and manage tables in DB2. That's flexibility!

Far more common than scripts that create and drop objects are the kind that actually manipulate the data stored. The common select, insert, update and delete statements that form the basis of this and many other projects can be created here, too. Start by invoking the wizard again; this time choose the SELECT template, choose the SQL Builder option, and then name it something like ShowEmployees. The familiar editing canvas will appear (refer to Figure 5-13), but an additional message shows in the middle of the dialog box:

```
To add a table, right-click in this pane and use the pop-up menu.
```

Well, go on! Right-click and you'll see the Add Table pop-up menu. Clicking it gives you access to a simple table browsing dialog box, as shown in Figure 5-14.

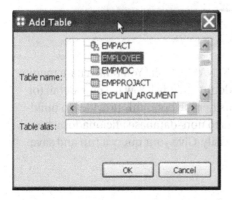

Figure 5-14. *The Add Table dialog box in the SQL Builder Wizard*

Drill down the tree as I have, and you'll see the tables you created and those that were created as part of the setup in Chapter 3 for SAMPLE. Pick EMPLOYEE (you can leave the Table Alias field blank) and you'll see the next trick Data Studio has up its computational sleeve, as shown in Figure 5-15: a nifty little column-picking interface that you might find very similar to other IDEs.

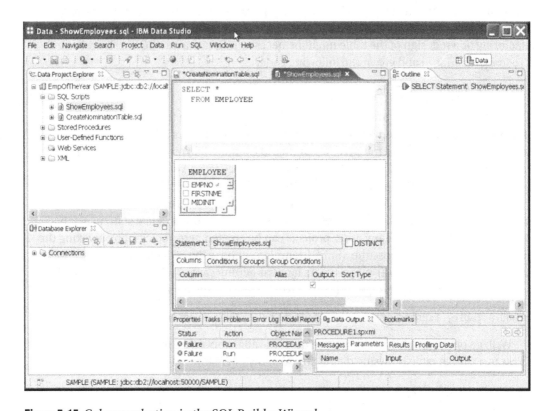

Figure 5-15. *Column selection in the SQL Builder Wizard*

Choose a few columns, such as FIRSTNME and LASTNAME. Voila! You built a data manipulation query. Such simple SQL is something you'll no doubt already know in some detail (or could quickly learn without Data Studio's help). But consider the boon this provides to building even more complex queries and think of the benefits to non–database aficionados who can build syntactically correct statements quickly and easily. Give your query a run and save the statement you built for later use.

New Stored Procedure Wizard

As easy as it is to put your many and varied SQL commands into one or more script files, it might become cumbersome when it comes to embedding this logic into your growing SAMPLE system. You wouldn't necessarily want to be continually opening text files to retrieve commands to execute them, and many of you know that several far superior approaches exist. The two key methods are embedding SQL in your application-level code and embedding the SQL in the database within logic constructs such as Stored Procedures and Functions.

I'll touch on SQL in higher-level programming languages in later chapters. Let's now write a procedure using the wizard that enables you to easily add a new nomination to the NOMINATION table. (If you have the same sick sense of humor I do, by now you're thinking you've seen enough wizards to populate a Harry Potter movie.)

Start the wizard by right-clicking the Stored Procedures folder in the Data Project Explorer window and select New ➤ Stored Procedure from the pop-up menu. You'll see the start dialog box for the wizard (see Figure 5-16).

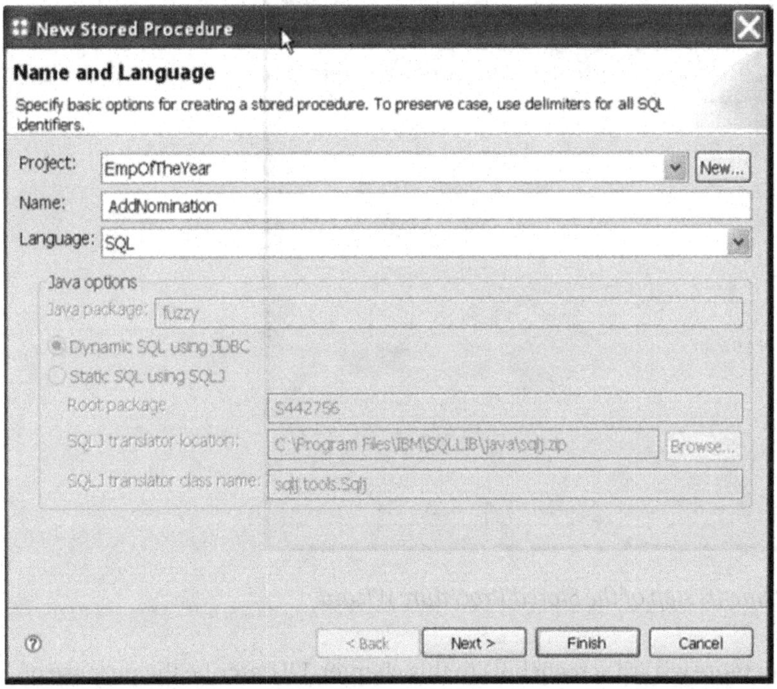

Figure 5-16. *The first dialog box of the New Stored Procedure Wizard*

Your choice for Project should be self-evident; it defaults to EmpOfTheYear if that is your currently open project. Choose a meaningful name—something similar to AddNomination. The last option is deceptively simple. Will your stored procedure be written in SQL or Java? The possibility of using Java will come as a revelation to some of you, but I'll leave that to the chapter that deals specifically with Java support. Choose SQL as your option and proceed.

Tip IBM added the capability to write stored procedures in Java a few years ago with the DB2 7 release. The DB2 engine enlists its own Java Virtual Machine (JVM) and supporting infrastructure to allow it to run Java stored procedures in a dedicated environment. See Chapter 16 for more details.

Now you'll appreciate my Harry Potter joke. There are wizards embedded within this wizard. Figure 5-17 shows you how the second dialog box of the wizard appears when opened. Don't panic! All the buttons and options have their purposes, and the good news is you rarely need to use more than a few of them unless you're writing more complex code.

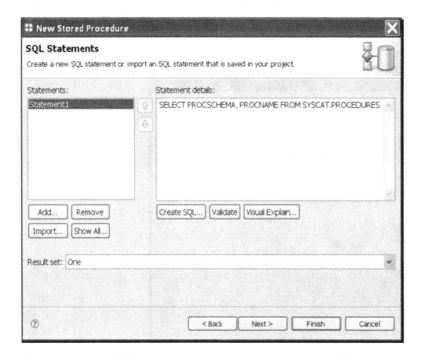

Figure 5-17. *The SQL Statements step of the Stored Procedure Wizard*

Instead of adding yet more wizard screenshots to this chapter, I'll describe the purpose of each feature in Table 5-1, and you'll be able to highlight which features are key to your likely future needs. It is designed to allow you to add all the SQL statements that will be used in combination to fulfill your business logic for a given procedure.

Table 5-1. *Features of the SQL Statement Step in the New Stored Procedure Wizard*

Feature	Purpose
Statements	Shows the list of statements available for this procedure.
Statement Details	Shows the code for the currently highlighted statement.
Add	Adds a new statement to the set.
Remove	Removes the currently highlighted statement.
Import	Imports SQL scripts saved in the project.
Show All	Shows a single view of all code, in order, for all the statements.
Create SQL	Launches the SQL Statement Wizard, similar to other SQL wizards.
Validate	Parses the current procedure text for syntactic correctness.
Visual Explain	Launches the utility that diagrammatically shows how the statements will be executed (learn more in Chapter 12).
Result Set	Shows whether the procedure returns any sets of data as a result of execution. If so, shows the number of sets.

All these features come together to help rapidly develop stored procedures. There is so much more detail to the art and science of DB2's stored procedure language and the capabilities provided that an entire chapter could be written on the topic. Chapter 8 is just such a chapter! So instead of deviating from this tour of the Data Studio for a very long discussion of SQL PL, the SQL-style stored procedure language for DB2, I'll instead offer a very simple piece of code to use in the current wizard:

```
INSERT INTO NOMINATION
(NominationID, Empno, Reason )
VALUES (:VAR01, :VAR02, :VAR03)
```

You'll delve into this in much greater detail in Chapter 8, but for now this insert statement expects to be able to insert three values into the NOMINATION table that will be passed to it via parameters provided when the procedure is called. The use of the colon prefix prior to the name, such as :VAR01, is the shorthand way of indicating that it is a parameterized value. Feel free to investigate the SQL Statement Wizard, invoked from the Create SQL button, which includes a GUI interface to specifying these parameters.

Regardless of the approach you take, moving to the next dialog box confirms the parameters that the procedure currently expects to receive when called (see Figure 5-18). It also allows you to change, add, and remove parameters if they require fine-tuning.

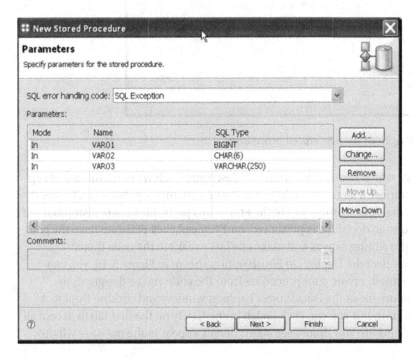

Figure 5-18. *Specifying parameters for stored procedures*

Because you have the necessary parameters described to match the insert statement, simply continue to the next dialog box.

Just as the SQL Script wizards allow you to build SQL statements without actually having to execute them, the Stored Procedure Wizard allows you to build all your logic without necessitating that the procedure be created or executed. The purpose of the Deploy Options dialog box is to explicitly take the initiative and tell the wizard that you do want the relevant create procedure statement run, so the procedure is actually created once the coding is complete. This dialog box pictured in Figure 5-19 allows you to provide for a different name and schema for deployment, which can be handy when working with multiple schemas for development, testing, and production.

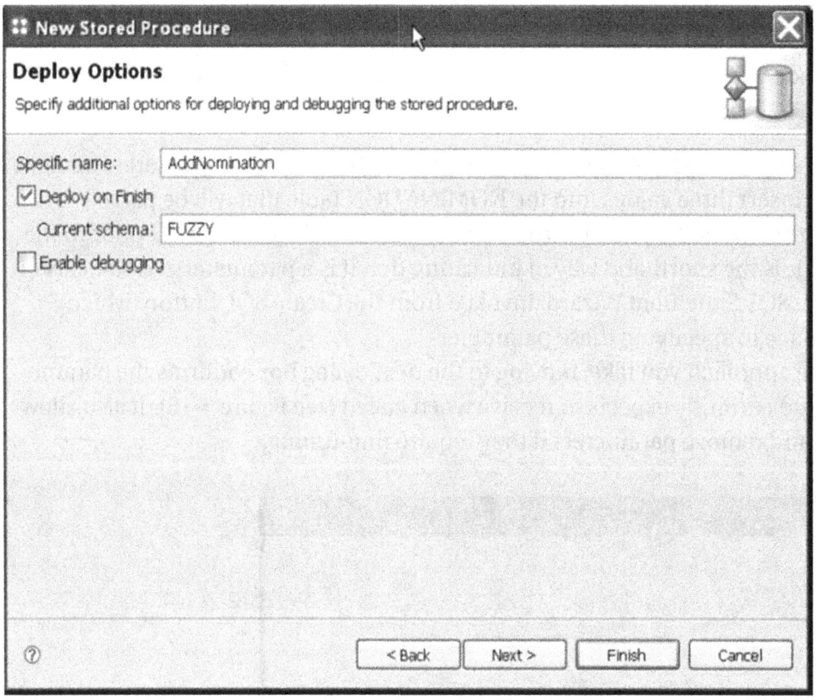

Figure 5-19. *Deployment options for new stored procedures*

The next dialog box, which I've omitted from this description, allows the gathering of separate parts of SQL to compose a larger procedure. You'll deal with this capability in Chapter 8.

Moving to the next dialog box brings you to the end of this powerful wizard. A summary of your stored procedure design decisions is presented, and you can click Finish to have the generated code placed on the editing canvas and make any last tweaks to the code there.

If you choose not to select the Deploy On Finish option shown in Figure 5-19, you can always deploy (that is, actually create your procedure from the code you've designed) by right-clicking the procedure file in the Data Project Explorer window and clicking Deploy. A deployment wizard will start, but you can click Finish immediately on the first tab to accept all the default deployment options. You should see status details appear in the message window like this:

```
FUZZY.ADDNOMINATION - Deploy started.

FUZZY.ADDNOMINATION - Create stored procedure completed.

FUZZY.ADDNOMINATION - Deploy successful.
```

Congratulations! You've just added business logic to your SAMPLE system. You can test it from any of your favorite DB2 query tools (and let's face it, you've now mastered four or five of these, so your beginner status is looking like a distant memory). Use the Call command to invoke the procedure, and pass four parameters to it like this:

```
db2 => connect to sample user fuzzy
Enter current password for fuzzy:

  Database Connection Information

 Database server        = DB2/NT 9.5.0
 SQL authorization ID   = FUZZY
 Local database alias   = SAMPLE

db2 => call addnomination (1, '000010',
 'Eileen designed the new company logo');

  Return Status = 0
```

That Return Status means that all is well (as you'd find in most other programming languages and environments). To prove that the procedure actually added the data, query the table:

```
db2 => select * from nomination;

NOMINATIONID          EMPNO  REASON
-------------------   ------ --------------------------------------
                    1 000010 Eileen designed the new company logo

  1 record(s) selected.

db2 =>
```

Hopefully that has sparked your interest in the power of stored procedures. You'll need to explore some of the other DB2 SQL and command capabilities before you return to a tour-de-force of stored procedures later.

Summary

IBM Data Studio is a powerful IDE that was created with actual database developers, administrators, and even users in mind. You have seen some of the power inherent in its many wizards, and there are at least a dozen more within the tool that you'll explore as the following chapters unfold.

Even though Data Studio has been released as a complementary stand-alone product that's suitable for working with both DB2 and other databases, it's easy to see how it leverages and supplements the power of the other tools delivered with DB2, and its wider development project capabilities will be invaluable to you for larger bodies of work you might undertake in the future. Happy developing!

CHAPTER 6

■ ■ ■

SQL for DB2: Part 1

A great deal of database work revolves around writing queries to do everything from populating your data to performing complex reports. The best place to start with a crash course or quick refresher on SQL is by learning about the data manipulation statements and seeing the additional capabilities DB2 offers with these statements. They then become the building blocks for further statements for object creation, database management, and more.

Manipulating Data with SQL

I've covered a range of SQL statements so far that are specific to DB2; for example, database creation, unique features of table and index creation, and other DB2-centric aspects of SQL. When it comes to manipulating the data in your database, there are additional special features and capabilities of DB2 with which you can take your SQL to even more productive extremes.

One thing I haven't covered is teaching you the fundamentals of the data manipulation language (DML) of SQL. And to be completely honest, I'm not going to! At least I won't provide a lengthy course on data manipulation with SQL because that would fill another book containing many more pages than this one. In fact, a book such as *Beginning SQL Queries: From Novice to Professional*, by Clare Churcher (Apress, 2008) fits that description perfectly as a contemporary in-depth book on pure SQL. What I'll do instead is quickly recap SQL basics with a quick primer on DML statements—select, insert, update, and delete—and then explore in more detail the power and features that DB2 brings to these common foundation statement types.

Note More recent adherents to SQL sometimes omit the select statement from the DML group, but that's more a passing fad than reality. Manipulation literally means *handling*, and a select statement can manipulate or handle data just as well as its related statements.

Using Select Statements

Select statements can be the easiest or most complex statements used with a database such as DB2. You'll explore the more complex aspects when I introduce the special features DB2 makes available, but for now let's review the basic structure. A select statement consists of up to six main sections:

- *select clause*: Enumerates the column names and related constructs

- *from clause*: Describes the target(s) from which the data will be gathered and how multiple targets should be joined

- *where clause*: Describes conditions known as predicates that the target data must meet in order to be included or considered for the query results

- *group by clause*: Describes how nonaggregated data will be handled in the presence of related aggregated data (sums, averages, and so on)

- *having clause*: Optional equivalent to the where clause, which is used as criteria to judge groups formed in the group by clause

- *order by clause*: Provides optional ordering to the otherwise unordered sets of data and results

Thus, the simplest of SQL select statements selects one or more values from a single table without any extra criteria, modification, or the like. Right now, you're probably asking, "How do I know from what table to select data?" The DB2 catalog—the internal collection of tables and other objects—comes to the rescue here. It includes specific tables that allow you to query the metadata about your system. *Metadata* is literally the data about data, and the system catalog tables includes such things as a table listing other tables, a table listing indexes on those tables, tables that reflect your permissions, and many more.

Table 6-1 provides a list of some of the most useful of the tables in the catalog, which you'll find yourself returning to again and again, whether you are an administrator, developer, or something else.

Table 6-1. *Useful DB2 System Catalog Tables*

Table Name	Schema	Purpose
SYSTABLES	SYSIBM	Information about all tables in the database
SYSINDEXES	SYSIBM	Information about the indexes on all tables
SYSVIEWS	SYSIBM	Information on all views in the database

While there are many specialized tables in the system catalog, the basic tables in Table 6-1 follow a simple pattern that you can see in the names used. For each type of object in the database, there's a SYS table to store metadata about them: SYSTABLES for tables, SYSVIEWS for views, and so on. If asked to guess what system catalog table might tell you about all the procedures or all the triggers in the database, you'd probably guess the names SYSPROCEDURES and SYSTRIGGERS. Your guess is correct!

There is also a set of views in the system catalog that provides read-only access to similar information. These views are in the SYSCAT schema, and there's a matching SYSCAT view for almost every table in the SYSIBM schema. Equivalent useful views in the system catalog are shown in Table 6-2.

Table 6-2. *Useful DB2 System Catalog Views*

Table Name	Schema	Purpose
TABLES	SYSCAT	Information about all tables in the database
INDEXES	SYSCAT	Information about the indexes on all tables
VIEWS	SYSCAT	Information on all views in the database
PROCEDURES	SYSCAT	Information on all stored procedures in the database
FUNCTIONS	SYSCAT	Information on all functions in the database

You now have the information you need to find out what tables and other objects exist in the SAMPLE database (and, in fact, any database). The most straightforward select statement to start a quick tour of SQL DMLs would ask for all columns using the asterisk shorthand notation and look like this:

```
select *
from sysibm.systables
```

Try that out for yourself from the DB2 Command Line Processor (CLP), Command Editor, or Data Studio. You'll get a nice graphical grid showing results in the two graphical tools, like the one shown in Figure 6-1 for the Command Editor.

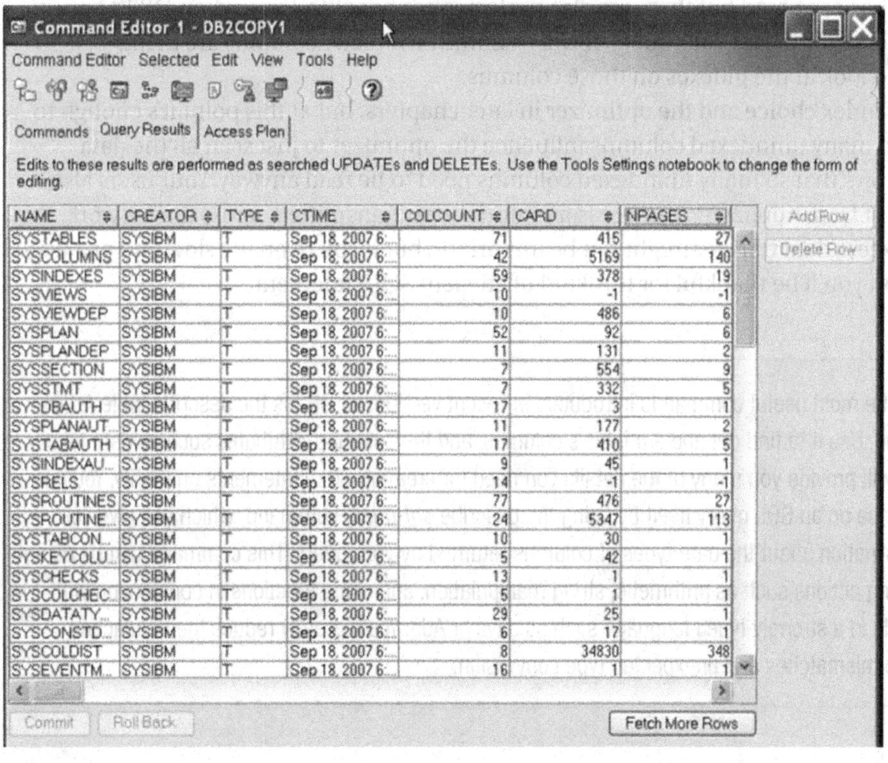

Figure 6-1. *Results of a select statement in the Command Editor*

If you try that same SQL command from the CLP, the results are somewhat frustrating. Screen upon screen of data scroll past, including countless lines of separators, blank screens, dashes, and so on. What's happening is a conspiracy of too much data for the small area of a typical command or shell window, plus the presence of several very long sets of data in the SYSIBM.SYSTABLES table.

Thankfully, you can opt to enumerate the columns in which you're interested in the select clause of the statement:

```
db2 => select name, creator, colcount
       from sysibm.systables

NAME                CREATOR COLCOUNT
------------------  ------- --------
SYSATTRIBUTES       SYSIBM        19
SYSBUFFERPOOLNODES  SYSIBM         3
SYSBUFFERPOOLS      SYSIBM         8
SYSCHECKS           SYSIBM        10
SYSCODEPROPERTIES   SYSIBM        12
...
```

The results are far more digestible from the command line. More importantly, dealing with specifically the data you need is one of the fundamental building blocks of writing efficient SQL. In relational algebra terms, the act of specifying columns is the equivalent of the Projection action. Additionally, in many user interface (UI) environments, your users will thank you for not inundating them with needless additional information. Not only does your SQL become easier to read but there are also performance benefits. First, when DB2's optimizer considers how to run your query, it will examine how many columns are being requested and look at the indexes on those columns.

I'll cover index choice and the optimizer in later chapters, but at this point it's enough to know that too many unindexed columns influence the optimizer to just scan all the data because it knows that so many unindexed columns need to be read anyway. Your users also directly benefit from not having unnecessary information transmitted across the network. On a fast LAN, excess data transfer might not be important, but if you're on the slow end of a dial-up connection you'll be thankful for this kind of efficient SQL statement.

Tip One of the most useful commands introduced in recent versions of DB2 is the describe table *table-name* command. Use it to find out about a table's columns, and the columns' attributes such as data type and size. This will provide you many of the details you need for creating SQL statements on the fly. You can even use describe on an SQL query itself by using the describe *sql-query* command, which will give you invaluable information about the data types of columns returned by your query. This command can be useful when performing actions such as arithmetic, string manipulation, and using functions in conjunction with application code in a strongly typed language such as Java or Ada. You'll greatly reduce the headaches caused by type mismatches and unexpected type conversion.

To complete the typical options used for the select line of a select statement, I'll introduce literals, rename columns, perform arithmetic, and even call some functions at this stage:

```
db2 => select name, creator, colcount as "No of Columns",
      abs(npages*4*1024) as "Bytes"
      from sysibm.systables

NAME                 CREATOR No of Columns Bytes
-------------------- ------- ------------- -----
SYSATTRIBUTES        SYSIBM            19  4096
SYSBUFFERPOOLNODES   SYSIBM             3  4096
SYSBUFFERPOOLS       SYSIBM             8  4096
SYSCHECKS            SYSIBM            10  4096
SYSCODEPROPERTIES    SYSIBM            12  4096
...
```

I'll cover which functions are acceptable in the select line of the select statement when I introduce scalar functions in Chapter 8. For the purposes of this example, you're using the absolute value function abs to calculate the size of database pages used by each table. That's reflected in the npages column; multiply by 4096 to get a value in bytes because by default you're dealing with 4KB page sizes. I'm using the abs function here because DB2 populates only the npages value when the runstats utility has been used on the table (more on runstats in Chapter 24). The npages column has the value -1 if runstats hasn't been used, and I want my output to reflect a "minimum" byte allocation of 4096 in those circumstances.

You can introduce conditions to be satisfied in the where clause, which acts as filtering predicates to return only a subset of data matching the criteria:

```
db2 => select name, creator
from sysibm.systables
where creator = 'FUZZY'

NAME                 CREATOR
-------------------- --------------------
ACT                  FUZZY
ADEFUSR              FUZZY
CATALOG              FUZZY
CHECKED_OPERATORS    FUZZY
CL_SCHED             FUZZY
CUSTOMER             FUZZY
DEPARTMENT           FUZZY
DEPT                 FUZZY
EMP                  FUZZY
EMPLOYEE             FUZZY
EMPMDC               FUZZY
EMPPROJACT           FUZZY
IN_TRAY              FUZZY
INVENTORY            FUZZY
OPERATORS            FUZZY
OPSEMPLOYEE          FUZZY
```

```
ORG                FUZZY
PRODUCT            FUZZY
PRODUCTSUPPLIER    FUZZY
PROJ               FUZZY
PROJACT            FUZZY
PROJECT            FUZZY
PURCHASEORDER      FUZZY
SALES              FUZZY
STAFF              FUZZY
SUPPLIERS          FUZZY
...
```

Eureka! With the first flexing of the where clause, you've narrowed down the list of known tables created when the SAMPLE database was put together. Of course, if you created the SAMPLE database as the instance owner (db2inst1 under Linux or db2admin under Windows) or have a different name, be sure to change your version of that command to use the right value in the where clause.

I could spend the rest of the chapter talking about just the where clause because it offers endless capabilities to mix and match criteria using Boolean AND, OR, and NOT operators; parentheses; and predicates such as IN and EXISTS. I won't tediously introduce each one separately because many of you will be familiar with them.

If you need a refresher, try starting with the following statement and then add more and more clauses to it to until you no longer get any results:

```
select name, creator, colcount as "No of Columns", abs(npages*4*1024) as "Bytes"
from sysibm.systables
where creator = 'SYSIBM'
and name like 'SYS%'
or (npages > 0 and colcount < 250)
and type not in ('A', 'O', 'X')
-- add as many more clauses as your query logic demands
```

You can use functions in the select clause and the shorthand asterisk (*) to represent all columns—as you saw previously with the use of the abs absolute value function. If you want to mix functions that aggregate data (such as SUM, MAX, MIN, COUNT and the like), presenting it with nonaggregate data, you need to introduce a group by clause. There are numerous definitions available that attempt to describe how group by works. A simple coherent explanation is best done by example.

Suppose that you want to know how much salary is paid to employees for each of the department codes listed in the SAMPLE database's employee table. Take a look at this table in the Control Center by using the describe table command or by using a full select statement. You can get the department code for an employee from the workdept column for the table and the relevant salary from the salary column of the same row. Although you can use the SUM function to do the arithmetic, how do you tell the SUM function that you want different sums for each of the department codes? Easy: you tell it to group its sums by each unique workdept value. That's the purpose of the group by clause.

```
db2 => select workdept, sum(salary) as newsalary
 from employee
 group by workdept
```

```
WORKDEPT NEWSALARY
-------- ---------------------------------
D11                       646620.00
A00                       354250.00
B01                        94250.00
E11                       317140.00
C01                       308890.00
D21                       358680.00
E01                        80175.00
E21                       282520.00
```

  8 record(s) selected.

You can use the having clause to apply criteria to aggregated groups. Think of the having clause as similar to the where clause, but applying only to the aggregate groups after they are formed by the group by clause. For instance, I might be interested only in the biggest spenders among departments, which spend more than $100,000 on salary. I can find them with the group by and having clauses as follows:

```
db2 => select workdept, sum(salary) DeptSal
  from employee
  group by workdept
  having sum(salary) > 100000
```

```
WORKDEPT DEPTSAL
-------- ---------------------------------
D11                       646620.00
A00                       354250.00
E11                       317140.00
C01                       308890.00
D21                       358680.00
E21                       282520.00
```

  6 record(s) selected.

Note that if you want to apply having criteria to your aggregate values, you need to use the equivalent aggregate function and columns in your having clause, even if you renamed your result column as I did with an alias.

Ordering must be applied if desired because relational theory and its implementation in SQL-based databases work with the notion of unordered sets. Thankfully, it's as easy as using the order by clause:

```
db2 => select workdept, sum(salary) DeptSal
  from employee
  group by workdept
  having sum(salary) > 100000
  order by workdept
```

```
WORKDEPT DEPTSAL
-------- ---------------------------------
A00                              354250.00
C01                              308890.00
D11                              646620.00
D21                              358680.00
E11                              317140.00
E21                              282520.00
```

    6 record(s) selected.

That's a very brief reminder for any of you who have forgotten the joy and thrill of using the select statement. Okay, perhaps I'm overselling the excitement level, but I think you get the idea. There are numerous additional concepts that apply to the select statement (and apply equally to the insert, update, and delete statements), but I'd quickly run out of room to cover them. You should at least be familiar with three larger building blocks of the select statement: joins, subqueries, and unions.

Joins bring together related data in separate tables for comparison, manipulation, and use. A straightforward example in the SAMPLE database is to join the data about an employee and the department in which the employee works:

```
db2 => select e.firstnme, e.lastname, d.deptname, d.location
 from employee e inner join department d on e.workdept = d.deptno

FIRSTNME     LASTNAME         DEPTNAME                               LOCATION
------------ ---------------- -------------------------------------- ----------------
CHRISTINE    HAAS             SPIFFY COMPUTER SERVICE DIV.           -
MICHAEL      THOMPSON         PLANNING                               -
SALLY        KWAN             INFORMATION CENTER                     -
JOHN         GEYER            SUPPORT SERVICES                       -
IRVING       STERN            MANUFACTURING SYSTEMS                  -
...
```

This example also uses aliases for tables in the SQL statement (the e and d shorthand notation for the table names), hopefully helping me and my readers avoid repetitive typing-strain related injuries. This example illustrates the most common join form, the inner or "equi" join, in which only rows that have equal compared attributes are used for later parts of the query or returned in results. Other types of joins that you'll be familiar with are left, right, and full outer joins.

ANSI JOIN SYNTAX VERSUS IMPLICIT JOINING

Those of you who have been using SQL for some time will note that I used the standard ANSI join syntax in the previous example instead of the implicit joining technique available by placing criteria in the where clause. I know some people who avoid the ANSI technique for inner joins and then struggle with the logic when they write outer joins when they're required.

One of the best ways to get comfortable with outer joins and the ANSI syntax is to think in terms of what each table is doing for you instead of just reading the syntax. A very useful technique is to think of the outer table as the "row providing table," from which result rows will primarily be generated. Think of the corresponding table as the "null supplying table," from which either supplemental matching data, or nulls, will be supplied. The outer table is the one mentioned on the *left* of the *left outer join* keywords for a left outer join, and the one mentioned on the *right* of the *right outer join* keywords for a right outer join.

Although using the older method of implied joins through predicates in the where clause is usable, available classic proofs show that using this approach will return incorrect results in a subset of circumstances, and only ANSI join syntax can provide the correct join semantics and predicate semantics to overcome such discrepancies. They do take a little longer to write, but they are far easier to read and give you the right answer every time.

Subqueries have multiple uses within SQL statements. They can be used as more complex criteria in a where or having clause, can act as virtual tables or views within the from clause at run time, and can even be used in various ways in the select clause.

```
select firstnme, surname
from employee
where empno in
(select mgrno from department)
```

The example finds all staff listed as departmental managers, and the mechanics are easily understood. Empno values from the employee table are compared against all of the mgrno values returned in the subselect on the department table. Many of you recognize that this subselect could be converted into a join—and that's true of a great many subselect constructs. It's important to recognize that there are logic differences when doing such subselect-to-join conversions. Using an IN predicate with a subselect in the previous example returns a given manager only once, no matter how many departments that employee manages. Converting it to a simple inner join returns the same employee as many times as they appear as a manager. (I'll talk more about the performance implications of subselects versus joins in Chapter 24.)

The union operations in SQL map to the set logic most of us learned in childhood. If you remember drawing circles and watching your teacher talk about Venn Diagrams, you have union operations mastered, whether or not you used databases before. Do you remember the Venn diagrams shown in Figure 6-2?

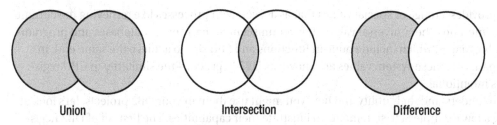

Union   Intersection   Difference

Figure 6-2. *Results of a select statement in the Command Editor*

These concepts form the basis of the union operators in almost all databases. DB2 supports the union set operations outlined in Table 6-3.

Table 6-3. *Union Operations in DB2*

Type	Behavior
Union	A merger of two sets of rows, so that one combined set is returned with identical rows (duplicates) removed
Intersect	A merger of only those rows that appear in both of the source sets—any row that appears in one, but not both, of the sets is discarded
Except	A pruning of one set by removal of all rows found in a second set (that is, set difference)

Users of other databases are familiar with the first three of those operations. The except technique—essentially, set-based subtraction—is known as *minus* is some other databases and is completely missing from several high-profile competitors of DB2. Each of these operations can be extended by using the ALL keyword (for example, UNION ALL, INTERSECT ALL, EXCEPT ALL). By using ALL, the union operation retains any duplicates that it otherwise would have discarded. Some examples of union operators are as follows:

```
Select firsname, surname from employee where salary < 80000
Union
Select firstnme, surname from employee where salary < 120000
```

That example is a little contrived because the same result could be achieved without a union, but it illustrates the point. An example of the intersect operation checks to see whether any employees have the same surname as someone else's first name:

```
Select surname from employee
Intersect
Select firstnme from employee
```

This raises a common limitation or requirement when using union operations. The number of columns in your union must match, and their data types must either be equivalent or complementary (so no combining integers with BLOBs, for instance).

Using DB2 Registers

DB2 provides a range of special values that assist you with processes like retrieving the current date, time, and other universal values. It is reminiscent of many other databases and programming languages, which include built-in functions and libraries to achieve the same end. In DB2 parlance, these system values are known as DB2 Registers—the similarity to CPU registers is intentional.

To understand their utility and how you might use them in your DB2 projects, let's look at using a few example SQL statements to illustrate their capabilities. The first set of DB2 Registers you'll look at are the date- and time-related registers: current date, current time, and current timestamp. The first attribute of these three registers to learn is that the naming intentionally matches the data type of the value returned. You can execute a sample query and immediately see proof of this:

```
db2 => select current timestamp from sysibm.sysdummy1
1
2007-08-27-13.10.21.263000
1 record(s) selected.
```

That certainly looks like a timestamp, doesn't it? And better still, it acts like a timestamp, too. This register and its companions, current time and current date, are particularly useful in circumstances in which you want to record the date and/or time an event happened, but don't want to burden the user with having to manually enter details.

Note The `sysibm.sysdummy1` table is a special table that exists in DB2 memory to take the place of a table in the from clause in which no real table is available or makes sense to use. This is analogous to features found in other databases, such as Oracle's "dual" table. The table `sysibm.sysdummy1` has only one column, IBMREQD, of data type `CHARACTER(1)`. There exists only one row in the table, with a value of Y. This data itself is almost never important; instead, it's the fact that there's only one row that matters.

Think about the physical design of the employee table in the SAMPLE database shown in Figure 6-3.

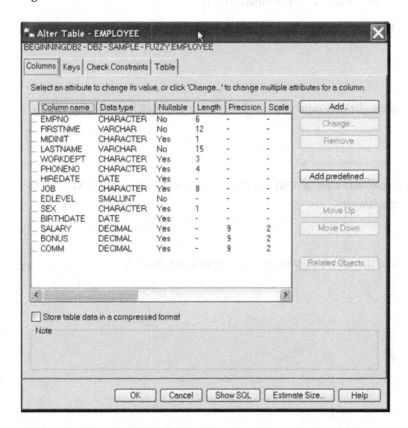

Figure 6-3. *The physical model for the table*

You can add a new employee to the table with an insert statement that looks like this:

```
Insert into employee
(empno, firstnme, lastname, hiredate, edlevel)
Values
('111111', 'Wolfgang', 'Mozart', '01/01/2007', 16)
```

While new employees expect to provide their personal details such as first name and surname, asking someone to key in their joining date will seem a little too much like hard work—they'll have experienced numerous systems that calculate this for them. Now you know DB2 can do this, too. You can change this insert statement to use an appropriate DB2 register to record it automatically, which has the added benefit of freeing you from worrying about how dates are written in various geographies and similar concerns. Let's add Mozart's good friend, Jimi Hendrix, to the system.

```
Insert into employee
(memberid, firstnme, lastname, hiredate, edlevel)
Values
('222222', 'Jimi', 'Hendrix', current date, 16)
```

The current date register does the work of determining the right value, and you're free to work on more interesting design and development issues. Just to prove that the current time register really tells the time, invoke the values command on it:

```
db2 => values current time
1
13:25:15
1 record(s) selected.
```

That's certainly the time right now (and you can infer the time of day I was writing this section).

Tip You can use the values command while working with DB2 Registers in any of the SQL execution environments with which you're now familiar.

Other DB2 Registers and the values they provide are shown in Table 6-4.

Table 6-4. *Other Useful DB2 Registers*

Register	Data Provided
Current degree	Controls the additional threads/processes spawned for intraquery parallel processing
Current path	The set of schemata DB2 will search for stored procedures and functions specified without a schema
Current query optimization	The current level of optimization, and therefore effort, used by DB2 for query plan generation
Current schema	The current default schema specified for the connection
Current server	The database for the current connection
Current timezone	The time zone in which the server is currently operating
User	The name of the currently connected auth ID

Using DB2 Functions and Procedures

You already saw a teaser about the kinds of functions and procedures that DB2 makes available in the column generation example. The upper() function exists to convert text to uppercase, regardless of its current form. There are literally hundreds of functions that are built in to DB2, as well as the ability to write your own (which we will cover in Chapter 8).

Instead of providing a list you can easily reference in the DB2 documentation or online, I'll cover the important factors that you should be aware of regarding functions. There are four broad types of functions, and their use differs along with the target information on which they can work.

- *Scalar functions*: Designed to take scalar parameters and return a single value. This seems to be a trivial statement, but the other function types take on more meaning in this light. Examples are upper(), floor(), and abs().

- *Column functions*: Designed to operate on an entire column of values and then return a single value based on well-understood rules of aggregation. You can see how these differ from scalar functions—it's a one-input versus many-inputs distinction. Examples include sum(), avg(), and max().

- *Table functions*: Designed to perform some operation and return a table-like set of data that can be used as a virtual table in the from clause of a select statement. An example is SQLCache_Snapshot(). Using a table function can be a very useful way of creating a table-like object based on complex business rules that don't sit easily in a table, materialized query table, or view. Even more useful is a table function's capability to react to parameters passed to it. (We'll cover this topic in more detail in Chapter 8.)

- *Row functions*: Designed to work with sets of data to transform them in rows of information based on built-in DB2 data types.

Broadly, you can use each type of function wherever their return type can legally be used in a SQL statement. Scalar and column functions that return scalar values can be used anywhere a single value can appear, such as in the select and where clauses; table functions can appear in the from clause of a SQL statement; and so on.

Using Insert Statements

You've already seen insert statements in action in this book, and many of you have used them in countless other systems. The basic syntax of an insert statement is straightforward:

```
insert into tablename (optional enumeration of columns) values (values)
```

The placeholders in italics are where you, as the writer of the insert statement, specify the table into which you are inserting data, the relevant columns if you aren't inserting values into all columns in the order in which they're specified in the table, and the actual values. So you can form insert statements such as this:

```
Insert into member
Values
('333333', 'Johann, 'S', 'Bach', 'A01', '555-1234', current date, 'Musician',
 16, 'M', '21/03/1685', 100000.00, 50000.00, 10000.00)
```

It does have two drawbacks. First, there's the minor drawback of the statement being less readable for the casual observer. More importantly, if you ever change the structure of your employee table in the future to add more columns, this statement will cause maintenance headaches because its implicit use of column order will no longer be valid. It's generally good practice to include column names. Where some fields in some tables allow nulls, you can omit values that you don't know. To do that, you must specifically enumerate the fields associated with the values you want to insert; otherwise, DB2 (just like every other database) can't correlate columns to values.

```
Insert into member
(empno, firstnme, lastname, hiredate, birthdate, edlevel)
Values
('444444', 'Louis', 'Armstrong', current date, '04/08/1901')
```

Perhaps most powerful of all, you can insert data in bulk by using the insert into ... select ... technique, in which the results of a select statement are used to feed data into the target table:

```
Insert into employee
(empno, firstnme, lastname, hiredate, birthdate, edlevel, salary, bonus, comm)
Select empno, firstnme, lastname, hiredate, birthdate, edlevel, salary, bonus, comm
From some-other-table-or-view
```

All very understandable, and all these examples can be extended with DB2-specific features (which I'll cover shortly). It should also be noted that the ability to use the insert into ... select ... technique extends to arbitrarily complex select statements. If you can compose a select statement as a stand-alone query, it can be used as part of an insert statement, no matter how complex it is.

DB2 supports multirow inserts via the insert statement, allowing you to add data in bulk via this technique. There tends to be a fuzzy boundary between the effort needed to insert just a few rows and the work required for mass data loading. The latter approach can use some of the dedicated tools such as the load and import utilities of DB2, which will be discussed in upcoming chapters. Inserting only a handful of rows highlights the overheads of these tools, but it is also cumbersome to write individual insert statements for each row of a modest set of data.

The multirow insert statement uses almost identical syntax to the typical insert statement, simply adding multiple groups of values after the leading insert stub. For example, you can load new departments into the department table in one statement:

```
insert into department
(deptno, deptname, admrdept)
values
('K22','BRANCH OFFICE K22', 'E01'),
('L22','BRANCH OFFICE L22', 'E01'),
('M22','BRANCH OFFICE M22', 'E01')
```

Using Update Statements

Update SQL statements, like their DML compatriots, can fall anywhere on the spectrum of complexity. To refresh your memory, their form looks generally like this:

```
Update tablename
Set column = value [ , (column = value) [, ...]]
Where criteria is met
```

Even that basic framework can be simplified because the where criteria are strictly optional. A sample update that's relevant to our employee table is the following:

```
Update employee
Set salary = 150000,
bonus = 50000
Where empno = '444444'
```

This example targets only one row for update (or so I hope), but update statements can affect any subset of a table. Update statements can also have their criteria based on any complex logic, up to and including subselects, joins, unions, and so forth. There is an equivalent syntax supported for the update statement that bundles the columns to be updated into one set and the required values into a second set.

```
Update employee
Set (salary, bonus) = (150000,50000)
Where empno = '444444'
```

Importantly, when using this form of syntax, the positions of the columns are matched to the positions of the new values, so it is important not to accidentally transpose values or mistype the order of your intended updates.

Using Delete Statements

Always my favorite statement, delete removes data from your chosen table. That's right; you go to all that effort crafting designs, building physical models, and coding a variety of tools to create and manage your data, and with one little statement you can remove the lot. Okay, melodrama aside, the delete statement's purpose is synonymous with its name—it removes unwanted data from a table. The delete statement takes this basic form:

```
Delete from tablename
Where criteria is are met
```

For those of you who've used other databases that are somewhat lax about standard and syntactical correctness, the word *from* is not optional. As with the other DML statements, the where clause is optional. By not specifying a where clause, all rows from a table will be removed. Using a where clause limits the rows deleted to those that match the specified criteria. A simple example using the where clause is the following:

```
Delete from employee
Where hiredate > '2009-01-01'
```

One interesting aspect of the DB2 delete and update implementation is that you'll see a warning if the criteria you specify don't match any rows; that is, if your delete statement won't actually delete any rows. You'll see this warning:

```
SQL0100W  No row was found for FETCH, UPDATE or DELETE;
or the result of a query is an empty table.  SQLSTATE=02000
```

Summary

You now know the ins and outs of DB2-specific features that you can use in normal select, insert, update, and delete statements. The material here should be enough to rekindle the memories of experienced SQL users and spark curiosity in those still coming to grips with SQL. You'll return to more features of SQL with DB2 in the following chapter on table creation, and again in Chapter 12, in which I'll discuss other objects such as indexes, views, sequences, and more.

CHAPTER 7

■■■

SQL for DB2: Part 2

With databases, tablespaces, and buffer pools mastered, you might want to get back to the real business of databases—working with data! I'm not one to stand in the way of progress, so let's examine the capabilities DB2 provides to the aspiring data wrangler (that'd be you), in terms of creating tables to hold your data and then working to insert, select, update, and delete your data.

Creating and Managing DB2 Tables

In earlier chapters, you dealt with the SAMPLE database and took a whirlwind tour of SQL to select, insert, update, and delete data. This might have been a refresher or a brief introduction if you are new to SQL. All the examples relied on the existing tables in the SAMPLE database, but knowing *how* those tables are created, and being able to design and create your own tables, are important skills to have when working with DB2. I'll recap the basic syntax for table creation and then build on it to illustrate the additional capabilities that are at your fingers. In the process, you'll be creating the tables that you'll use in later examples.

The fundamental syntax for table creation is as follows:

```
Create table table-name (element list [or other more advanced options])
 [even more advanced options]
```

You need to know about the *data types* DB2 supports in order to enumerate the columns of data that make up the "element list" in the create table syntax outline. In the DB2 context, data types are nearly identical to the concept in other databases and are analogous to variable typing in programming languages. Just as in these other areas, DB2 data types govern the data domain of a given attribute, allowed values, permissible operations, and so on.

Data Types in DB2

DB2 comes delivered with many native data types. It also supports user-defined data types, which I'll cover in a later chapter. The native data types are grouped into broad categories of similar data, such as numeric types, temporal (date and time) types, and so on. Each native data type has a reserved word that describes it and is used in table, function, and other definitions; explicit casting; and other situations.

The Numbers

The native numeric types in DB2 are as follows:

- SMALLINT: As the name suggests, the smallest numeric data type that DB2 supports. These values use 2 bytes of storage (16 bits) and are interpreted as 2s-complement signed numbers, providing a range between –32768 and 32767.

- INTEGER: A 32-bit signed number. The range of permissible values is –2147483648 to 2147483647.

- BIGINT: The biggest form of integer supported by DB2. These values are 64 bits, providing a huge range: from –9223372036854775808 to +9223372036854775807. If your integers fall outside that range, I'd love to hear what data you're modelling!

- REAL: The first of the noninteger types; floating-point numbers with single precision. They provide an approximation to 32 bits for any number from the extremely small positive or negative 1.175E-37, to the extremely large positive or negative 3.402E+38. Zero is stored precisely.

- DOUBLE/FLOAT: Using 64 bits to approximate nonintegers, these values provide for double-precision floating point numbers as well as exact zero values. The numeric range supported is ±1.175E-37 to ±3.402E+38.

- DECIMAL/NUMERIC: Used for storing exact noninteger values so that no data is lost in the precision rounding that other floating point types encounter. These types are specified with a scale (the number of digits before the decimal point) and a precision (the number of decimal places). They use a packed storage notation. The scale must at least be 1 (i.e., at least the first digit in the packed storage is for the scale), and the precision must be no more than 31 digits. In practice, this means that values in the range $\pm 10^{31}$ can be stored.

- DECFLOAT: New to DB2, this is a newly introduced variant of the DECIMAL type. It does not differ in semantics or exactness. This type was created to allow explicit use of the new floating-point hardware IBM introduced in the POWER6 CPU. Unless you're planning to use DB2 on that platform, you will probably never use this data type.

The Strings

No, not a section of an orchestra; I'm actually talking about textual string data types in DB2. The native string data types are as follows:

- CHAR: This fixed-length data type allows you to store up to 254 bytes as a string, depending on the length you specify at the time of definition. CHAR data types pad any unused space in a string up to that length, so if you declare a CHAR value of 50 bytes, but only store the words "Hello World", DB2 pads that value with 39 spaces for storage *but not for comparison purposes*. That comparison part sometimes catches people out because it is more friendly behavior than you might find in other databases. DB2 always ignores trailing spaces in CHAR and VARCHAR columns. Your application will still fetch these trailing spaces when retrieving the data, so it's best to be mindful of this when working with that data in development languages such as Java or C#.

- VARCHAR: This variable-length data type allows you to store up to 32672 bytes as a string, depending on the length you specify when defining the column or variable. However, the size you specify must be able to fit on one database page when being stored by DB2, and page sizes range from 4KB to 32KB. I'll talk more about database pages when I describe physical storage in Chapter 18, but there's a small overhead to each page, so in practice your VARCHAR types are limited to 4005 bytes on 4KB pages, 8101 bytes on 8KB pages, and so forth—up to the 32672-byte size limit on 32KB pages. Unlike a CHAR, VARCHAR doesn't pad your data with spaces to fill unused bytes.

- LONG VARCHAR: This variable-length data type allows you to store up to 32700 bytes as a string, depending on the length you specify when defining the column or variable. It is only slightly longer than a VARCHAR, so you might wonder why the effort of an entirely separate data type. The short explanation is that a standard VARCHAR has historically been able to hold much less data. It is also stored on disk in a way not affected by the page size limitation of VARCHAR, so you might use up to the full length regardless of your page size. A limitation of a LONG VARCHAR is its incapability to be used with predicates such as equals, greater than, and so on. You are limited to simple tests for nullability.

- CLOB: The largest of the string types, this type can store up to 2 gigabytes of textual data. There are some functional limitations on what CLOB can achieve, including the comparison limitations listed previously for LONG VARHAR. I'll discuss more about these limitations as you start using this data type in later chapters.

The Double-byte (or Graphical) Strings

Double-byte string data types exist to support ideographic scripts such as Kanji and Hangol. The native data types for double-byte strings are GRAPHIC, VARGRAPHIC, LONG VARGRAPHIC, and DBCLOB, and they each can store approximately half as many double-byte characters as their single-byte equivalents (so a GRAPHIC can store up to 127 double-byte characters in comparison with a 254 single-byte characters of a CHAR).

The Binary Data Type

In a category of its own, but closely related to the other large object types, is the BLOB. No, it's not a character in a science fiction film; it's a binary large object that can store up to 2 gigabytes of information that will be treated as a binary stream of ones and zeros.

The Date and Time Data Types

The basic temporal data types that allow you to store the information about past and future times and dates. The three principal data types are the following:

- DATE: Stores year, month, and day data. Possible values range from 01-01-0001 to 31-12-9999. DB2 also enforces strict and accurate date validation, meaning that you'll never suffer the flaws found in other databases that allow February 30 and January 0 as dates.

- TIME: Similar to the DATE data type, this data type stores hour, minute, and second data. Possible values range from 0:00:00 to 23:59:59. Special allowance is made for 24:00:00, which equates to 0:00:00. This special handling is quite sensitive, so ensure that you are dealing with the TIME data type when expecting this behavior, not DATE or TIMESTAMP.

- TIMESTAMP: Designed to support International Organization for Standardization (ISO) standardized temporal information. A TIMESTAMP stores year, month, day, hour, minute, second, and microsecond. Optional support exists for time zone information as well.

Esoteric Data Types

Not really a category of related types; more just the leftovers that don't fit anywhere else. This category includes the following:

- DATALINK: Provides special semantics for storing links to information that is housed outside of the database. Can include items such as URLs pointing to HTTP-based information on an external web server or files on a file system stored either locally to the database server or on another server.

- XML: Not to be confused with the pureXML features discussed later, it is a limited data type that exists primarily for historic reasons. It allows XML data to be input into a CLOB data field by use of a special function: XML2CLOB.

Data Type Summary

As you might expect, there are more layers of detail about data types that will become apparent as you start to use them, but I'll cover those details as they become relevant instead of weighing you down with yet more theory. In short, aspects such as implicit and explicit conversion of values between types, and the implications for column and variable assignment, are the main areas of further discussion. Some of the data types, such as LONG VARCHAR, have usage limitations that I'll also discuss as they are introduced. For now, you're armed with the knowledge you need to work with a physical data model.

Your First Table

Now you know what's required to create a table, as well as more details about the tables that already exist in the SAMPLE database, such as the employee and department tables. To make the following examples relevant and to get you thinking about the kinds of systems in which you might be interested, you'll extend the schema in the SAMPLE database for a fictional sales organization. You'll build the tables (and later design the application logic) to provide for an Employee of the Year system. Browsing the SAMPLE database shows a lot about staff members, where they work, and how much they sell and earn. But you need extra tables to track information (such as which employees are nominated for Employee of the Year), a table to count votes, and naturally some way of storing details about the prizes offered.

Let's start with a nomination table to track nominees for our awards. You can develop a table creation statement of the following form:

```
Create table nomination
(
nominationID INTEGER Not Null,
nominee char(6) Not Null,
nominator char(6) Not Null,
reason VARCHAR(250),
nomdate date Not Null
)
```

The SQL for the nomination table seems easy. Go ahead and execute it; numerous DB2 activities take place under the hood to ensure that this table is created. First, all the storage requirements for the table are handled implicitly. I'll delve into how DB2 handles storage with tablespaces and their containers in Chapter 18. For now, you'll appreciate that these low-level details were handled for you without bothering you for specific details. I'll cover the options available for specifying explicit storage shortly.

The other details managed for you were those that govern who has permission to create tables. The rules governing this range from the simple to the complex, and I'll cover them in detail in Chapter 11. For now, for you to successfully create tables, you must

- be a member of the SYSADM group for the instance; or

- be a member of the DBADM group for the specific database; or

- have the CREATETAB authority in the specific database and USE privilege in the desired tablespace, as well as potentially requiring several other privileges.

You can appreciate that beyond this point the caveats and conditions become significantly more complex and will drag you away from the details of table creation. So for now, I trust that you'll connect to your database as your instance owner—or grant yourself SYSADM or DBADM privileges if you skip ahead to read Chapters 9 and 10.

There are numerous options that can be used at table creation time, and instead of hitting you with them all in one mammoth statement, I'll build up examples introducing successively more features. I'll show you the most common features used when defining DB2 tables. There are more than 60 pages of documentation on the create table statement alone at the DB2 Information Center, and I'm sure you don't want an equally long regurgitation of that. Once you've mastered the basics, be sure to consult the DB2 Information Center for more advanced and esoteric options.

Naming DB2 Tables

This is by far the simplest part of creating tables in DB2. You must specify a name for the table you want to create and it needs to abide by these rules:

- Start with an alphabetic character

- Use alphanumeric and permitted punctuation characters

- Be no longer than 128 characters

- Be a unique name within the schema

For example, using CREATE TABLE NOMINATION... is fine, but CREATE TABLE _MY!NOMINEES ... breaks multiple rules and is not okay. A schema in DB2 acts like a namespace in programming environments, providing a realm in which names must be unique. If you don't specify an explicit schema when creating objects such as tables, DB2 will default to the AuthID name you used when connecting to the database.

Specifying Column Details and Constraints

The columns for your table—referred to as *elements* in DB2 syntax diagrams of the create table statement—have a basic form that is very familiar to you already, both from examples in earlier chapters, and possible previous experience you might have had with other database types:

```
Create table tablename
(column_name data_type constraint_details,
column_name data_type constraint_details
...
[or other more advanced options])
```

Determining column names is largely a matter for you to decide and should be done as a natural consequence of a design process. A column name must start with an alphabetic character and be no longer than 30 characters. Duplicate column names within the same table are not allowed.

Working with Null Data

Data types were discussed in depth earlier in this chapter, and again your design usually dictates the physical implementation and data type choices. In reality, you could stop right there and start issuing create table statements with just this information:

```
db2 => drop table nomination
DB20000I  The SQL command completed successfully.

Create table nomination
(
nominationID BIGINT,
nominee char(6),
nominator char(6),
reason VARCHAR(250),
nomdate date
)
DB20000I  The SQL command completed successfully.
```

DB2 implicitly determines column constraints if they're not explicitly specified. In short, it automatically allows nulls wherever a column is specified without constraints. This leads naturally to discussing which explicit constraints you *can* specify.

As well as the not null constraint, which directs DB2 to enforce the presence of a value for a given column, you can also specify a referential constraint—also known as a foreign key relationship—or a check constraint, which is usually a small piece of business logic that must be satisfied for the value to successfully pass the constraint:

```
db2 => drop table Instrument
DB20000I  The SQL command completed successfully.

Create table nomination
(
nominationID BIGINT Not Null,
```

```
nominee char(6) Not Null,
nominator char(6) Not Null,
reason VARCHAR(250),
nomdate date Not Null
)
DB20000I  The SQL command completed successfully.
```

Primary Key Constraints

If you have a data modelling background, you know that of all the attributes for a given entity, one or more of them should be able to uniquely identify each occurrence of that entity. These unique attributes are known as candidate keys. Picking one (or one group) to be the canonical arbiter of uniqueness is the act of declaring your primary key (i.e., the primary set of values that will decide whether an entity is unique). This is then modelling physically by declaring one or more fields to constitute the physical primary key in a table. As a byproduct of this declaration, DB2 automatically creates a unique index (discussed in Chapter 12) to enforce the uniqueness of your primary key values, as well as to boost performance.

DB2 supports the normal SQL syntax for declaring primary keys at the time of table creation by using the primary key modifier, either inline with a single field or as a separate clause to enable a subset of fields to be declared the primary key.

An example of the inline technique looks like this:

```
Create table nomination
(
nominationID BIGINT Not Null Primary Key,
nominee char(6) Not Null,
nominator char(6) Not Null,
reason VARCHAR(250),
nomdate date Not Null
)
```

Using the separate clause technique looks like this, where there can be one or more values in the last set of parentheses:

```
Create table nomination
(
nominationID BIGINT Not Null,
nominee char(6) Not Null,
nominator char(6) Not Null,
reason VARCHAR(250),
nomdate date Not Null,
Primary Key (nominationID)
)
```

Instead of dropping and re-creating the nomination table to try these out, you can also begin to explore the alter table command to effect this kind of change. You can alter the existing nomination table to add the primary key, like this:

```
db2 => alter table nomination add primary key (nominationid)
DB20000I  The SQL command completed successfully.
```

As with most relational databases, primary keys must exist for another kind of constraint to be utilized: the foreign key (or referential integrity) constraint.

Referential Constraints

A referential constraint instructs DB2 to compare a value being inserted, updated, or even deleted with a corresponding value in a related table. This concept, which probably isn't new to you, is found in almost every database that supports the SQL standards. To recap, referential constraints are often used to enforce parent-child relationships between data or supertype-subtype relationships. The key is to ensure that the parent or supertype always exists before a child or subtype refers to it. Referential constraints are usually called foreign keys, and the two terms are interchangeable.

To illustrate, I'll evolve the model slightly to include a category table and change the nomination table to reference it in a constraint. The logical model for the category is very simple and is shown in Table 7-1. It translates to the equally simple physical model shown in Table 7-2.

Table 7-1. *Logical Modelling for Category Table*

Attribute	Nature of Attribute	Comments
CategoryID	Unique Number	Uniquely identifies a category
CategoryName	Textual	The name of the category
Eligibility	Textual	Eligibility requirements for this category

Table 7-2. *Physical Modelling for Category Table*

Attribute	Data type	Nullability
CategoryID	INTEGER	Primary Key, Not Null
CategoryName	VARCHAR(50)	Not Null
Eligibility	VARCHAR(250)	Nullable

The create table statement now looks like this:

```
Create table category
(
CategoryID INTEGER Not Null Primary Key,
CateogryName VARCHAR(50) Not Null,
Eligibility VARCHAR(250)
)
```

The nomination table can now be modified to incorporate the CategoryID instead of a country name. Now every time a category changes its name, you needn't revisit every nomination you know about to make the change. This is classic data modeling. If you are new to the topic, hopefully my little example shows some of the real-world applications of DB2's capabilities in this regard. You could now go ahead and add nominations, but you would have to manually ensure that CategoryIDs used to reference corresponding categories actually existed in the category table. This is where *declarative* referential integrity comes into play. You can use DB2's SQL features to declare that the CategoryID field of the nomination table actually exists in the category table. With the category table in place, you can make the necessary changes to the nomination table to incorporate ready-made referential integrity:

```
db2 => alter table nomination
add column categoryid integer not null

SQLO193N  In an ALTER TABLE statement, the column "CATEGORYID" has been
specified as NOT NULL and either the DEFAULT clause was not specified or was
specified as DEFAULT NULL.  SQLSTATE=42601
```

Oops! Stopped in your tracks. I let this error occur to illustrate one caveat that you need to deal with when using ALTER TABLE to add columns to an existing table. If you choose to enforce the NOT NULL constraint, DB2 will insist that you deal with the consequences for any possible existing rows. DB2 doesn't actually check to see *whether* there are existing rows; it simply assumes there are, so you must therefore handle what the default value for this new column would be for those rows.

Let's try again, this time specifying a default category of 1. Before I create the referential integrity constraint, I'll need to deal with an associated row of data in the category table:

```
db2 => alter table nomination
add column categoryid integer not null default 1
DB20000I  The SQL command completed successfully.
```

We can now add declarative referential integrity, having this column reference the categoryid column of the category table.

```
db2 => alter table nomination add foreign key CategoryExists (categoryid)
 references category (categoryid)
DB20000I  The SQL command completed successfully.
```

In this example, I am implicitly referencing the category table within the current schema. I have also given my constraint a name, CategoryExists, so that future administration is a little easier. The name is optional, however, and DB2 will generate a cryptic string on your behalf if you don't include it. Cross-schema referential integrity is feasible, but it requires additional permissions (I'll cover them in the next chapter).

From these examples, you can see that the foreign key clause has this general form:

```
Foreign key optional constraint name (column name)
references reference table (reference column name)
 additional on-change rules
```

As you might have experienced in other systems, DB2 provides the usual "on change" rules to accompany the constraint. In practice, this means that when the parent (referenced) field is updated or deleted you can set rules that automatically resolve any possible data inconsistencies before they happen. The most common example of this is dealing with child rows if the parent is deleted. In this case, if a category is deleted for whatever reason, you might not necessarily want its related nominations deleted. Instead, you might want to reference another category, reference some "not applicable" value (although that breaks quite a few data modelling norms), or you might want the nomination to take on a null CategoryID so that you're implying you just don't know what to do but want a sensible structure reflected in the database. You have to change the `CategoryID` definition in the `nomination` table to allow nulls in this last case. You can extend the foreign key clause to use an on delete ... option; in this case, the set null technique will be used.

```
db2 => alter table nomination drop constraint CategoryExists
DB20000I  The SQL command completed successfully.
```

```
db2 => alter table nomination add foreign key CategoryExists (categoryid)
 references category (categoryid) on delete restrict
DB20000I  The SQL command completed successfully.
```

There are two sets of "rule clauses" you can apply in this way. The on delete ... rules include no action, which literally doesn't attempt to resolve any conflicts; restrict, which prevents the operation from completing; cascade, which instructs DB2 to delete subordinate children of the parent row; and the set null option you used. Equivalent rules can also be specified for the on update ... rules, but there are only two options from which to choose—no action and restrict—which do nothing and prevent the action, respectively. You'll note that in order to affect this change, I had to use the alter table command twice—once to remove the existing constraint and a second time to reintroduce it with the desired rule clause. Currently, there's no notion of an "alter constraint" command in DB2.

It's quite possible to go to town on referential integrity, especially if you used the normalization techniques for a data model and it has evolved to third or higher normal form.

Check Constraints

Check constraints allow you to enforce business rules in the definition of your tables. This is no different from what you might have encountered with other databases, but a quick overview will help anyone who isn't familiar with their use. The general form of a check constraint is the following:

```
Check (column column-constraints)
```

Simple logic, including arithmetic operators, comparisons such as <, > and =, and more complex predicates like IN, EXISTS, and BETWEEN are all suitable. A relevant example for the Employee of the Year environment is to use a check constraint on the nominee and nominator, ensuring that people aren't trying to nominate themselves.

```
Create table nomination
(
nominationID BIGINT Not Null Primary Key,
nominee char(6) Not Null,
nominator char(6) Not Null,
reason VARCHAR(250),
nomdate date Not Null,
categoryid INTEGER Not Null,
check (nominee != nominator),
Foreign Key CategoryExists (categoryid)
 references category (categoryid) on delete restrict
)
```

That table creation statement looks like quite a comprehensive command. Of course, instead of having to drop the table and re-create it using this statement, you can use the alter table command to add the check constraint to the existing table:

```
db2 => alter table nomination add constraint
 NoSelfNomination check (nominee != nominator)
DB20000I  The SQL command completed successfully.
```

Disabling Constraints and Constraint Deferral

DB2 has special capabilities that allow it to tolerate constraint violations when a referential or check constraint is declared (and post-creation during operations such as bulk data load). All constraints are implicitly created in enforced mode, in which the database ensures that the rules dictated by the constraint are followed. You can also explicitly add the enforced keyword after the constraint. There are times when you don't necessarily want a constraint enforced, such as when you know another system is guaranteeing the same outcome provided by your constraint. In this circumstance, you can declare the constraint but mark it as not enforced:

```
db2 => alter table nomination drop constraint NoSelfNomination
DB20000I  The SQL command completed successfully.

db2 => alter table nomination add constraint
 NoSelfNomination check (nominee != nominator) not enforced
DB20000I  The SQL command completed successfully.
```

You might wonder why you'd specify a constraint that wasn't enforced. Even though DB2 might not be governing the data using the rules from your constraint, there are other benefits that a constraint provides that are still in play. If you choose, you can tell DB2 to use the information about the constraint in determining how it will optimize the execution of your queries, whether or not the constraint is active. The syntax to control this includes the keywords enable query optimization and disable query optimization. Without pre-empting later chapters on performance tuning, one way to illustrate how it might be used is as follows:

```
db2 => alter table nomination drop constraint NoSelfNomination
DB20000I  The SQL command completed successfully.

db2 => alter table nomination add constraint
 NoSelfNomination check (nominee != nominator)
 not enforced enable query optimization
DB20000I  The SQL command completed successfully.
```

So we're not enforcing the check constraint, but signaling to DB2 that it should use the constraint information to help it optimize queries. Now imagine a simple select statement like this:

```
Select * from nomination where nominee = nominator
```

DB2 could optimize the execution of this statement without even reviewing the data in the table. DB2 determines that because of the constraint rules no data in theory can exist where the nominee and nominator are equal for a row, even though the constraint is not enforced! By recognizing the query optimization setting, DB2 knows the value in the query does not satisfy the check constraint. It doesn't need to access the data in the table because it knows it won't find a match. Of course, this might not be true when constraints are disabled, so carefully consider the impact of switching these off.

Automatic Value Generation for Columns

DB2 provides several advanced features that enable columns to generate their own values when a row is inserted into a table. Broadly, this capability is governed by the generated modifier for the column. With this modifier a column can be set to generate values in two different ways. First, the concept of an identity can be used to allow numbers in a certain series to be automatically placed in the column. This can be as simple as an incrementing number that starts at a given point, but it can also be more complex. A common use for the identity option is to provide a substitute value to use as the primary key for a table, either because the natural primary key is unwieldy, or because the data has been difficult to model and no natural primary key presents itself.

Alternatively, the generated clause can use arbitrary techniques and functions that you specify in order to generate a value. The general format of the generated clause looks like this:

```
column definition generated {always | by default}
 as {identity identity rules | using your rules}
```

Let's take a look at an example that uses the identity technique. My design for most of the tables you've seen incorporates an identifier number as the primary key. Let's use the generated modifier to have DB2 provide this by way of an identity:

```
db2 => drop table nomination
DB20000I  The SQL command completed successfully.

Create table nomination
(
nominationID BIGINT Not Null Primary Key generated always as identity,
nominee char(6) Not Null,
nominator char(6) Not Null,
reason VARCHAR(250),
nomdate date Not Null,
categoryid INTEGER Not Null,
check (nominee != nominator) not enforced enable query optimization,
Foreign Key CategoryExists (categoryid)
 references category (categoryid) on delete restrict
)
DB20000I  The SQL command completed successfully.
```

In this instance I instructed DB2 to always generate the value for NominationID. It will no longer allow you to specify an explicit value in an insert or update statement. The alternative, by default, will generate a value if one isn't explicitly provided in an insert or update. Another technology mastered! Well, not quite. There are numerous modifiers that the identity technique can use. Table 7-3 summarizes these modifiers for you.

Table 7-3. *Available Options for Identity Columns*

Identity Modifier	Effect
Start with n	Sets the starting number, n, for the identity.
Increment by n	Specifies the value, n, by which the identity increments every time it is used.
Minvalue n	An explicit lower bound assigned to the identity. Generated values cannot be lower than this value.
No minvalue	The lower bound (either 1 or the Start with value if different) for the identity.
Maxvalue n	An explicit higher bound assigned to the identity. Generated values cannot be higher than this value.
No maxvalue	The higher bound (either –1 or the Start with value if different) for the identity. Note that –1 is a symbolic reference to a value higher than all positive values.
Cycle	Indicates that ascending values that exceed the maximum, or descending values that exceed the minimum, will implicitly cycle around and start from the highest/lowest applicable value for the field's data type.
No cycle	Indicates that once the identity column reaches the maximum or minimum value, no further identity values will be generated, and an error will be returned instead. This is the default.
Cache n	Nominates n values for the identity that will be calculated and cached in the DB2 instance's memory, ready for use. This provides a high-performance option for using identity values, with the balancing factor being that cached values can be lost (and not regenerated) if the server abnormally terminates for any reason.
No cache	Disables the caching of identity values and requires their use to be logged per normal transactional processing in the DB2 logs. This provides lower performance, but guarantees no lost identity values in the event of instance failure.
Order	Specifies that identity values must be generated in strict order. This has a slight impact on the performance of concurrent identity generation requests.
No Order	Indicates that strict order is desired, but not mandated. Strict concurrency is sacrificed for the sake of performance.

The category table is a prime candidate for using the various features of identity columns. Here are we replace the existing trivial physical category table with one that uses all the identity bells and whistles:

```
db2 => drop table category
DB20000I  The SQL command completed successfully.

Create table category
(
CategoryID INTEGER Primary Key  Generated Always as Identity
 (Start With 1 Increment by 1 minvalue 0 maxvalue 999999999
 no cycle cache 5 no order),
CateogryName VARCHAR(50) Not Null,
Eligibility VARCHAR(250)
)
DB20000I  The SQL command completed successfully.
```

There are times when you don't want to play with just numbers. Let's say you have a particular need to overcome case sensitivity because of an unavoidable collation or codeset requirement. You could use your own generation rules to create values for a generated column, such as this:

```
db2 => alter table category add column
UpperCatName VARCHAR(50) generated always as (upper(CategoryName))
DB20000I  The SQL command completed successfully.
```

In this example, I used the upper() function to take the value of the CategoryName column and generate the uppercase version for storing in the UpperCatName column. This is a trivial example, but there are quite a few options available for generated columns as long as you follow their basic limitations. In short, your rule must reference a deterministic function, previously declared column, or other "non-exotic" source from which to determine its value. There's a comprehensive discussion on this in the DB2 documentation, so if you're interested you might want to read more there.

Specifying Table Storage Characteristics

The last area to look at in some detail is the physical and logical storage for a table. You have a chicken-and-egg situation, in which you need to learn about the concept of tablespaces as the logical storage for tables. But you also need to know about tables in order for tablespaces to serve any purpose. A detailed discussion of tablespaces will wait until Chapter 18. For now, you can relax in the knowledge that there are far fewer options to consider than those you just learned for column definitions.

There are essentially three types of tablespaces you can declare a table to use during its creation. First, you can nominate in which regular tablespace the normal data for a table is stored. You can optionally nominate a separate regular tablespace in which all the indexes for a table will be placed. Finally, you can allocate a large tablespace for housing the large objects of a table.

The general syntax for the tablespace storage characteristics of a table is as follows:

```
Create table tablename
(various column names and attributes)
[in tablespace-name]
[Index in tablespace-name]
[Long in tablespace-name]
```

The first thing to note is the square bracket notation, which highlights that specifying *any* tablespace assignment is optional. For data and indexes, failure to specify a tablespace results in the create table statement using the default tablespace for the table's creator. An example using all possible tablespaces would take this form:

```
Create table AwardWinner
(AwardWinnerID integer Primary Key Generated Always as Identity
 (Start With 1 Increment by 1),
DateWon Date Not Null,
TotalVotes Integer Not Null,
Picture BLOB)
in userspace1
Index in userspace1
Long in picturelobs
```

The user creating the table must have use privileges in any tablespace referenced. I'll discuss more about these privileges in Chapter 10.

Other Table Characteristics

I've explored many of the common and useful features specific to tables in DB2, and you can start using them now in Express-C or in other editions of DB2 for some advanced features. But there are more features available that could literally fill the rest of this book. Instead of leaving you with nothing else but table options for chapter after chapter, I'll summarize some of the remaining options and their uses.

Dimension Organization allows DB2 to cluster data together in the same page of data on disk, based on the values of multiple columns. This is usually known as multidimensional clustering (MDC). This is useful when you often access the same information by some common factors in tandem, such as working with employees based on their workdept and edlevel values.

DB2's data-partitioning capabilities allow you to create a logical table that spans physical storage under the control of multiple database instances. This is the shared-nothing approach to scaling out database capabilities.

Drop restriction uses the simple clause with restrict on drop added to your table to prevent ordinary users with administrative privileges from dropping a table.

Logging control allows tables to be set to not log their activity (inserts, updates, and deletes). While this can compromise recovery, it is a common technique used when first creating a database that you know will have bulk data loaded from some external source. If the load fails, the tables will be unrecoverable if the not logged initially option is used, but consider that you haven't really lost anything—you can re-create and reload the tables. The payoffs to using this approach are faster loading and reduced log space consumption.

Other Techniques for Table Creation

There are times when tables need to be created—not from detailed designs such as those we've already seen, but based on the content and/or structure of other tables or parts thereof. This can be very useful for quickly testing ideas, taking samples of data, and so forth.

Two options DB2 provides that are always useful are the create table ... as select ... approach (sometimes referred to as CTAS), and the create table ... like ... approach. They have slightly different uses, so let's explore them.

Creating a table based on a select statement allows you to implicitly construct the table columns based on the definition of another table (or more particularly the final results of your select statement), and populate your table at the time of creation if you want. To create a table using a select statement, simply append the select statement following the normal table cre- ation syntax that lists your column definitions using the as (select statement) definition only technique:

```
db2 => Create table EmployeeCopy
as (select firstnme, lastname from employee)
definition only
DB20000I  The SQL command completed successfully.
```

This essentially creates an independent table that has no further relationship to any other tables referenced in the select statement at the time of creation. You can achieve the same results with the create table ... like ... command. This command is a little different in that it doesn't allow you to select individual columns to include. Instead, you get all the columns from the source table. However, you do get control over whether or not to inherit the genera- tion rules used for identity columns and column defaults.

```
create table EmployeeCopy3 like EmployeeCopy2
including column defaults
excluding identity column attributes
DB20000I  The SQL command completed successfully.
```

Finally, you can also use DB2's materialization features to create and periodically refresh a table like this. The concepts of materialized query tables take us well beyond the realm of a beginners' book, so we'll leave that topic for the sequel.

Summary

You now know the ins and outs of table creation in DB2, and (like me when I first explored the topic) you're probably feeling a bit swamped by all the options available. You'll return to more features of SQL with DB2 in Chapter 12, in which I'll discuss other objects such as indexes, views, sequences, and more.

CHAPTER 8

■■■

Developing Functions and Stored Procedures in DB2

You might have heard horror stories about the complexities of building stored procedures and functions, involving the need for arcane compiler configuration, mastery of long-forgotten notions of computer architecture, and understanding millions of inscrutable commands. The reality is that procedural logic in DB2 is a snap, and the real challenge will be to avoid solving every problem with a procedure or function.

I'll cover the basic syntax, calling semantics, management, and administration of stored procedures and functions so you'll have a firm ground on which to learn more. Entire books have been written on those individual aspects, and the DB2 website and online documentation host a wealth of knowledge on the topic. If the procedural aspects of DB2 development catch your eye, I strongly suggest you bookmark the IBM DB2 permalink at http://publib.boulder.ibm.com/infocenter/db2luw/v9r5/. Visit it frequently to learn more.

DB2 Stored Procedures

SQL Procedural Language (SQL PL) is the IBM implementation of one of the least-loved aspects of the ANSI standards for SQL; the so-called SQL Persistent Modules (SQL PM). You'll probably never hear or read about the term *SQL PM* again unless you're a keen fan of the academic monographs that are issued at the end of standards committee meetings, but you'll certainly get to know and love SQL PL.

Creating Stored Procedures in DB2

A walkthrough of all the syntactic options for stored procedure creation would be long and likely to put you to sleep. So I'll target what you need to get going quickly and trust that you can explore further if you want to know more.

The big picture syntax of a SQL PL procedure looks like this:

```
create procedure procedure_name
parameters
options that modify procedure behavior
body of procedure
```

If I scared you with my tale of horror in the preamble to the chapter, you're probably thinking, "What was he talking about? This seems both sensible and simple." You're right; it is both of those things. Let's look at the four broad sections of the procedure syntax, and get a fresh procedure written to work on the SAMPLE database. You'll make one that tallies votes for employee of the year.

The create procedure line is fairly self explanatory. You need to be aware that the normal identifier rules apply for the procedure name, so your procedure must start with an alphabetic character, be composed of any alphanumeric or underscore characters, and be no longer than 128 characters. So far, so good.

If you don't specify an explicit schema, DB2 will default to using your schema (or optionally the schema set most recently via SET CURRENT SCHEMA). To use an explicit schema, simply prefix your procedure name using dot-notation. You can also pass NULLID as the schema. NULLID is a default built-in schema created with every database by default, to which the PUBLIC group is granted permissions for object creation. Think of NULLID as a handy namespace to which all users normally have access instead of anything particularly special.

```
create procedure nullid.employee_vote ...
```

Parameters for a procedure have three parts: a mode, a name, and a data type. Modes can be IN, OUT, or INOUT (see Table 8-1).

Table 8-1. *Parameter Modes*

Mode	Behavior
IN	Value passed to procedure, scoped internally, and not returned to caller
OUT	Placeholder for value generated internally and returned to caller
INOUT	Value passed to procedure, potentially modified, and returned to caller

Multiple parameters are separated by commas, and the set of parameters for a procedure is enclosed in parenthesis. You are free to choose any name you like; the data types are per those already covered for DB2.

```
create procedure employee_vote
(IN employee_id char(6),
 OUT current_votes integer)
...
```

DB2 takes strong typing of parameters to its logical (and useful) extreme by allowing you to have procedures of the same name *in the same schema* as long as the number of parameters to the procedure differs. For developers this is standard procedural overloading, although it stops short of allowing the same number of parameters of different types as a valid overload. So you could also create a procedure that allows you to vote for an employee based on first and last name:

```
create procedure employee_vote
(IN employee_fisrtname varchar(50),
 IN employee_lastname varchar(50),
 OUT current_votes integer)
...
```

One other aspect of parameters is also central to managing stored procedures. Unlike some other stored procedure languages in other relational databases, DB2 does not require you to nominate a parameter to hold result sets generated by queries within the procedure that you want to return to the calling party. By using a common database technique called cursors, procedures can simply declare how many result sets will be returned using the DYNAMIC RESULT SETS option that will be explored shortly.

A stored procedure can have its behavior altered by using one or more of the modifiers available in the SQL PL syntax. The modifiers are the following:

SPECIFIC *name*

DYNAMIC RESULT SETS *n*

{MODIFIES | READS} SQL DATA | CONTAINS SQL

[NOT] DETERMINISTIC

CALLED ON NULL INPUT

INHERIT SPECIAL REGISTERS

{OLD | NEW} SAVEPOINT LEVEL

LANGUAGE SQL

[NO] EXTERNAL ACTION

PARAMETER CCSID {ASCII | UNICODE}

The SPECIFIC *name* option allows you to include an additional unique name to help identify procedures that have been overloaded—two or more procedures sharing the same procedure name, but with different numbers of parameters. Its two key uses are to distinguish which procedure to use and to allow you to uniquely identify a procedure for the drop procedure statement. Without using a SPECIFIC *name* clause, the only way to drop overloaded procedures requires inclusion of the string of data types to match. I provide an example of this when I discuss dropping procedures.

The DYNAMIC RESULT SETS *n* parameter tells DB2 how many open cursors (that is, result sets of select queries) will be available when this procedure completes. The number provided can be zero or a positive integer. The DYNAMIC keyword provides great flexibility for letting the consuming application decide when and in what order to access the result sets.

The options MODIFIES SQL DATA, CONTAINS SQL, and READS SQL DATA act as a simplistic indicator to DB2 about the behavior of the procedure. Think of READS SQL DATA as a very simplistic control that prevents the procedure from changing data. The default option MODIFIES SQL DATA encompasses almost anything you want to do, and securing procedures should be done at other levels.

Using the DETERMINISTIC option for a procedure tells DB2 that it returns the same set of outputs every time for a given set of inputs. This allows the database to optimize future invocations of a procedure by caching the results of the first execution. Using NOT DETERMINISTIC (the default) results in the procedure being executed in full each time it is called.

The default CALLED ON NULL INPUT and INHERIT SPECIAL REGISTERS do what they describe, and there's no real variability involved. IBM has future plans for these options, but until then they are simply esoteric extras.

{OLD | NEW} SAVEPOINT LEVEL allows control over nesting of actions within a unit of work. Savepoints allow you to set markers so that you need not fully roll back actions when problems occur, instead reverting to a known savepoint.

LANGUAGE SQL indicates that the code for the procedure will be provided by a SQL PL body. DB2 also supports Java, C, and other languages, but you'll deal with them in the later development chapters.

Flagging EXTERNAL ACTION or NO EXTERNAL ACTION helps with minor optimizations when invoking the procedure. By flagging a procedure as EXTERNAL ACTION, you highlight to DB2 that consequences beyond its control and boundaries are likely from invoking this procedure, such as synchronous dependency on other processes and lack of transactional control at the DB2 level. At this stage I'll steer clear of procedures that act externally, which means you can run with the default of NO EXTERNAL ACTION.

PARAMETER CCSID {ASCII | UNICODE} allows your parameters to have a different collation to the default for your database. This can be useful in transitioning logic when making the move to Unicode or when you need to work in complex environments that lack Unicode support.

Using the most common modifiers in action, here is a stored procedure skeleton for returning the current standings in votes for employee of the year. It's missing the procedure body between the begin and end statement, but I'll cover that shortly.

```
create procedure emp_vote_standings()
specific all_emp_standings
dynamic result sets 1
reads sql data
not deterministic
called on null input
language sql
begin
...
end
```

Before fleshing out the body of this procedure, let's create a table to hold the votes cast and relate it back to the employee table:

```
create table emp_votes
(empno char(6) not null references employee(empno),
timeofvote date not null)
```

Now you can complete some of the earlier procedures. First, the employee_vote procedure that takes an employee_id, tallies the vote for the given employee, and returns that employee's current number of votes:

```
create procedure employee_vote(in employee_id char(6), out current_votes integer)
specific emp_vote_by_id
dynamic result sets 0
modifies sql data
not deterministic
language sql
begin atomic
```

```
    insert into emp_votes values (employee_id, current date);
    select count(*) into current_votes from emp_votes where empno = employee_id;
end
```

You'll note a few new points about stored procedures, particular the approach to writing their body statements. In the employee_vote example I can use the parameter employee_id (and any other parameter) without special referencing, leading punctuation such as semicolons, and so on. This makes reading and writing DB2 stored procedures somewhat easier, but be careful. If your parameter names are ambiguous or if they match column names in tables or views that you want to reference in the procedure, you'll find yourself making more than your fair share of coding snafus.

The second thing you'll notice about the procedure is that the return value was assigned to the OUT parameter using the into clause. This is similar to a number of other programming environments. The good news with DB2 is that there are in fact four ways to set a variable, be a parameter, or simply a local variable for the procedure:

- *Select count(*) into current_votes*: The previous technique

- *Values current date into mydatevariable*: A simple assignment using the values command

- *Set current_votes = 0*: Using the set command (per many other languages) on an already defined variable

- *Declare vote_total integer default 100*: Define and set a variable in one go

Choosing which method to use is often dictated by where you plan to source the data and what purpose it will serve once you have it. So in practice, you'll find yourself using the Declare, Set, and Values approaches interchangeably, and using the Select approach most often when retrieving your data from a table or view.

■**Tip** DB2 has a neat trick for the select ... into ... approach, letting you set multiple variables in one go. The syntax simply extends the normal form to select some_value, some_other_value into my_first_var, my_second_var from my_table. Simple and efficient.

Finally, notice the keyword atomic used with the begin statement. This keyword directs DB2 to treat all the statements at that nesting level—in this case, the entire procedure—as one block of statements that either must all succeed or all roll back. This is a trivial case in this example, but in more complex procedures it can be important to rely on this capability in addition to the normal transaction semantics that DB2 provides. You almost cannot take this too far. Consider always using the atomic operator to group commands because they not only protect your data and logic but also assist readers of your code to see what commands are logically grouped together.

Moving on to complete the emp_vote_standings procedure, you need to introduce a cursor to handle the pending result set of the current vote standings to whomever or whatever called the procedure. There are two parts to the process. First, declare a variable of the special type CURSOR WITH RETURN FOR and include the select statement that will provide the result set.

Then instruct the procedure to OPEN the cursor. This effectively leaves it "dangling" and ready to be collected and used by the caller. Here's what the emp_vote_standings procedure looks like:

```
create procedure emp_vote_standings()
specific all_emp_standings
dynamic result sets 1
reads sql data
not deterministic
called on null input
language sql
begin
  -- declare the cursor
  declare vote_cursor cursor with return for select * from emp_votes;
  -- open the cursor for return to the caller
  open vote_cursor;
  -- We're at the end of the procedure.  Any open cursors at this point are returned
end
```

Put those two procedures together to prove you have a working voting system. First vote for one of the employees. Dian has an employee id of '200010', so let's vote for that employee:

```
db2 => Call employee_vote('200010',?)

  Value of output parameters
  --------------------------
  Parameter Name  : CURRENT_VOTES
  Parameter Value : 1

  Return Status = 0
```

That's a successful call of the procedure from the CLP. Note that the question mark is used as a placeholder for any OUT parameters (they are then enumerated when the procedure is called). Let's see how many votes have currently been tallied:

```
db2 => call emp_vote_standings()

  Result set 1
  --------------

  EMPNO  TIMEOFVOTE
  ------ ----------
  200010 10/09/2007

  1 record(s) selected.

  Return Status = 0
```

No surprises there—just the first vote for Dian. You can vote again and again, and now that you have the procedure in place, you don't have to grant insert or select permissions on the table to allow users to vote nor expect them to write their own SQL statements. You can simply grant execute privileges on the voting procedure and add another standard layer of security to your environment by doing so.

So far, you've constructed procedures that handle DML statements and cursors for returning result sets to the caller. There are quite a few other logic constructs that can be used within a procedure, covering all the usual constructs you'd find in a procedural language such as loops, if-then statements, and so on.

I'll implement the second employee_vote procedure and include several of these constructs to demonstrate their operation. Don't let the length of the procedure fool you—I'll simply be using different types of procedural elements one after another so you can digest their meaning in small steps. I included comments in the code to illustrate what's happening.

```
create procedure employee_vote
(IN employee_firstname varchar(50),
 IN employee_lastname varchar(50),
 OUT current_votes integer)
specific emp_vote_by_name
dynamic result sets 0
modifies sql data
not deterministic
language sql
PVOTE: begin
  -- the PVOTE: text acts to label the entire body of the procedure

  declare my_name varchar(50);
  declare employee_id char(6);
  declare matches integer default 0;
  declare ok_to_vote integer default 0;
  declare current_votes integer default 0;
  values current user into my_name;

  -- example case statement, to see if you are voting for yourself
  case my_name
    when employee_firstname then
      set ok_to_vote = 0;
    when employee_lastname then
      set ok_to_vote = 0;
    else
      set ok_to_vote = 1;
  end case;

  -- sample for loop, to find users with matching names
  for employee as emp_cursor cursor for
  select empno
  from emp
  where firstnme = employee_firstname
  and lastname = employee_lastname do
    call my_notify_procedure();
  end for;
```

```
  -- example if-then test, and use of labels, leave and goto
  if ok_to_vote = 0 then
    goto invalid_emp;
  elseif ok_to_vote = 1 then
    goto valid_emp;
  else
    leave PVOTE; -- something disasterous happened, leave the procedure
  end if;

invalid_emp:
  -- We can deal with our own failure logic, by jumping to this label
  return -1;

valid_emp:
  -- We can deal with our own success logic, by jumping to this label
  Select empno into employee_id from emp
  where firstnme = employee_firstname
  and lastname = employee_lastname;
  insert into emp_votes values (employee_id, current date);
  select count(*) into current_votes from emp_votes where empno = employee_id;
  return current_votes;

end
```

That's a lot of code to digest, but break it down into the separate sections and you'll get some idea of how each procedural element works.

The case-when and if-then syntax is much like any other programming language you have used. As usual, you can include additional when cases or elseif clauses.

The for loop example uses the ability to declare a cursor over a result set as the basis for iteration. You can also omit the cursor part and simply use syntax like this:

```
For emp in select * from employee do ...
```

This is just one of the loop constructs available to DB2. The others are the while-do-end while command, the repeat-until command, and the loop command. These commands obey the normal iteration rules that come with these names—the while command tests the looping condition at the start of the loop, and the repeat-until command tests the condition at the end of the loop.

Some of the other control structures displayed in the employee_vote example were the use of labels and the goto command. They allow procedural flow to jump as directed.

Caution I'll warn you now that the goto statement in the DB2 stored procedure language carries all the baggage of goto statements in other languages. They break the normal logic flow, leave your code open to wildly inexplicable behavior, and in general should be avoided like the plague unless there's absolutely no alternative for the logic you have in mind. I hope that isn't too subtle for you to get my meaning.

All these flow control statements also provide context for the leave command. The example used the leave command to exit the entire procedure (given the label PVOTE:). But it's also possible to label inner-nested sets of commands and use the leave command to exit elements such as loops, just as you would use the break-style of command in other programming languages.

More sophisticated development will see you wanting to call one procedure from another. This is perfectly possible, but you need to consider what needs to be done to accommodate any result sets returned by open cursors from the called procedure. This simple case allows you to simply call a procedure that doesn't return any result sets:

```
...
begin
  call some_procedure()
end
```

More advanced uses allow you to retrieve the result sets of called procedures if they return them. This requires the use of the associate resultset locator command to link a local result set variable to hold the result set returned from the called procedure. To then use that result set, the allocate command is used to create a cursor. You can then use that cursor just as you would any other, in for loops, fetch statements, and so on.

```
...
begin
  call emp_vote_standings();
  ...
  associate resultset locator(vote_standings) with procedure emp_vote_standings;
  allocate vote_cursor cursor for resultset vote_standings;
  ...
  -- further logic that works with the cursor vote_cursor.
end
```

Procedures can also include their own error management and exception handling by using the signal, resignal, and condition statements; and handlers for various SQLSTATE conditions. An entire chapter could be written solely on error handling, but I'll illustrate an immediately useful case in just a few lines. The previous stored procedure could detect an abnormal case in the if-then clause:

```
...
if ok_to_vote = 0 then
  goto invalid_emp;
elseif ok_to_vote = 1 then
  goto valid_emp;
else
  leave PVOTE; -- something disasterous happened, leave the procedure
end if;
...
```

Instead of just leaving the procedure when abnormal behavior was detected, you could signal the problem so that higher-level DB2 error control and management could trace and rectify the problem. It's as simple as adding the signal command to the procedure:

```
...
if ok_to_vote = 0 then
  goto invalid_emp;
elseif ok_to_vote = 1 then
  goto valid_emp;
else
  signal sqlstate '99001';
  leave PVOTE; -- something disasterous happened, leave the procedure
end if;
...
```

This will flag the sqlstate 99001, chosen because it's above the range of values used by DB2. This will be returned to the caller, and might also appear in any trace files or the DB2 diagnostic log, depending on the severity of the problem.

Finally, you can handle the exception internally with the declaration of a handler for a given condition. In this case, you declare that when an action returns SQLSTATE 02000, the code that means "no more data to fetch," you'll trigger a continue handler that in turn sets a flag variable called end_of_data. You then test that variable in your further logic when expecting data and leave the relevant code when you notice it:

```
...
declare employee_id char(6);
declare not_found condition for sqlstate '02000'
declare continue handler for not_found set end_of_data = 1;
declare employee as emp_cursor cursor for
  select empno
  from emp
  where firstnme = employee_firstname
  and lastname = employee_lastname;

open employee;

inloop: loop
  fetch employee into employee_id;
  if end_of_data then leave inloop;
...
```

Dropping Procedures

Your procedures are bound to evolve over time, and some might even reach obsolescence. At that point, you'll want to drop procedures that are no longer of use. You can drop procedures from the CLP using the drop procedure command, but watch out for the case where you have overloaded procedure names.

```
db2 => drop procedure employee_vote
```

```
DB21034E  The command was processed as an SQL statement because it was not a
valid Command Line Processor command.  During SQL processing it returned:
SQL0476N  Reference to routine "FUZZY.EMPLOYEE_VOTE" was made without a
signature, but the routine is not unique in its schema.  SQLSTATE=42725
```

In this case, you can use the specific keyword, matching the specific attribute of the procedure in question, or you can include a list of parameter data types in the drop statement, which DB2 will use to match to the correct overloaded procedure. To drop the specific emp_vote_by_name procedure, use this:

```
drop specific procedure emp_vote_by_name
```

Or to drop the corresponding procedure that works with empno, use this:

```
drop procedure employee_vote(char, int)
```

This requires knowing more about the detail of a procedure, and you might find yourself managing procedures written by all manner of developers. In these scenarios, the DB2 Control Center offers an excellent way to choose the procedures to drop. Figure 8-1 shows the default view you'll see when you browse procedures within a database.

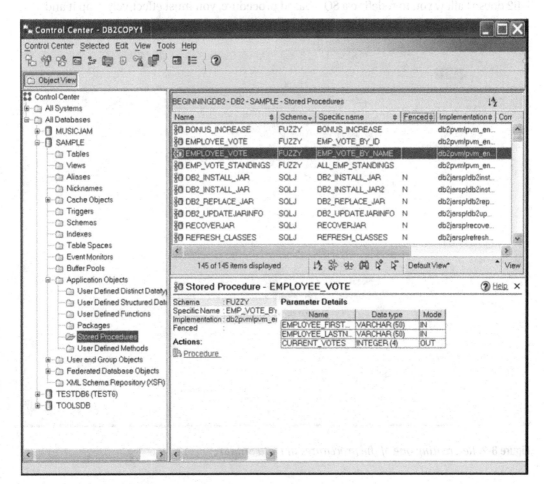

Figure 8-1. *Using the Control Center to identify a procedure to drop*

Note that the list of procedures includes the specific name of each procedure in the list at the top right, and the detail view in the bottom right lists the parameters for the highlighted procedure. In one view you can see all the distinguishing features about a procedure, which enables you to select the one you want to drop. Right-click the procedure and choose drop to drop it. You can even select multiple procedures and drop them in one step. Don't panic if you accidentally choose drop when meaning to select one of the other menu options because you'll be prompted to confirm your action.

Managing Procedures

Ongoing management of your procedures can be done by any of the tools with which you're now familiar. But you'll probably agree that grappling with specific clauses for manual drop statements, or juggling the Control Center and Command Editor, can get a little cumbersome. You already experienced the capability of the IBM Data Studio; managing procedures (and functions, which I'll soon cover) is where it really comes into its own.

Chapter 5 covered the basics of using the New Procedure Wizard to create a new stored procedure. One important feature of the Deploy option within Data Studio is to seamlessly handle the existence (or otherwise) of procedures as you refine and redeploy them. Because DB2 doesn't allow you to redefine a SQL-based procedure, you must effectively drop it and re-create it. You can just as easily create your procedure, as shown in Figure 8-2.

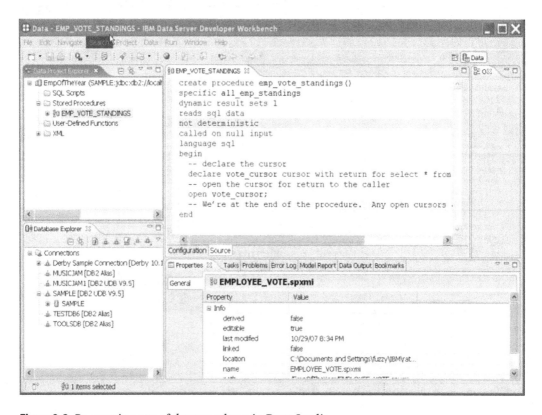

Figure 8-2. *Re-creating one of the procedures in Data Studio*

Right-click the procedure and choose deploy; the Deploy Wizard will take care of creating the procedure in the schema of your choice, as well as handling the existence of procedures with the same name and calling signatures in case of overloading. This is the Duplicate Handling radio button you see in the Deploy Wizard (see Figure 8-3).

Figure 8-3. *Using duplicate handling in the stored procedure deployment screen*

You'll see duplicate handling in action in the messages window if you do deploy a duplicate with identical name and overloading signature. For this example, the messages are the following:

```
FUZZY.EMP_VOTE_STANDINGS - Deploy started.
DROP SPECIFIC PROCEDURE FUZZY.ALL_EMP_STANDINGS
FUZZY.EMP_VOTE_STANDINGS - Drop stored procedure completed.
FUZZY.EMP_VOTE_STANDINGS - Create stored procedure completed.
FUZZY.EMP_VOTE_STANDINGS - Deploy successful.
```

Further Reading on DB2 Stored Procedures

A section of one chapter cannot possibly do justice to such a large topic. If you are interested in learning more about DB2 stored procedures, I thoroughly recommend these in-depth materials from IBM:

- IBM DB2 Information Center:
  http://publib.boulder.ibm.com/infocenter/db2luw/v9r5/index.jsp

- IBM Redbook sg245485, Cross-Platform DB2 Stored Procedures: http://www.redbooks.ibm.com/

- IBM developerWorks tutorials on DB2 Stored Procedures: http://www.ibm.com/developerworks

- Yip et al., *DB2 SQL PL: Essential Guide for DB2 UDB for Linux, UNIX, Windows* December 2004, IBM Press

The only problem you're likely to have is restraining yourself from solving every problem presented to you with a procedure. Fortunately, there are alternatives, such as DB2 user-defined functions!

User-Defined Functions in DB2

User-defined functions (UDFs) and stored procedures have a similar relationship in DB2 to their existence in other databases or programming environments. By far the biggest advantage you'll encounter as you work with user-defined functions is their wide-ranging capability to be specified over an externally written piece of code, such as C or COBOL, and to have DB2 reference that code to perform the functions operation. In this discussion, I'll deal only with writing user-defined functions wholly within DB2 using SQL PL. Branching out to cover other languages would require a long detour into the programming of C, Java, or some other language that will distract you from DB2.

A difference between SQL PL procedures and functions is the stipulation that a function return one result only or (more accurately for DB2) one set of results only. Compare this with the open cursor capability of stored procedures, which allow you to return as many result sets as you can consume. On the flip side, user-defined functions can be called from many more places in SQL logic, and even from external tools such as the export utility, which I'll cover in later chapters. Let's look at the different types of user-defined functions you can create in DB2.

Types of User-Defined Functions in DB2

DB2 supports three types of user-defined functions, shown in Table 8-2, which represent the structure of the data that is returned by the function; and therefore how they can be used in SQL statements, stored procedures, and other code.

Table 8-2. *User-Defined Functions*

Type	Behavior
Scalar	Returns a single value per call
Row-typed	Returns one row of data per call
Table-typed	Returns an entire table structure per call

The function types dictate from where they can be called. As you'll see in the following sections, you can call a scalar UDF anywhere a normal DB2 expression can, a row-typed UDF anywhere a full row of data can be references, and a table-typed UDF anywhere a table can be referenced.

Creating User-Defined Functions in DB2

The general syntax pattern for creating DB2 user-defined functions is as follows:

```
create function function_name
parameters
options that modify function behavior
return body specification
```

You'll see that it is broadly similar to the template for procedures, but there are important differences. The parameters of a function are implicitly all in-style parameters, and from a processing logic point of view you should assume that they are passed by value, not reference. For nonprogrammers, that means anything provided as a parameter to a function will not be changed by the function directly. It also means that you don't use the IN, OUT, or INOUT markers when specifying your parameters. So the start of the function would be the following:

```
create function emp_current_votes
(employee_id char(6) )
...
```

The options that modify function behavior have significant overlap with their procedural equivalents. The options all apply when writing user-defined functions:

SPECIFIC *name*

{MODIFIES | READS} SQL DATA | CONTAINS SQL

[NOT] DETERMINISTIC

CALLED ON NULL INPUT

INHERIT SPECIAL REGISTERS

LANGUAGE SQL

[NO] EXTERNAL ACTION

PARAMETER CCSID {ASCII | UNICODE}

You'll note that DYNAMIC RESULT SETS *n* is missing from that list, and that matches the earlier statement that functions return only one value or one set of values. There are important additional options that exist for user-defined functions. The most significant is the RETURNS option, which must be specified with one of the following forms:

RETURNS *data type*

RETURNS ROW (*row definition*)

RETURNS TABLE (*table definition*)

These options correspond to the scalar, row-typed, and table-typed functions. The table and row definitions are in a set of field names and data types specified in a manner similar to that used for a simple table definition. Additional options include the following:

STATIC DISPATCH

PREDICATES (*specification*)

INHERIT ISOLATION LEVEL {WITH | WITHOUT} LOCK REQUEST

The STATIC DISPATCH option instructs DB2 to evaluate the choice of functions using the static parameter types at run time. The PREDICATES option controls inheritance of special behaviors by external functions, which takes you beyond the scope of this introductory discussion. The INHERIT ISOLATION LEVEL {WITH | WITHOUT} LOCK REQUEST option controls lock specification inheritance from the calling statement. The default is the ...WITHOUT... variant, and at this stage you won't need to concern yourself with the vagaries of this option.

Given this slightly altered set of options, you can flesh out the skeleton of the emp_current_votes function like this:

```
create function emp_current_votes
(employee_id char(6))
returns integer
specific emp_curr_votes_int
not deterministic
language sql
...
```

Almost there! In fact, you might already be at the point of filling in the missing function body. You want to count the number of votes for an employee, so a simple count() function in a SQL select statement will do the work for you:

```
create function emp_current_votes
(employee_id char(6))
returns integer
specific emp_curr_votes_int
not deterministic
language sql
return select count(*)from emp_votes where empno = employee_id
```

That's a fairly simple example of a scalar user-defined function, but it shows how easy it is to code a function. You can adapt it to a row-typed function that returns a person's empno and current vote count. This would be useful if you have some rather vain employees who want to know how they're faring in the polls.

```
Create function emp_current_votes_row(employee_id char(6))
returns row (empno char(6), votecount integer)
specific emp_full_votes
not deterministic
language sql
called on null input
```

```
return select empno, count(*) votes
   from emp_votes
   where empno = employee_id
   group by empno
```

When called, this function will return a row of information, such as ('200010', 5). You can use this anywhere a row of information can be used, such as in the values clause of an insert statement. What happens in the event of a tie vote? The row-typed function does have a blind spot there. You could overcome this gap by writing a table-typed function to return the full set of results for the election or one that returns all the "winners" in the event of a tie:

```
create function emp_vote_results()
returns table(empno char(6), votecount integer)
specific emp_results
not deterministic
language sql
called on null input
   return select empno, count(*) votes
   from emp_votes
   group by empno
```

Very similar to the row-typed UDF, but in this case returns the entire set of results from the emp_votes table. This function provides the equivalent of the power of a raw select statement on the emp_votes table. There are options that the function provides that will come in handy. For instance, you can always increase the complexity of the SQL statement while shielding your users from the need to know and use more complex SQL.

Calling User-Defined Functions in DB2

Having built these functions, it's time to prove they actually have some use. First, let's examine the use of the scalar function defined here: emp_current_votes. You can use this function anywhere a scalar expression can be used (that is, anywhere a single value is expected by DB2). So you can use it in a select clause:

```
db2 => select firstnme, lastname, emp_current_votes(empno) from employee

FIRSTNME      LASTNAME        3
------------  --------------- -----------
CHRISTINE     HAAS                      1
MICHAEL       THOMPSON                  0
SALLY         KWAN                      0
...
WING          LEE                       0
JASON         GOUNOT                    0
DIAN          HEMMINGER                 2
GREG          ORLANDO                   0
KIM           NATZ                      0
KIYOSHI       YAMAMOTO                  0
```

Because it's a scalar function, emp_current_votes is evaluated for every row in the result set, based on the current row's value of empno. It can be used almost everywhere a scalar value can be used. One important limitation is the use of user-defined scalar functions in an order by clause. To provide a usable ordering function, the UDF must be deterministic. If you attempt to order by a nondeterministic scalar function, you'll get error code SQL0583N.

Let's jump to the other extreme and see how to use the table-typed user-defined function. There is one important difference when calling a table-typed UDF, compared with referencing a regular table. You can invoke its use by referring to it anywhere you would normally use a table or view. However, to allow DB2 to refer to the results of the function call in predicates, join conditions, and so forth you must provide a correlation alias and use the table() function as a wrapper to call the underlying table-typed UDF. This is more easily understood when you see an example:

```
db2 => select * from table(emp_vote_results()) as t

EMPNO   VOTECOUNT
------  -----------
000010            1
200010            2

  2 record(s) selected.
```

In this example, t is the correlation alias. You can use it in other clauses, just as you would use a normal table alias. Let's query the table-typed function for only those votes belonging to empno 200010:

```
db2 => select * from table(emp_vote_results()) as t where t.empno = '200010'

EMPNO   VOTECOUNT
------  -----------
200010            2

  1 record(s) selected.
```

Voila! Just like using a table or view. To take the use of functions to the logical extreme, you can use multiple functions and types of functions in the same statement:

```
Select emp_current_votes(t.empno) from table(emp_vote_results()) as t

1
-----------
          1
          2

  2 record(s) selected.
```

That's a contrived example of the results of one function feeding the input of another, but it reinforces the idea that functions are ubiquitous and you should feel free to use them wherever and whenever the situation demands. Of course, you might want to check your sanity if every statement you write ends up referencing nothing but functions!

Managing and Deleting User-Defined Functions

This will be a very short topic. You're intimately familiar with how to manage stored procedures, and exactly the same tools and techniques can be used to manage user-defined functions. Naturally, the syntax of the DDL statement for dropping a function uses the keyword `function`, as follows:

```
drop function emp_vote_results
```

The same rules apply for using the specific clause for overloaded functions, and the Control Center and IBM Data Studio can be used in identical ways to manage your growing collection of user-defined functions.

Summary

You have come a long way since the start of this chapter, moving into the procedural world of DB2 to master SQL PL for stored procedures and user-defined functions. As I highlighted in the introduction, there is a wealth of material I haven't covered, particularly surrounding the use of external procedures and functions written in other programming languages such as C, COBOL, or Java. If you have interests in this area, I strongly recommend the materials available on the IBM website. You can also find helpful material in the later chapters of this book that deal with application development using some of these languages with DB2.

CHAPTER 9

■ ■ ■

Controlling Access to DB2

It's time to discuss the topic of access control—or more formally how users are authenticated .
when trying to access DB2—and the mechanisms used to control who can connect to databases, who can attach to instances, and the baked-in powers available to special groups and
users.

Like many other databases and many other software systems in general, the concepts of
access security and privileges in DB2 are divided into two distinct areas. First, authentication
is the process of determining that you are who you say you are when you attempt to perform a
privileged action, such as connecting. Once authenticated, the second area of authorization
determines what you can do.

This chapter deals with the first area, authentication, and a number of related topics pertaining to operating system security and your DB2 processes. Chapter 10 will deal with the
topic of authorizations and cover topics such as who can add, change, and delete data from
tables and structures in your databases.

Authentication and authorization act in a layered effect. Your ability to connect to a particular DB2 database and the powers you have over objects within it are composed like layers
of an onion to provide you with a working set of powers and capabilities. Figure 9-1 shows the
overall picture of where various powers and privileges originate and provides a useful model
for the next two chapters.

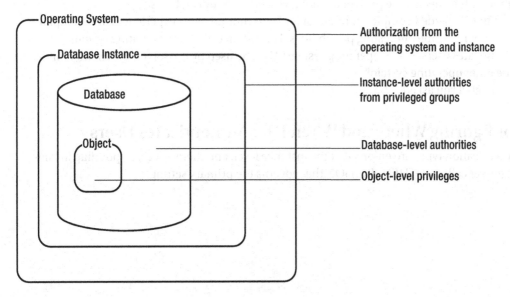

Figure 9-1. *The layers of authentication and authorization in DB2*

It's time to find out *who you are*!

DB2 Building Blocks for Authentication

DB2 bases authentication of users on external facilities instead of using an internal list of users and passwords that you might have experienced with other databases. In practice it means that DB2 will use the operating system users (and groups) for authentication purposes, and can use third-party authentication facilities such as Kerberos and RADIUS to properly authenticate users in more advanced configurations.

During normal operation, DB2 keeps data on what users and groups have been nominated for authentication. These users and groups are known as *authorization IDs* (*authids* for short). When one of those users shows up asking to be "let in" to see your precious data, DB2 refers the request to the external authenticating system to give it the all-clear. There are advantages and disadvantages to this approach.

The advantages are pretty obvious. DB2 doesn't track password information, so you're freed from having to remember yet another password. You're also freed from the timeless issues of password synchronization, different password "strength" requirements, different password lifetimes or mandated change cycles, and so forth. DB2 uses operating system user names, so once you know your operating system user name, you automatically know your DB2 user name. By not storing redundant copies of passwords or other sensitive credentials, you also reduce the possible surface area for security vulnerabilities and hacker attacks. In general, some pretty strong advantages.

The disadvantages are a little more subtle, but worth knowing. To add a user or group to a DB2 database, that user or group needs to be known to your operating system or other external security facility. If you're wearing multiple hats as a database administrator and systems administrator, you have the power to perform these multiple steps. But if adding operating system–level users is someone else's job, you are now dependent. Not necessarily a huge problem, but a complication nonetheless. You are afforded the flexibility of granting privileges and authorizations to users and groups in DB2 before they exist in the operating system, but ultimately they need to be present at both levels before they can be used.

While the added complexity might differ from your previous experiences, it does open up the door to some interesting possibilities. For instance, if it's the operating system that authenticates users, *which* operating system? The one used by the server, the client, or indeed some other operating system?

I'm glad you asked!

Configuring Where and When DB2 Authenticates Users

Authentication types are enforced at the instance level, and there is a corresponding instance parameter called AUTHENTICATION that governs the primary setting.

SERVER Authentication Type

The SERVER authentication type is the default setting for your instance. With this option, users are authenticated based on the DB2 server's operating system. DB2 can determine whether you're connecting remotely or locally, and will allow local connections based implicitly on your current user name.

SERVER_ENCRYPT Authentication Type

The SERVER_ENCRYPT authentication type is a special variant on the SERVER type, where one of a particular approved set of cryptographic schemes must be used in conjunction with the DB2 environment. IBM keeps a published list of the approved mechanisms—essentially, those that are technically capable and have demonstrated interoperability—including such facilities as cryptographic coprocessors, cryptographic chipsets, cryptographic security tokens, JavaCard cryptographic tokens, and cryptographic software from IBM. Only a user's password will be encrypted during authentication; data and user names still transmit unencrypted.

CLIENT Authentication Type

Do you trust your clients? It's a question often asked, not just in the software world. With the CLIENT authentication setting, DB2 is set to rely on the client operating system to handle authentication and will trust that the client operating system has done its job—it won't force a user to prove *bona fides* again.

You might be wondering what happens in environments in which untrusted operating systems prevail or where operating systems with no inherent security exist, such as Windows 98 or Windows ME. The CLIENT authentication behavior is modified by two further parameters, TRUST_ALLCLNTS and TRUST_CLNTAUTH, to help deal with these scenarios.

TRUST_ALLCLNTS is a Yes/No/Maybe style parameter (where Maybe in this instance means the term *DRDA*). It basically determines how strict DB2 will be when trusting clients. The TRUST_CLNTAUTH parameter, which takes the values CLIENT or SERVER, dictates where clients of "dubious trust" will be asked to authenticate themselves.

WHAT IS DRDA?

The *Distributed Relational Database Architecture (DRDA)* is the IBM protocol for the distribution of parts of a logical conceptual database across many physical databases, not necessarily running on the same software or hardware architecture.

DRDA is supported by all IBM DB2 products (and indeed many of IBM's other database offerings), and one of its key features is the capability to specify and enforce rules that govern how data spread across multiple systems such as mainframes, minicomputers, UNIX hosts, Linux hosts, and Windows hosts will be managed. It is enough to know at this stage that the protocol exists because I won't deal further with it in this book.

A prose description of how the three values for TRUST_ALLCLNTS and the two for TRUST_CLNTAUTH work together with CLIENT authentication, *and* whether you supply a user name and password or implicitly use your nominal current user name, rapidly becomes confusing. I think you'll agree that even that warning about confusion is confusing. Table 9-1 illustrates where a user will be authenticated (depending on the settings for these parameters) in common Windows, Linux, UNIX, and similar environments.

Table 9-1. *Authentication Type Combinations and Resulting Authentication Location*

TRUST_ ALLCLNTS Setting	TRUST_ CLNTAUTH Setting	With Implicit User Credentials		User Supplies Explicit Credentials	
		Trusted Client	**Untrusted Client**	**Trusted Client**	**Untrusted Client**
YES	CLIENT	CLIENT	CLIENT	CLIENT	CLIENT
YES	SERVER	CLIENT	SERVER	CLIENT	SERVER
NO	CLIENT	SERVER	SERVER	CLIENT	CLIENT
NO	SERVER	SERVER	SERVER	CLIENT	SERVER

DRDA clients, those mainframe/otherworldly entities that you might never encounter, are strictly authenticated at the client if implicitly connecting with no user name and password, and obey the setting of TRUST_CLNTAUTH if a user name and password is explicitly provided. That is, server-side authentication if TRUST_CLNTAUTH is set to SERVER; client-side if it is set to CLIENT. Perhaps counterintuitively, the TRUST_ALLCLNTS setting is irrelevant for DRDA clients, even if that parameter has a suspiciously similar named setting of DRDA available. Don't say I didn't warn you about the confusion.

KERBEROS Authentication Type

The KERBEROS authentication type is available if both the DB2 server and client operating systems support Kerberos. In such an environment, DB2 bases authentication on service tickets issued by a Kerberos server and honors those tickets granted to holders of appropriate ticket-granting tickets. Most modern operating systems supported by DB2 also support Kerberos, and it is increasingly popular in environments that desire single sign-on across diverse systems (if you haven't encountered it already, it's bound to pop up in a system near you soon).

KRB_SERVER_ENCRYPT Authentication Type

You can probably glean the operation of KRB_SERVER_ENCRYPT from what's been mentioned previously. This setting prefers Kerberos authentication if it's available and allows falling back to SERVER_ENCRYPT for suitably configured clients. If none of these options is available, clients receive a connection error and can't connect.

DATA_ENCRYPT Authentication Type

Confused yet? Believe it or not, DATA_ENCRYPT will be perfectly understandable given your existing knowledge. It is identical to SERVER_ENCRYPT, but it includes wire-protocol–level encryption of data, including SQL statements, variables, data returned, and associated codes and messages. So with native DB2 protocols you don't need to worry about network snooping or interception because all over-the-wire traffic is encrypted. If you are used to using secure tunnels, port forwarding, and similar types of security apparatus you might find this option significantly easier and more straightforward to administer. In all other respects, DATA_ENCRYPT acts like the SERVER authentication type.

DATA_ENCRYPT_CMP Authentication Type

Are you still with me? The smorgasbord of authentication types is almost at an end. DATA_ENCRYPT_CMP is in essence a clone of DATA_ENCRYPT, except that its underlying compatibility is with SERVER_ENCRYPT. Just think of it as authentication paranoia coupled with data transfer paranoia. A tinfoil hat for every occasion. In practice, DB2 seeks to use DATA_ENCRYPT with clients, but settles for the lesser protection of SERVER_ENCRYPT for those clients unable to support DATA_ENCRYPT.

More-Exotic Members of the Authentication Family

By now, you're probably wondering how much more exotic things can get. The remaining members of the authentication family are GSSPLUGIN and GSS_SERVER_ENCRYPT. These authentication types support plug-in authentication systems and act by providing a client attempting to connect with a list of supported authentication plug-ins. If the client also supports one of these plug-ins, it is used; otherwise, authentication falls back to Kerberos. Failing that, if GSS_SERVER_ENCRYPT is used, authentication falls back to SERVER_ENCRYPT.

I've never seen either of these options used in practice, but they have a following out there in the DB2 community.

Choosing Your Authentication Option

The bewildering array of authentication types has doubtless left you wondering how you'll ever choose between them. Let me put your mind at ease, at least at this early stage in your DB2 career. The vast majority of deployments I have seen use SERVER or CLIENT authentication, with some movement toward KERBEROS. I can almost guarantee that my e-mail inbox will be filled with protests from those who use the other options, and they certainly have their place. But that doesn't detract from my admittedly anecdotal experience.

Don't let my jaded view of being spoiled for choice of authentication types influence your decision. Your data should be protected by whatever means you think appropriate. Think about what approach to security is taken generally in your environment—and which DB2 authentication type will work best with it and your data security goals. In practice, most DB2 administrators lean toward the SERVER group of authentication options because the level of trust and belief in some client operating systems and their capability to reliably authenticate users with a CLIENT setting without threat from attacks or vulnerabilities is sometimes too much to ask.

Before delving into some examples of changing the authentication, it is useful to understand the complementary area of instance-level privileged groups.

DB2 Instance-Level Privileged Groups

Authentication and authorization work as complementary techniques to ensure that your
data is always protected. While we are primarily discussing authentication in this chapter, one
area that blurs the line between the two is the set of special privilege groups that can be linked
to operating system groups. Being a member of one of the associated operating system groups
can allow for authentication where this otherwise might not succeed (thus the discussion
here). I also need to warn you against certain modifications to authentication type and these
groups' settings made at the same time—but first, a description of what you'll deal with.

These groups are known as SYSADM, SYSCTRL, SYSMAINT, and SYSMON. You can think
of these groups as different kinds of instance supergroups, members of which have special
powers over the instance, the operation of its databases, and in some cases access to data. I'm
not sure we'll see a Hollywood film about these superpowers any time soon.

Following is a description of each group:

- *SYSADM Group*: The SYSADM authority provides a nominated user with total control
  over all the resources and data controlled by the associated instance. This is the highest
  level of built-in privilege associated with a DB2 instance, and it encompasses all the
  privileges granted to the other groups—SYSCTRL, SYSMAINT, and SYSMON—as well
  as several database-level privilege sets. Importantly, it includes all privileges over the
  actual data in the database by default.

- *SYSCTRL Group*: Users with membership of SYSCTRL have a broad set of powers over
  the instance processes and behavior, without any access to the actual data in associated databases. So a user with SYSCTRL membership can stop and start the instance,
  change most instance parameters, quiesce databases, change database parameters,
  and create and drop databases. They have no inherent access to the underlying data in
  the databases, however, so this role is perfect for operational control over a system.

- *SYSMAINT Group*: A user granted membership to SYSMAINT has database-level powers
  over all databases associated with an instance, but no powers over the instance itself.
  Again useful for operational tasks such as database backups, restores, quiescence, and
  so forth. Members of this group also have SYSMON privileges. No data access is provided to members of this group.

- *SYSMON Group*: The last of the instance-level special privilege groups, SYSMON membership allows users to use and control the monitoring and snapshot tools that are used
  for database and instance diagnostics. Members of this group have no access to data
  within the monitored databases.

Now that you're familiar with those privilege groups, you're probably thinking that this topic has more to do with authorization than authentication. For the most part you're correct, but one important aspect of the implementation of these privilege groups can affect who is authenticated, and with what privileges, for a given instance.

Each of the groups can be governed by a database manager (that is, instance-level) parameter that can reference a group from your operating system. The parameters (SYSADM_ GROUP, SYSCTRL_GROUP, SYSMAINT_GROUP, and SYSMON_GROUP) control the privilege level associated with their name. For example, members of the group specified in SYSADM_ GROUP are those that inherit SYSADM privileges.

At this point, you can probably foresee the responsibility implicit in these powers. If you set one of these parameters to an operating system group, all members of that operating system group have the relevant privileges *and* can successfully authenticate to exercise those powers, even if they've never been explicitly granted permissions to connect or attach to databases or your instance by their authids.

I'm probably being overly cautious about this, but it's important to remember the authentication implications if you want (or need) to change one of these parameters.

Changing Your DB2 Authentication Parameters

The concepts involved in changing the authentication and special privilege group parameters are no different from the changes you've made to parameters in previous examples. There are some useful features of DB2 that are worth quickly exploring to show how they can make your life easier, however.

Caution Now for the all-important warning about setting the AUTHENTICATION and SYSADM_GROUP parameters. These are parameters much like any other set at the instance level for your system. And as a suitably authorized user (say, SYSADM) you're well within your rights to modify these parameters. My advice (from long, at times frustrating, at other times funny experience) is this: *Never change both parameters at the same time!* There's no technical reason preventing you from making simultaneous parameter changes; instead it is simple human nature that at some point you will make a mistake, and one of the outcomes of missetting these parameters in tandem is the possibility that users are totally and irrevocably locked out of your instance until the instance owner intervenes to correct these settings! Okay, perhaps a more realistic suggestion is to make sure you know what you're doing and to have a complete fallback strategy in case something goes wrong.

With that warning out of the way, let's look at the tools for working with these parameters.

Using Control Center to Manage Authentication Parameters

Starting and using the Control Center should now be a familiar experience for you, so I trust you can open up the Configure Parameters option for your instance. Figure 9-2 shows that the Control Center actually lists all the relevant authentication parameters at the top of the dialog box—you don't even need to scroll to see what you need to work with.

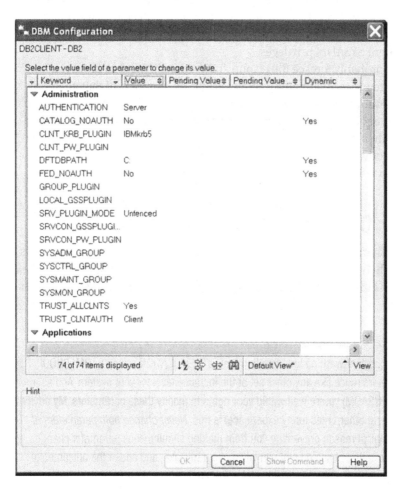

Figure 9-2. *The Control Center management of authentication parameters*

None of the group level parameters is set. By implication, no operating system groups have any of these privileges by default. Only the instance owner has any of the special privileges—they start with implicit SYSADM rights.

To change the authorization setting, click the ellipsis button next to the current setting. The dialog box shown in Figure 9-3 appears, presenting you with the predefined options available.

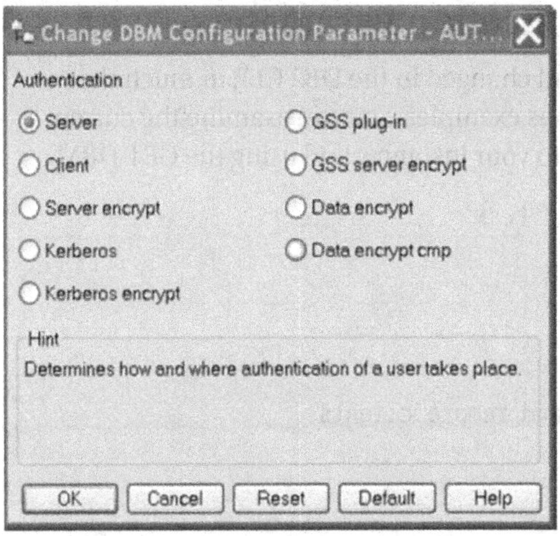

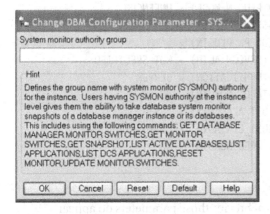

Figure 9-3. *The defined authentication types can be selected in the Control Center.*

I don't recommend changing your current setting away from SERVER until you create a few groups and users in later steps, but at least now you're familiar with this process.

Now take a look at what happens when you select one of the privilege group settings (for example, SYSMON_GROUP) for changing. You're presented with a simple dialog box, as shown in Figure 9-4. Note that the field in which you specify the group name is a free-form text field.

Figure 9-4. *The free-form field for setting SYSMON_GROUP in the Control Center*

You can probably appreciate the warning in more depth now because there is no protection provided against accidentally mistyping the group name. So it might be possible to unintentionally exclude all current SYSADMs from the system when modifying the SYSADM_GROUP parameter. If you don't notice this until after you save the change and exit the Control Center, you could also lose the ability to query this DBM parameter, so you might not know which group now has the privileges! Admittedly, that's a far-fetched scenario, but it has happened more than once.

Using DB2 CLP to Manage Authentication Parameters

The values for these parameters can be viewed and changed in the DB2 CLP, in much the same way the other parameters were set in previous examples. You can examine the current settings by starting a DB2 CLP session, attaching to your instance, and using the GET DBM CFG command:

```
db2 => get dbm cfg

            Database Manager Configuration

     Node type = Database Server with local and remote clients

...

    SYSADM group name                      (SYSADM_GROUP) =
    SYSCTRL group name                     (SYSCTRL_GROUP) =
    SYSMAINT group name                   (SYSMAINT_GROUP) =
    SYSMON group name                      (SYSMON_GROUP) =

    Client Userid-Password Plugin         (CLNT_PW_PLUGIN) =
    Client Kerberos Plugin               (CLNT_KRB_PLUGIN) = IBMkrb5
    Group Plugin                            (GROUP_PLUGIN) =
    GSS Plugin for Local Authorization   (LOCAL_GSSPLUGIN) =
    Server Plugin Mode                    (SRV_PLUGIN_MODE) = UNFENCED
    Server List of GSS Plugins      (SRVCON_GSSPLUGIN_LIST) =
    Server Userid-Password Plugin        (SRVCON_PW_PLUGIN) =
    Server Connection Authentication        (SRVCON_AUTH) = NOT_SPECIFIED
    Database manager authentication       (AUTHENTICATION) = SERVER
    Cataloging allowed without authority  (CATALOG_NOAUTH) = NO
    Trust all clients                     (TRUST_ALLCLNTS) = YES
    Trusted client authentication         (TRUST_CLNTAUTH) = CLIENT
    Bypass federated authentication           (FED_NOAUTH) = NO

...
```

While I've truncated the output for the sake of brevity, those parameters do appear as a contiguous block as shown when using the GET DBM CFG command.

An example of changing your current authentication settings is to alter the AUTHENTICATION type to SERVER_ENCRYPT:

```
db2 => update dbm cfg using authentication server_encrypt
DB20000I  The UPDATE DATABASE MANAGER CONFIGURATION command completed
successfully.
SQL1362W  One or more of the parameters submitted for immediate modification
were not changed dynamically. Client changes will not be effective until the
next time the application is started or the TERMINATE command has been issued.
Server changes will not be effective until the next DB2START command.
```

Note that DB2 will warn you if your authentication or authorization changes can't take immediate effect. Normally this means an instance restart or client reconnection.

Once again, the warning against careful changes to these parameters is of value. While changing the AUTHENTICATION type will be parsed by the DB2 CLP for syntactic correctness, changes to the privilege group parameters such as SYSADM_GROUP can pass such a syntactic test and point to an operating system group that doesn't exist. Take care!

Group Authentication Issues

All this talk of authentication and the suggestion of more detail to come when I discuss authorization probably leaves you wishing for the simple life. The good news is that DB2 has the sophisticated security mechanisms I've discussed, but also includes sensible streamlining of security by using familiar techniques. One of the primary approaches to authentication management is to base privileges upon group membership instead of individually granting authid's access and later granting those individuals further authorizations over data, stored procedures, and so forth. There are some group-level considerations with which you'll need to be familiar.

Configuring DB2 to Use Local or Global Groups

Another topic that straddles the authentication/authorization boundary is determining where DB2 seeks group information when allowing users access to the system. In Windows operating systems, groups can be present as local security features or can be sourced from a global security service such as Active Directory, and they can be nested so that local groups have members that are themselves global (domain) groups and other combinations.

A DB2 registry value named DB2_GRP_LOOKUP controls at what level DB2 seeks group membership details when authenticating a user. This can be set for each instance on a server and globally for all instances on a server.

By default, this value is empty, which equates to a universal approach to group membership resolution. DB2 examines both local and domain-level groups for membership when this default configuration is used. It is sometimes desirable to change it so that only local (or only domain) group enumeration is used.

To make such a change, you can invoke the db2set utility from the command line, specifying the option you want to use. For example, the following db2set command alters all instances on a server to use only domain-level groups for authentication:

```
C:\ db2set -g DB2_GRP_LOOKUP=DOMAIN
```

Similarly, this example changes the instance name DB2 to using only local group membership resolution:

```
C:\ db2set –i DB2 DB2_GRP_LOOKUP=LOCAL
```

There are more complex settings for this parameter that are designed to support token-based authentication schemes. They are well beyond the scope of a beginner's book, so I encourage you to look them up in the DB2 Information Center if they are of interest to you.

64 Groups Limitation

A scenario that is sometimes encountered in very large organizations is excessive nesting of groups within groups and proliferation of groups. This is often done to represent or convey project membership, cross-team responsibilities, or similar associations. DB2 enumerates only the first 64 groups it encounters for membership purposes, meaning that it doesn't honor membership in groups "beyond" 64. You're probably wondering who would assign more than 64 groups to a given user. Somewhere, someone has done this and doubtless will do so again.

At least you're now aware of this limitation if it ever becomes an issue in your environment.

Support for Windows AD Domain Features

DB2 supports many of the features provided by Active Directory (AD) and also supports concepts such as trust relationships, domain lists for domain preferences, and explicit support for authentication of users directly with backup domain controllers.

If you plan to operate DB2 in a Windows AD environment, there are additional resources available that describe capabilities, functions, and limitations in the DB2 Information Center, and also in a dedicated IBM Redbook titled *DB2 UDB V8.2 on the Windows Environment*. While this Redbook is nominally for the previous major version of DB2, many of the concepts are still valid in DB2 9.5.

Security Context of the DB2 Server

One last area to consider when securing your DB2 environment is the actual operating system user under which your DB2 software runs. Under Linux, you saw in Chapter 2 and Chapter 3 how instances are configured to be owned and run by a nominated user account. Consider for a moment the implications of using the root user for this purpose. No doubt some of you just yelled *WHAT!?* at the top of your lungs, and rightly so. One of the key mantras of any security environment is to never grant privileges that are not needed and, by implication, to never assume a role more powerful than necessary to get a job done.

Entire books have been written on the topic of good security practice, outside of just DB2 considerations. I'm sure that each one of them contains a line like this: *don't run anything as root unless you absolutely have to!* DB2 is fundamentally designed to not need this level of power for normal operation of existing instances, so resist the temptation to run as root. You'll need root privileges for installation and instance creation, but use security common sense beyond that.

Windows presents a parallel issue: it has several built-in accounts that are often used for operating services. Two in particular are often used for other facilities and services in a Windows environment: *Local System* and *Network Service*. Microsoft has an enormous volume of information available about the security features and considerations of both of these accounts, so I don't propose to repeat all that here.

I'll summarize the reasons to not use either of these accounts for your DB2 instance services in one simple sentence: the Local System user has no network access privileges in a Windows environment, and the Network Service user has *unfettered* network access privileges. Basically, Local System lacks sufficient power for the needs of DB2 services needing network access, and Network Service has too much power for the tasks required. Some of the services specific to the local environment run as Local System under a Windows operating system, such as the licensing service, but I recommend that you run the DB2 instance services as the user you nominated when installing the software.

Summary

Security will always be one of your leading concerns when working with sensitive data and DB2 databases. This chapter started you on the path to appreciating all the factors and subtleties that come into play when determining who your users are and what permissions they have to connect to your DB2 environment.

The details on authorization considerations that control what a user can do once they have access (discussed in Chapter 10) complement the details found in this chapter. Even after reading both chapters, you'll almost certainly find that there are always more details and more security factors that will govern your future use of DB2. Keeping up with the shifting world of security is one of the key aspects of successfully managing databases.

CHAPTER 10

■ ■ ■

Securing Data in DB2

You've seen how DB2 authentication determines who you are, and to which instances and databases you have access. You've looked at the special authorities vested in SYSADM, SYSMAINT, and others. But what about day-to-day access to normal data, and common privileges such as the ability to create tables, run SQL statements that change what's stored in the database, and so on?

Managing Authorities and Privileges in DB2

In DB2, this third area of securing the database and its contents is the domain of database and object privileges, and they control most of the activities you'd expect when a user tries to select, update, insert, and delete data; as well as perform common management tasks on database objects such as tables, views, and procedures.

Preparing to Use Authorities and Privileges

This chapter uses two operating system users and one operating system group to explore the inner workings of DB2 privileges. Using the Computer Management applet for Windows, the domain/Active Directory management tools, or the useradd and groupadd commands for Linux, you can create the following users and group:

- THEUSER: You'll use this user to perform normal end-user tasks.

- THEBOSS: You'll use this user to show how higher-level privileges change your capabilities with DB2.

- AGROUP: You'll use this group to provide its members with inherited privileges.

Database-Level Authorities

Certain privileges exist at the database level, baked in to each DB2 database. These privileges are known as *database authorities* to remain consistent with the naming for instance-level equivalents. There are ten database level authorities available to grant to any registered user of the database:

- *DBADM*: Think of DBADM as the superuser authority at the database level. It allows the possessor to do almost anything in a given database and provides full control over all objects in the database.

- *CREATETAB*: A user with this authority is allowed to create tables in the database.

- *BINDADD*: Someone with this authority can add code packages to the database with the bind command.

- *CONNECT*: As simple as it sounds. This authority allows you to connect to a database.

- *QUIESCE_CONNECT*: A more powerful form of the connect authority. With QUIESCE_CONNECT, you can connect to the database even if it has been placed in the quiesced state.

- *CREATE_EXTERNAL_ROUTINE*: This authority allows its grantee to create a procedure in the database that relies on external code.

- *CREATE_NOT_FENCED_ROUTINE*: This authority allows a user to create a user-defined function (UDF) that runs in the same address space as the instance itself (a so-called "unfenced" function).

- *IMPLICIT_SCHEMA*: With this authority, a user no longer has to explicitly create a schema using the create schema command before objects can be placed within it.

- *LOAD*: Provides the necessary authority to use the bulk data load utilities for DB2 (but does not cover the use of the Insert SQL statement).

- *SECADM*: Possibly the most important new addition to the database-level authorities in DB2 9. The SECADM privilege is the only authority that can configure and perform database-level auditing (instead of just control where audit details are written). SECADM also controls the use of Label-Based Access Control (LBAC), which I'll discuss shortly.

One very important aspect of database authority management is to consider the implied privileges that accompany any of the preceding explicit authorities. The first and most confusing implication is that if you grant users any of the authorities listed, they will implicitly be given connect authority to the database. If you look back over that list, you'll understand that implicit connect authority isn't really opening up the database to any unwanted access—none of those authorities make sense if you can't actually connect to the database. The second important implication is that DBADM authority provides many of the other privileges implicitly. (The only exception is the SECADM authority, which can be granted only by instance-level SYSADM authority holders.)

To round out implications and assumptions, there is one crucial difference between DB2 authorities and other privileges when compared with other databases. Privileges and authorities are assumed to be denied if not granted. There is no explicit way to deny a privilege (other than to revoke it from someone who has that privilege, but that is an action instead of a setting). It means that you cannot override the cascading authorities I mentioned in the previous paragraph. You also don't have to worry about competing levels of granted and denied authorities after I start talking about inheritance of privileges and authorities from groups. You might not think this is a big deal right now, but it means you'll never have to play "hunt the denied privilege," as you sometimes have to do in other database systems. DB2 wins again!

Viewing Database Authorities

Database-level authorities are easily managed through the Control Center, but there is an interesting Catch-22. To manage the database authorities for a given database, you must be a member of the SYSADM group for the instance or already hold DBADM authority in the database. Log in to your machine as the instance owner for DB2, and launch the Control Center. Drill down to find the SAMPLE database, and select Authorities from its context menu to call up the database authority management dialog box, as shown in Figure 10-1.

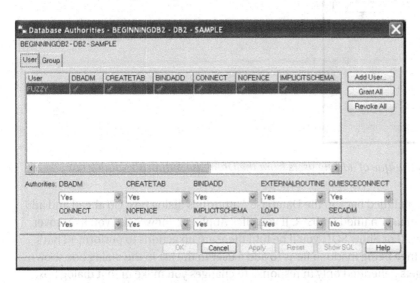

Figure 10-1. *Database Authorities dialog box*

This dialog box is one of the most useful presented in the Control Center. You can see all the users known to the database and their fixed authorities. Remember, there's no concept of "denying" a user access. If you don't see ordinary users in this list, it is because they have not been granted an authority. Special users, such as those who are members of the SYSADM or SYSMAINT groups, might not show up here, but will still hold those authorities over your database. Strangely, these special users will show up in the Users folder in the Control Center. Just a quirk you'll have to live with.

Changing Database Authorities

The same dialog box also serves as your point of control to add users, change authorities, or revoke authorities from users. The interface is intuitive enough that you won't need copious screenshots to walk you through it. Simply highlight the user you're interested in changing (or the group on the group tab) and use the drop-down lists below to set a given authority to Yes or No. Note that the green ticks and red crosses you see onscreen show you what the *outcome* of your changes will be *if* you go ahead and apply your various modifications—they show only the current state of authorities when the dialog box is first opened, before you start altering values.

To introduce a user to DB2, click the appropriately named Add User button. This calls up the abbreviated version of the Add User facility. It's abbreviated because (as you can see in Figure 10-2) you're given the options to name the operating system (or other external) user account you want to use.

Figure 10-2. *Express technique of adding users from the Database Authorities dialog box*

The user is then included back in the Database Authorities dialog box. Go ahead and add your operating system user named THEUSER. If you click Apply (or Show SQL), you'll discover that nothing happens. (For Show SQL, you'll be told there are no actions to perform.) That's because the only change being made so far is to add a user to the list in the dialog box shown in Figure 10-1. SQL gets generated only in response to changes you make in that dialog box. You basically have a two-step process here: 1) add a user to the list shown in the Database Authorities dialog box; 2) grant authorities to that user. Step 2 is what triggers SQL to actually make changes to your database.

Remember that authorities and privileges are implicitly denied. If you don't grant any authorities to THEUSER, that user implicitly has no powers within DB2 and isn't considered a user. Think of this disappearing act as efficient housekeeping. The user will even disappear from the list of users in the Database Authorities dialog box.

For purposes of example, change the CONNECT setting for THEUSER to Yes, which will grant the authority to connect to the database. If you choose Show SQL at this point, you'll see that the equivalent SQL statement takes this form:

```
GRANT CONNECT ON DATABASE TO USER THEUSER
```

That statement should make perfect sense. The general form of the SQL commands that grant authorities is the following:

```
GRANT AUTHORITY[, AUTHORITY ...] ON DATABASE TO { USER | GROUP } USER_OR_GROUP_NAME
```

The equivalent of the Database Authorities dialog box's capability to set an authority to No is to use the revoke command, which takes this form:

```
REVOKE AUTHORIT Y[, AUTHORITY ...] ON DATABASE FROM USER_OR_GROUP_NAME
```

You can nominate users and groups using the same general syntax, and the Database Authorities dialog box allows you to create either with ease. This reflects DB2's reliance on the underlying operating system to manage groups and their members. In essence, DB2 is passing group management responsibilities to the operating system, in much the same way it trusts the operating system to manage the notion of a user and all that entails. Don't confuse an operating system group with a DB2 *role*. I'll cover roles shortly.

Try using the DB2 Command Line Processor (CLP) to issue the following command to grant the group AGROUP the CONNECT and CREATETAB privileges:

```
db2 => connect to sample user db2admin
Enter current password for db2admin:

   Database Connection Information

 Database server       = DB2/NT 9.5.0
 SQL authorization ID  = DB2ADMIN
 Local database alias  = SAMPLE


db2 => grant connect, createtab on database to group AGROUP
DB20000I  The SQL command completed successfully.
```

Whether you used the Control Center's Database Authorities dialog box or the equivalent SQL command, THEUSER should now have the ability to connect to the SAMPLE database. Test it to prove that you haven't missed anything (such as clicking Cancel instead of OK in the dialog box):

```
db2 => disconnect sample
DB20000I  The SQL DISCONNECT command completed successfully.
db2 => connect to sample user THEUSER
Enter current password for THEUSER:

   Database Connection Information

 Database server       = DB2/NT 9.5.0
 SQL authorization ID  = THEUSER
 Local database alias  = SAMPLE
```

That means success! Naturally, granting and using the other database authorities follow a similar path, as you'd expect. Now for a brain teaser. At the moment, you know that you've granted CONNECT authority to THEUSER. From what you know of DB2 authorities, because it doesn't have CREATETAB authority, it shouldn't be able to create tables, right?

```
db2 => create table try_it_out (mynumber integer)
DB20000I  The SQL command completed successfully.
```

What on earth is going on? Have I lied to you about authorities for half a chapter? Thankfully, the answer is no; I haven't led you astray. Instead, the mystery is solved by understanding how groups allow users to inherit authorities and permissions in DB2, and the particular culprit in this example: the PUBLIC group.

Group Behavior in DB2

Any permissions or privileges system worth its salt makes the life of administrators easier by allowing powers to be granted in bulk, to groups or roles, instead of expecting every ability to be granted to every single user who might need it. In DB2, this efficiency is gained by using groups that, like users, map directly to your operating system's (or authentication system's) set of groups.

A user's group membership is determined at the operating system level—DB2 itself doesn't add an extra layer of membership management. DB2 also offers the ability to plug in a separate group management facility, which can be nominated at the instance level using the GROUP_PLUGIN configuration parameter. This takes the name of a dynamic link library (DLL) under Windows or shared object under Linux that will resolve all group membership lookups.

A user's group membership is picked up at login time when DB2 attempts to determine whether a user has CONNECT privileges.

Group Lookup in DB2 on Windows

If normal operating system users and groups are used, DB2 takes additional steps when looking for groups in a Windows environment. Your Windows DB2 server will normally be part of a domain or Active Directory enterprise environment. As such, users can be created locally using the Computer Management tool or in Active Directory using the relevant tools there. When a user connects to DB2, the DB2 instance will implicitly look for groups in the same context from which the user comes—local groups for local users or Active Directory/domain groups for global users.

Of course, Microsoft is the master of providing options, so you naturally can nest global groups inside local groups, and global users inside either. Add to that the ability to name global and local groups identically (Windows considers that they have totally separate namespaces) and you might find that your group lookups become problematic. Another common environment you might encounter, as a new developer or administrator, is using a domain-level user on a laptop that is temporarily disconnected.

A DB2 registry setting that covers all instances on a server is provided, which directs DB2 to consider only local groups, or local groups and any cached credentials from a domain in a disconnected state. This is particularly useful if you want to keep group membership local to the DB2 server or disambiguate local and global groups that share names. It's also useful for people who tinker with DB2 while on the move. The registry setting is called DB2_GRP_LOOKUP, and is set using the db2set utility as follows:

```
c:\> db2set DB2_GRP_LOOKUP=LOCAL
```

This invocation sets the variable to LOCAL, telling DB2 to consider only local groups. You can also examine the value of the variable by calling db2set with the parameter name:

```
c:\> db2set DB2_GRP_LOOKUP+
LOCAL
```

The additional parameter TOKENLOCAL can be used to tell DB2 to use the cached credentials of domain users.

One limitation that you should be aware of (even if you might never encounter it) is the degree of group nesting that DB2 can navigate when resolving privileges. With group nesting, one group is made a member of another group. Currently, the limit of traversing such nested groups in DB2 stands at 64 groups, which sounds like more than you can ever imagine nesting, but in large enterprise environments, this limit is sometimes hit.

The PUBLIC Group

What about the mystery of THEUSER being able to create tables without the CREATETAB authority? Take a look at the at the Group tab in the Database Authorities dialog box in the Control Center, as shown in Figure 10-3.

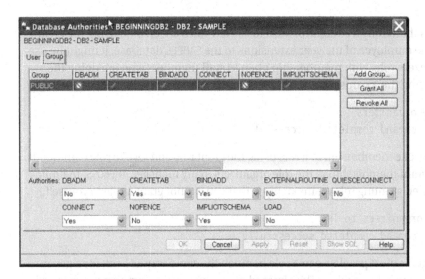

Figure 10-3. *The group and its authority*

There's the culprit: the pseudo-group PUBLIC! Every DB2 database has this group provided, and it comes packaged with a set of basic privileges. This group does not map to any operating system or authentication packages idea of a group. Instead it is provided as a de facto common group for all users of a given database. As you can see from the Database Authorities dialog box, it includes the CREATETAB privilege.

By default, every user is a member of this group. That's where THEUSER got the power to create tables. But that's not all that gets provided through the PUBLIC group. Select privileges on a wide range of system catalog tables are also provided (those that belong to the SYSIBM schema).

■**Note** DB2 administrators, old and new, have to decide what they do with the PUBLIC group and its privileges and authorities when managing security for their environments. There's no concrete rule regarding how it should be treated; many organizations leave it configured in its default fashion. But best-practice security would suggest that blanket privileges of the kind it grants are not the best way to harden a system, and any authority that isn't explicitly needed or granted should be removed. You won't tinker with its settings now, but as your DB2 career moves ahead, this is something to consider.

Roles in DB2

With the advent of DB2 9.5, a complementary feature to groups has been introduced that also happens to provide additional flexibility and control for DB2 administrators. Roles in DB2 are another way of collecting users together, so that privileges can be managed in concert, instead of individually. While they are very similar to groups, roles do have some important differences, which you'll explore shortly.

Managing Roles

Role management is thankfully a straightforward task. New roles are created using the create role statement. In the employee of the year extensions to the SAMPLE database, it might be useful to have an organizers role, with membership open to staff members who are doing the hard work of organizing the awards:

```
db2 => create role organizers
DB20000I  The SQL command completed successfully.
```

You grant and revoke membership in a role using the grant role and revoke role commands. In this example, I'll grant membership in the role organizers to my manager, THEBOSS. (A limitation to remember when granting role membership is that you cannot grant a role to yourself.)

```
db2 => grant role organizers to THEBOSS
DB20000I  The SQL command completed successfully.
```

Finally, I can grant object privileges to a role in much the same way as I can for a group. Granting and revoking privileges takes effect immediately, so existing members of a role will gain new privileges with no delay.

```
db2 => grant select, insert, update, delete on nomination to organizers
DB20000I  The SQL command completed successfully.
```

In practice, roles then behave much as groups do, providing a streamlined system for permissions management.

The Benefits of Roles over Groups

There are two main benefits that roles provide, over and above the features they have in common with groups. First, roles do not rely on operating system groups to control membership. All membership of roles is managed in the DB2 system catalog, which frees DB2 administrators from some of the burden of having to either become system administrators as well or bother those who perform that role to manage groups in ways that suit the database and its users.

The second set of benefits relates to a limitation on permission inheritance with groups. Privileges, when granted to a group, are not recognized for the purposes of particular tasks in DB2. The affected tasks are

- View creation

- Materialized Query Table creation

- Routine, trigger and package creation (where static SQL is used)

The new roles in DB2 do not have this limitation, and these tasks can be performed under the auspices of privileges and authorities inherited from a role.

Managing Object Privileges in DB2

In DB2, database objects such as tables, views, the schemas in which they are housed, and the procedures that work on them have their access controlled by privileges that operate with varying degrees of granularity.

Working with Privileges on DB2 Objects

DB2 collects the privileges a user can have on objects into several logical sets: those that relate to tables, those that relate to tables and views, privileges for schemas, privileges for programmatic procedures and functions, and miscellaneous privileges. Let's start by looking at the privileges that relate specifically to tables and views, as shown in Table 10-1.

Table 10-1. *Table/View Object Privileges*

Privilege	Purpose
SELECT	Users can select information from the table or view.
INSERT	New information can be inserted into the table or view.
UPDATE	Changes can be made to the existing rows in the table or view.
DELETE	Rows can be removed from the table or view.

No surprises there. These privileges equate exactly to the SQL statements of the same name. If you have the privilege, you can perform the eponymous command. A related collection of privileges shown in Table 10-2 are those that act on tables themselves, which specifically control managing the structure and supporting objects.

Table 10-2. *Table Object Privileges*

Privilege	Purpose
ALTER	Allows a user to change the definition and structure of a table using the alter command.
INDEX	A user can create an index on the table.
REFERENCES	A user can refer to this table using referential integrity (foreign keys).

The only one of these privileges that needs further explanation is the REFERENCES privilege. It is required on the restrictive "end" of the relationship, so the table acts as the parent in a parent-child design. These three privileges deal with powers over existing objects. When it comes to general powers over anything that might now or in the future exist in a schema, the following set of privileges in Table 10-3 is used.

Table 10-3. *Schema Object Privileges*

Privilege	Purpose
CREATEIN	A user can create a new object (table, view, and so on) in a schema.
ALTERIN	A user can alter any existing or future objects in a schema using the relevant alter command.
DROPIN	Objects in a schema can be dropped, notwithstanding any constraints.

The schema privileges are a very convenient set to provide to developers. It allows freedom to continuously refine objects within the parameters of the schema. For day-to-day use of programmatic constructs, several privileges are key, as shown in Table 10-4.

Table 10-4. *Procedure/Function Object Privileges*

Privilege	Purpose
EXECUTE	Applies to packages, procedures, and functions, granting the user the ability to execute the named code.
BIND	Empowers the user to rebind a package to the database.

The EXECUTE privilege is a very important one to keep in mind. In many design environments, it is preferable to control all data access using just procedures and functions. So instead of providing users direct SELECT, INSERT, UPDATE, or DELETE powers over the underlying data, they are just granted a controlled set of EXECUTE permissions on code that performs these tasks in controlled ways. This ensures that your data is protected by consistent business logic. DB2 calls this indirect privilege, and you'll see this mentioned in the core DB2 documentation.

The last set of privileges shown in Table 10-5 relates to most objects and is used as a catch-all technique to manage groups of privileges simultaneously.

Table 10-5. *Miscellaneous Privileges*

Privilege	Purpose
CONTROL	This gives full power over an object to the user, allowing any compatible privilege to be used implicitly. It also allows the user to grant further privileges, including CONTROL, to others.
ALL	A shorthand phrase that equates to all non-CONTROL privileges on an object.

The CONTROL privilege is clearly quite powerful, so use it with care. The ALL shorthand makes it easy to grant or revoke lots of privileges at once, so you don't have to type SELECT and INSERT and UPDATE and DELETE in one giant SQL statement.

Now that you're familiar with the available object privileges, let's grant them and see them in action.

Granting Object Privileges to Users

Simply recite the magic phrase "Control Center" and you're done. Well, okay, it's not quite that easy, but it comes close. Within any database folder in the Control Center, you'll see a User and Group Objects folder. Within this folder are separate folders for both DB Users and DB Groups, and you'll see all known users and groups to whom privileges have been granted within their respective subfolders. Right-click either folder or the whitespace below the listing of known users/groups, and the context menu will open with only two options: Add or Refresh. Do this in the DB User folder of the SAMPLE database, choose Add, and the Add User dialog box will appear (see Figure 10-4).

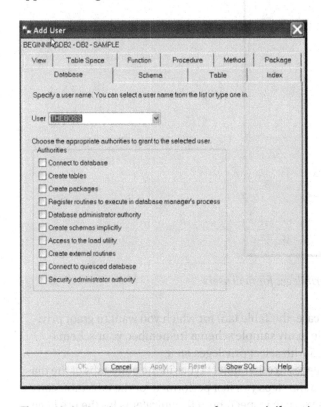

Figure 10-4. *Nominate a new user and grant privileges in the Add User dialog box.*

Don't be put off by the ten tabs in this dialog box. They exist so that you can perform all your privilege management for a user or group at once if you find that convenient. The first tab allows you to nominate the user whose permissions you want to manage. I chose THEBOSS because the remaining login from the start of this chapter is yet to be configured. The ten check boxes on this tab link directly to the fixed database authorities you learned about at the start of the chapter. Simply check the authorities you want THEBOSS to have. I chose CONNECT, CREATETAB, and BINDADD (shown in the more readable English as Create Packages in the dialog box).

The other nine tabs allow you to add relevant privileges to the user for a particular class of object. Figure 10-5 shows the tab for Table, but all the other tabs have similar functionalities.

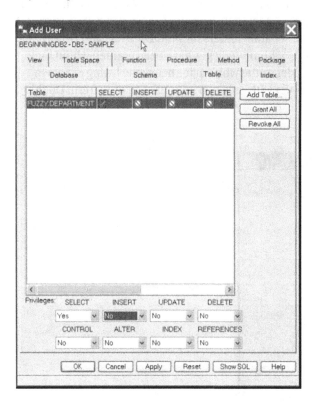

Figure 10-5. *Selecting individual object privileges for new users*

First, select the object type (in this case, the Table tab) for which you want to grant privileges. I chose the FUZZY.DEPARTMENT table in my sample schema (remember, your schema name might differ) and provided THEBOSS with select privileges on it.

You can continue to add other privileges to other object types in the other tabs of the dialog box because the process is a repeat of the steps you just performed for the table. You can go ahead and click OK (if you're curious you can inspect the SQL equivalents for the privilege granting you're about to perform). This is a fantastic and useful feature because it allows you to walk through a process in the Control Center, graphically selecting the options you want. You can then call up the equivalent SQL commands and use them from the CLP as well as store them away in scripts for later use.

The general form of the SQL statement that grants privileges is as follows:

```
GRANT PRIVILEGE[,PRIVILEGE...] ON OBJECT TO { USER | GROUP } USER_OR_GROUP_NAME
```

Simply use the relevant privilege, object, and user/group designation, and you've achieved parity with the Control Center GUI. In this example, granting privileges to THEBOSS results in this SQL:

```
CONNECT TO SAMPLE;
GRANT  CREATETAB,BINDADD,CONNECT ON DATABASE TO USER THEBOSS;
```

```
GRANT  SELECT ON TABLE FUZZY.DEPARTMENT TO USER THEBOSS;
CONNECT RESET;
```

You can prove that it has taken effect by trying a little SQL yourself. Let's query the DEPARTMENT table as THEBOSS to prove the privileges are working:

```
db2 => disconnect sample
DB20000I  The SQL DISCONNECT command completed successfully.
db2 => connect to sample user THEBOSS
Enter current password for THEBOSS:

   Database Connection Information

 Database server        = DB2/NT 9.5.0
 SQL authorization ID   = THEBOSS
 Local database alias   = SAMPLE

db2 => select * from fuzzy.department

DEPTNO DEPTNAME                               MGRNO  ADMRDEPT LOCATION
------ -------------------------------------- ------ -------- ----------------
A00    SPIFFY COMPUTER SERVICE DIV.           000010 A00      -
B01    PLANNING                               000020 A00      -
C01    INFORMATION CENTER                     000030 A00      -
...

  14 record(s) selected.
```

Privilege granted and successfully used. Privileges such as these are dynamic, and their resulting powers take effect as soon as they are granted. If I revoke the SELECT privilege on FUZZY.DEPARTMENT from THEBOSS, even while that user is still connected, the power to query that table will be immediately lost. Try it for yourself: in the Control Center, change THEBOSS to remove the select power on this table or run the relevant revoke command from another DB2 CLP session. For example:

```
(in second session, connecting as instance owner)
db2 => connect to sample user db2admin
Enter current password for db2admin:

   Database Connection Information

 Database server        = DB2/NT 9.5.0
 SQL authorization ID   = DB2ADMIN
 Local database alias   = SAMPLE

db2 => revoke select on fuzzy.department from THEBOSS
DB20000I  The SQL command completed successfully.
```

Now try the same select statement in the first session as THEBOSS and see the change take effect immediately:

```
(in the original session, connected as THEBOSS)
db2 => select * from fuzzy.department
SQL0551N ""THEBOSS"" does not have the privilege to perform operation ""SELECT""
on object ""FUZZY.DEPARTMENT"".  SQLSTATE=42501
```

You achieved instant rejection, and ideally that's what you want when managing privileges because any delay could result in all kinds of chaos. There is only one criticism sometimes made of the information DB2 reports when you lack privileges on an object, particularly the SELECT privilege on tables and views, and the execute privilege on procedures or functions. DB2 will report a different error depending on whether you lack privileges to a known object (as above) or to an object that does not exist. For example, here's what you'll get when you query a table that does not exist:

```
db2 => select * from THEBOSS.notatable
SQL0204N ""THEBOSS.NOTATABLE"" is an undefined name.  SQLSTATE=42704
```

Very informative and friendly, but the message does allow an unscrupulous user to discover the names of the objects to which they don't have privileges. Knowing that tables, procedures, and so on exist can sometimes be a security concern, but that discussion takes you beyond beginning DB2.

Label-Based Access Control in DB2

The third and final realm of privilege management in DB2 9 involves the new powers it introduced to manage permissions at the row and column level of a table. This is known as Label-Based Access Control because it uses a set of security policies and rules to label individual data components to control access. It is commonly abbreviated as LBAC, although that's not necessarily easier to pronounce.

Building Blocks of LBAC

LBAC is composed of three interrelated parts: the policy component definition, the policy itself governing data access, and the fine-grained labels of the policy that can be applied to data, and granted to users.

LBAC policy components themselves come in three flavors (the recurrence of the number three is purely coincidental), each with slightly different behaviors. Set-based policy components use a collection of labels that have no order or priority, thus the use of the term *set*. They act like a collection of privileges that can be granted individually or severally to control data access. Array-based components imply an order, where leading components of the collection imply all the powers of the subsequent elements of the array. Tree-based components act in a hierarchy, in which the higher-level components aggregate the powers of their child components.

The behavior of an LBAC policy is better illustrated with an example. Currently, graphical tools such as the Control Center have no special interfaces for working with LBAC, so your trusty DB2 CLP comes to the rescue. You'll follow an example that has real-world application. Let's presume that it is time for the employees of the SAMPLE database to have their annual salary review, and that new salary data must be protected at the individual row level—a real case that mirrors real-world requirements to keep such sensitive data private.

Defining an LBAC Label Component

To manage label-based access control, a user needs to have the SECADM database authority. Only users with SYSADM instance authority can grant this privilege, so at this stage you should connect to your database as the instance owner (or other SYSADM user) and use the Control Center or the DB2 CLP to grant SECADM to another user. In my case, I chose my fuzzy authid:

```
db2 => grant secadm on database to fuzzy
```

With this in place, you can connect to the SAMPLE database as this user to create an LBAC label component.

In the salary review example, you'll use the premise that individuals should be able to see only their own salary review information, and no others. The exception is the manager deciding on the salary increases, who naturally knows this information for all employees already, and needs access to set and review new salaries. To keep the examples manageable assume that it's only department C01 that's undergoing salary review. If you examine the EMPLOYEES table in the SAMPLE database, you'll see there are four employees in this department; assume that THEBOSS is their manager. This requirement is best covered using the tree-based label component model because it follows a complementary hierarchy.

The following command defines a tree-based label component, creates a root that will stand as the most powerful label, and creates four child labels that will be used for individual employees in the C01 department:

```
create security label component salreview_comp tree
(
''C01'' ROOT,
''KWAN_SR'' under ''C01'',
''QUINTANA_SR'' under ''C01'',
''NICHOLLS_SR'' under ''C01'',
''NATZ_SR'' under ''C01'')
```

The structure is mostly self explanatory, with the overall component name and label names being anything you choose. The keyword tree indicates that it is a tree-based label component model.

Defining an LBAC Policy

An LBAC policy is the object that governs the overall privilege scope that you want to use for a table. A table can have only one policy in force at any one time, but it can consist of multiple label component models. You'll stick to the single component approach to keep this example flowing. A policy is given a name related to label components, and classed as enforcing the DB2 label security with SQL as follows:

```
create security policy salreview_policy
components salreview_comp
with db2lbacrules
restrict not authorized write security label
```

With a policy defined, you can now derive individual labels from it, which are the privileges you can then grant to users.

Defining LBAC Labels

You need to define a label for each element you specified in the label component model. In this case, you had five different items in the tree, so you'll need five labels. You can create them as follows:

```
create security label salreview_policy.all_sr component salreview_comp ''C01''
create security label salreview_policy.natz_sr component salreview_comp ''NATZ_SR''
create security label salreview_policy.kwan_sr component salreview_comp ''KWAN_SR''
create security label salreview_policy.quintana_sr component
salreview_comp ''QUINTANA_SR''
create security label salreview_policy.nicholls_sr component
salreview_comp ''NICHOLLS_SR''
```

The general structure allows you to provide an individual label name using the dotted notation following the label component name, and then use the keyword component to reference the point in the label component model to which a given label relates.

LBAC in Action

You have now successfully created the policy and associated labels for use. To get value from them, however, you need data structures that can actually hold your new LBAC values, so that DB2 can enforce them. In the example of row-based label security, you'll need to create a table that has a column using the special DB2SECURITYLABEL data type. Because it is the manager who will be doing the salary review work, you'll need to connect as THEBOSS. You'll create a work table just for the salary review information, like this:

```
db2 => connect to sample user THEBOSS
Enter current password for THEBOSS:

   Database Connection Information

 Database server      = DB2/NT 9.5.0
 SQL authorization ID = THEBOSS
 Local database alias = SAMPLE

db2 => create table salary_review
(firstnme varchar(12) not null,
 lastname varchar(15) not null,
 workdept char(3),
 newsalary decimal(9),
 salreview_label db2securitylabel)
 security policy salreview_policy
```

The two key additions to your already wide knowledge of table creation are the use of the DB2SECURITYLABEL data type and the security policy clause that identifies the LBAC policy that will govern this table. With a table in place, you now need to add data. But before you can do that, THEBOSS must actually be granted privileges to work with your security policy because when you defined it, you enforced the "write restriction" power of LBAC, and your new table will prevent inserts—even from its creator—without a relevant label access control being satisfied.

Open a second DB2 CLP session, and connect as your user that has SECADM powers (in my case, the user fuzzy). You can now grant one of the labels from your policy to THEBOSS. Because you know the manager is meant to have rights to see and work with all salary information, you can naturally choose the label at the top of the tree hierarchy: salreview_policy.all_sr. The command is as follows:

```
grant security label salreview_policy.all_sr to THEBOSS for all access
```

Most of that syntax is self-explanatory. The one subtle part is the second-to-last word (*all*). The grant security label command can use read, write, or all to convey the ability to select data, change it, or both. With this privilege in place, return to your CLP session for THEBOSS and run the following insert statements:

```
insert into salary_review select firstnme, lastname, workdept, salary*1.1,
  seclabel_by_name(''SALREVIEW_POLICY'', ''KWAN_SR'')
  from fuzzy.employee where workdept = ''C01'' and lastname = ''KWAN''

insert into salary_review select firstnme, lastname, workdept, salary*1.1,
  seclabel_by_name(''SALREVIEW_POLICY'', ''NATZ_SR'')
  from fuzzy.employee where workdept = ''C01'' and lastname = ''NATZ''
```

Wow, where did that weird function come from? LBAC labels are stored in the database in a binary form to allow for high-performance security checks during DB2 data processing. Instead of forcing you to speak the same binary patois, the function seclabel_by_name() exists to allow you to use the human-readable policy and label names you've become familiar with.

Another important point is the effect of the tree-based label component in action. Even though THEBOSS was granted access to the ALL_SR label, it inherits its child labels and their powers because it is the root of the tree model you defined, so THEBOSS can use the KWAN_SR and NATZ_SR labels as if they were explicitly granted.

You can see for yourself that the data is there—and also the unfriendly binary representation of the label—using a common select statement:

```
select * from salary_review

FIRSTNME     LASTNAME         WORKDEPT NEWSALARY   SALREVIEW_LABEL
------------ ---------------- -------- ----------- -------------------

SALLY        KWAN             C01         108075. x''0000000000000001''
KIM          NATZ             C01          75262. x''0000000000000008''

  2 record(s) selected.
```

Now it's time to prove that LBAC does what it claims—in this case, provide row-level access controls. In preparation for the proof, I want you to grant THEUSER authid select privilege on the salary_review table of THEBOSS:

```
grant select on THEBOSS.salary_review to THEUSER
```

Now open a new query window (either the Command Editor or DB2 CLP) and connect as THEUSER. You just granted this user select access on your table, but what do you see if THEUSER issues a typical select statement?

```
db2 => select * from THEBOSS.salary_review

FIRSTNME     LASTNAME        WORKDEPT NEWSALARY    SALREVIEW_LABEL
------------ --------------- -------- ----------- ---------------

  0 record(s) selected.
```

You're not seeing things—that's LBAC at work! And you can already guess that it is not just an all-or-nothing affair. Let's finish the example by granting THEUSER the label KWAN_SR, so the user can see the salary review details for Sally Kwan. In your CLP session logged in as THEBOSS, issue this command:

```
grant security label salreview_policy.kwan_sr to THEUSER for read access
```

Now rerun your select statement as THEUSER. What do you see?

```
db2 => select * from THEBOSS.salary_review

FIRSTNME     LASTNAME        WORKDEPT NEWSALARY    SALREVIEW_LABEL
------------ --------------- -------- ----------- -------------------
SALLY        KWAN            C01          108075. x''0000000000000001''

  1 record(s) selected.
```

Voila! LBAC does it again. Theuser is seeing only the rows to which the granted labels permit access, and nothing more. You can revoke the label just as easily, using common revoke syntax:

```
revoke security label salreview_policy.kwan_sr from THEUSER
```

As you can see in following this example to its conclusion, label-based access control can take a little effort to set up, but once the label components, policy, and labels are in place, they then can be used to grant and revoke privileges in much the same way as normal table-level privileges, and the flexibility and control provided is truly amazing.

There is more to LBAC than this chapter can cover, including column-based controls and exception mechanisms. I heartily recommend that you consult the following for more information: online DB2 documentation; IBM RedBooks; and *Understanding DB2 9 Security*, by Bond et al., IBM Press, 2006 (ISBN 0131345907).

Summary

In this chapter you ran the gamut of database privileges, from the highest database-level power to the lowest LBAC label. Along the way, you saw how authorities, privileges, and LBAC can completely secure the data in your database and provide the right powers and capabilities to perform the actions required to work with your data.

CHAPTER 11

■■■

Using XML with DB2

Do you remember where you were when Armstrong landed on the moon? What about when the Berlin Wall fell? How about the day you first heard about XML—that it would relieve world hunger, bring global peace, and solve Fermat's last theorem, all before breakfast? Those heady days of the late 1990s were full of dot-com mania, with a liberal dose of XML to grease the wheels of ... well ... just about anything!

Of course, the great promises never quite materialized, but somehow XML hung on and became the de facto tool for many kinds of information interchange. At about the same time, many people in the database industry predicted the death of relational databases because XML was "the way of the future." Of course, a few wise old heads noted that XML was exactly like the hierarchical databases of 20 and 30 years prior, and they'd quickly ceded the data processing world to the likes of DB2.

For the next 10 years, XML and relational databases did a sort of dance around each other, with vendors—including IBM—slowly moving closer to dealing with the XML as first-class kind of data. With the release of DB2 9, IBM has brought XML into the heart of the database, with its pureXML technology that enables simultaneous storage and processing of relational and XML data with seamless interplay between the two.

There are some great tools supporting XML in the DB2 pureXML features. Some of the related technologies around XML are not as well known as XML or the SQL features in the database. So I'll spend some time covering XQuery and XPath to make sure you're best equipped to work with pureXML, too!

Exploring XML in the Sample Database

Before we dive into the depths of working with the XML and DB2 pureXML technology, it is worth taking a quick tour of the SAMPLE database to see how IBM has used its new technology to provide you a fast track to learning about these great new features. You can also see how tools such as the Control Center and Command Editor natively support XML and allow you to work with it easily.

Make sure that you are logged in as instance owner (db2admin under Windows, db2inst1 under Linux if you've followed the defaults) and fire up the Command Editor from within the Control Center. Connect to the SAMPLE database:

```
connect to sample
```

```
Database Connection Information
```

```
Database server        = DB2/NT 9.5.0
SQL authorization ID   = DB2ADMIN
Local database alias   = SAMPLE
```

A JDBC connection to the target has succeeded.

The SAMPLE database includes three tables—CUSTOMER, PRODUCT, and SUPPLIERS—that include XML columns as well as working data that was populated when you created the SAMPLE database. If you query one of these tables using a normal SQL query, you'll see how the Command Editor provides some slick tools for working with your XML data. Try selecting the contents of the PRODUCT table:

```
select * from product
```

The output will appear as shown in Figure 11-1, but you can't see any data in the DESCRIPTION column. Instead, you see the word XML and an ellipsis button (the one with the three dots). That's not because the products lack data for the description; the data is in XML form.

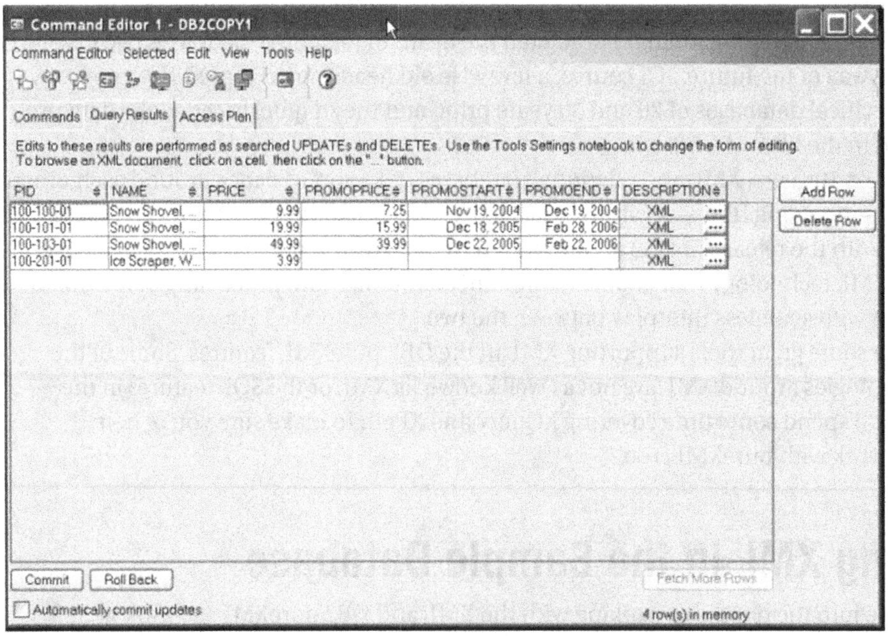

Figure 11-1. *Command Editor results, including XML data*

The Command Editor knows that XML has complex presentation requirements and has a built-in Document Viewer that understands how to traverse data in XML form and present it in a meaningful way. Remember that unlike SQL, XML has concepts such as hierarchy and order, and this is where the Document Viewer really helps. Click the ellipsis button for the first row in the results, and you'll see the Document Viewer spring to life, as shown in Figure 11-2.

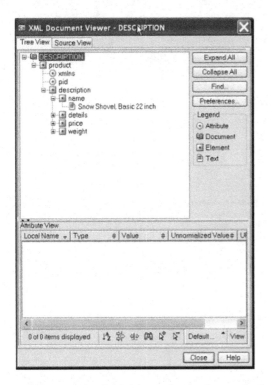

Figure 11-2. *Displaying XML data columns in the Document Viewer*

By default, the Document Viewer shows you the pictorial version of the XML tree, allowing you to see the structure of the data first. In this example, you see that a product's description has a <product> element at the root of the XML, with pid and xmlns (namespace) attributes. It then has a child element of <description> that in turn has child elements <name>, <details>, <price>, and <weight>. The values for an element aren't shown by default, but simply clicking on the plus sign next to an element name will expose the data for this row, as I did for the <name> element in Figure 11-2.

The Document Viewer also allows you to see the raw XML by choosing the Source view. Click the Source View tab, and the view will change to that shown in Figure 11-3.

If your XML text is displayed in a single line that scrolls off the screen, click the Preferences button and choose the Format Text option. This procedure invokes the parsing capabilities of the Document Viewer and it formats the elements in the much more user-friendly way you see in Figure 11-3.

You'll be pleased to know that the Document Viewer for XML is built in to the Control Center. If you launch the Control Center and drill down to the CUSTOMER table in the SAMPLE database, you can right-click it and choose Open. You'll see the same output for XML columns here—the code XML and an ellipsis button inviting you to explore the XML.

Figure 11-3. *Viewing raw XML data in the Document Viewer*

Note If you installed the original DB2 9 release, code-named Viper, your Document Viewer will require an extra step to process XML. You'll see a Fetch XML button on any result screen (from either the Command Editor or the Control Center); you have to click it before the XML placeholder and ellipsis button become visible. If you automatically see them and not the Fetch button, you're already benefiting from DB2 9.5 and the great new Viper 2 features!

The Document Viewer is a very handy tool for investigating and exploring individual XML results, but you're certain to want to work with XML data in bulk at some stage. I think you'll agree that having to navigate through dialog boxes for every row of a large set of results might quickly become tedious. As you expect, DB2 offers powerful pureXML features you can use from your favorite query tool and within your application code to work with XML en masse!

Querying Your XML Data

With the introduction of XML into relational databases, there was a need to adapt the query language to enable the hierarchical nature of XML to be exploited. While some attempt was made to add features to SQL, a complementary approach was also developed to enable data manipulation with an XML focus.

The DB2 pureXML support offers multiple ways to work with your data, meaning that you can leverage any existing knowledge you already have. If you're new to the whole idea of mixing XML in your relational database, you have choices about a variety of tools to help you.

There are two main query dialects supported by pureXML in DB2: the XQuery and Xpath dialects.

XML IN THE SAMPLE DATABASE

IBM refines the data in the SAMPLE DB2 database with each release. One change that has occurred in the DB2 9.5 release is the inclusion of an explicit XML namespace in all the sample XML data that wasn't present in the 9.1 release. In lay terms, this means the XML is peppered with an additional attribute in the top level of a given schema. It is the namespace attribute, xmlns, which appears like this in the data (in this example, a <customerinfo> element from the info column of the customer table):

```
<customerinfo xmlns="http://posample.org" Cid="1000">
```

In these circumstances, all XQuery and XPath queries need to be prefaced with a namespace declaration. If you are using a SAMPLE database created with DB2 9.5, every XQuery and XPath example needs to start with the following additional statement, instead of just the keyword xquery:

```
XQUERY declare default element namespace "http://posample.org";
```

Because this statement expands every query to a multistatement one, you'll need to set an alternative statement terminator. I recommend using the pipe symbol (|) because it won't conflict with anything else and using the semicolon to separate each individual statement in the unit of work; for example:

```
XQUERY declare default element namespace "http://posample.org";
db2-fn:xmlcolumn('CUSTOMER.INFO')/customerinfo |
```

Using XQuery for XML

XQuery is a language designed to work intimately with the XML in your database. It shares some similar concepts with SQL, but also has important differences to deal with the unique nature of XML data.

I'll start with a discussion of some of the unique capabilities of XQuery. First and foremost, XML has structure, and XQuery has methods of working with this structure. In particular, XML documents have a hierarchy, so one element can be contained within another. XML also has implied order—the sequence in which the elements, data, and so forth appear in the document is part of the metadata about that document. In other words, order is important. This is a distinct difference from relational data and SQL.

To deal with these particular characteristics, XQuery uses a simple slash character (/) to allow you to navigate through XML hierarchies and structures. It also provides predicates similar to those used in SQL. Most importantly, DB2 wraps these basic constructs in two pureXML functions: db2-fn:xmlcolumn and db2-fn:sqlquery. Each function can form the core of an XQuery statement, along with a set of clauses that are colloquially known as the "F-L-W-O-R" commands.

XQuery builds around the foundation functions using clauses similar to those in SQL, but they are slightly different in name and function, as shown in Table 11-1.

Table 11-1. *The F-L-W-O-R Clauses of XQuery*

Clause	Purpose
for	Introduces the alias by which data will be manipulated
let	Introduces working values and variables for data manipulation
where	Introduces additional predicates (similar to the SQL where clause)
order by	Provides ordering rules (similar to the SQL order by clause)
return	Indicates aliases and values to return to the caller (the results)

Understanding XQuery is always easier with some examples, so let's build up your knowledge using the CUSTOMER table you've already explored.

First, the most SQL-like technique. You can use XQuery code to invoke an SQL statement that targets XML data. There's no reason you need to approach XML data retrieval this way for simple data retrieval, but there are more complex uses you'll explore later that rely on the ability to do this. Using the keyword xquery, you introduce to DB2 that you're about to invoke the pureXML features. The db2-fn:sqlquery function allows you to pass a SQL statement to be issued. These results are formatted for ease of reading and flow on the page. The following statement invokes an SQL statement from XQuery, and that SQL statement returns the INFO column, which is the column in the CUSTOMER table containing XML data:

```
xquery declare default element namespace "http://posample.org";
db2-fn:sqlquery("select info from fuzzy.customer")|

INFO
--------------------------------------------------------------------------------
<customerinfo xmlns="http://posample.org" Cid="1000">
 <name>Kathy Smith</name>
 <addr country="Canada">
  <street>5 Rosewood</street>
  <city>Toronto</city>
  <prov-state>Ontario</prov-state>
  <pcode-zip>M6W 1E6</pcode-zip>
</addr>
<phone type="work">416-555-1358</phone>
</customerinfo>
<customerinfo xmlns="http://posample.org" Cid="1001">
 <name>Kathy Smith</name>
 <addr country="Canada">
  <street>25 EastCreek</street>
  <city>Markham</city>
  <prov-state>Ontario</prov-state>
  <pcode-zip>N9C 3T6</pcode-zip>
 </addr>
```

```
  <phone type="work">905-555-7258</phone>
</customerinfo>

...
```

The beauty of the db2-fn:sqlquery function is its capability to leverage what you already know. The only caveat, and the key difference between just issuing your SQL directly, is that db2-fn:sqlquery must return only XML data. In its simplest form, it's just like a wrapper around a select statement. To use the equivalent db2-fn:xmlcolumn function, you need to introduce the first two of the F-L-W-O-R clauses: FOR and RETURN. The general syntax looks like this:

```
xquery namespace-clause
for alias in db2-fn:xmlcolumn('table-and-xml-column-name')/optional-predicates
return alias
```

An alias is simply a placeholder variable that allows you to conveniently refer to the XML data as it is refined down to those items you want to see. An alias starts with a dollar sign ($) and can then contain almost any name you like. The table and column name is specific in typical DB2 dotted notation. They are not case sensitive, in line with normal references to tables and columns in regular SQL. The optional XQuery predicates allow you to specify matching criteria, wildcards, elements, attributes, and so forth. Because XML is case sensitive, this part of an XQuery is also case sensitive. This case sensitivity isn't just a factor of DB2 pureXML; you'll encounter it whenever you work with XML.

You can build an equivalent statement to the first db2-fn:sqlquery function as follows:

```
xquery declare default element namespace "http://posample.org";
for $x in db2-fn:xmlcolumn('FUZZY.CUSTOMER.INFO')
return $x |
```

Remember to use the schema name appropriate for your database, as you're unlikely to be using FUZZY as your schema. If you created the SAMPLE database as the instance owner, you'll likely be using DB2INST1 under Linux or DB2ADMIN under Windows if you followed the default. Because you were interested in all the data in the INFO column, you didn't need to specify any predicates to refine the result. When you execute this statement, the results look very familiar:

```
INFO
---------------------------------------------------------------------------------
<customerinfo xmlns="http://posample.org" Cid="1000">
 <name>Kathy Smith</name>
 <addr country="Canada">
  <street>5 Rosewood</street>
  <city>Toronto</city>
  <prov-state>Ontario</prov-state>
  <pcode-zip>M6W 1E6</pcode-zip>
 </addr>
 <phone type="work">416-555-1358</phone>
</customerinfo>
<customerinfo xmlns="http://posample.org" Cid="1001">
```

```
<name>Kathy Smith</name>
<addr country="Canada">
 <street>25 EastCreek</street>
 <city>Markham</city>
 <prov-state>Ontario</prov-state>
 <pcode-zip>N9C 3T6</pcode-zip>
</addr>
<phone type="work">905-555-7258</phone>
</customerinfo>
...
```

No surprises here; you're seeing the same data you browsed through in the Document Viewer. Naturally, you're not always interested in all the data, and XQuery supports the use of predicates, conditions, and similar constructs to refine your queries. The equivalent of selecting columns in SQL is to use the / character and the names of the element you want to see. So if you're interested only in the names of your customers, extend the XQuery as follows:

```
Xquery declare default element namespace "http://posample.org";
for $x in db2-fn:xmlcolumn('FUZZY.CUSTOMER.INFO')/customerinfo/name
return $x |
```

Here, you're instructing the XQuery processor to walk through the document and pick out the <name> child elements of the <customerinfo> top-level elements. The results look like this (with a little touchup of the formatting):

```
1
--------------------------------------------------------------------------------
<name>Kathy Smith</name>
<name>Kathy Smith</name>
<name>Jim Noodle</name>
<name>Robert Shoemaker</name>
<name>Matt Foreman</name>
<name>Larry Menard</name>

  6 record(s) selected.
```

You might immediately think that the logical extension is to select multiple columns. That's where the analogy with SQL stops—or takes a little detour because you're not dealing with tabular data, but with a tree. To fetch elements that are "peers," or from different branches of the XML document, use the let clause of the F-L-W-O-R syntax:

```
Xquery declare default element namespace "http://posample.org";
for $x in db2-fn:xmlcolumn('FUZZY.CUSTOMER.INFO')/customerinfo
let $cname := xs:string($x/name)
let $cprovince := xs:string($x/addr/prov-state)
return ($cname, $cprovince) |
```

The xs:string notation is similar to data type casting in regular SQL—you're indicating that the data to be retrieved should be treated as a string. The let clause can leverage the alias that you declare for the matching elements in the for clause, saving you from having to type that full function, table, and element path every time you want to refer to your matched XML. The results are the names and provinces of your customers:

```
1
--------------------------------------------------------------------------------
Kathy Smith
Ontario
Kathy Smith
Ontario
Jim Noodle
Ontario
Robert Shoemaker
Ontario
Matt Foreman
Ontario
Larry Menard
Ontario


  12 record(s) selected.
```

Importantly, the results are not treated as a table of name/province pairs. Instead, the matching elements are returned as the XML is navigated, so first a name will be returned, then its child province(s), then the next city name, and so on. Depending on the complexity of the XML schema, this could mean you get distinctly hierarchical data instead of tabular data. This can take a little getting used to, but after awhile, you'll be picturing trees of data in your mind.

I'll now introduce another of the F-L-W-O-R clauses. The where clause enables you to add predicates and conditions to filter the data being returned. The normal range of options is available—from equality, greater than and less than, to Boolean operators. You can construct a simple where clause for the XQuery to exclude one of your customers. Let's leave Jim Noodle out of the picture for the time being (no offense, Jim):

```
Xquery declare default element namespace "http://posample.org";
for $x in db2-fn:xmlcolumn('FUZZY.CUSTOMER.INFO'')/customerinfo
where $x/name != 'Jim Noodle'
return $x/name |
1
--------------------------------------------------------------------------------
<name>Kathy Smith</name>
<name>Kathy Smith</name>
<name>Robert Shoemaker</name>
<name>Matt Foreman</name>
<name>Larry Menard</name>


  5 record(s) selected.
```

You asked the XQuery to seek out all <customerinfo> elements and compare the <name> child element with the text 'Jim Noodle' by using the handy alias $x. You returned the child element <name> from our alias. Quite straightforward, and the logic translates across from SQL quite nicely.

Ordering your data is something that's bound to crop up as a requirement, and the order by clause of the F-L-W-O-R syntax is reminiscent of SQL and fits with the XQuery techniques you already learned. I'll also introduce another of the special functions of XQuery.

```
xquery declare default element namespace "http://posample.org";
for $x in db2-fn:xmlcolumn('FUZZY.CUSTOMER.INFO')/customerinfo
where $x/name != 'Jim Noodle'
order by $x/name/text()
return $x/name |
1
-------------------------------------------------------------------------------
<name>Kathy Smith</name>
<name>Kathy Smith</name>
<name>Larry Menard</name>
<name>Matt Foreman</name>
<name>Robert Shoemaker</name>

  5 record(s) selected.
```

The text() function returns the actual text of a given element. In this case, you wanted to use that text as the basis for ordering your results. You can go to town on the F-L-W-O-R clauses, building more elaborate and complex commands as your comfort of XQuery grows. For these purposes, I covered the basics of every clause and how to combine them together to query your XML data.

Using XPath Queries for XML

The easiest way to think of XPath queries, in comparison with XQuery style queries, is to strip away the F-L-W-O-R constructs and just think of the bare predicates that invoke the xmlcolumn function or other pureXML procedures.

You might be confused because XPath queries are also flagged with the keyword xquery when passing the query text to the Command Editor or the Command Line Processor (CLP). To illustrate, here's the equivalent search for customer info that you modeled with the preceding XQuery dialect.

```
xquery declare default element namespace "http://posample.org";
db2-fn:xmlcolumn('FUZZY.CUSTOMER.INFO') |
```

The results look remarkably similar to those from the earlier XQuery example:

```
INFO
-------------------------------------------------------------------------------
<customerinfo xmlns="http://posample.org" Cid="1000">
<name>
 Kathy Smith
</name>
<addr country="Canada">
 <street>
  5 Rosewood
 </street>
```

```
<city>
 Toronto
</city>
<prov-state>
 Ontario
</prov-state>
<pcode-zip>
 M6W 1E6
</pcode-zip>
</addr>
<phone type="work">
 416-555-1358
</phone>
</customerinfo>
...
```

The key difference between XQuery and XPath is the added flexibility XQuery offers with its FOR, LET, WHERE, ORDER BY and RETURN options. But XPath is powerful in its own right and can perform many of the same tricks.

XPath expressions can access any element or attribute in an XML document stored in DB2. To illustrate traversing to lower-level elements, look at the postal codes for those customers already in the SAMPLE database. The approach should be familiar: just append the element names, separated by forward-slash characters, to the XPath statement. The results are formatted to appear a little more readable and concise:

```
xquery declare default element namespace "http://posample.org";
db2-fn:xmlcolumn('FUZZY.CUSTOMER.INFO ')/customerinfo/addr/pcode-zip |

INFO
--------------------------------------------------------------------------------
<pcode-zip>M6W 1E6</pcode-zip>
<pcode-zip>N9C 3T6</pcode-zip>
<pcode-zip>N9C 3T6</pcode-zip>
<pcode-zip>N8X 7F8</pcode-zip>
<pcode-zip>M3Z 5H9</pcode-zip>
<pcode-zip>M4C 5K8</pcode-zip>

6 record(s) selected.
```

Voila! A set of postal codes as requested.

Using XPath Predicates

You can construct XPath queries based on the data values using [...] predicates, just as you can with XQuery. Let's find the city for the customer with Cid, an attribute of the <customerinfo> element, of 1004. To do this, you use the @ symbol to lead the attribute name.

```
xquery declare default element namespace "http://posample.org";
db2-fn:xmlcolumn('FUZZY.CUSTOMER.INFO')/customerinfo[@Cid=1004]/name |
```

```
1
--------------------------------------------------------------------------------
<name xmlns="http://posample.org">
Matt Foreman
</name>

1 record(s) selected.
```

And you're not restricted to single values. XPath supports the normal Boolean combination for attributes and other criteria. So you can query for two Cid values like this:

```
xquery declare default element namespace "http://posample.org";
db2-fn:xmlcolumn('FUZZY.CUSTOMER.INFO')/customerinfo[@Cid=1004 or @Cid=1005]/name |
```

```
1
--------------------------------------------------------------------------------
<name xmlns="http://posample.org">
Matt Foreman
</name>
<name xmlns="http://posample.org">
Larry Menard
</name>

  2 record(s) selected.
```

XML documents have implied order, unlike data in normal relational storage. Your customer, Matt Foreman, actually has two phone numbers listed. You can use a positional predicate to pick the second one. In this query, the first predicate, [@Cid=1004], selects Mr. Foreman by Cid reference, and the second predicate, [2], chooses the second <phone> child element:

```
Xquery declare default element namespace "http://posample.org";
db2-fn:xmlcolumn('FUZZY.CUSTOMER.INFO')/customerinfo[@Cid=1004]/phone[2] |
```

```
1
--------------------------------------------------------------------------------
<phone type="home">
416-555-3376
</phone>

  1 record(s) selected.
```

Using XPath Wildcards

XPath supports the asterisk (*) as a universal wildcard for any element. It also supports the function text() to return the actual text of an element. So you can retrieve the text of all the elements below <addr> as follows:

```
Xquery declare default element namespace "http://posample.org";
db2-fn:xmlcolumn('FUZZY.CUSTOMER.INFO')/customerinfo/addr/*/text()
```

```
1
-----------------------------------------------------------------------------------
5 Rosewood
Toronto
Ontario
M6W 1E6
25 EastCreek
Markham
Ontario
N9C 3T6
...
```

Finally, XPath supports // as the "myself or any of my descendants" placeholder. The customer data illustrates a useful application of this feature. Customers have their own phone
numbers in the <phone> element. Customers can also have assistants, who in turn might also
have their own phone numbers. Using the // wildcard lets you retrieve all phone numbers at
any arbitrary level at or below <customerinfo>. Again, I formatted these results to save a few
trees:

```
xquery declare default element namespace "http://posample.org";
db2-fn:xmlcolumn('FUZZY.CUSTOMER.INFO')/customerinfo//phone |

1
-----------------------------------------------------------------------------------
<phone type="work">416-555-1358</phone>
<phone type="work">905-555-7258</phone>
<phone type="work">905-555-7258</phone>
<phone type="work">905-555-7258</phone>
<phone type="home">416-555-2937</phone>
...
<phone type="home">416-555-6121</phone>

  11 record(s) selected.
```

More pureXML Features for Querying Data

Naturally, there are more pureXML features than just the db2-fn:xmlcolumn function. One of
the more useful features is the ability to parse your XML data and present it as a virtual relational table using the XMLTable function. Here's an example query to show how this function
works:

```
select x.name, x.city
from customer,
xmltable(XMLNAMESPACES(DEFAULT 'http://posample.org'),
 '$cust/customerinfo' passing info as "cust"
 columns
  "NAME" varchar(50) PATH 'name',
  "CITY" varchar(50) PATH 'addr/city'
) as x
```

The XMLTable function takes as a starting point a directive for the XML namespace using the XMLNAMESPACES function. It then nominates a starting element at a particular level of an XML schema, which is provided by an alias to the base table in which the XML data resides. So the from clause is essentially saying you want to construct a virtual table based on the <customerinfo> element that's referenced from the INFO column of the customer table using the alias "cust". You then state what you want the virtual table to look like using normal SQL column names and data types, and use the PATH option to link them to the source elements in the XML data.

Finally, the XMLTable function is a table-typed function, so it returns a table that needs an alias—you used X for this purpose. The select clause is then just like any other, simply listing the columns you'd like to see. The data looks like this:

```
X.NAME           X.CITY
------------------------
Kathy Smith       Toronto
Kathy Smith       Markham
Jim Noodle        Markham
Robert Shoemaker  Aurora
Matt Foreman      Toronto
Larry Menard      Toronto
```

So when you need to work with your XML data as if it were in tabular form, XMLTable is the function to call on.

Changing XML Data

Now that you've conquered the world of XQuery and XPath, you're ready to round out the complementary statements that allow you to add, change, and remove your XML data. Each of them can be related to equivalent action in SQL, and you'll see how the two languages blend to tackle some of these tasks.

Inserting XML Data

There are several approaches to inserting XML into databases such as DB2, with choices revolving around whether you have to compromise your XML to store it in relational structures or whether you're lucky enough to have features such as pureXML that let you have the best of both worlds. The "shredding" of XML is where the information is ripped out of the elements that form XML documents to be placed into one or more relational tables.

Thankfully, pureXML allows true XML storage, so while it supports shredding or decomposition, you will probably find the native XML handling capabilities of greater use and more intuitive after you adopt the XML mindset.

Regular insert statements can be used to enter XML data into tables defined with XML fields. Figure 11-4 shows the structure of the customer table with which you've been practicing XQuery commands.

Figure 11-4. *XML columns in the table*

Of the three fields, `Cid` is a mandatory integer, and the Info and History fields are of type XML. The `customer` table in the `SAMPLE` database is configured by default to be permissive about the adding of data to the XML fields. You'll examine the more complex options for XML insert shortly, but right now you can actually go ahead and use a simple SQL insert statement to add data, including XML, to this table:

```
insert into customer values (1006, '<my_xml>Hello</my_xml>','<more_xml/>')
DB20000I  The SQL command completed successfully.
```

That's just like dealing with simple text data. (And let's face it, that's *exactly* what XML is—text!) DB2's pureXML features are at work here, though, because even though I haven't yet invoked the advanced features of XML, DB2 is still ensuring that the data inserted into an XML typed field is well formed. If you try to insert data that fails the XML well-formed test, DB2 rejects it:

```
insert into customer values (1006, '<my_xml>Hello</wrong_tag>','<more_xml/>')
SQL16129N  XML document expected end of tag "my_xml".  SQLSTATE=2200M
```

The XML purists among you will know that there are two tests for determining the correctness of XML. The well-formed test, as you've seen, ensures tag matching and closure. The second test is validation, in which XML is compared with a definition for a particular type of XML document. In the early years of XML, these were Data Type Definitions, or DTDs. Later as XML matured, the XML schema standard emerged, allowing the definition of an XML document to itself be described in XML. DB2's pureXML supports validation of XML against both DTDs and XML schema.

To invoke validation, the insert statement is extended using the xmlvalidate function. I abbreviated this example to spare you several pages of raw XML data and to keep the structure understandable:

```
Insert into customer (cid, info)
values (1006,
xmlvalidate(source-xml-data according to xmlschema id "http://www.myschema.com"))
```

In this example, the validation is invoked using a publicly available schema on the Internet. DB2's pureXML capabilities extend to registering schemata (and DTDs) within DB2, so validation can complete locally. The xmlvalidate function is modified to call a schema ID in this case:

```
Insert into customer (cid, info)
values (1006, xmlvalidate(source-xml-data according to xmlschema id "CUSTOMER"))
```

Where do these schemata reside? I'm glad you asked.

XML Schema Registration in DB2

Each DB2 database includes support for XML schema objects, in the XML Schema Repository, or XSR. In the Control Center, under the object types for your SAMPLE database, you'll see the XSR listed as the last folder, as shown in Figure 11-5.

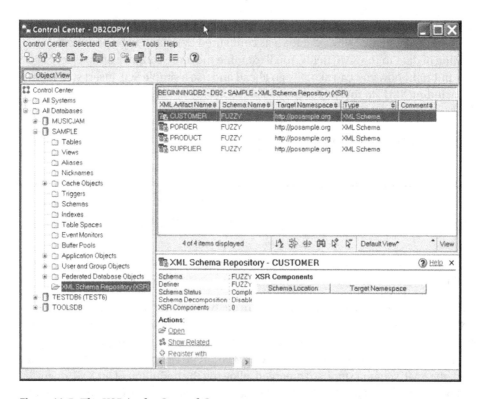

Figure 11-5. *The XSR in the Control Center*

Open the XSR folder; you'll see XML schemata registered. The CUSTOMER schema is the one in which you're interested, so right-click it and choose View Document. Figure 11-6 shows that your old friend the XML Document Viewer is called in to service to display the schema.

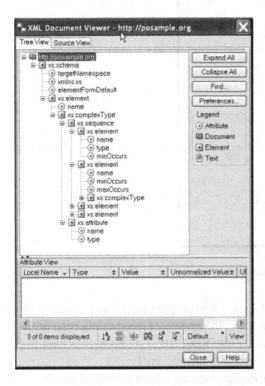

Figure 11-6. *Viewing an XML schema in the Document Viewer*

Registering a new XML schema is a quick process, and you'll use the CUSTOMER schema as a shortcut. Switch to the Source View tab of the Document Viewer and click the Save button, which prompts you to save the text file of the CUSTOMER schema. Call the file recipient.xsd. Once the file is saved, click Close to close the Document Viewer. Open the file recipient.xsd using your favorite text editor (Notepad, KWrite, and so on). The third line of the file reads as follows:

```
<xs:element name="customerinfo">
```

Change it to read as follows:

```
<xs:element name="recipientinfo">
```

Congratulations, you just defined a new XML schema. Okay, in real life you might put more effort into it, but because the discussion is about DB2, not XML schema design, it works for your purposes. Return to the Control Center; from the XSR Folder, right-click and choose the Register With XSR option. The dialog box shown in Figure 11-7 appears.

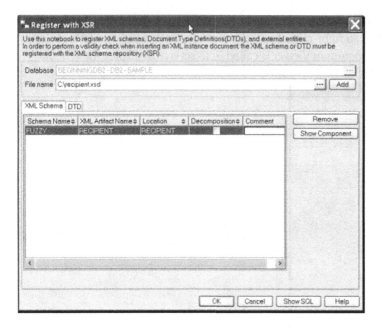

Figure 11-7. *Registering a new XML Schema with the XSR*

Click the ellipsis button and browse to find the `recipient.xsd` file you created. Make sure that you click the Add button to add this file's schema to the one you'll register. You then need to enter values for XML Artifact Name and Location. Enter **RECIPIENT** for both. Now click the OK button in the dialog box, and the registration process will commence.

You might be presented with an error (not a warning) that the schema doesn't map any attributes to a table, but the schema will actually be loaded into the XSR, and you can further refine it and its relationship to your tables and XML fields at a later point. That process takes you a little beyond the scope of this book, so I'll stop the coverage of schema registration there.

Updating XML Data

Changing XML data structures is one of the areas in which developing XML data-manipulation standards have been a little lacking, but DB2 is leading the way with pushing the standard forward. To be brief, to update a column with XML data type, until recently you had to replace the whole XML document for that row and column; you couldn't just alter the data within one element.

The good news is that there are simple ways to update your XML data. The first is an old-fashioned SQL update, just like this:

```
update customer set info = '<my_xml>Hello</my_xml>' where cid = 1006
```

Again, DB2 performs a test for well-formed XML, so there are pureXML features helping you even with this straightforward technique. The second approach is to use the pureXML `XMLPARSE` function to take a given string and convert it to the XML data type for insertion. Think of this as an explicit conversion instead of the implicit one used by the standard SQL update statement:

```
Update customer
set info = xmlparse (document '<my_xml>Hello</my_xml>' preserve whitespace)
where cid = 1006
```

Forgive the simple structure of the XML here, but it allows you to concentrate on the syntax and semantics instead of on pages of XML text.

DB2 9.5 is the first database to support the new in-place update standard, allowing you to make a change to the elements of an XML column without the need to totally replace it. This saves a huge overhead in resources such as logging, extracting, and reinserting the same data. The general syntax is as follows:

```
update table-name
set column-name = xmlquery
( '[transform] copy $new-XML-placeholder := $XML-column-placeholder
    modify do replace value of $new-XML-placeholder/element/... with value
    return $placeholder-for-new-XML ')
[where normal-SQL-criteria];
```

While that looks somewhat more complex than a regular SQL update statement, the benefit comes from the capabilities of the modify option you see used in the xmlquery invocation. This modify clause does the hard work of making the updates in place, taking its instruction from the English-looking syntax options that follow it, such as "replace value of ... with ..." That should be quite understandable.

An example will help clarify how the command works. Update your previously updated data using this new method:

```
update customer
set info = xmlquery('transform copy $mynewxml := $INFO
 modify do replace value of $mynewxml/my_xml with "Hello Again"
 return $mynewxml')
where cid = 1006
```

Deleting XML Data

There are no special standards for deletion based on XML properties—element text, attributes values, and so on. You can base your delete statements on one of the traditional relational columns of your table; for example:

```
Delete from customer where cid = 1006
```

You can also use other XML functions, such as XMLEXISTS, to evaluate XML-based criteria to help you determine data to be deleted:

```
delete from customer
where xmlexists('$doc/my_xml/text()="Hello" ' PASSING info AS "doc")
```

Your criteria might well be much more complicated, but the principle is the same. Identify what you want to delete by using the SQL or XQuery capabilities that best help you target it.

Summary

You now have a firm grounding in handling XML data within your DB2 database, including the capabilities of the pureXML functions and the utility of XQuery and XPath queries. Because XML will be more prevalent in all forms of data and database management in the future, this knowledge should be useful in your dealings with DB2 and beyond.

CHAPTER 12
■ ■ ■

Indexes, Sequences, and Views

Storing data in tables and managing its manipulation with stored code are only some of the aspects of working with data in a DB2 database. In this chapter, I'll introduce the supporting cast of objects that round out DB2's capabilities and provide some of its most subtle and powerful features.

Indexes are used to allow DB2 to provide fantastic performance with enormous amounts of data, as well as additional capabilities in query optimization and even data integrity.

Sequences cover a classic use pattern in data management: the need to generate numbers guaranteed to be unique based on a given algorithm or business rule.

Views are some of the oldest and most widely used features of any database. By providing neat shorthand to cover complex sets of data and filtered versions of information, views allow users and developers more efficient access to the data they desire most.

Working with Indexes

DB2 shares fundamental aspects of data access common to many data management systems, including the ways in which it can access data in tables and the shortcuts it can take to answer your queries as quickly as possible. The most important tool in this regard is the index object. You might have previously encountered the very common analogy used to illustrate the power of indexes in databases by comparing them to an index in a book. The idea is almost identical. In effect, keep a list in some order that you can later reference to find desired items in less time than if you examine every item at random until you happen upon the right one.

You can see why the analogy with a book is used. DB2's implementation of indexes incorporates several useful and different features, which you'll explore.

Creating Indexes

The syntax for index creation is some of the most straightforward found in DB2. The general form has the following structure:

```
create [unique] index index_name
on table_name (column_name [options], column_name [options] ...)
[further options]
```

In practice, many indexes are created with only the basic options for the syntax: a name, table reference, and list of columns. In the evolving employee of the year system, a number of the tables would benefit from indexes. For example, the nomination table acts to highlight those employees who have been nominated for various awards. The empno column of this table is the foreign key in the relationship to the employee table. If you were to run a query that sought details on whether a given employee had been nominated by looking for a specific empno value, DB2 would have to read all the values in the nomination table to find your answer in the absence of an index.

You'll create an index shortly to illustrate the syntax and usage of an index, but first let's prove that in doing so, you'll improve the performance of working with the underlying data. You can use the built-in access plan feature of the Command Editor to see what's happening for a query against the nomination table. Let's assume that I want to find nominations of the employee Christine Haas, who has an empno of 000010. This simple query would return all the nominations:

```
select * from nominations where empno = '000010'
```

If you type this query into the Command Editor, and then click the Access Plan button, you'll see a graphical representation appear in the Access Plan tab (see Figure 12-1).

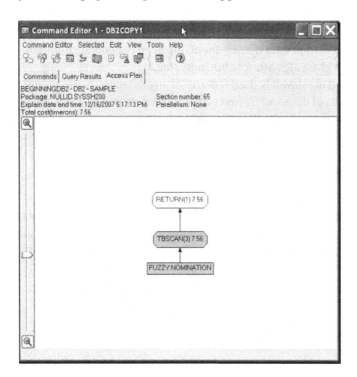

Figure 12-1. *Query access plan without the benefit of an index*

Note that this access plan shows the table being accessed, FUZZY.NOMINATION, and the access method, which in this case is tbscan. That's DB2 shorthand for table scan, in which all the data in the table has been read to resolve the query. This might be fine for tables with relatively small amounts of data, but think for a moment what might happen if you worked for a large company, and thousands or even tens of thousands of nominations are made over the year. Would you really want to read all that data just to find Christine's nominations? An index to the rescue!

If you create an index on the empno column of the nomination table, you should see an immediate difference:

```
create index nom_empno on nomination (empno)
```

While the time to create an index like this varies in line with the volume of data being referenced, it's safe to say at this point that this command should complete within a few seconds. Now that this index is in place, rerun the Access Plan tool on the original select statement. Depending on how many rows of data are in the nominations table, and whether system utilities such as runstats have been run (discussed in more detail later), you might see the index used in the new access plan, as seen in Figure 12-2.

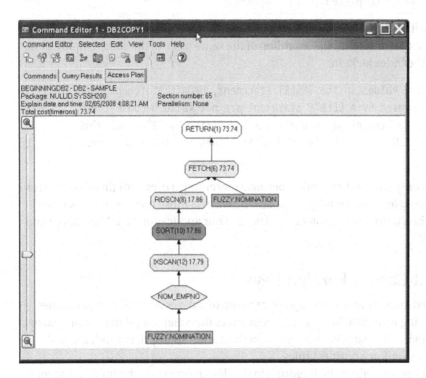

Figure 12-2. *Query access plan with the benefit of an index*

You can now see that the tbscan has changed to an ixscan (an index scan), and an extra polygon has been added to the access plan that indicates which index was used. In this case, it's the nom_empno index.

Enforcing Unique Values

On of the other primary reasons for using an index is to enforce uniqueness. While other options are available, including check constraints and triggers, almost all cases of uniqueness are best controlled through the unique property of an index.

In the working system it would be sensible to ensure that the awards in various categories are awarded only once to each person. It would be a little embarrassing to award the same prize multiple times to the same person. In the award_result table, you hold the relationship between employees and the category of award they won by using empno and categoryid. By creating a unique index on this combined set of fields, you not only improve general data access performance, but with the `unique` attribute, you enforce a "one award per employee per category" policy.

```
create unique index award_result_pairs on award_result (empno, categoryid)
```

I can illustrate how this helps the business rule by entering some award results. Let's assume that Eileen Henderson (empno 000090) has won employee of the year (award category 1). You could then record this in the `award_result` table with a simple insert:

```
insert into award_result values (1, '000090', 1, current date)
DB20000I The SQL command completed successfully.
```

You're greeted with the familiar success message. But if you try executing the same query again to reflect accidental or intentional awarding of the same prize to the same employee, the unique attribute of the index kicks in:

```
SQL0803N  One or more values in the INSERT statement, UPDATE statement, or
foreign key update caused by a DELETE statement are not valid because the
primary key, unique constraint or unique index identified by "2" constrains
table "FUZZY.AWARD_RESULT" from having duplicate values for the index key.
SQLSTATE=23505
```

Typically, this is only part of the solution because presenting a user with this kind of error message might be considered unfriendly. Because DB2 will use those precise SQL CODE and SQLSTATE values when uniqueness protection kicks in, your application can detect them and respond accordingly.

The Important Case of Foreign Keys

As already highlighted, one of the main reasons for the use of indexes is to improve access performance when working with data. Many people remember this when they design their systems, ensuring that fields that often participate in query predicates are appropriately indexed and using unique indexes to enforce business rules.

One aspect that can sometimes be forgotten in the design process is the impact that referential integrity has on working with data. A good rule of thumb for development is to always create an index for the foreign key columns of a child table at the same time you define the referential integrity. Without it, DB2 has the necessary information to enforce your constraint, but must always work with the whole child table's data. This is best illustrated by a delete of a row from a parent table. DB2 must make sure that no matching child rows reference this parent row before allowing the delete to proceed. With an index, it's as simple as performing a seek on the relevant value in the index to find whether such a row exists in the child table. Without a supporting index, DB2 must perform a table scan.

Once you perform this index-to-foreign-key matching, review how many indexes you have. If you now have dozens of indexes, you might want to compromise. Because each index must be maintained as data changes, there comes a point where too many will start affecting your performance. Unfortunately, there's no absolute maximum number of indexes recommended for each table. As your system develops, and performance can be measured, it becomes a tuning and balancing exercise.

Understanding Other Index Features

Indexes provide numerous other useful features that help cater to specific circumstances in your design, including customized and flexible sorting, traversal, and more. In the opening syntax description, I flagged them as "Further Options." Let's explore what the most important are, or at least the ones you'll want to know about first in your DB2 career.

Ordering

Until now, I've been omitting any ordering semantics when creating indexes. In doing so, I allowed DB2's default behavior of *ascending indexes* to take effect. You can also explicitly declare that you want an index to be ascending or descending for a given column by using the asc and desc options of the create index statement.

```
drop index nom_empno
create index nom_empno on nomination (empno asc)
```

You can also mix ascending and descending columns as you require in the index definition:

```
drop index award_result_pairs
create unique index award_result_pairs on award_result (empno asc, categoryid desc)
```

■**Note** I haven't used alter index to perform these changes because there is no alter index statement in DB2. The reasoning is sound. Any time you change an index, you most likely affect the way the items in it are sorted and/or stored, necessitating a complete rebuild of the index's structure by DB2. By omitting an alter index statement, DB2 subtly reminds you of the amount of work required if you need to change an index.

Reverse Scans

The ordering of an index has implications for how DB2 will elect to use that index when satisfying a query. When you create an index, you either choose the default ascending ordering, or explicitly choose ascending or descending ordering to suit your needs. Another default behavior kicks in at the same time with DB2 9.5, where DB2 will permit itself to traverse your index in reverse order to help it with queries. If you're still on DB2 9, the database is a little retentive and won't allow reverse scans by default. This default had its foundation in the overhead in storage and computation to allow walking an index in both directions.

You can override this aversion to reverse scans prior to version 9.5 by adding the allow reverse scans option to the index definition:

```
drop index nom_empno
create index nom_empno on nomination (empno asc) allow reverse scans
```

This still creates the index in the order indicated (in this case, ascending), but adds additional pointer information to the structure to allow the index to be traversed in the opposite (descending) order. This additional metadata is very small, and the benefit of reverse scans far outweighs any impost of additional storage.

You can also explicitly disallow such reverse scans by using the disallow reverse scans option.

Included Columns

As you explore more avenues in search of performance and efficiency in DB2, you might find yourself extending your indexes to cover more and more data in the hope that you can avoid unnecessary table scans or poor execution plans for queries, and the burden that goes with them. There might come a time when you have so many indexes (and your indexes contain so many columns) that you're actually adversely affecting your system. This might be because you are using vastly more storage than you wanted or because DB2's own optimizer is swamped with a choice of near-identical indexes and might not always choose the best one for a particular query. While you can then play with configuration parameters and other controls to improve behavior, there is another option.

DB2 indexes might include other columns in their structure that don't form part of the main ordering information for that index. Why would you want to have added baggage in your index? If you know that you'll often have a query that is predicated on a given value, but needs to return one or more other columns for the matching results, you can include those columns in the index, thus allowing DB2 to satisfy the query by only referencing the index. In performance terms, that means DB2 won't have to go to the underlying table to collect the other data needed, and in theory, your query should be faster and/or more efficient.

To include one or more columns, the include clause is used with the names of the columns in parentheses. As an example, when you look for the person who won employee of the year, you also might want to see the date of the award. But you don't really care about the order of dates and don't need to burden your index with the ordering overhead of the date_collected column; you just want that column included for the performance benefit:

```
drop index award_result_pairs
create unique index award_result_pairs on award_result (empno, categoryid)
 include (date_collected)
```

This example highlights the one key limitation of the include option: you might use it only on indexes that are unique. That might not be as big a limitation as you might think. All (or almost all) your tables will have a primary key, which by definition is unique. It's a useful design trick to think about a few columns that could be included in the primary key to benefit common queries.

Clustering

The last major area of indexes I'll cover is the clustering feature. *Clustering*, which is common to almost every significant database, has been a cornerstone of DB2 since its early days. One of the key concepts of relational and set theory, on which much of the world of contemporary databases is based, is that there is no basic concept of *order*. If you need the data in your tables ordered, you use constructs such as indexes and query clauses such as the order by clause to achieve your desired outcome.

When database developers were thinking about the various ways in which performance could be improved for a database, someone realized that as soon as a single index is defined for a given table, an indication has been given about at least one preference for how that table's data might be ordered. In other words, if you create one or more indexes on a table, you're telling DB2 that sometimes ordering the data in line with those indexes is a *good thing*. The developers seeking ways to improve database performance then recognized that instead of leaving data in random order on disk, it could be laid out using the order of one of these indexes to allow any data access using that index to benefit from sequential reading of data from disk. That's clustering—to order the data on disk to benefit one index in order to make access by that index as fast as possible.

To nominate an index as the clustering index for a table, simply include the cluster clause in the index definition:

```
drop index nom_empno
create index nom_empno on nomination (empno asc) cluster allow reverse scans
```

This will override any other index that might previously have been nominated as the clustered index. Over time, the clustered index will gradually have its contiguous clustering degrade as users add, remove, and change data. This means that some small but growing fraction of the data has to incur a little more seek time. DB2 provides two utilities to detect and reorganize suboptimal clustering: reorgchk and reorg. I'll cover these utilities in more depth in Chapter 24.

Using Design Advisor

To this point, much of the discussion regarding indexes has revolved around what you can do, but not necessarily *why* you might want to construct indexes in a given way. I could launch into a great discussion on index theory, relational design, and performance management art and science. But this book is about beginning life with DB2 and getting the most out of it quickly. In the realm of indexes, one of the best features of DB2 is the Design Advisor.

The *Design Advisor* has a number of major features, but the one in which you are interested is the index advisor facility. The Design Advisor can observe how a given set of queries interacts with your tables and data, and (following a configurable timeframe of testing your workload against your data) can advise on useful indexes to add to your tables.

In the best tradition of "learning by doing," let's point the Design Advisor at the nascent employee of the year work to see what advice it can provide. To prepare, I'll drop the nom_empno index from the nomination table. This will leave this table with no indexes. Now you're ready to see what the Design Advisor can do for you.

To start working with the Design Advisor, run the Control Center and drill down to the SAMPLE database. Right-click the SAMPLE database and you'll see that Design Advisor is one of your options (see Figure 12-3). Choose it to launch the Design Advisor.

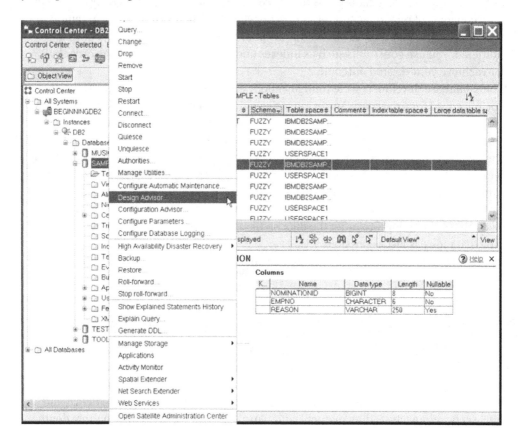

Figure 12-3. *Launching the Design Advisor*

You'll be presented with the Design Advisor splash screen, which acts as a glorified Next button. It does provide useful links to call up the Information Center help on its capabilities, but for your purposes, just click the Next button to move to the actual design advice facilities. You then move to the second dialog box, shown in Figure 12-4.

The Design Advisor can assist with index design and also with materialized queries and multidimensional clusters. Those last two topics are outside the scope of this chapter and even beyond the realm of beginning DB2. Deselect them so that Indexes is the only chosen performance feature and then click Next. You'll be presented with the workload specification dialog box shown in Figure 12-5.

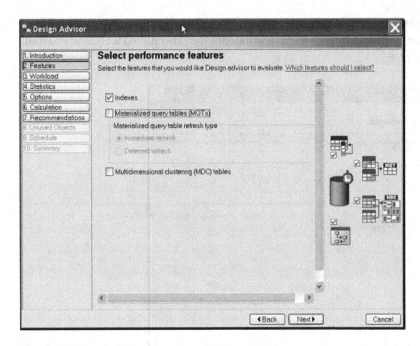

Figure 12-4. *Feature selection in the Design Advisor*

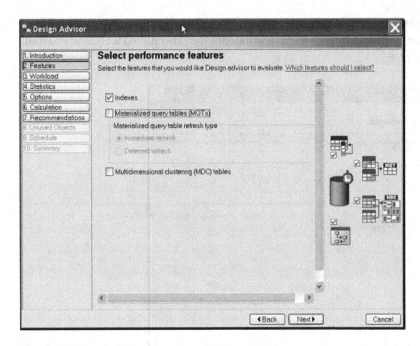

Figure 12-5. *Workflow specification in the Design Advisor*

If you previously created a workload, you'll see it listed with a Change Workload button available. With or without existing workloads, you also have the option to create a new workload. It's here where you can spend a great deal of your time. A *workload* is simply a collection of queries that you want the Design Advisor to use in simulation, so it can make its recommendations. For this example, I suggest using a query along these lines:

```
select * from nomination where empno = '000010'
```

Choose your schema (FUZZY, in this case) and provide a frequency value that will tell DB2 how often this command will run in your sample workload. Your completed workload will look something like Figure 12-6.

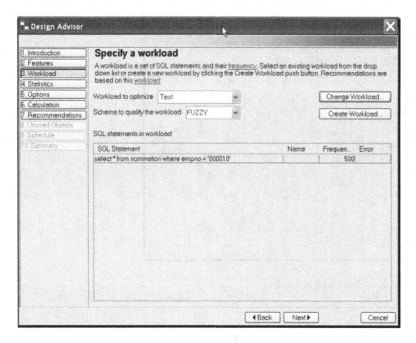

Figure 12-6. *A completed workflow specification in the Design Advisor*

Next you see the Update Catalog Statistics dialog box. Without pre-empting the discussion on statistics that I'll get to in Chapter 24, you need a little background here. In short, statistics provide information about your data, so that DB2 can determine how best to process your queries. Think about things such as number of rows in a table, frequency of a given value in a column, and so forth. For now, I recommend choosing your entire schema (FUZZY, in this case) for statistics generation, as shown in Figure 12-7. This will give the Design Advisor the best set of information upon which to make its recommendations.

Moving to the next dialog box in the wizard brings up the recommendation options. The main option to control is how much space you're willing to allocate to any recommendations the Design Advisor might make. Note that this is space for resultant objects (new indexes, in this case), not working space for the Design Advisor to do its work. I normally leave this space blank, as shown in Figure 12-8, and then consider afterward whether I'm happy with the amount of space that accepting a particular recommendation entails.

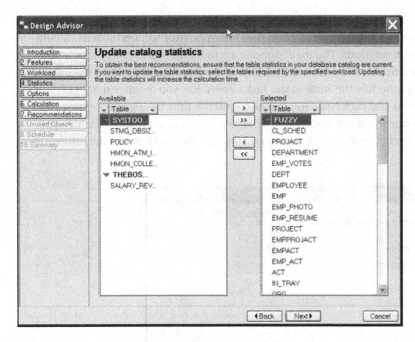

Figure 12-7. *Statistics generation in the Design Advisor*

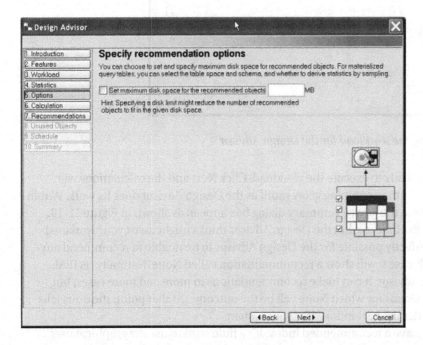

Figure 12-8. *Constraining space for recommendations in the Design Advisor*

Clicking Next takes you to the penultimate dialog box of the wizard. The calculation tab shown in Figure 12-9 allows you to control when the Design Advisor will perform its calculations to provide recommendations. The main options are to do the work now or to schedule the work for later. If you do schedule the work for later, the wizard will divert to a few extra screens to allow you to schedule the work in the Task Center. But you're interested in instant gratification, so go ahead and click Now. You can also limit the time the Design Advisor will have in which to run your workload. Because you made your workload relatively small, you won't need to impose such a limit. But when you create complex workloads in the future, this does come in handy.

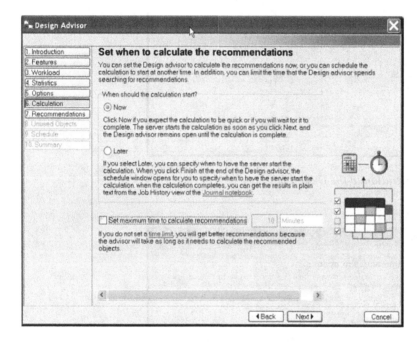

Figure 12-9. *Scheduling the workload for the Design Advisor*

Drum roll! You're ready to execute the workload. Click Next and the calculations will begin. You'll see the common spinning gears motif as the Design Advisor does its work. Within a few minutes, you'll see the advice summary dialog box appear, as shown in Figure 12-10. Here you get a list of the indexes that the Design Advisor thinks might assist your workload.

Note that it is perfectly possible for the Design Advisor to be unable to recommend anything useful, in which case it will show a recommendation called None. Naturally, as IBM improves the Design Advisor, it can make recommendations in more and more cases, but there will still be workloads for which None will be the outcome. At that point, the onus falls back on you to consider the best indexes for your system.

In this case, you have a recommended index. It's a little hard to use the graphical user interface (GUI) to see what's being suggested, so I find it useful to highlight each recommendation and use the Show button for a textual description:

```
CONNECT TO SAMPLE;
CREATE INDEX "FUZZY    "."IDX712170455590000"
 ON "FUZZY    "."NOMINATION"
 ("EMPNO" ASC, "REASON" ASC, "NOMINATIONID" ASC)
 ALLOW REVERSE SCANS ;
CONNECT RESET;
```

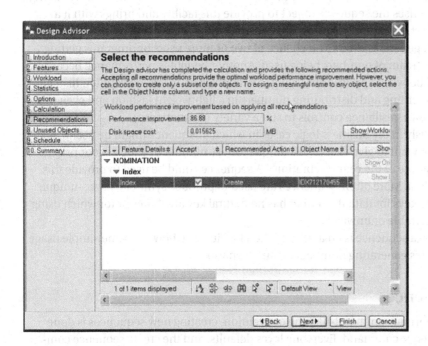

Figure 12-10. *The Design Advisor's recommendation summary*

Based on the workload that queried the nomination table by empno value, the Design Advisor is recommending a compound index with empno as the leading column. That's sensible and replicates the index you created manually and dropped prior to the Design Advisor exercise. You could continue to the Unused Objects, Schedule, and Summary dialog boxes to go ahead and create this index, or you could time the index's creation for a later point. I'll leave those dialog boxes for you to explore on your own.

Index Wrap Up

There are some features of indexes not covered in this discussion, including free page allocation and customized indexing extensions, which are well beyond the basics of DB2. For now, you should feel confident about the standard capabilities of indexes and enjoy using (and abusing) them.

Working with Sequences

When working with data and databases, the ability to simply keep a running counter or sequence is sometimes useful. This can be as simple as a count of one-two-three; or more complex with offsets, unusual starting cases, incrementing by large numbers, and so on.

While this is often easily done using programming logic in C++, Java, or other programming languages, real problems crop up if this counter needs to be shared concurrently among numerous users. DB2 uses the sequence object to provide this facility and brings with it a bunch of benefits. First, by centrally storing and controlling the sequence (and therefore the stream of numbers it generates) there's no chance of two or more users or programs getting out of pace with the stream of numbers being used. Another benefit is performance because there is no overhead between applications trying to keep track of an agreed counter. Instead, DB2 performs incrementing and distributing numbers in a lightweight fashion and even provides a few performance/resilience controls to suit a variety of situations.

There are obviously many business logic cases in which a sequence might be useful. For instance, let's say you want to give everyone a unique lottery number or a lucky door prize number for the employee of the year celebrations. A sequence could be used to provide this kind of user-facing data. More often, sequences are used to produce synthetic keys—unique identifiers or primary keys for data that either has no natural key attributes or for which using a natural key is undesirable or unwieldy.

Let's explore how a sequence is created, and then I'll illustrate how the same simple usage pattern accommodates generating numbers for any scenario.

Creating Sequences

Following the DB2 normal command-naming convention, creating new sequences is done with the create sequence command. Everyone loves defaults, and the create sequence command is very friendly in this regard. Let's say you simply want a basic sequence to hand out lucky door prize numbers for all the employees attending celebrations for employee of the year. The following statement creates a simple sequence for this purpose:

```
db2 => create sequence doorprize
DB20000I  The SQL command completed successfully.
```

To illustrate what's been created, let's cover two of the basic concepts of working with sequences. Any sequence can be asked for the immediate previous number it generated. This is known as the previous value, or prevval for short. A sequence can also be asked to generate the next logical number based on its generation rules. This is known as the next value, or nextval.

You can refer to prevval and nextval using the SQL fragments PREVVAL FOR SEQUENCENAME and NEXTVAL FOR SEQUENCENAME. You can use this in a simple values statement to see how our new sequence behaves:

```
db2 => values nextval for doorprize

1
-----------
          1

  1 record(s) selected.
```

It seems that the doorprize sequence starts with the number 1. Repeating the call to nextval should reveal more:

```
db2 => values nextval for doorprize


1
-----------
          2


  1 record(s) selected.
```

Eureka! You are incrementing the value returned by doorprize by one each time. And to be honest, you could read the manual to have learned that default, but seeing it in action is tangible proof of a working sequence.

The starting value and increment are not the only attributes available for a sequence. The attributes available are as follows:

as *datatype*: Specifies a data type for the values generated by the sequence, and is limited to one of integer (the default), smallint, bigint, or decimal with zero points of precision.

start with *n*: Indicates the starting value issued by the sequence on its first invocation with nextval. The default is 1.

increment by *n*: The factor, n, by which the sequence values will increase or decrease with successive use of nextval. By using a negative number, the sequence will decrease instead of increase.

no minvalue | minvalue *n*: The default behavior, no minvalue, leaves the minimum value past which the sequence will not descend controlled by the datatype specified. Using minvalue *n* introduces an explicit floor value.

no maxvalue | maxvalue *n*: Similar to minvalue, maxvalue can either be determined by the data type or specified explicitly.

[no] cycle: A sequence set to cycle will "wrap around" if invoking nextval exceeds the minvalue or maxvalue of the sequence. If set to no cycle (the default), once a sequence reaches its minvalue or maxvalue, future uses of nextval will return SQL Code SQL0359N, with the message "The range of values for the identity column or sequence is exhausted. SQLSTATE=23522".

no cache | cache *n*: To provide high performance, DB2 can cache values in advance of them being requested for a sequence. The default is 20 and it can be set from as low as 2. Caching of values can be disabled using the no cache option.

[no] order: Another factor influencing performance is guaranteed ordering. High numbers of simultaneous requests to a sequence can be satisfied more quickly without the overhead of strict ordering. This doesn't mean that the values handed out are random. The default can be overridden by using the order clause, which introduces serialization.

You can use any of these attributes you want to explicitly control and leave the remainder at the DB2 defaults. The values for start value, increment, cycling, and so forth exist mainly to provide flexibility to handle the arithmetic that suits the kind of number you want to generate. Maybe you want only even numbers, or maybe you're simulating some sort of countdown timer.

The cache and order clauses deserve a little more attention because they have implications for resilience and performance. Caching certainly acts to increase performance when referring to sequences because DB2 needs to log the generation of values only once per cache quantity. The drawback is that if DB2 crashes (for instance, by the host computer suffering power failure), the database engine does not have a record of which values from the cache have been used. To ensure integrity, DB2 assumes that *all the values* were used and starts generating from the next value above maximum (or minimum for a descending sequence) theoretical value that would have been in the cache.

Often this won't bother you because the performance benefits will outweigh any "gaps" in your sequence. This is true when using sequences for synthetic key generation and similar scenarios, in which the number itself has no special meaning; only its uniqueness matters. But some people will attach meaning or logic to the generated values in other scenarios, and for them gaps due to cache loss will be unsuitable. In those circumstances, the no cache option is the key because it essentially serializes the generation (and logging for recovery purposes), or one sequence value at a time.

Also related to performance and integrity is whether values need to be strictly issued in order of calling or whether it really doesn't matter if two near-simultaneous nextval invocations return in strictly the order of request. Both parties still get values, and for most scenarios that's all that's required. However, I can think of a small subset of cases, particularly having to do with auditing and tracing, that might warrant the small overhead that the order option brings to enforce a rigorous first-come, first-served distribution of values.

The syntax of the create command simply strings the options one after the other, optionally separating the options with commas. Let's drop the doorprize sequence and re-create it with some sensible explicit values:

```
db2 => drop sequence doorprize
DB20000I  The SQL command completed successfully.
db2 => create sequence doorprize start with 10 increment by 1
     maxvalue 25000 no cycle
DB20000I  The SQL command completed successfully.
```

Voila! A well-specified sequence, ready to use either stand-alone or as part of a program or application.

Altering Sequences

Dropping and re-creating a sequence to change it is cumbersome and can also be problematic in systems that reference a sequence multiple times per second. You really don't want your program to suffer or to return an error because it can't find a sequence it needs to use in order to make a change. Naturally, IBM thought ahead and supports the alter sequence command. In order to alter a sequence, you need to be either its creator or hold the alterin schema privilege, or sysadm or dbadm authority.

The syntax for the alter sequence command allows exactly the same clauses as the create sequence command. So you can alter the doorprize sequence like this:

```
db2 => alter sequence doorprize minvalue 0 maxvalue 50000 no cycle no cache no order
DB20000I  The SQL command completed successfully.
```

There is one additional clause that is available to the alter sequence command. The restart clause allows you to reset the sequence to its starting value, effectively letting you "reset the clock" if you have the need:

```
db2 => alter sequence doorprize restart
DB20000I  The SQL command completed successfully.
```

For the doorprize sequence, you originally specified that it start with 10, and following the restart command, it will revert to 10 as the next value it issues and continue to follow its generation rules from there. You can also use the with *n* modifier for the restart clause. This allows you to both restart number generation and change the base generation point with the same clause:

```
db2 => alter sequence doorprize restart with 20
DB20000I  The SQL command completed successfully.
```

This change will not affect the sequence's configured minvalue or maxvalue, which would require additional clauses in the alter statement to change.

Using Sequences

I briefly introduced the nextval and prevval operators at the start of the discussion on sequences. While using the values call to retrieve the desired number is useful to illustrate how a sequence works, it would be a little cumbersome to have to use it to source a sequence value and then hold it temporarily in a program while building a dynamic SQL statement or passing it back as a parameter.

Fortunately, both operators can be used in place of numeric literals within other SQL statements. So within select, update, and insert statements, you can both generate and use a sequence number in one step. As an example, you can give all employees lucky door prize numbers as follows:

```
db2 => select firstnme, lastname, (nextval for doorprize) as "Lucky Door Prize"
  from employee
```

```
FIRSTNME      LASTNAME         Lucky Door Prize
------------  ---------------  ----------------
CHRISTINE     HAAS                           10
MICHAEL       THOMPSON                       11
SALLY         KWAN                           12
JOHN          GEYER                          13
IRVING        STERN                          14
EVA           PULASKI                        15
...
REBA          JOHN                           46
ROBERT        MONTEVERDE                     47
EILEEN        SCHWARTZ                       48
MICHELLE      SPRINGER                       49
HELENA        WONG                           50
ROY           ALONZO                         51

  42 record(s) selected.
```

With prevval, you can check the last door prize number that was issued. You might want to do this so the master of ceremonies can let the audience know how many tickets have been distributed:

```
db2 => select prevval for doorprize as "Last Ticket" from sysibm.sysdummy1

Last Ticket
-----------
         51

  1 record(s) selected.
```

The prevval operator has a scope governed by the current connected session. This has two important implications. First, your prevval can be different from the one reported by another connection. The reason for this goes back to the concept of speed and freedom from cross-process checking discussed previously. If DB2 had to keep telling every session every number that had been generated—even if most sessions didn't care—the overhead would seriously affect sequence performance. A second more subtle issue is the usefulness of prevval in environments that use connection pooling. Here, you can't even rely on prevval in your own "session" because you're sharing your actual connection with other application users, and they might be generating sequence values at the same time you are. There's no telling whose prevval you've actually retrieved.

One other minor caveat with prevval is that it can't be successfully used by a session until nextval has been called at least once on a given sequence in the same session. Attempting to do so returns an SQL0845N SQL Code with the error message "A PREVVAL expression cannot be used before the NEXTVAL expression generates a value in the current session for sequence *your sequence id*".

A sequence can also easily be used in an insert or update statement. For instance, let's assume that you actually need to store the lucky door prize information for later use. You could create a table as follows to reference existing staff information in the employee table:

```
create table empdoorprize (empno char(6), prizeno integer)
DB20000I  The SQL command completed successfully
```

With that in place, you could allocate all staff a door prize number with one insert statement using the doorprize sequence:

```
insert into empdoorprize select empno, nextval for doorprize from employee
DB20000I  The SQL command completed successfully
```

A quick examination of the new `empdoorprize` table shows the desired effect:

```
db2 => select * from empdoorprize

EMPNO   PRIZENO
------  -----------
000010         52
000020         53
...
200310         91
200330         92
200340         93

  42 record(s) selected.
```

You can easily join this table back to the `employee` table to find the human-readable details you need, such as given names and surnames.

Sequence Wrap Up

Prior to this chapter, you wouldn't have thought that simply counting numbers was as complex a feature as it has turned out to be. But it is such a common requirement in databases that you'll find yourself dreaming up new uses for sequences in no time.

Working with Views

Views in DB2 follow the principle often found where views are implemented elsewhere: whenever you need a way to work with a subset of data, defined by a consistent rule or query, a view can substitute for a table. In practice, views are very useful tools for providing a customized subset of data for users to work with, removing distractions from extraneous data and even hiding data to which a user shouldn't have access.

Defining Views

The principle of creating a view is to decide on the query that will act to define the data accessible through the view. That query can be as simple as a short select statement, all the way up to complex joins, common table expressions, and more. The basic syntax for view creation is the following:

```
create view view_name
as (tailored column names for your view)
select statement for your view
other view options
```

The only problem with such a simple flexible structure is imagining a concrete example. Let's use a common scenario in which you want to see a subset of the data in a given table. The employee table in the SAMPLE database covers employees of all departments. If I were working in one department (say, Operations), a view based on a query that only selected operations staff could help my day-to-day work with the data. The workdept atttribute of an employee is the foreign key to department, and examining the department table shows that the code for Operations is E11. You can see the employees in this department with a simple select statement:

```
select * from employee where workdept = 'E11'
```

EMPNO	FIRSTNME	MIDINIT	LASTNAME	WORKDEPT	PHONENO	HIREDATE	JOB
000090	EILEEN	W	HENDERSON	E11	5498	08/15/2000	MANAGER
000280	ETHEL	R	SCHNEIDER	E11	8997	03/24/1997	OPERATOR
000290	JOHN	R	PARKER	E11	4502	05/30/2006	OPERATOR
000300	PHILIP	X	SMITH	E11	2095	06/19/2002	OPERATOR
000310	MAUDE	F	SETRIGHT	E11	3332	09/12/1994	OPERATOR
200280	EILEEN	R	SCHWARTZ	E11	8997	03/24/1997	OPERATOR
200310	MICHELLE	F	SPRINGER	E11	3332	09/12/1994	OPERATOR

```
  7 record(s) selected.
```

To create an equivalent view, you simply place this select statement into the view definition:

```
create view opsemployee
as select * from employee where workdept = 'E11'
```

You can now use this view in just about every conceivable place where you could use the underlying table. For example, to query the staff of the Operations division, you only need to query the view:

```
select * from opsemployee
```

EMPNO	FIRSTNME	MIDINIT	LASTNAME	WORKDEPT	PHONENO	HIREDATE	JOB
000090	EILEEN	W	HENDERSON	E11	5498	08/15/2000	MANAGER
000280	ETHEL	R	SCHNEIDER	E11	8997	03/24/1997	OPERATOR
000290	JOHN	R	PARKER	E11	4502	05/30/2006	OPERATOR
000300	PHILIP	X	SMITH	E11	2095	06/19/2002	OPERATOR
000310	MAUDE	F	SETRIGHT	E11	3332	09/12/1994	OPERATOR
200280	EILEEN	R	SCHWARTZ	E11	8997	03/24/1997	OPERATOR
200310	MICHELLE	F	SPRINGER	E11	3332	09/12/1994	OPERATOR

```
  7 record(s) selected.
```

Surprise! Exactly the same data as if you issued the underlying query for the view. And that's the essence of normal view operation. The view itself acts as a stored query without duplicating the actual data referenced in the base tables.

DB2 supports views based on views, so you could define a view that was for operators in the Operations department on top of the opsemployee view:

```
create view operators
as select * from opsemployee where job = 'OPERATOR'
```

Further View Options

There are some quite complex capabilities available for views, which stretch beyond your scope. One worth covering at this point, however, involves whether or not a view is update-able, and if so, to what degree.

In general, a view defined on a given table will by default allow the full range of data manipulation language (DML) statements to operate against it, transforming the underlying table. So if you delete, insert, or update an employee via the opsemployee view, or even the operators view, you can make a change that would render the new data invisible to the view. That means the following query against the operators view in turn attempts to update the opsemployee view, which in turn attempts to update the employee table:

```
db2 => update operators set job = 'MANAGER' where empno = '000280'
DB20000I  The SQL command completed successfully.
```

It succeeds, and now you'll note that Ethel Schneider no longer appears in the view for operators because she is now a manager and thus falls outside the criteria for the view:

```
db2 => select * from operators
```

EMPNO	FIRSTNME	MIDINIT	LASTNAME	WORKDEPT	PHONENO	HIREDATE	JOB
000290	JOHN	R	PARKER	E11	4502	05/30/2006	OPERATOR
000300	PHILIP	X	SMITH	E11	2095	06/19/2002	OPERATOR
000310	MAUDE	F	SETRIGHT	E11	3332	09/12/1994	OPERATOR
200280	EILEEN	R	SCHWARTZ	E11	8997	03/24/1997	OPERATOR
200310	MICHELLE	F	SPRINGER	E11	3332	09/12/1994	OPERATOR

```
  5 record(s) selected.
```

But often you want the criteria that define a view to act as a safeguard against changing data through that view, so changes that are mutually exclusive to the view definition are pre-vented. This can be achieved with the with check option, and in more complex cases, using the with cascaded check option.

The with check option treats the view as both a stored query and a pseudo-check con-straint that must be satisfied when changing data through the view. If you create a new view called checked_operators that enforces the job type of operator, you'll see the behavior in action:

```
create view checked_operators
as select * from opsemployee where job = 'OPERATOR'
with check option
```

Now attempting to promote another operations employee to manager will be checked by the view definition, and prevented. Let's use Philip, with an empno of 000300 to illustrate it:

```
db2 => update checked_operators set job = 'MANAGER' where empno = '000300'
SQL0161N  The resulting row of the insert or update operation does not conform
to the view definition.  SQLSTATE=44000
```

Very useful because this saves on the complexity of having to create separate views and check constraints. You also benefit from the inherent security that views can provide. I now have several views built over the employee table. Currently, my user called theuser has no select privileges on the employee table or any of the views built on it. By granting select privileges to one of the views, I can effectively limit and control the data theuser can see, without needing to implement more fine-grained options:

```
db2 => connect to sample user fuzzy
Enter current password for fuzzy:

  Database Connection Information

 Database server        = DB2/NT 9.5.0
 SQL authorization ID    = FUZZY
 Local database alias    = SAMPLE


db2 => grant select on opsemployee to theuser
DB20000I  The SQL command completed successfully.
db2 => revoke select on employee from theuser
DB21034E  The command was processed as an SQL statement because it was not a
valid Command Line Processor command.  During SQL processing it returned:
SQL0556N  An attempt to revoke a privilege, security label, exemption, or role
from "THEUSER" was denied because "THEUSER" does not hold this privilege,
security label, exemption, or role.  SQLSTATE=42504
```

That error was expected; I'm just explicitly showing that theuser cannot select from the base table: employee. Now I connect as theuser, and see what I can see:

```
db2 => connect to sample user theuser
Enter current password for theuser:

  Database Connection Information

 Database server        = DB2/NT 9.5.0
 SQL authorization ID    = THEUSER
 Local database alias    = SAMPLE


db2 => select * from fuzzy.employee
SQL0551N  "THEUSER" does not have the privilege to perform operation "SELECT"
on object "FUZZY.EMPLOYEE".  SQLSTATE=42501
db2 => select * from fuzzy.opsemployee
```

EMPNO	FIRSTNME	MIDINIT	LASTNAME	WORKDEPT	PHONENO	HIREDATE	JOB
000090	EILEEN	W	HENDERSON	E11	5498	08/15/2000	MANAGER
000280	ETHEL	R	SCHNEIDER	E11	8997	03/24/1997	MANAGER
000290	JOHN	R	PARKER	E11	4502	05/30/2006	OPERATOR
000300	PHILIP	X	SMITH	E11	2095	06/19/2002	OPERATOR
000310	MAUDE	F	SETRIGHT	E11	3332	09/12/1994	OPERATOR
200280	EILEEN	R	SCHWARTZ	E11	8997	03/24/1997	OPERATOR
200310	MICHELLE	F	SPRINGER	E11	3332	09/12/1994	OPERATOR

```
  7 record(s) selected.
```

Presto! As theuser I can query only via the view. In practice I don't need to worry about the fact it is a view, not a table.

View Wrap Up

Views can become significantly more complex and can include the notions of multiple rules for updateability, insertion, and deletion. There are also type hierarchies that can be introduced, allowing superviews and subviews to be defined. While powerful, they tend to be some of the more esoteric features of views, and I'll leave their study as an exercise for the reader.

Summary

The supporting cast of objects in a DB2 database includes a variety of useful features. Indexes play a vital role in streamlining data access and enforcing the uniqueness of data where necessary in your database. The simple act of counting is taken to new heights with the capabilities of sequences, and you'll never have to rely on your own arithmetic again to provide a roll call of numbers to suit your business needs. Views are a fantastic stored query technique, allowing you to hide the complexity of data access and business logic from users and developers, and optionally providing extra security against accidental or deliberate change.

PART 4

■■■

Programming with DB2 Express Edition

CHAPTER 13

■■■

PHP with DB2

PHP is one of the "P" languages that for more than a decade have collectively formed one of the pillars of the web and the explosion of online content and sites. PHP excels at the heavy lifting required to dynamically create content, but has traditionally lacked features that let it work with relational databases such as DB2. Some time ago, database vendors such as IBM started releasing libraries of database connectors and associated functions to enable PHP to talk to databases such as DB2. More recently, IBM has invested considerable developer effort in both developing a revamped connection library, IBM_DB2, and also supporting third parties developing more-sophisticated PHP development tools.

PHP and Zend Core for DB2

While it is possible to source the IBM_DB2 PHP extensions in isolation, IBM has recently promoted the bundle provided by Zend with the Zend Core framework for DB2. This package includes the traditional PHP extensions, as well as the mind-boggling large framework that Zend has constructed to support a diverse range of PHP development requirements.

The current release of Zend Core for IBM is 2.0.4. Zend currently validates its product for a wide range of Linux distributions, as well as Windows and AIX. You'll take advantage of Zend's bundling to explore the numerous options available for PHP development with DB2. Navigate your favorite browser to the Zend website at www.zend.com. There, you can search for "Zend Core for IBM" (its official name) or navigate to the downloads page and choose the IBM option. You should eventually see a download page that is approximately the same as shown in Figure 13-1.

The installation for Windows amounts to approximately 80MB and for Linux around 66MB.

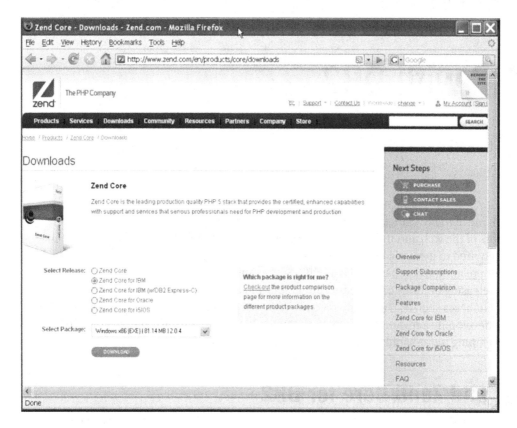

Figure 13-1. *Zend Core download selection*

Starting an Install of Zend Core

One of the important choices to make when downloading from the Zend site is whether to choose the bundled version of DB2 Express-C. You know by now that Express-C is a great DB2, but you already have DB2 Express-C installed and probably don't need another copy. You are also more likely to get the absolute latest version of DB2 Express-C from the IBM website. I'd advise grabbing the Zend Core for IBM installer that is the slimmed-down version, skipping the bundled DB2 Express-C installer. Choose your target platform—Linux, or Windows—and wait for the package to download.

Under Windows

Unpack the zip file, and you'll see a single executable file. Run this to begin the installation. After the usual welcome splash screen and license agreement, you'll see the utilitarian typical or custom installation question. Choose the custom option to follow because it will give you the best grounding in what's included in the package, particularly surrounding web servers. You'll be prompted for an installation directory, and the default is fine.

The installer will then probe your system to determine which, if any, web servers are currently installed. Zend Core is written so it plugs in to all major versions of Apache and Microsoft IIS. If you have an existing web server installed, you can choose to use it or you can install a new instance of Apache to use as a dedicated web server for Zend Core.

Under Linux

Installation under Linux provides the usual comprehensive set of options you'd expect. Key among them are the choice of text-based installer, or "Text GUI" installer akin to that used under Windows, with the graphics somewhat skewed toward ASCII art. Unzip and untar the imaginatively named source file, ZendCoreForIBM-2.0.4-linux-glibc21-i386.tar.gz, and you'll see two installation scripts in the directory in which you unpack the archive.

The ./install script will launch the "Text GUI" installation tool, shown in Figure 13-2.

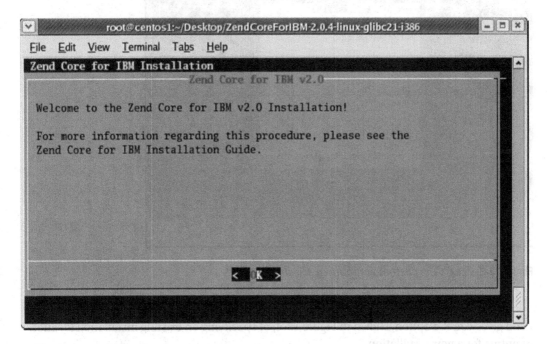

Figure 13-2. *Zend Core download selection*

If you want to use a text-only installation, use the ./install-tty option instead. Using either approach, you'll be asked the same questions, and the meaning matches those questions you'll see in the graphical installation outlined in the following section.

Continuing the Installation

Figure 13-3 shows a typical installation choice on a Windows XP box. I recommend choosing the Zend framework in addition to the default components because it provides the greatest flexibility for any future PHP on DB2 development you want to explore, and you'll also be using it in the examples later in this chapter. It's also only 90MB in size, which is tiny by modern standards.

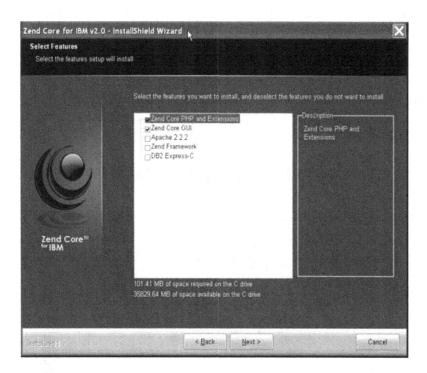

Figure 13-3. *Zend Core custom component selection*

With the components selected, you then need to determine which web server to use. Zend gives you the option, shown in Figure 13-4, of specifying an existing installation location or opting for a new installation.

Following web server selection, a dialog box appears that asks for the port on which the web server will listen. You can go with the default of 80 if you know that your chosen web server is either the default or is definitely listening on this port. If you elected to install an additional web server, be sure to choose a different unused port.

Clicking Next brings you to the file extension specification dialog box shown in Figure 13-5. PHP has evolved over a number of years, and in that time PHP scripts have taken on file extensions under different naming schemes. The most common is .php, which was the original extension. When PHP version 4 was released, there was a brief fad entailing naming with a .php4 extension to signify whether a script utilized features found only in that version. The same thing happened with the release of PHP version 5. More recently, a kind of role reversal has happened—people writing scripts based on older versions tend to mark their scripts with the extension .php3, leaving the "vanilla" .php extension to indicate a script designed for contemporary versions.

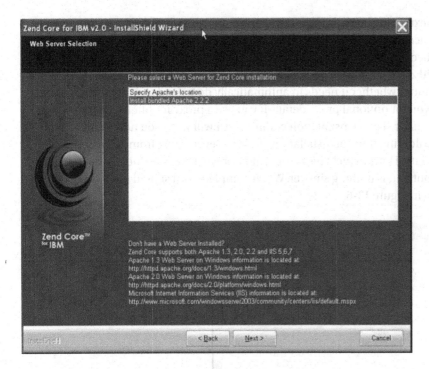

Figure 13-4. *Zend Core web server selection*

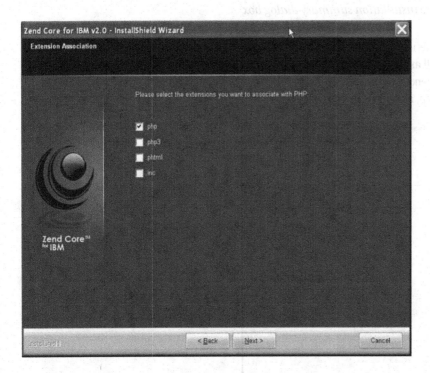

Figure 13-5. *Zend Core PHP file extension selection*

I recommend that you select all the extensions shown to minimize future administrative work if you inherit code written by others that might use extensions such as .phtml and the like.

Moving to the next dialog box brings you the Zend Core administrator password dialog box, which controls access to the graphical administration console. Specify a password you're likely to remember because you'll be using it shortly. The following dialog box asks whether you subscribe to paid Zend support; if you do, it offers to let you enter your details. The installer then determines whether it needs to automatically download any additional components and prompts you for optional proxy details if you use a proxy for Internet connectivity.

Finally, you'll actually see the installation commence. I will warn you now that you will potentially see a bewildering array of installation choices—everything from Microsoft Visual C++ to Windows Update. Don't panic! This is the Zend Core installer's included dependencies sorting themselves out and is nothing sinister. When complete, you should see a summary dialog box, as shown in Figure 13-6.

Figure 13-6. *Zend Core installation summary dialog box*

This is a very useful summary because it gives you starting points to see exactly what you just installed, as well as the location of samples that will come in handy. Point your browser at http://localhost/ZendCore (be careful to match that case), and you'll see the Zend administrative login interface, as shown in Figure 13-7.

Figure 13-7. *Zend Core administration login screen*

Enter the password you chose during installation (you do remember it, right?), and you'll be presented with the administrative summary dialog box you see in Figure 13-8.

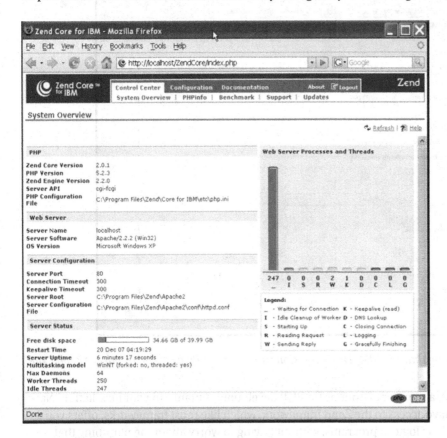

Figure 13-8. *Zend Core web server information dashboard*

Post-Installation Checks

Once the installation is complete, and you have logged in to the Zend Core administration page, it is worth checking that the IBM_DB2 PHP extensions and the DB2 bindings have been correctly installed and configured. This should have happened automatically through the actions of the installer, but it's worth checking now to save you angst and unexplained errors later.

From the Zend Core home page, navigate to the Configuration menu, and choose Extensions. The page of registered extensions will be displayed. Scroll down the page, until you spot the ibm_db2 – IBM DB2 Database Access entry, as shown in Figure 13-9. Open it by clicking the plus symbol, and you should see values for ibm_db2.binmode and ibm_db2.instance_name. The IBM_DB2 PHP extensions can work with only one instance at a time, and your current DB2INSTANCE value should have been detected automatically, and placed in the ibm_db2.instance_name field. If for some reason this auto-detection failed, ensure that this value is set to your desired instance's name. The ibm_db2.binmode parameter controls how binary information will be returned from DB2 to PHP. The default value, 1, indicates that the binary data is transferred natively, with no special handing. Other values are possible, for instance to convert all binary data to hexadecimal strings, or nulls, but the default value is fine for all these examples. The little light bulb icon on the right hand side should be lit, and the sliding switch icon should be "up" and colored green.

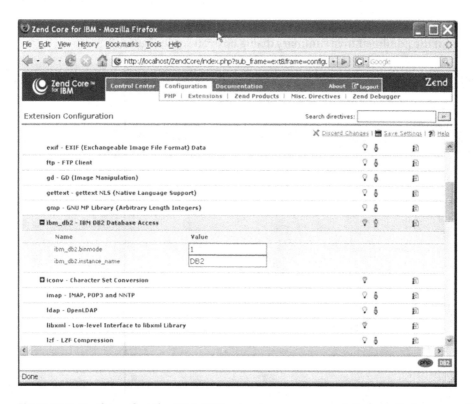

Figure 13-9. *Verifying that the IBM_DB2 extensions are successfully installed as part of Zend Core*

You now have a number of options for PHP development thanks to your installation. Naturally, you now have access to the Zend framework, which like most frameworks, offers you a structure to build the logic of programs, without having to worry about the plumbing that connects your web server to your PHP code, and onward to your DB2 database. But as part of the Zend Core installation, you have installed the IBM_DB2 extensions for PHP, which also enables you to write vanilla PHP code that can work with the objects, methods, and features that IBM provides for working with databases from PHP. You'll take a look at development using this approach and touch on the Zend options toward the end of the chapter.

Developing with the IBM_DB2 PHP Extensions

The IBM_DB2 PHP extensions, which are some of the oldest forms of integration between DB2 and PHP, are so reliable that Zend bundles them in with the installation you've performed. As such, they are also one of the most well-tested and reliable set of tools for wiring your web applications to your DB2 database. The IBM_DB2 extensions are a set of functions that allow you to manage connections to DB2, execute SQL stored procedures and functions, and work with result sets and responses from your DB2 server.

Connecting to a Database

To start familiarizing you with the functions and to get you up and running in the shortest possible time, I'll introduce the connection management functions in a working PHP file, so you can walk through the code and learn the IBM_DB2 PHP extensions as you go.

The first function to learn, db2_connect, manages the connection from the PHP engine to DB2. Its general form is as follows:

```
db2_connect ( string connection_details, string uid, string pwd )
```

The function name is sensibly self-descriptive, but the connection string details need further explanation. The following components are concatenated in the string, separated by semicolons to form the full connection string:

DRIVER: The name of the underlying driver used to create the connection

HOST: The host name for your DB2 server

DATABASE: The catalogued database name for the DB2 database

PROTOCOL: The network protocol to use for connectivity

PORT: For port-orientated protocols (for example, TCP/IP), the port of the DB2 listener

UID: The DB2 authid (user name) to use for the connection

PWD: The password for the user

You'll note that the user name and password (UID and PWD) can be included in the connection string or passed as separate parameters to the db2_connect function. This example includes everything in the connection string and passes empty strings for the latter two parameters:

```php
<?php
$driver = "{IBM DB2 ODBC DRIVER}";
$database = "SAMPLE";
$hostname = "localhost";
$port = 50000;
$user = "fuzzy";
$password = "fuzzy";

$conn_string = "DRIVER=$driver;DATABASE=$database;";
$conn_string .= "HOSTNAME=$hostname;PORT=$port;PROTOCOL=TCPIP;";
$conn_string .= "UID=$user;PWD=$password;";

try
{
  $conn = db2_connect($conn_string, '', '');
  if (! $conn)
  {
    echo db2_conn_errormsg();
  }
  else
  {
    echo "Hello World, from the IBM_DB2 PHP extensions!";
    db2_close($conn);
  }
```

```
}

catch (Exception $e) {
  echo $e;
}
?>
```

There are several important things to note about that small code example that will further your understanding of how the IBM_DB2 extensions will aid your PHP coding. First, the password value is in plain text, which is helpful if you want to explicitly provide authentication details for your connection. An alternative is to allow the user running your web server to implicitly be used by providing no user name or password. There are further security considerations to think about if you do go down this path. First, very highly privileged accounts, such as root under Linux, and Local System and Administrator under Microsoft Windows, are usually not recommended for running facilities such as web servers (okay, that's an understatement). At the other end of the spectrum, accounts such as nobody under Linux and the Network Service account under Windows, bring some awkward usability issues to the fore as well. You might find that for the purposes of learning and developing test code, using explicit authentication credentials acts as a practical compromise. When deploying your code to any form of production environment, make sure that you revisit these credentials and choose a setup that meets your security and functional needs.

Next you'll notice that along with db2_connect, I introduced two more IBM_DB2 PHP functions: db2_conn_errormsg and db2_close. The db2_close function should be mostly self-explanatory, but just to reinforce its message, it explicitly closes a connection object, which releases all its locks, resources, and pending results. Closing connections is good coding behavior, but you'll shortly look at more advanced methods of connection management.

The db2_conn_errormsg function allows you to access the details of the last error (or information statement or warning) returned from any connection. If your code has multiple connection objects instantiated at one time, you can differentiate between connections by passing the connection handle as an optional parameter to the db2_conn_errormsg function.

Finally, you'll note that the value provided for the DRIVER portion of the connection string is the hard-coded value "{IBM DB2 ODBC DRIVER}". This special value corresponds with the IBM DB2 ODBC driver that IBM recommends using for underlying connection management. Other options are available, such as OLE DB providers under Windows, but the ODBC option is the most reliable, the most portable, and is the top recommendation of the options provided by IBM.

I saved my sample PHP code to a file called ch13ex1.php and placed it in the root directory of my Apache browser (the htdocs directory). Similarly, if you're using Microsoft IIS, you can save the code to a file of the same name into the wwwroot directory. Figure 13-10 shows the results in a web browser of the PHP code successfully negotiating a connection to my DB2 database, and returning the near-ubiquitous Hello World message as a sign of success.

All good testers will tell you that it's just as important to test the error and exception handling of your code as it is to test the path of success. If you change the previous code to include an incorrect password, you'll see the db2_conn_errormsg function in action. I changed my code to modify the password like this:

```
$password = "wrongvalue";
```

Figure 13-10. *A successful Hello World test of the IBM_DB2 PHP extensions*

If you reload the test page, you should see the message shown in Figure 13-11.

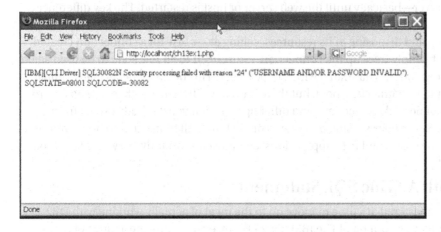

Figure 13-11. *Successfully testing and trapping a connection problem*

CODING BEST PRACTICE FOR CONNECTION CODE AND MANAGEMENT

My examples show the details of how to fully specify the connection string for PHP in each of the code snippets. In more sophisticated development environments, good coding practice would highlight this code as both recurring and sensitive, and refactor it into a separate file that could provide the connection details—or better still, a fully fledged connection object—to other parts of code that require it. This results in much cleaner, more secure, and more maintainable code, and is certainly a practice I recommend. Follow my example style only as long as you need to in order to understand the mechanics.

Managing IBM_DB2 PHP Connections

While the code for creating and closing connections is easy, thanks to the db2_connect and db2_close functions, the processing effort and resources consumed in creating connections is always significant. At the PHP processing end, the PHP engine must detect the driver to use, load the driver into memory, invoke the underlying connection API, and optionally also trigger credential lookup or exchange from the operating system for authentication. The DB2 instance must authenticate the user making the connection attempt, including negotiating the trust rules covered previously, allocate memory and other resources for the connection, invoke or allocate DB2 agents and other server-side resources, and return connection details to the caller. That's a lot of effort to do every time a PHP page is rendered.

More importantly, it's a lot of effort wasted every time the PHP and associated objects are discarded after rendering. Using reusable connections in a connection pool is the technique normally used to provide better connection and resource management when working with DB2, and the IBM_DB2 extensions provide a function to allow approximately that.

The db2_pconnect function has the same calling semantics as the db2_connect function, so the connection string and associated authentication credentials are treated the same way. The db2_pconnect function creates a persistent connection that lives for the life of the PHP engine within the web server—basically until the web server or host is restarted. The key difference in use comes when db2_close is then called on the resulting connection. Instead of actually closing the connection and disposing of its resources, calling db2_close on a connection created with db2_pconnect simply frees up the connection, returning it to an idle state to be used again when next a connection is instantiated with db2_pconnect. This behavior bears many similarities to the concept of a connection pool, but there are a few differences—there are no controls over the number of pooled connections and other options that you'd usually expect from a connection pool. Nevertheless, using persistent connections will translate into better resource management for your DB2 and PHP applications, and most importantly, they'll be faster too!

Working with Ad Hoc SQL Statements

With connections mastered, it's time to move on to the meat of actually working with DB2 from PHP: manipulating your data! The IBM_DB2 PHP extensions provide a range of functions for working with ad hoc SQL through to stored procedures; as well as dealing with the results, transactions, and associated housekeeping. The first function that you'll find useful is the db2_exec function, which has the following form:

```
db2_exec (resource connection_object, string statement)
```

The db2_exec function is passed the connection object for the connection to use to execute the statement and the string representing the statement to execute. The db2_exec function returns a result resource. An important point to make regarding the SQL statements passed to the db2_exec and other functions is that the IBM_DB2 PHP extensions don't include the concept of embedded SQL, which you'll find in other languages such as SQLJ. Instead, all your statements and calls to stored procedures rely on simple string values, representing your SQL, being passed to the relevant functions. This makes for a lighter weight set of extensions because no additional preprocessing is required—all the complexities of SQL execution are left to the DB2 engine.

With a statement executed, there's a matching need to then gather and work with the results. This is where the options start flourishing with the IBM_DB2 extensions. There are several ways to work with your results, so there's bound to be an option that suits you:

db2_fetch_row: Allows manual iteration through a result set or movement to an explicit row. Used in conjunction with db2_result to return actual row data.

db2_result: Returns the row of data at the provided row parameter. Used in conjunction with db2_fetch_row.

db2_fetch_assoc: Returns a column-name-indexed array from a result, so that columns are accessed by name.

db2_fetch_array: Returns a column-position-indexed array from a result. Column one has position zero (0) in the array, column two has position 1, and so forth.

db2_fetch_both: The best of both worlds—provides an array indexed by both column-name and column-position.

db2_fetch_object: Returns an object with properties matched to the result row's column names.

The first two functions, db2_fetch_row and db2_result, are used in combination to manually iterate the pointer to the current result row and subsequently fetch its value. This is a rather laborious technique, and like me, you'll probably prefer one of the array-fetching functions instead. I find db2_fetch_both to be the best all-around choice because it provides the flexibility to refer to columns in my results by either position or column name interchangeably. The one downside is that it requires slightly more memory and processing time to set up the twin indexes for the array, so if you are counting every byte in an effort to make your application super efficient, you might prefer db2_fetch_assoc or db2_fetch_array.

The db2_fetch_object function is a slightly different beast. Instead of returning an array of results, you instead receive an object that has properties named to match the result columns. Think of this as the extreme object-oriented fetching technique.

All these descriptions make more sense in action. The following code executes a SQL statement to return the employees in your organization, who are in the running for employee of the year:

```php
<?php
$driver = "{IBM DB2 ODBC DRIVER}";
$database = "SAMPLE";
$hostname = "localhost";
$port = 50000;
$user = "fuzzy";
$password = "fuzzy";

$conn_string = "DRIVER={IBM DB2 ODBC DRIVER};DATABASE=$database;";
$conn_string .= "HOSTNAME=$hostname;PORT=$port;PROTOCOL=TCPIP;";
$conn_string .= "UID=$user;PWD=$password;";

try
{
```

```php
  $conn = db2_pconnect($conn_string, '', '');
  if (! $conn)
  {
    echo db2_conn_errormsg();
  }
  else
  {
    echo "Candidates for Employee of the Year:";
    $result = db2_exec($conn, "select firstnme, lastname from fuzzy.employee");
    if ($result)
    {
      while ($row = db2_fetch_both($result))
      {
        echo "<p>".$row[0]." ".$row[1]."</p>";
      }
    }
  db2_close($conn);
  }
}

catch (Exception $e) {
  echo $e;
}
?>
```

This example is only fractionally longer than the simple Hello World example, but it achieves quite a bit more. The call to the db2_exec function includes the SQL statement "select firstnme, lastname from fuzzy.employee". If you're following these examples, be sure to use the correct schema name for your database. All the execution and fetching methods in the IBM_DB2 extensions return Boolean false when there are no results or no more results, so the shorthand if ($result) test allows you to work with results if you have them. The key to building the PHP page then lies in this block of code:

```php
    while ($row = db2_fetch_both($result))
    {
      echo "<p>".$row[0]." ".$row[1]."</p>";
    }
```

Using the db2_fetch_both function to iterate over the results until they are exhausted, you then build up rows to include in the final HTML document by simply echoing the necessary HTML markup and the values from each row using column positioned lookups. Because I used the db2_fetch_both function to build my result array, I could have achieved the same output using column names like this:

```php
    while ($row = db2_fetch_both($result))
    {
      echo "<p>".$row[FIRSTNME]." ".$row[LASTNAME]."</p>";
    }
```

If I use the column-name-based indexing, I need to use uppercase column names to match those returned from DB2 in the result set. The final page should look like Figure 13-12 in your browser.

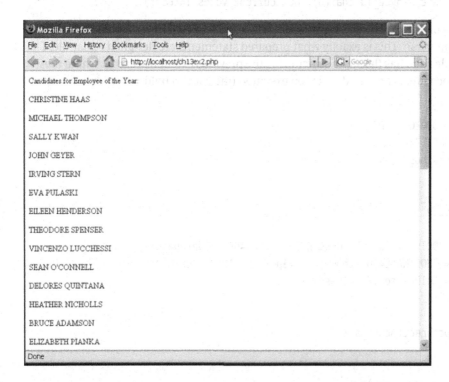

Figure 13-12. *Results from executing a SQL statement via the IBM_DB2 PHP extensions*

Working with Prepared Statements and Stored Procedures

While handcrafting every SQL statement is fun the first few times, you'll eventually get tired of it and want to get maximum benefit from all the hard work you placed into your stored procedures and functions. There are also times when you want to use the same SQL statement over again, only changing the values used in various predicates instead of the overall logic itself. Both of these scenarios are covered using the functions db2_prepare and db2_execute.

■**Caution** db2_exec is *not* shorthand for db2_execute in the IBM_DB2 PHP extensions; they are distinct function calls. db2_exec is used for executing dynamic SQL passed as a parameter directly to the function. db2_execute is used only for executing a statement previously prepared with db2_prepare.

Let's get straight to it with an example. Let's assume that Eileen, one of the employees in the SAMPLE database, thinks that she can really increase her votes by putting up a simple PHP page that lets other staff vote for her by visiting that page. To do that, the page will need to invoke the previously written employee_vote stored procedure, which has two specific versions: one that can be invoked using a person's first and last name, and another that takes the employee's empno as a parameter. The signature for the latter version is the following:

```
employee_vote (IN employee_id char(6), OUT current_votes integer)
```

Right away, you're probably asking yourself, "How do I let PHP know that the procedure works with parameters?" This is exactly what prepared statements are designed to handle. The following example code has the same structure as the previous examples, except where the actual stored procedure is prepared and then executed (the code in bold):

```php
<?php
$driver = "{IBM DB2 ODBC DRIVER}";
$database = "SAMPLE";
$hostname = "localhost";
$port = 50000;
$user = "fuzzy";
$password = "fuzzy";

$conn_string = "DRIVER={IBM DB2 ODBC DRIVER};DATABASE=$database;";
$conn_string .= "HOSTNAME=$hostname;PORT=$port;PROTOCOL=TCPIP;";
$conn_string .= "UID=$user;PWD=$password;";

try {
  $conn = db2_pconnect($conn_string, '', '');
  if (! $conn)
  {
    echo db2_conn_errormsg();
  }
  else
  {
    echo "<p>You've voted!</p>";
    $eileens_empno = "000090";
    $eileens_votes = 0;
    $pstmt = db2_prepare($conn, "CALL fuzzy.employee_vote(?, ?)");
    $result = db2_bind_param($pstmt, 1, "eileens_empno", DB2_PARAM_IN);
    $result = db2_bind_param($pstmt, 2, "eileens_votes", DB2_PARAM_OUT);
    $result = db2_execute($pstmt);
    if ($result)
    {
      print "Eileen now has $eileens_votes votes!";
    }
  db2_close($conn);
  }
}

catch (Exception $e) {
  echo $e;
}
?>
```

Let's examine each line so you become comfortable with the techniques. After echoing a friendly message, I set up a simple variable to hold the return value from the procedure's OUT parameter, current_votes, and a variable that holds Eileen's empno for passing to the stored procedure (you can verify that this is Eileen's empno by issuing the relevant select query against the employee table). I called them $eileens_empno and $eileens_votes to make it clear that you can use any name you like—you don't have to match the name in the procedure's definition.

Next, I prepare the statement that invokes the stored procedure. This uses exactly the same SQL code you could run from the DB2 CLP and uses the question mark (?) to indicate the placeholders for the IN and OUT parameters. I then invoke the db2_bind_param function, assigning the output to my yet-to-be-populated result object. The db2_bind_param function has the following general form:

```
db2_bind_param (statement handle, 1-based parameter number,
  variable placeholder, parameter type [, precision and scale options])
```

The statement handle is the variable from the prepared statement. The parameter number is a one-based count of the particular parameter you're binding. This means that if you have a function that requires multiple parameters, such as the employee_vote procedure, you need to call db2_bind_param for each parameter in turn. This is identical to almost every other programming language, so it should be familiar. When binding the parameter values, the options DB2_PARAM_IN and DB2_PARAM_OUT indicate to the IBM_DB2 PHP extensions how to work with the parameters, enabling successful passing of IN and OUT parameters between your PHP code and DB2.

Finally, with the statement fully prepared, you execute it using the related db2_execute function. The results look similar to the output shown in Figure 13-13.

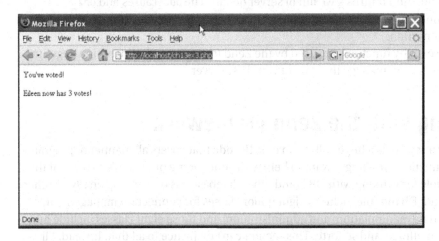

Figure 13-13. *Preparing and executing a stored procedure via PHP*

Other IBM_DB2 PHP Functions

You can naturally go further than the simple examples, extending your PHP to call and invoke all manner of SQL statements, procedures, and functions. To that end, the IBM_DB2 PHP extensions provide a host of additional functions.

Transaction management is supported using the db2_commit, db2_rollback, and db2_autocommit functions. These functions allow you to take full control of transaction logic, explicitly committing or rolling back where required, or simply setting autocommit to rely on every statement being committed, come what may.

THE PERILS OF AUTOCOMMIT

It's very tempting to set any programming or query environment you work with to automatically commit changes you make as you make them. This so-called autocommit setting is attractive because you can get on with executing your code without having to remember to commit your changes.

You never make mistakes, right? You certainly never execute code in a production environment when you thought you were connected to a test environment. And if you've ever accidentally pressed the Enter key before adding that vital where clause to your delete statement, that means the difference between deleting one and one million rows.

I think you get my drift. Be absolutely certain you can live with the consequences before you succumb to the autocommit temptation. If it were me, it would be the first thing I turn off!

You can probe and manipulate your results in great detail using the db2_field_* group of functions. These include db2_field_type, db2_field_name, db2_field_precision, and many more, enabling you to precisely evaluate and display text, numbers, dates, times, and more.

There are also functions that allow you to check the settings and behavior of the tables on which you are working, and the database and server themselves. Functions such as db2_client_info return useful code page, version, and driver information. The db2_server_info function returns a wealth of server details. The db2_tables and db2_procedures functions are useful for examining which tables and procedures are available to the current connection.

Many of these utility functions are used by the Zend framework administration pages to enable you to browse and manage the state of your DB2 server.

Developing with the Zend Framework

The Zend PHP framework is a huge collection of PHP code that covers all manner of programming tasks and functions you might want to help with your coding project. It's so big that the module responsible for working with DB2 (and other databases) is one among nearly 50 other modules. The Zend_Db module includes eight major classes for connection management, SQL statements, data manipulation, and administration; and those eight classes include hundreds of options, methods, and so forth. This section can't do justice to all that. Instead, I'll follow examples that will get you started quickly with connections and statements, and hopefully whet your appetite enough to let you explore further on your own.

Configuring the Zend Framework

One area that is still heavily under development by the Zend Core team is the out-of-the-box configuration for Zend core. Don't get me wrong, things have moved ahead in leaps and bounds over the last year. If you installed the latest Zend Core, there's only one manual configuration task you'll need to perform to use the Zend Core option for PHP and DB2.

The current installation creates a preconfigured `php.ini` master configuration file, complete with almost every configuration option you require to get Zend Core operating out of the box. Indeed, you can see the fruits of the developers' efforts in the configuration and administration dialog boxes shown in Figures 13-8 and 13-9. However, one option in the `php.ini` file might need attention.

To find the library files that the PHP engine needs to leverage the Zend Core, the installation creates a custom [Zend] stanza in the `php.ini` file. This describes several configuration values, among them include_path (which dictates the paths searched to find files referenced in require), require_once, and other PHP directives. The default installation will have a line that looks like this:

```
include_path=".;C:\Program Files\Zend\Core for IBM\ZendFramework-0.8.0"
```

The problem is that the installation under Windows does not correctly search subdirectories under the paths listed. And the Zend Core files actually sit in a directory named `C:\Program Files\Zend\Core for IBM\ZendFramework-0.8.0\library\Zend`. To allow the Zend Core libraries to be found, you need to modify include_path and add this directory explicitly. So include_path should look like this:

```
include_path=".;C:\Program Files\Zend\Core for IBM\ZendFramework-0.8.0;
              C:\Program Files\Zend\Core for IBM\ZendFramework-0.8.0\library "
```

That is one single line—it is split here to fit on the page. With this in place, you should be good to go.

Tip If you encounter more problems with loading the Zend Core files, you'll typically see your pages come up blank thanks to the PHP engine deciding it needs to abort page generation. If this happens, refer to the diagnostic log for your web server to see what might be happening. For Apache, the `error.log` and `access.log` files provide invaluable information.

Managing Connections with the Zend Framework

Many of the principles of the Zend framework look identical to those you encountered using the IBM_DB2 PHP extensions. The framework needs to know database names, host names, ports, user names, and passwords to manage connections. There is one important difference, however: instead of supporting a special-purpose DB2 connection object, the Zend framework uses a class factory and a set of supported database adapters to allow one class to instantiate connections to a wide variety of databases, including DB2. An example will best illustrate this, and the following code is the Zend Core equivalent of the connections made earlier in the chapter:

```php
<?php
require_once 'Zend/Db.php';

try
{
  $db = Zend_Db::factory('Db2', array(
```

```
      'host'     => 'localhost',
      'username' => 'fuzzy',
      'password' => 'fuzzy',
      'dbname'   => 'SAMPLE'
  ));
  $db->getConnection();
}
catch (Zend_Db_Adapter_Exception $e)
{
  echo "adapter exception: $e";
}
catch (Zend_Exception $e)
{
  echo "general Zend framework exception $e";
}
?>
```

The Zend_Db::factory method of the Zend_Db class is the core of the connection generation. It takes two parameters: a string, representing the name of the desired database adapter
(and therefore target database) for the connection, and an array of values to provide to negoti-
ate the connection. Note the different style here, using the name=>value pair notation to build
the array.

Caution A connection with this code might fail if your host doesn't have localhost registered to resolve
the local machine. Either add that to your host's file or change the previous example to use the loopback IP
address: 127.0.0.1.

Executing Statements Using the Zend Core Framework

The mechanics of query execution and result manipulation also benefit from a wide range
of supporting classes and methods in the Zend framework in a similar fashion to the way
IBM_DB2 PHP extensions, classes, and methods exist to manage queries, fetch results by a
number of methods, examine the client and server environment, and so on. It won't surprise
you to learn that this is because many of the Zend framework options wrap the underlying
IBM_DB2 extensions that serve the same purpose.

There are additional helper methods for the Zend_Db object that help greatly simplify
query execution: Zend_Db::query(), ::insert(), ::update(), and ::delete(). As the names
suggest, they are designed to streamline running their respective SQL statements. Let's
examine executing a select statement using the ::query() method, and you'll see how
straightforward it makes working with your DB2 environment:

```
<?php
require_once 'Zend/Db.php';

try
{
  $db = Zend_Db::factory('Db2', array(
```

```
    'host'     => '127.0.0.1',
    'username' => 'db2admin',
    'password' => 'db2admin',
    'dbname'   => 'SAMPLE'
  ));
  $db->getConnection();
}
catch (Zend_Db_Adapter_Exception $e)
{
  echo "adapter exception: $e";
}
catch (Zend_Exception $e)
{
  echo "general Zend framework exception $e";
}
  $sql = "select firstnme, lastname from fuzzy.employee";
  $result = $db->query($sql);
  while ($row = $result->fetch())
  {
    echo "<p>".$row['FIRSTNME']." ".$row['LASTNAME']."</p>";
  }
?>
```

After setting up the connection per the previous example, you create a string for the SQL statement and then invoke the ::query() method with it as a parameter. This returns a result object, which you can then iterate over using the fetch() method. The results look suspiciously like the first and last names of the employees, as shown in Figure 13-14.

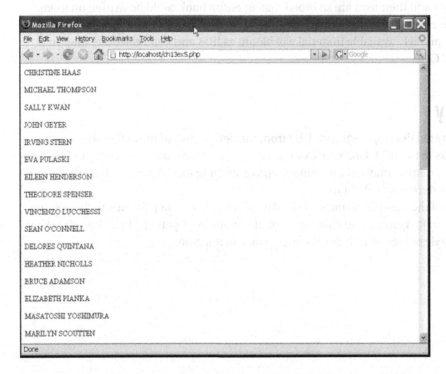

Figure 13-14. *Results of a SQL statement executed with the Zend Core framework*

Familiar results—that's reassuring because the framework is just another approach to working with your data and shouldn't be mysteriously changing it. Zend Core also supports fetching methods to allow column access by name, position, or object parameter: ::fetchAll(), ::fetch_assoc(), ::fetch_num(), ::fetch_both(), and ::fetch_obj(). Take a second look at them and refer to the list of fetching functions that the IBM_DB2 PHP extensions provided. Looks similar, doesn't it? And apart from the names and class->method invocation, you pretty much understand the semantics of these methods.

Other Major Classes in the Zend Core Framework

There are several other major classes in the Zend_Db module of the framework:

Zend_Db_Statement: Allows for statements to be prepared and executed, including stored procedures and other statements using bind variables

Zend_Db_Profiler: A class for instrumenting PHP code to track execution times and related details

Zend_Db_Select: A class specifically tailored to select SQL statements and the processing of their results

Zend_Db_Table: A table-orientated approach to manipulating the data in a table, including selecting, inserting, updating, and deleting in bulk

Zend_Db_Table_Row: An object representing one row of a table or result set

Zend_Db_Table_Rowsets: The special class returned by the ::find() and ::fetchAll() methods, consisting of the resulting rows from the related query

These classes and their uses are so broad that an entire book could be written on them. The Zend Core framework has developed so quickly that such a book has not yet been written, but I'm sure the publicly available material will bloom as IBM and Zend celebrate their new releases of Zend Core.

Summary

This chapter covered development with DB2 from the perspective of the PHP web scripting language. Thanks to the IBM_DB2 PHP extensions, wiring a DB2 database directly to PHP web pages is easy and mimics many of the common programming techniques used in other, more mature database development libraries.

The advent of the Zend Core framework takes development a step further, with a foundation of database management and data manipulation options as part of a huge framework for just about any style or type of web development you can imagine.

■■■

DB2 on Rails

Are you a Ruby revolutionary? Do you ride Rails or know what I mean when I say *RoR*? If any of this sounds familiar, chances are you've joined the followers of the development environment that enjoys the fastest growth rate in the world. Ruby the language, and Rails the framework, leverage a Model/View/Controller (MVC) development approach to get you building applications in a hurry. At the risk of another cheesy analogy, the concepts of fabulous tools and rapid development leading to great outcomes are also hallmarks of DB2. Is it any wonder that since 2006, IBM has had a DB2 on Rails toolkit available to enable Ruby developers to wire up their DB2 databases to make their applications RoR?

Okay, I promise no more cheesy jokes. What I'll do instead is give you a tour of acquiring, installing, and configuring the DB2 on Rails toolkit, and developing applications in quick-fire fashion to show how useful this environment can be. If you're not yet a Ruby developer, don't despair. Ruby is so easy to learn, and Rails is so good at catapulting your development to the next level, that you'll be able to work with these examples right away.

Installing Ruby and Rails

IBM provides the Starter Toolkit for DB2 on Rails as a current Alphaworks project. You can find the download for the toolkit here: `http://www.alphaworks.ibm.com/tech/db2onrails`.

This isn't one of IBM's permalinks, so it might change in the future, especially if the toolkit is promoted from an Alphaworks project to a "mature" member of the DB2 toolset. A search on the IBM website for "DB2 on Rails" finds the Alphaworks link as hit number one, and I trust such a search will track down the toolkit if the good folks at IBM decide to move it. Follow the download link to find the download page shown in Figure 14-1.

You know the routine from here. Choose the toolkit for your platform—Linux or Windows—and wait for the download to complete.

■**Note** The version of DB2 you have is important. If you have DB2 9.5—the Express-C version you've been working with throughout the book—you'll be set for immediately using the IBM_DB Ruby adapter straight away. If you're using earlier versions of DB2 or the IBM_DB Ruby adapter, I strongly recommend that you upgrade to avoid some minor issues with how certain data types are exchanged with the Ruby adapter that can cause problems.

Figure 14-1. *Sourcing the Starter Toolkit for DB2 on Rails*

Unpack the installer and then run the included executable or binary. On Windows, this is a self-extracting zip file that reveals the true installation package. Once you've completed these multiple levels of unpacking and unzipping, start the installer, which installs all the key components you require: Ruby, RubyGems, Rails, and the IBM_DB adapter that allows Ruby and Rails to talk to DB2. You need a working Internet connection to allow the installer to do its job because it will download the necessary packages at run time. The resulting install takes a little over 500MB of disk space when all the subinstallers have completed their work.

Starting the installation package presents you with a familiar-looking web page, as shown in Figure 14-2.

The Starter Toolkit for DB2 on Rails home page has a bunch of features, including prerequisite information, migration details, documentation, and more. It offers the ability to install DB2 Express-C if you don't already have it—this option downloads the Express-C installer at run time if you need it. The link to Ruby and Rails takes you to the page dedicated to the installations you need to perform, as shown in Figure 14-3.

The Ruby and Rails page has a self-explanatory list of the three installations that need to be performed. Make sure that you install in the order presented and note the warning regarding installation directories.

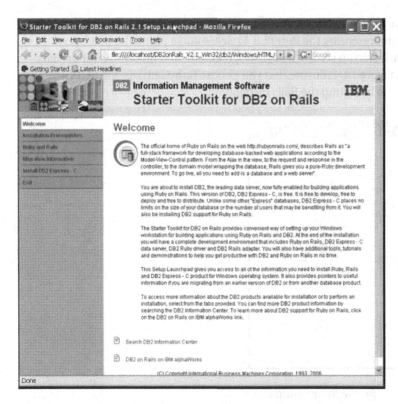

Figure 14-2. *Installer home page for the Starter Toolkit for DB2 on Rails*

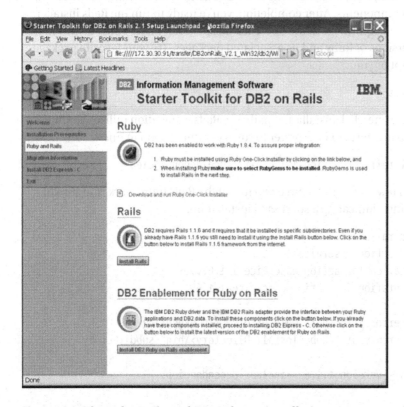

Figure 14-3. *The Ruby, Rails, and DB2 Adapter installation page*

On Windows, start with the Ruby one-click installer, which is 30MB in size. Its name will be similar to ruby184-20, representing the Ruby 1.8.4 release and a particular patch level. It will present a typical splash startup screen, a license agreement, and finally the option selection dialog box shown in Figure 14-4. Ensure that you choose RubyGems as one of the install options because it is used to bootstrap the Rails installation.

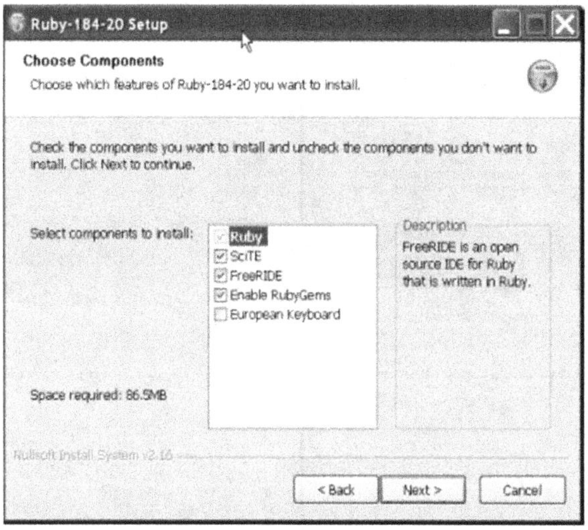

Figure 14-4. *Selecting options for the Ruby installation*

After choosing a location for installation, the Ruby one-click installer starts downloading and installing the Ruby components. After completion, you're ready to run the Rails installer.

Under Linux, there's no equivalent to the one-click installer. But many Linux distributions support prepackaged versions of Ruby and its associated packages. Try your favorite package manager; for example, apt or yum:

```
$ yum install ruby rails
```

If you're following the one-click installation path, the Rails installation utilizes your new Ruby environment, invoking the gem interpreter to run a command akin to this:

```
Executing "gem install rails --version 1.1.6 --include-dependencies"
```

It should take only a few seconds to source and install the Rails framework. You should see output along these lines, indicating a successful installation:

```
Successfully installed rails-1.1.6
Successfully installed actionwebservice-1.1.6
Installing ri documentation for actionwebservice-1.1.6...
Installing RDoc documentation for actionwebservice-1.1.6...

Review the output for errors. If there were errors, try executing
the following command from your "<Ruby Install Directory>\bin" subdirectory:

 gem.bat install rails --version 1.1.6 --include-dependencies.

<Press any key to continue>
```

Finally, you're ready to install the DB2 Ruby driver and DB2 Rails adapter. Again you see a splash screen, license agreement, and directory selection dialog boxes. Follow the defaults; installation will then begin and take approximately one minute.

Developing with Ruby, Rails, and DB2

Let's get straight to it. Instead of rehashing previous examples to show you how Ruby differs in doing identical tasks—which is not much—a better way to get working with Ruby right now is to look at one of its most appealing features for developers and database administrators.

Rails includes a fantastic feature that is slowly making its way into other development environments. The Rails team *knows* that working with real-life projects, databases, and systems involves working on code and data structures that evolve over time. New versions, new features, and even plain old bug fixes mean that things change; and Rails includes a feature loosely called *schema evolution* that addresses the need to make these kinds of changes to your database tables, indexes, and more from directly within your Rails development project.

Schema evolution doesn't just handle the ability to change things in the future; it also percolates all the way down to the Ruby code level, making your code "version-aware" and able to work with different incarnations of your database structures.

Creating a Project with Rails

If you're running on Windows, you might need to reboot to have environment changes take effect. Under Linux, it should be sufficient to start a new shell. The first step in your exploration of Rails, regardless of what you plan to do with it, is to create a project to house your Rails components. This is exactly the same "project" concept you'd find in any other integrated development environment (IDE), so think of it as akin to the previous projects you created in IBM Data Studio.

Open a shell or command line, and change to the directory in which you've installed Ruby and Rails. In my environment, for example, it's c:\ruby. A lot of the work I'm about to cover involves invoking the rails utility and working with many of its options. To start with, try just issuing the command rails to see the available help:

```
C:\ruby>rails
Usage: c:/ruby/bin/rails /path/to/your/app [options]

Options:
    -r, --ruby=path                 Path to the Ruby binary of your choice
      (otherwise scripts use env, dispatchers current path).
                                    Default: c:/ruby/bin/ruby
    -d, --database=name             Preconfigure for selected database
      (options: mysql/oracle/postgresql/sqlite2/sqlite3/ibm_db2).
                                    Default: ibm_db2
    -f, --freeze                    Freeze Rails in vendor/rails from the
      Gems generating the skeleton
                                    Default: false
```

```
General Options:
    -p, --pretend                   Run but do not make any changes.
        --force                     Overwrite files that already exist.
    -s, --skip                      Skip files that already exist.
    -q, --quiet                     Suppress normal output.
    -t, --backtrace                 Debugging: show backtrace on errors.
    -h, --help                      Show this help message.
...
```

You'll learn a bunch of these options as you progress, so I won't linger over options that you can read about and investigate on your own. Creating a project is as simple as providing a name for the */path/to/your/app* argument, which the rails interpreter will examine, determine that there's no existing project of that name, and immediately perform the necessary project-creation steps. You want a project for the employee of the year system, so call it Empofyear:

```
C:\ruby>rails empofyear
      create
      create  app/controllers
      create  app/helpers
      create  app/models
...
```

You'll see about 70-odd lines of create messages scroll past. This is Rails building the framework for the Empofyear project on the fly. Congratulations; you've mastered your first bit of Rails and Ruby, and you actually have some working code already for your project. You should also have an empofyear directory as a subdirectory of the rails directory. In this case, it's c:\ruby\empofyear. Before you look at how your project looks on the web, though, you can add some additional code to wire this up directly to the SAMPLE database.

Connecting a Rails Project to DB2

The project creation for the Empofyear project has created many files. Most of the configuration information required by the project will be stored in the config subdirectory. One of these files is database.yml (the .yml extension is usually pronounced *yamel*, which rhymes with *camel*). This file controls the connection properties for the project.

The default database.yml file includes a default definition for hypothetical development, test, and production databases. At this point, you're interested only in the development database entry. The default configuration appears as follows:

```
# IBM DB2 Database configuration file
#
# Install the IBM DB2 driver and get assistance from:
# http://www.alphaworks.ibm.com/tech/db2onrails
development:
  adapter: ibm_db2
  database: empo_dev
  username: db2admin
  password:
  schema:
```

```
# If connecting through tcp/ip
# uncomment the following two lines
# host:
# port:
```

Note that the # character acts as a comment marker, so there are five active values available under the development heading:

- **adapter**: The Rails adapter name—ibm_db2 in this case

- **database**: The DB2 database name (within the current DB2INSTANCE instance)

- **username**: The authid to use for the connection

- **password**: The password for the authid

- **schema**: An optional explicit schema to use for all object references

You'll immediately spot my favorite bugbear: the plain-text entry for a password. I'll spare you another discourse on why this is poor design. Protect this file using your operating system's security, such as using chmod under Linux to make it readable only by your application server. For your environment, you'll need these settings:

```
adapter: ibm_db2
database: sample
username: fuzzy # ensure you use your AuthID here, not mine.
password: fuzzy # ensure you use your password here, not mine.
schema: fuzzy # use your schema here, not mine.
```

You're now ready to start performing *migrations*, the act of evolving your schema from one incarnation to the next with Ruby on Rails. To actually have something to do, you need to design a table as a starter case for the project.

Designing DB2 Tables in Rails

The employee of the year system is designed to reward your hard-working staff with suitable recognition. One part of that reward, from your original design, is the idea of a prize awarded in a given category. The Prize table is a perfect example for exploring the power of Ruby on Rails with DB2.

If I were to model the Prize table normally for DB2, I'd probably come up with something akin to the definition in Table 14-1.

Table 14-1. *Design of the Prize table*

Attribute	Data Type	Nullability
PrizeID	INTEGER	Not Null
PrizeName	VARCHAR(255)	Not Null
Description	VARCHAR(255)	Nulls allowed
Value	INTEGER	Nulls allowed
Picture	BLOB	Nulls allowed

Normally, I would now write the equivalent SQL to create that table and execute it from a project in Data Studio or from the DB2 CLP or the Command Editor. But I don't need to do that in this case. I'll have Ruby do the work for me and keep track of changes to this structure to boot!

Change the directory into your project directory, which in this case is c:\ruby\empofyear. To have Ruby then take charge of the Prize table, you need to invoke its generate tool and tell it to create a migration for the Prize table. The command and its results look like this:

```
C:\ruby\empofyear>ruby script/generate migration prize_table
      create  db/migrate
      create  db/migrate/001_prize_table.rb
```

You should now find that your project's db folder has a new subfolder called migrate, and within that folder is the file 001_prize_table.rb. This file is the first incarnation of your table, representing its initial state (thus, the 001_* naming style). Right now, the contents of this file are very Spartan. It simply contains the skeleton that must be fleshed out for the first incarnation of the Prize table:

```
class PrizeTable < ActiveRecord::Migration
  def self.up
  end

  def self.down
  end
end
```

To turn this into a working migration, you need this file to encode the attribute definitions needed for creating the table (the self.up action), and the action you want to perform when downgrading (the self.down action). This involves writing a Ruby class to describe the table using Ruby's pseudo-English declarative syntax:

```
class PrizeTable < ActiveRecord::Migration
  def self.up
    create_table :prizes do |t|
      t.column :prizesname, :string, :null  => false
      t.column :description, :string
      t.column :value, :integer
    end
  end

  def self.down
    drop_table :prizes
  end
end
```

If you've scratched your head over that code, wondering why I changed from the singular, Prize, to the plural, Prizes, wonder no more. A strange side effect of working with Ruby on Rails is that it implicitly works with the plural version of the table's name, even though some of the migration and other commands use the singular form. I'm not sure it's clever enough to know about atypical plurals, so if you're ever modeling *bureaux*, you might want to use the incorrect but practical plural form (*bureaus*).

The form of the ActiveRecord class is fairly straightforward if you're familiar with any other object-oriented development language. In this case, PrizeTable is a child class of ActiveRecord. It contains two methods: self.up and self.down, and those methods have functional actions associated with them. For PrizeTable, it is to create a Prizes table with the definition shown when self.up is called and to tear that table down when self.down is called.

If you're observant, you'll see that some things are missing. Where is the definition for the PrizeID column, and where is the definition for the Picture column? Ruby on Rails includes a neat feature in which it always creates a column called ID to act as the primary key for the table. As such, the PrizeID attribute I modeled is redundant, and I'll let Ruby's automatic feature take care of it instead. Be careful about automatically assuming that this is appropriate for your tables and database design because it can lead to proliferation of autogenerated ID columns all over your databases, when in fact they might not be needed at all. These examples won't suffer from their inclusion, but be careful to make sure that you don't give up your design prerogatives in general when dealing with this behavior. As for the Picture attribute, I intentionally left that out so I can show you what a subsequent schema evolution looks like in a later step. Ruby on Rails does include nice features for more elaborate DDL, including managing table placement in tablespaces.

Executing a Migration in Ruby for DB2

With your table definition in place, you're ready to run your migration and have Ruby interpret your project, interrogate the database, and move your schema to the current incarnation. That's a long-winded way of saying that Ruby will create your Prizes table. The command to achieve this is the rake command and it takes the parameter db:migrate to indicate that it should be operating on the specifications in the files under the empofyear/db/migrate directory.

I always thought that the choice of the name *rake* was somewhat Zen-like. I picture a calming Japanese rock garden every time I run this command. I'm not sure this kind of calming influence was what the Ruby developers expected, but it's definitely a bonus for me. The execution of the rake command should look something like this:

```
C:\ruby\empofyear>rake db:migrate
(in C:/ruby/empofyear)
== PrizeTable: migrating =========================================================
-- create_table(:prizes)
   -> 1.7350s
== PrizeTable: migrated (1.7350s) ================================================
```

You can check that your migration completed successfully by opening your favorite DB2 query tool and calling up your schema, or querying the (currently empty) Prizes table.

```
db2 => select * from prizes

ID          PRIZENAME DESCRIPTION VALUE
----------- --------- ----------- -----------

  0 record(s) selected.
```

A table—as if by magic! There's no data in that table yet, but Ruby on Rails has a surprise in store for that as well.

Evolving Your DB2 Schema with Ruby on Rails

Having intentionally left out the `Picture` attribute for the `Prizes` table, it's time for me to amend it and ensure that lucky staff members can see what they've won. Ruby keeps successive changes to a project's schema in successively numbered files in the migration directory. You can give them meaningful names to help self-document your changes as you go. I'll use this command to create the Ruby skeleton for adding the Picture column to the `Prizes` table:

```
C:\ruby\empofyear>ruby script/generate migration prize_table_add_picture
     exists  db/migrate
     create  db/migrate/002_prize_table_add_picture.rb
```

As promised, Ruby has created the skeleton file with the autonumber prefix to help it (and you) keep track of schema versions. You need to edit this file to tell Ruby to add columns when evolving to this schema incarnation and to drop them if devolving back to an earlier incarnation. Here's what the contents of the `002_prize_table_add_picture.rb` file should look like:

```
class PrizeTableAddPicture < ActiveRecord::Migration
  def self.up
    add_column :prizes, :picture, :binary, :limit => 2.megabytes
  end

  def self.down
    remove_column :prizes, :picture
  end
end
```

The steps are quite readable in their Ruby form. When upgrading to this version, add a column called picture, of type binary, with a size limit of 2 megabytes to the `Prizes` table. If you downgrade to lower than this version, remove this column. If you're feeling Zen, it's time to rake again.

```
C:\ruby\empofyear>rake db:migrate
(in C:/ruby/empofyear)
== PrizeTableAddPicture: migrating =========================================
-- add_column(:prizes, :picture, :binary, {:limit=>2097152})
   -> 0.4530s
== PrizeTableAddPicture: migrated (0.4530s) ================================
```

The rake claims to have done the trick, and you can verify it again. I'll use the Control Center to prove the schema has been modified, as shown in Figure 14-5.

You probably guessed that I chose the Control Center because viewing BLOBs (even empty ones) in the DB2 CLP is rather frustrating. Ruby, rake, and the Control Center make this whole experience very Zen-like and calming, indeed.

Figure 14-5. *A view of the Prizes object after the second schema migration with Ruby*

The Schema_Info Table for Ruby on Rails

Running the Control Center wasn't a complete coincidence in the previous example. There's another object to look at, thanks to your use of Ruby on Rails. When you first run a migration with Ruby, it creates a tracking table in your nominated schema so it can keep track of the current incarnation of the database, compared with its migration scripts.

The schema_info table is a very simple table. It has only one column, called version, with an integer data type. Ruby simply uses a single number in this table to correlate with the equivalent migration level from the project. In my Empofyear project, I ran through two migrations, and the schema_info table now looks like this:

```
db2 => select * from schema_info

VERSION
-----------
          2

  1 record(s) selected.
```

Predictable—and also useful if you want to know at what version your current schema is when compared with your project files.

Reverting to Earlier Schema Incarnations

To complete the picture of schema management with Ruby on Rails, it's useful to know how to devolve to earlier incarnations of the schema. The same rake command shown for evolution can be used in reverse. In the case of devolution, an additional parameter called version is used to indicate what incarnation to target. In this example, I want to remove the entire Prizes table, so I chose the theoretical version zero, which is the version representing the state of the system prior to any migrations:

```
C:\ruby\empofyear>rake db:migrate VERSION=0
(in C:/ruby/empofyear)
== PrizeTableAddPicture: reverting ============================================
-- remove_column(:prizes, :picture)
   -> 5.7960s
== PrizeTableAddPicture: reverted (5.8120s) ===================================

== PrizeTable: reverting ======================================================
-- drop_table(:prizes)
   -> 0.3910s
== PrizeTable: reverted (0.4060s) =============================================
```

You can see the self.down actions in motion here, first removing the added picture column and then dropping the Prizes table. I recommend that if you follow this example in your own environment, you proceed to run your migrations again, so that you end up with a complete Prizes table. The rest of this chapter will be less fun without a working Prizes table.

Ruby on Rails Scaffolding for DB2

Having explored the table creation and schema management features of Ruby on Rails for your DB2 world, it's time to turn your attention to how quickly you can get some useful Ruby on Rails code up and running to work with your data structures. It might surprise you to learn that this will be fast. In fact, not just fast, but *very* fast. Through the Rails framework, it will take approximately one line of text to get a working useful environment up and running. You aren't misreading that. I mean one line, and it's not even a line of code. I say approximately one line because if I was pedantic, I would have to say it is two lines. I'll need a second command to start Ruby's own web server to show off the results of the first line.

How is all this possible? Ruby on Rails includes a feature called *scaffolding*, which creates all the classes necessary to enable selecting, inserting, updating, and deleting basic objects such as the prizes in the Prizes table. Naturally, you can then go on to write more sophisticated Ruby code, modifying the scaffolding, to incorporate all kinds of business logic. However, I'll stick to the elements of Ruby on Rails that directly relate to DB2 instead of turning this chapter into a generic Rails tutorial. That would be far too long for the space available.

Generating the Scaffolding

Generating scaffolding relies on the same generate command you used previously, invoked with a scaffold parameter. For the Empofyear project, you can create the scaffolding using this invocation:

```
C:\ruby\empofyear>ruby script/generate scaffold prize
     exists   app/controllers/
     exists   app/helpers/
     create   app/views/prizes
     ...
     create   app/helpers/prizes_helper.rb
     create   app/views/layouts/prizes.rhtml
     create   public/stylesheets/scaffold.css
```

You'll once again see a few dozen lines of output for the create actions of the scaffold invocation. After it completes, you'll have working scaffolding that can be hosted by a web server and used to browse and manage the data for your Prizes table.

Ruby on Rails Scaffolding in Action with DB2

With the scaffolding created for your prizes, you can now see which features are created for you automatically. To do this, you need to start the built-in WEBrick web server that's included with Ruby, which is started by invoking the script/server option with the ruby command:

```
C:\ruby\empofyear>ruby script/server
=> Booting WEBrick...
=> Rails application started on http://0.0.0.0:3000
=> Ctrl-C to shutdown server; call with --help for options
[2008-01-08 22:11:43] INFO  WEBrick 1.3.1
[2008-01-08 22:11:43] INFO  ruby 1.8.4 (2006-04-14) [i386-mswin32]
[2008-01-08 22:11:43] INFO  WEBrick::HTTPServer#start: pid=3120 port=3000
```

WEBrick attempts to communicate on TCP port 3000, but if it is already taken on your system, it tries incremental ports above 3000 until it finds one free. It is worth checking the output of the script/server command to ensure that you know what port is being used (I marked the value in bold in the sample output).

Point your browser to the URL http://localhost:3000/. Be sure you use the correct port if different from 3000. You should see the Ruby on Rails and IBM DB2 Welcome Aboard page, as shown in Figure 14-6.

Figure 14-6. *The Welcome Aboard page for the WEBrick web server for Ruby on Rails*

The Ruby environment is now running the WEBrick server properly. But you're doubtless far more interested to see your Prizes table in action. Navigate to the URL http://localhost:3000/prizes/list; you should see the contents of the Prizes table that is currently empty, as shown in Figure 14-7.

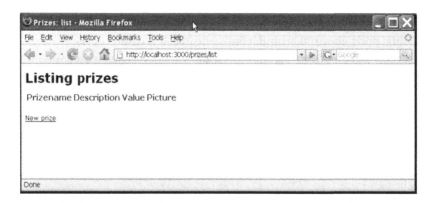

Figure 14-7. *The Prizes table interface via Ruby on Rails scaffolding*

Browse around, follow the links for new items, and so on, and you should get a feel for what the scaffolding offers you for free. Some actions, such as inserting and updating existing rows, require further customization. However, listing values, counting totals, and deleting information are all free. Figure 14-8 shows how the default display logic shows your information for free as you use the Prizes table.

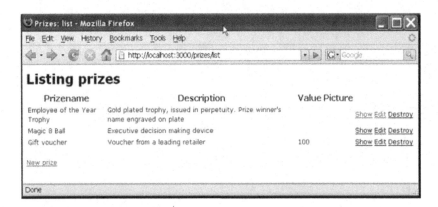

Figure 14-8. *A populated Prizes table interface via Ruby on Rails scaffolding*

Summary

The Starter Toolkit for DB2 on Rails and Ruby on Rails provide some great features for working with your DB2 database. A novel way of creating and managing your database structure is one of the key features of the Rails' way of working. With a simple command line, it's possible to treat your database schema like a time machine, rolling forward and backward through its incarnations.

The Rails scaffolding offers a great way to start building a web interface to your data, without the need to drill right down to the level of application code unless and until you want to customize beyond the default capabilities offered automatically.

Ruby on Rails is a huge topic and its relationship with DB2 is getting stronger. I hope this chapter has set you firmly behind the controls of your own Rails locomotive!

CHAPTER 15

■■■

DB2 Development with Microsoft Visual Studio.NET

When Microsoft releases new operating systems and development environments, one database is first to jump to support them: DB2. I'll bet that's not the database you expected me to name. But it's true. During past releases of Microsoft Windows XP and Microsoft Visual Studio, the first database to be verified by its vendor to be unconditionally supported in those environs has been DB2. Is it any surprise that IBM has made sure that the ability to develop within Visual Studio is as easy as possible for DB2 application developers and database administrators? Windows is a popular development platform, and IBM knows that matching it with arguably the most popular database (certainly by volume of data stored) makes for a knockout combination.

You'll take a tour of the integration offered between DB2 and Visual Studio, and how it lends itself to writing great applications for Windows and the web that harness languages such as C# and ASP.NET. Throughout the chapter, I'll assume that you're more interested in the nuances of DB2 and its capabilities through Visual Studio instead of Visual Studio itself.

Installing IBM Database Add-Ins

When showing you the features and capabilities of many of the other tools that work with DB2, I walked you through the installation in some detail. As you've progressed through database management and development topics, I've cut back on that detail because reading my prose about the joys of clicking buttons called Next is something I think will challenge the stamina of even the most avid reader.

In this chapter, I'll show you how *not* to install the IBM Database Add-Ins for Microsoft Visual Studio 2005. To explain, I haven't come up with some magical method to have the integration components appear on your computer by osmosis or through some quirk of quantum mechanics. Instead, the installation of Visual Studio and IBM Database Add-Ins is so straightforward that there's no need for endless screenshots of license agreements and the like.

What I *will* explain is how to avoid the common pitfalls that prevent you from installing the IBM Database Add-Ins for Microsoft Visual Studio 2005. There are a few finicky steps between installing Visual Studio and later installation of the IBM Database Add-Ins, which if done incorrectly will drive you to distraction and frustrate even the most patient soul.

Let's begin with some assumptions. You need to source Microsoft Visual Studio 2005, Professional Edition or higher, and have it installed. I also recommend the latest Service Pack for Visual Studio from Microsoft, although the IBM Database Add-Ins will operate with the unpatched, or release to manufacturing (RTM), version. At the time of writing, Microsoft is six or more months away from releasing Visual Studio 2008.

While it could be an interesting challenge to attempt installation of the IBM Database Add-Ins with release candidates or beta versions of this new edition of Visual Studio, your chances will improve as the general release of Visual Studio 2008 gets closer. IBM has already listed Visual Studio 2008 as a supported platform for the IBM Database Add-Ins. The examples in this chapter are all predicated on using Visual Studio 2005, but you should be able to generally apply them to Visual Studio 2008 once you have your hands on it.

With Visual Studio 2005 in place, you're almost ready to begin installing the IBM Database Add-Ins for Visual Studio. Remember way back in Chapter 2 when you went through the exercise of using the IBM DB2 Express-C installation Launchpad to install DB2 on your chosen computer? Figure 15-1 recaps the Launchpad installation screen you saw at the time.

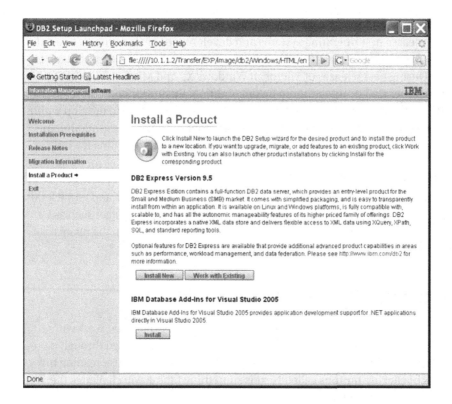

Figure 15-1. *IBM Database Add-Ins installation screen*

That image should jolt your memory. The lower half of the screen includes an enticing Install button for the IBM Database Add-Ins for Microsoft Visual Studio 2005. *Don't click that button!* That's right, I said don't click it—not yet, at least.

Registering the IBM Data Server Provider for .NET

Before the IBM Database Add-Ins can successfully register with Visual Studio's extension framework, the IBM data server provider for .NET must be registered in the .NET framework's machine.config. This provider is usually abbreviated to the DB2 .NET provider. You might already have the DB2 provider installed on your machine, depending on which custom options you choose for installing DB2 in the first place, or if you're using another client machine it might have had the provider registered when the DB2 client was installed. Instead of taking the chance, you'll go ahead and explicitly register the DB2 .NET provider so your IBM Database Add-Ins work perfectly first time.

IBM provides a shortcut for you to register the DB2 .NET provider in your DB2 Set-up Tools program folder. From the All Programs option of the Start folder under Windows, choose IBM DB2 ➤ DB2COPY1 (default) ➤ Set-Up Tools ➤ Configure DB2 .NET Data Provider. This launches a utility that performs the registration task for you. It's nice that the registration of the DB2 .NET provider is neatly encapsulated this way, but one of the drawbacks is that you're given no positive or negative feedback about the process. It will succeed or fail silently. Fortunately, there's an easy option to see the process in action and receive the explicit feedback I prefer.

The Configure DB2 .NET Data Provider program folder shortcut simply invokes the db2nmpsetup.exe utility, located in the Bin directory of your DB2 server or client installation. The program folder shortcut doesn't pass any arguments to the invocation, but the db2nmpsetup.exe utility will take a -l *logfilename* pair of parameters, which in turn gives you much more detail about what happens at registration time for the DB2 .NET provider.

Take my advice. Instead of just running the Start menu shortcut, open a command line and run the utility yourself with the log option:

```
db2nmpsetup.exe -l db2nmpsetup.log
```

You can then review the db2nmpsetup.log file (or whatever name you choose to use for your logging), and see results like these:

```
Tue Jan 1 21:32:25 2008

Start logging ...

The db2 install path is: "C:\Program Files\IBM\SQLLIB"
To register Data Provider into machine.config. The command line is:
"C:\Program Files\IBM\SQLLIB\BIN\db2nmpcfg.exe" -register -level 9.5.0 -db2path
  "C:\Program Files\IBM\SQLLIB" -migratev8
 Return code from db2nmpcfg.exe is: 0
Data Provider is registered to machine.config successfully.

End logging
***************
```

The registration utility calls another executable, db2nmpcfg.exe, with a set of parameters. More importantly, you should see the message that the provider has been registered successfully in the machine.config component of the .NET framework on your computer. This might seem like a long-winded approach to what could otherwise be achieved with the program folder shortcut, but you won't regret it if things go wrong. For instance, without a successful registration, if you return to the DB2 Launchpad and attempt to install the IBM Database Add-Ins, you'll receive this error message:

```
1: ERROR:To install IBM Database Add-Ins for Visual Studio 2005, you must have
 one of the following providers installed:

IBM Data Server Provider for .NET
```

You are now armed with the knowledge required to tackle this error if and when you see it.

Testing DB2 .NET Connectivity

You can now go one step further and ensure that the DB2 .NET provider can locate and connect successfully to your DB2 instance and database. The testconn20.exe utility bundled with DB2 server and client versions is designed to check that all the end-to-end components are in place for operating in a .NET environment. This is also a useful tool to know about when it comes to application deployment because after you build your applications and websites in Visual Studio with IBM Database Add-Ins, you might be deploying your application to computers that don't have these development tools. The testconn20.exe application is invoked as follows:

```
C:\Program Files\IBM\SQLLIB\BIN>testconn20.exe "User ID=fuzzy;Password=fuzzy;
   Database=SAMPLE;Server=localhost;ServerType=db2;pooling=false"
```

The text in quotes is a *connection string* and is used for all .NET database connectivity, not just for DB2. In this case, the options should be self-explanatory. Simply replace my user name and password with the ones appropriate for your system. The output of a successful connection attempt looks as follows:

```
Step 1: Printing version info
        .NET Framework version: 2.0.50727.42
        DB2 .NET provider version: 9.0.0.2
        Capability bits: ALLDEFINED
        Build: 20070524
        Factory for invairant name IBM.Data.DB2 verified
        Elapsed: 7.15625


Step 2: Connecting using "User ID=fuzzy;Password=fuzzy;Database=SAMPLE;
Server=localhost;ServerType=db2;pooling=false"
        Server type and version: DB2/NT 09.05.0000
        Elapsed: 4.640625


Step 3: Selecting rows from SYSIBM.SYSTABLES to validate existence of packages
   SELECT * FROM SYSIBM.SYSTABLES FETCH FIRST 5 rows only
        Elapsed: 0.890625
```

```
Step 4: Calling GetSchema for tables to validate existence of schema functions
        Elapsed: 1.78125
```

Test passed.

The most-common problems you'll encounter are likely to be incorrect user name or password, or no registered DB2 .NET provider. The error in the latter case appears as follows:

```
Could not load file or assembly 'IBM.Data.DB2, Version=9.0.0.2, Culture=neutral,
 PublicKeyToken=7c307b91aa1 3d208' or one of its dependencies.
 The system cannot find the file specified.
```

You might also encounter an error in which multiple DB2 copies are present, but your current default DB2 copy doesn't have the .NET provider available, or it has an older version. In these circumstances, the Default IBM and DB2 Default Client Interface Selection Wizard, db2swtchg.exe, can be used to point to your desired DB2 copy. The steps earlier in this chapter show you how to deal with the case of an unregistered DB2 .NET provider.

Completing the Installation

With the DB2 .NET provider installed, registered, and tested, you are now ready to complete the installation of the IBM Database Add-Ins for Microsoft Visual Studio. The installation requires that all DB2 components installed on a machine, and any other software such as IIS or Apache that might have loaded those components, be stopped for the duration. You needn't do this up front, but the installer will prompt you to halt numerous processes halfway through its work if you don't.

Now you're ready to press that Install button from Figure 15-1! Run the DB2 Launchpad (just as you did in Chapter 2) and begin. If you haven't kept the full installation source for DB2 handy, don't fret. You can also download the Visual Studio Add-In installer, vsai.exe, from the IBM download site for DB2. You'll see the normal array of boring installation screens, starting with a splash screen, a license to which you must agree, installation location on disk, and a confirmation screen. When installation is complete, don't forget to restart your DB2 database and other components if they were stopped on this computer prior to or during installation.

Testing the Database Add-Ins

Now that you've gone to the effort of ensuring a smooth installation for the IBM Database Add-Ins, it would be nice to see the fruits of your labor. Get started by launching Visual Studio. If you pay careful attention, you'll notice that as the splash screen flies by, it has an extra item in its component list: IBM Database Add-Ins. Thankfully, you don't have to rely on your reflexes. As soon as Visual Studio starts, you should see all the hallmarks of the add-ins in your working environment. For instance, the Tools menu will now include a top-level IBM DB2 Tools folder, containing links to the DB2 Control Center, the Command Editor, and so on. The Help menu includes a direct link to check for DB2 updates.

Most telling of all, however, is a new project type available to you. Follow the File ➤ New ➤ Project menu. The resulting New Project dialog box, as shown in Figure 15-2, includes a new IBM Projects project type and a subordinate DB2 Database Project template.

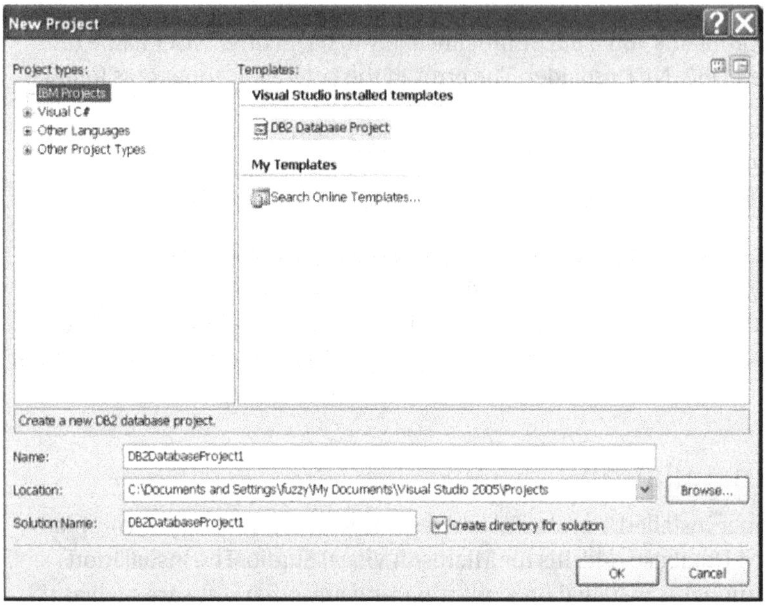

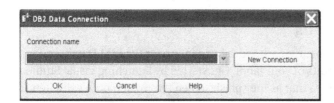

Figure 15-2. *Creating a new DB2 Database Project in Visual Studio*

Depending on the vintage of your installation, you might see IBM Database Project as the template name. It's just a cosmetic change and is functionally almost identical, so don't fret. Choose a meaningful project name (or accept the default: DB2DatabaseProject1) and click OK. Visual Studio generates all the skeleton files for your project, and the IBM Database Add-Ins kick in immediately to help you configure a connection to the DB2 database for your project. Figure 15-3 shows the DB2 Data Connection dialog box, which lets you select a previously configured connection or allows you to define a new one for your project.

Figure 15-3. *DB2 Data Connection definition for a DB2 Database Project*

Because this is the first project you created, there are no existing connections from which to choose, so go ahead and click New Connection to define one. The Choose Data Source dialog box appears, as shown in Figure 15-4.

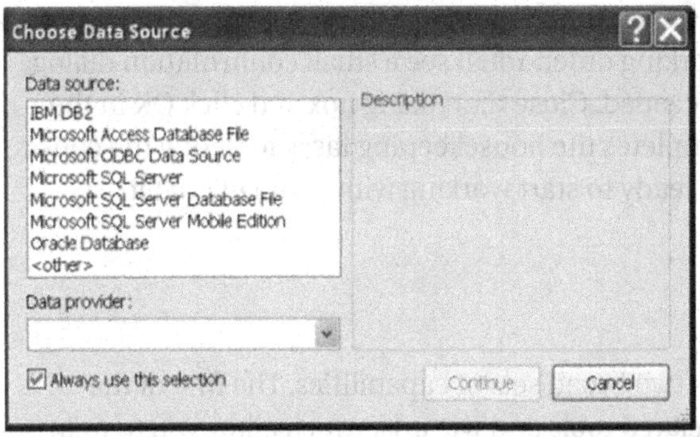

Figure 15-4. *Data Source selection for a project's connection*

This dialog box has a slightly misleading title. Strictly speaking, you're not selecting a data source. Instead, you're selecting the inferred data source type based on the underlying .NET provider (whose name isn't shown). For the purposes of a DB2 Database Project, you'll almost always want to select IBM DB2 here, although there are other options that you'll explore toward the end of this chapter. With IBM DB2 selected, click Continue. The Add Connection dialog box, shown in Figure 15-5, appears.

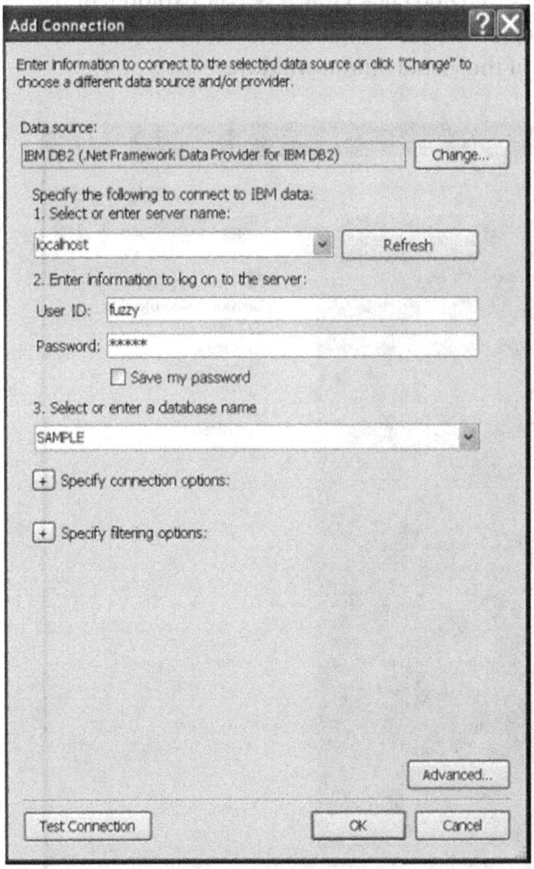

Figure 15-5. *The Add Connection dialog box for a project's connection to DB2*

Once you're happy with the credentials and other details, use the Test Connection button, which is provided to ensure that all is in working order. You'll see a small confirmation dialog box appear that reads Test Connection Succeeded. Close that dialog box and click OK in the Add Connection dialog box; the wizard completes the housekeeping tasks to define the connection object for your project. You're now ready to start working with your DB2 database.

Managing DB2 Objects

The integration with Visual Studio provides two broad sets of capabilities. The first of the capability sets is the Server Explorer with related tools and wizards, which allow you to manage DB2 tables, views, indexes, stored procedures, XML schema, and other members of the DB2 family of database objects. At this point, you're probably thinking that the last thing you need is yet another tool for managing your database. However, when used in conjunction with the second area of capability provided by the Add-Ins—application development for .NET languages—developers can manage all their work for a given development project with DB2 from one central location. In this way IBM ensures that no matter what type of development you want to undertake, you should be able to perform all the tasks of development from the integrated development environment (IDE) or tool of your choice: Visual Studio.

To start working with the Server Explorer, ensure that the IBM DB2 Data Project you created earlier in this chapter is open in Visual Studio. Then click View ➤ Server Explorer, or use the keyboard shortcut Ctrl+W, L to open the Server Explorer. Figure 15-6 shows the Server Explorer's default view, pinned to the left side of the Visual Studio window.

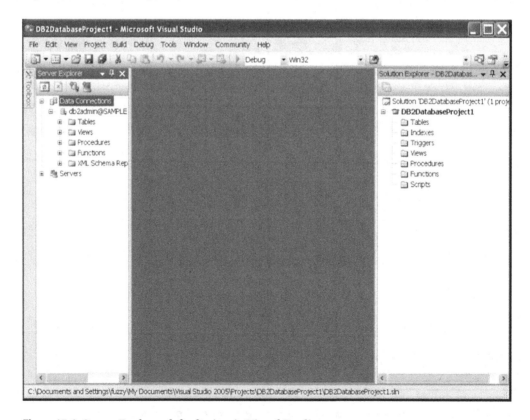

Figure 15-6. *Server Explorer default view in Visual Studio*

The Server Explorer allows you to browse the objects in your DB2 database much as you would with the Control Center. It does this within the context of the permissions for the defined connection, so you'll see those tables, views, and other objects to which the authid for the connection has access. Expand the tables folder and you'll see all the tables with which you've already been working in the SAMPLE database for the employee of the year project. Choose a table such as EMP_VOTES and right-click to see a range of familiar options. These options include the ability to explore the table definition, generate data definition language (DDL) SQL, and view the current contents. There are also two options specific to the IBM Database Add-Ins: Generate Web Methods and Deploy IBM Web Service, covered in the next section.

The DB2DatabaseProject1 project is a DB2 Database Project designed to let you manage the objects within your database. On the right pane of the window, the project solution tree includes folders for each of the types of objects you can manage. From any of these object types, such as tables, stored procedures, and views, you can right-click and choose Add ➤ New Item to launch the new item wizard.

■**Note** It doesn't really matter which folder you pick first because the first screen of the wizard allows you to switch your choice between table, view, and so on.

Creating a New DB2 View Object

You'll create a new view to fulfill the project's need to show a summary of current voting. You'll use this view in the latter sections of this chapter on Windows and web form programming, so you'd better get it right. Select the View folder, right-click, and choose Add ➤ New Item. The first screen of the Add New Item Wizard appears (see Figure 15-7).

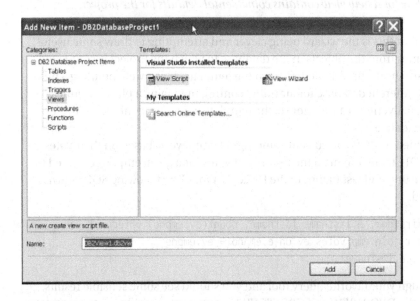

Figure 15-7. *The Add New Item Wizard for DB2 Database Projects in Visual Studio*

Choose the View Script option and a meaningful name for the script file. After a brief moment of processing, Visual Studio presents you with the new script, complete with ready-made template SQL for creating the new view (see Figure 15-8). Confusingly, the SQL for the view template uses objects such as NAME, DEPARTMENT, ID, and so forth.

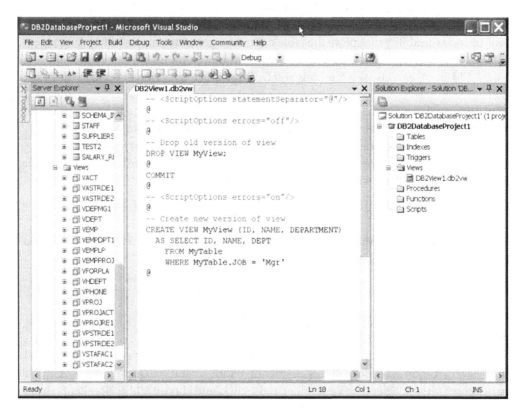

Figure 15-8. *The template for a new view contains coincidental defaults for the project.*

You might think that this is the wizard being clever and attempting to draw some useful table and column names from the objects in the database to which the project is connected. Unfortunately, they are simply hard-coded items in the template. If you were building a new view on a completely different database for air traffic control, managing a pharmaceutical company, or tracking deliveries to a warehouse, the template would be identical. So these names are just a coincidence.

The view is designed to show the current standings of employees, based on their votes recorded in the EMP_VOTE table. You need the number of votes for a given employee, joined to their human-readable first and last names in the EMPLOYEE table. The following SQL returns exactly what you need:

```
select e.firstnme firstnme, e.lastname lastname, count(ev.empno) votecount
from employee e inner join emp_votes ev on e.empno = ev.empno
group by e.firstnme, e.lastname
```

Try that out through your favorite query tool and you should see some sensible results. Now you can replace the DROP VIEW and CREATE VIEW statements provided in the template with the relevant commands for your project. Call this view Emp_Vote_Standings, which means that the full set of SQL and comments in the new view should be as follows:

```
-- <ScriptOptions statementSeparator="@"/>
@
-- <ScriptOptions errors="off"/>
@
-- Drop old version of view
DROP VIEW Emp_Vote_Standings;
@
COMMIT
@
-- <ScriptOptions errors="on"/>
@
-- Create new version of view
CREATE VIEW Emp_Vote_Standings (FIRSTNAME, LASTNAME, VOTECOUNT)
as
 select e.firstnme firstnme, e.lastname lastname, count(ev.empno) votecount
 from employee e inner join emp_votes ev on e.empno = ev.empno
 group by e.firstnme, e.lastname
@
```

Building the DB2 Database Project

You're ready to build your project. For a DB2 Database Project, the act of building the project executes all the SQL statements included in the various project files. So by choosing the build option in Visual Studio, the view should be created. Go ahead and build your project now and watch the results in the Output message pane in the lower-left corner of the Visual Studio window. My Output pane looks like this:

```
---- Build started: Project: DB2DatabaseProject1, Configuration: Debug Win32 ----
Compiling...
DB2View1.db2vw
Succeeded
========== Build: 1 succeeded, 0 failed, 0 up-to-date, 0 skipped ==========
```

If you have a problem, the succeeded line will be replaced by a line that reads as follows:

```
Refer to the 'IBM DB2 Output Message Pane' for additional information.
```

You can access the IBM DB2 Output Message Pane at any time, by selecting it from the Show Output From drop-down list in the Output pane. You can even do this when your build succeeds to get more information about what transpired for your build. In the case of the successful build for the Emp_Vote_Standings view, the IBM DB2 Output message pane reads as follows:

```
Executing Script.
Executing SQL:DROP VIEW Emp_Vote_Standings;
Error occurred: ERROR [42704] [IBM][DB2/NT] SQL0204N  "FUZZY.EMP_VOTE_STANDINGS"
 is an undefined name.  SQLSTATE=42704
```

```
: IBM.Data.DB2: -2147467259
O: Error occurred: [IBM][DB2/NT] SQL0204N  "FUZZY.EMP_VOTE_STANDINGS"
 is an undefined name.  SQLSTATE=42704
: -204: IBM.Data.DB2: 42704
Executing SQL:COMMIT
Executing SQL:CREATE VIEW Emp_Vote_Standings (FIRSTNAME, LASTNAME, VOTECOUNT)
as
 select e.firstnme firstnme, e.lastname lastname, count(ev.empno) votecount
 from employee e inner join emp_votes ev on e.empno = ev.empno
 group by e.firstnme, e.lastname
Successfully completed execution.
```

Interestingly, you'll note several errors in the supposedly successful build that relate to the DROP VIEW Emp_Vote_Standings command in the script. The first time you build your project (and therefore the first time the script is run), this view almost certainly won't exist unless you manually created it via another tool. However, note the two SQL comments that precede and follow the DROP VIEW statement. While they are treated as comments by DB2, the actual text of the comment is interpreted by Visual Studio and the IBM Database Add-Ins, thanks to the double leading dashes. You probably can guess that the ScriptOptions errors="off" comment tells Visual Studio to ignore errors, thus enabling it to trap and ignore the failure of the DROP VIEW statement. Similarly, the ScriptOptions errors="on" comment instructs Visual Studio to start paying attention to errors again.

You can make explicit use of these script option comments, and others such as the statementSeparator="@" option, anywhere you see fit in your DB2 Database Project scripts. Your view is now alive and kicking! Let's use this view as the basis for exploring the other capabilities of the IBM Database Add-Ins for Microsoft Visual Studio: building Windows and web applications wired up to DB2.

Building .NET Windows Applications with DB2

Building .NET applications for the Windows environment is naturally very easy with Visual Studio. The IBM Database Add-Ins extend this ease to include wiring your Windows applications to your DB2 database. A range of graphical user interfaces (GUIs) and wizards can make this process so simple that no actual coding is required. The classes and concepts that drive this ease are also exposed for you to work with at the code level, so you can customize and craft sophisticated applications to work exactly as you want.

To get started, create a new project in Visual Studio and choose a Visual C# Windows Application as the template. Give your project a meaningful name (along the lines of WindowsDB2Application1 or a similar name). Click OK; Visual Studio will spend a few minutes putting together the solution file, templates, and skeleton files for your new C# project. When it's done, you'll be at the familiar blank Form1 canvas that is the basis of every new Windows C# application.

Binding DB2 Objects to Windows Controls

To bring the Windows application to life, I want to display the current standings in voting for employee of the year on a grid on my form. From the toolbox, I selected a DataGridView and dropped it on my form, as shown in Figure 15-9.

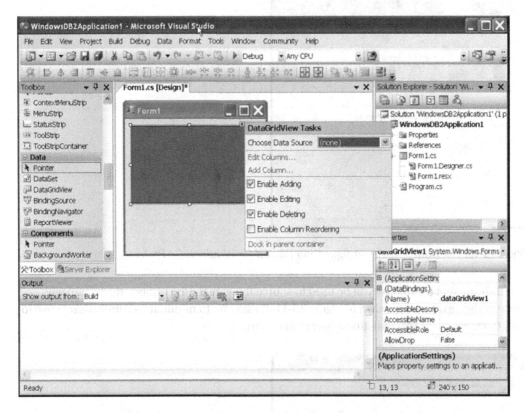

Figure 15-9. *Sample DataGridView for presenting data from a DB2 database*

The DataGridView is not currently connected to any data source, so I need to select the Choose Data Source drop-down list, at which point I'm presented with the option to add a project data source for this project. A friendly pointer if you're unfamiliar with Visual Studio: the Choose Data Source drop-down list is activated by the minuscule little arrow you see at the top of the DataGrid control.

Specifying a DB2 Connection for a Windows C# Project

Clicking the Choose Data Source link initiates the Data Source Configuration Wizard shown in Figure 15-10.

Figure 15-10. *The Data Source Configuration Wizard for Windows C# Projects*

Indicate that a database will be used to source the data for the project; the wizard will move to the next screen, shown in Figure 15-11. It asks you to nominate a connection to use to your database or for you to define a new connection.

Figure 15-11. *Selecting an existing or new connection for Windows C# projects*

Naturally, the connection defined for the early DB2 Database Project is available for use. You must specify whether "sensitive" information will be included in the connection string. In plain English, this is asking whether you want the password for the connection to be included in the connection string, which will be in plain text in the source file for your project. By now you know my feeling on strong security, so in a production environment you would choose not to include this sensitive information in the connection string. For this example, you'll allow it so that you can focus on the tools and outcomes.

By choosing this option, you're then presented with the dialog box shown in Figure 15-12, which allows you to move the connection string to a specific configuration file. This enables you to change connection details in isolation from the other code, which means you could point your application at another database and/or schema, or use different login credentials, without having to rebuild your application.

Figure 15-12. *Using a configuration file for connection string settings*

Finally you're asked what database objects you want to make available via this connection object. You can choose as many or as few tables, views, and other objects as you want. Typically you'll choose most (if not all) your objects because this connection can be reused by all the controls and logic you deploy in your application. You would normally restrict what's available only to add another layer of protection to some objects. However, this isn't a substitute for proper authorization and privilege management (covered in Chapters 9 and 10). In Figure 15-13, I chose the Emp_Vote_Standings view created earlier.

Figure 15-13. *Specifying objects available via a database connection in Visual Studio*

Clicking Finish completes the process of defining the connection.

Exploring a Connection's Related Objects

With the database connection defined for your project, you'll notice a few changes. Not only does your DataGridView now appear to know about your DB2 Emp_Vote_Standings view but three new objects have also sprung to life on the IDE canvas: a DataSet object, a TableAdapter object, and a BindingSource adapter. If you're familiar with database development in Visual Studio, you'll have a firm grounding in the purpose of each of them; if you're new to both DB2 and Visual Studio, a quick explanation is in order.

The BindingSource object is an abstraction layer that sits between the application and all the database objects selected for use through the defined connection. By acting as an intermediary layer, the BindingSource object allows you to wire your controls to your data at a logical level while providing the ability to redirect the underlying physical source of data to a different schema, database, or even a different server. All this is made possible without having to change the properties of any of your user interface (UI) objects.

The DataSet object acts as a temporary staging resource for the source data. Your .NET application enables people to work with the data in the DataSet object—browsing, changing, adding and removing values—without needing to persist each of these changes individually to DB2. When a user or application has finished manipulating the data in the DataSet object, a single method call can be used to synchronize all the net changes to DB2 in one go and using only one transaction.

The TableAdapter object acts as the work horse behind the scenes for the DataSet object. A TableAdapter object includes definitions for all the necessary insert, update, delete, and select statements required to process data changes to an underlying table. A TableAdapter object can also be extended to handle customized actions for various logical changes to your data. This kind of customization takes you well into the realm of Visual Studio development instead of DB2, so I'll leave that topic for another book.

Building and Running the Windows Project

You're ready to build and run your project, but you haven't typed a line of C#. That's one of the key points of the IBM Database Add-Ins, and you're experiencing one of its key goals in being able to develop quickly without being bogged down in the minutiae of C# coding.

You can either build your solution immediately (F6 if you've chosen C# key bindings) or start in debugging mode (F5) to see your application in action. If you've followed along to this point, you shouldn't encounter any build errors, and your application should appear as mine does in Figure 15-14.

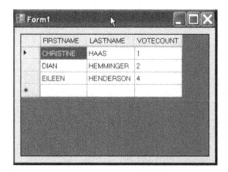

Figure 15-14. *Building and running the completed application*

Naturally, the actual data you see in the DataGridView will be affected, depending on how many votes you registered in your own database. Nevertheless, you should see something.

Building .NET Web Applications with DB2

Having mastered the art of building a Windows application with the IBM Database Add-Ins and DB2, it won't surprise you to learn that building an equivalent web-based application is even easier. The same facilities that provide simple wiring of code, objects, and databases are available in ASP.NET, with web-specific wizards in Visual Studio to help you out.

To get started building a web interface to the vote standings for employee of the year, choose File ➤ New ➤ Web Site in Visual Studio. From the resulting New Web Site screen, choose the ASP.NET Web Site template and give your new project a meaningful name such as **DB2WebSite1**. Your new project will be created and you'll be presented with a skeleton for the default.aspx page that will form the basis of your new website.

Switch to Designer view in Visual Studio and add a title text box with some meaningful text, such as **Current Standings in Employee of the Year**. You can then choose a data control to show the data available through the Emp_Vote_Standings view, just as you did with the DataGridView in the C# Windows applications example. In the ASP.NET case, choose a Grid-View data control and drop it on your website canvas. Your prototype page should look roughly like the one shown in Figure 15-15.

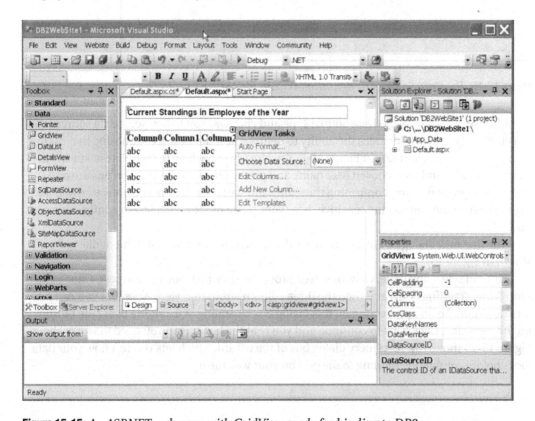

Figure 15-15. *An ASP.NET web page with GridView ready for binding to DB2*

Binding DB2 Objects to Web Controls

That sense of déjà vu you're feeling is warranted because the process of laying out controls on the web canvas and binding supporting data objects to them is analogous to the process for Windows forms. In this case, click the Data Source drop-down list and choose New Data Source. You'll see the Data Source Configuration Wizard (see Figure 15-16).

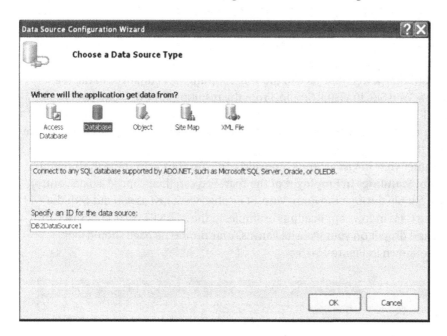

Figure 15-16. *The Data Source Configuration Wizard for ASP.NET projects*

Choose Database as the Data Source Type and click OK. You'll then see a data source selection screen, which includes the ability to define a new data source. Choosing that option brings up the screen you saw in Figure 15-5. You already know how to complete it: specify the SAMPLE database and your chosen user name and password. The following screens are also identical to previous ones, confirming the shorthand name for your new connection and asking your preference for storing sensitive data (your password) in the relevant configuration file.

The first new dialog box in the wizard is the Configure The Select Statement dialog box, shown in Figure 15-17.

You can select any table, view, or stored procedure to which you have access. Choose the Emp_Vote_Standings view and then the three columns from that view. Note that you can perform additional query processing on this dialog box by adding SQL criteria using the buttons on the right side. Click Next to continue and you're at the last screen you need to worry about. Figure 15-18 shows the Test Query dialog box of the wizard, which lets you test how your data looks before completing binding to the grid on your web form.

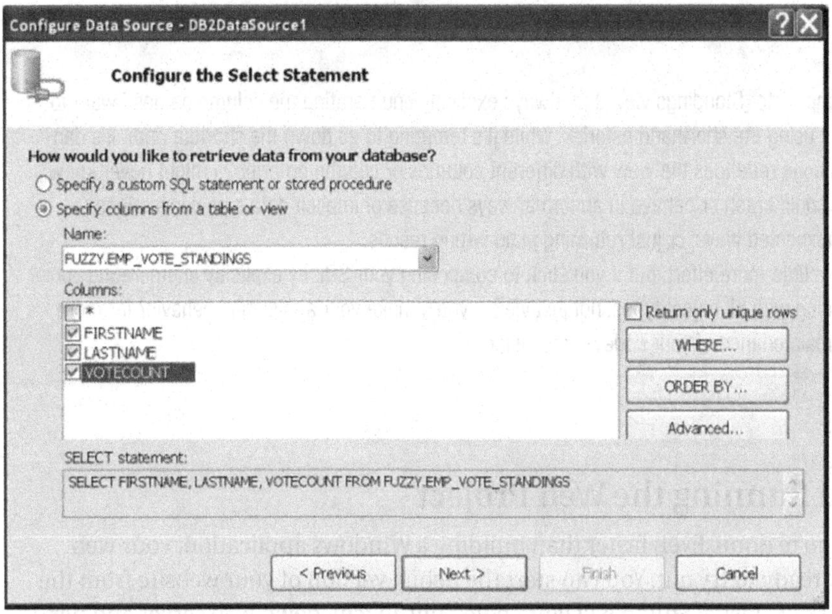

Figure 15-17. *Configuring the select statement for your ASP.NET data binding*

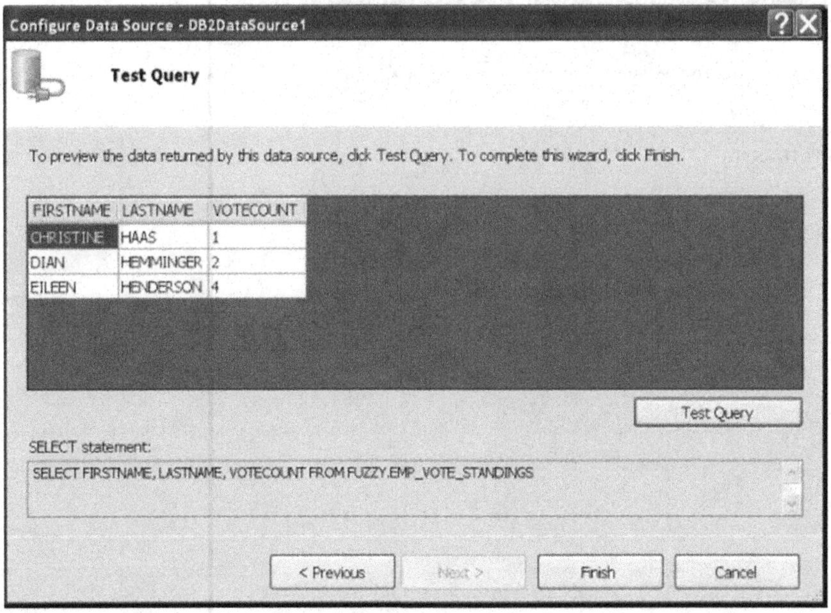

Figure 15-18. *Testing the results of the ASP.NET data binding*

Assuming that your results look acceptable, and no error is presented, click Finish to complete the wizard's work.

ENUMERATING COLUMNS IN SQL

When I query my Emp_Vote_Standings view, I'm always explicitly enumerating the column names I want to work with instead of using the shorthand asterisk. While it's tempting to go down the shortcut path, it's dangerous. What if someone redefines the view with different columns or column ordering? I might never know, and my application could crash or behave in abnormal ways because of implicit data type conversions, exposing data in unexpected ways, or just returning plain wrong results.

It might seem a little more effort, but if you stick to composing your SQL by explicitly enumerating your columns when working with all object types, not just views, you'll make your application behavior far more reliable and future maintenance of your code much easier.

Building and Running the Web Project

Believe it or not, you're done. Even faster than building a Windows application, your web application is now ready to try out. You can start the debug version of your website from the menu or just choose F5. Visual Studio will launch its built-in, cut-down web server and perform all the magic to present your finished product. It should look similar to the browser window shown in Figure 15-19.

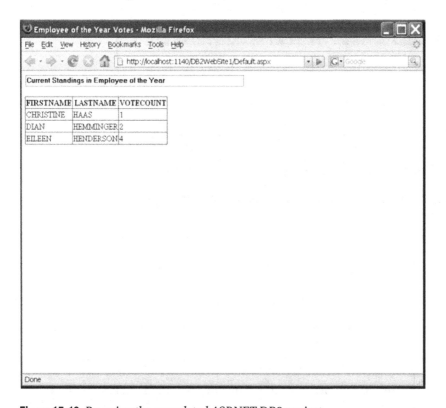

Figure 15-19. *Running the completed ASP.NET DB2 project*

You'll notice two things immediately. First, it worked! Your data is now live on the web, and your users now have the choice of monitoring the voting either via a Windows application or a website. Second, I am no great loss to the graphic design industry. My website design is a little plain, but I'm sure your imagination is brimming with possibilities here.

Summary

By this point in the chapter, you're probably struggling with the wide variety of options the IBM Database Add-Ins for Microsoft Visual Studio provides you in your development work. Whether it's building and managing objects within a DB2 database, or designing quick and easy-to-use Windows applications and websites to work with your data, there's sure to be something that's grabbed your attention. And you've just scratched the surface. With the examples you've now built, you can return and add more features and functionality—and leverage more of the DB2 database—as and when you need to.

IBM has consistently updated the IBM Database Add-Ins as Visual Studio evolves, so be sure to keep your eye out for new versions to match future versions of Visual Studio.

CHAPTER 16

■ ■ ■

Developing Java Applications with DB2

The realm of developing Java applications is a truly huge domain. As one of the premier development languages in use today, you'd expect nothing less. When it comes to developing Java applications with DB2, there are tools and techniques to suit every possibility, from the smallest utility to the largest enterprise application.

Java development with DB2 can be grouped into several major areas, each offering something for the avid Java developer. Traditional Java development—from "plain old Java objects" through to Java Enterprise edition (historically called J2EE)—benefits from DB2's long standing support for JDBC, the Java Database Connectivity (JDBC) APIs, and associated drivers and libraries such as SQLJ for static embedded SQL. Database purists are spoiled by the Java stored procedure capabilities of DB2, allowing all procedural and application logic to be stored in DB2, along with data. As if all that weren't enough, with the introduction of DB2 9, IBM released the power of pureQuery, allowing you to seamlessly blend Java with static and dynamic SQL in one easy-to-use framework.

I'll cover all four of these Java and DB2 combinations in this chapter, allowing you to pick a few favorites by the end. To wrap up this introduction, welcome back to you readers who were so keen to get to the Java chapter that you skipped the previous chapter on .NET.

CHOOSING YOUR JAVA DEVELOPMENT TOOLS

For all the examples in this chapter (up to but not including the pureQuery work), the choice of Java development environment is really up to you. You can use the latest and greatest incarnation of Eclipse, use your preferred alternative (perhaps even one you craft yourself), or even take the venerable approach of using a text editor and the javac command-line compiler.

That said, if you've followed the examples in the book to this point, you already installed one of the best Java development environments to be had: Eclipse-based IBM Data Studio. I recommend giving it a try for the exercises in this chapter. If it's not already your favorite development tool, it will be by the time you're done.

Writing JDBC Applications for DB2

JDBC was one of the earliest technologies designed for Java database development. Sun modeled much of the initial design along the lines of other popular APIs for database work, such as Open Database Connectivity (ODBC), DB2 CLI, and so on. So the concepts of connection objects, command/query objects, result sets, and so forth translate quite easily across technologies. JDBC took the technology further in its capability to cater for a variety of client installations (and "clientless" installations) through the concept of different *types* of JDBC drivers.

JDBC Driver Types

Sun's original JDBC design and specification allowed for 4 types of JDBC implementation, categorized into JDBC types 1 though 4:

- **JDBC type 1 driver**: A type 1 driver acts as a wrapper layer over the top of some other database interface or binding layer. The most common implementation of JDBC type 1 is the JDBC-ODBC Bridge Driver. This driver allows a very generic JDBC driver to operate with any underlying ODBC implementation, but it suffers from the varying support for ODBC (and other database-binding technologies) offered by respective vendors. There is no native DB2 JDBC type 1 driver available from IBM, and I recommend against using this driver in any of your projects.

- **JDBC type 2 driver**: A type 2 driver is built as a direct interface into a native database API. In the case of DB2 for Linux, UNIX, and Windows, the DB2 JDBC type 2 driver maps directly to the core DB2 CLI. This makes it a "first-class citizen" for binding to DB2 databases. IBM makes JDBC type 2 drivers for all supported DB2 platforms, and they are usually bundled with all server and client installations.

- **JDBC type 3 driver**: A type 3 driver is implemented solely in Java. It uses an intermediary component—usually a middleware server of some form—to proxy requests to the underlying database. In much the same fashion as a type 1 driver, the type 3 driver allows for a very generic implementation across all types of databases, but has the same drawback in relying on the capabilities of another component for completeness of functionality.

- **JDBC type 4 driver**: A type 4 driver is also implemented entirely in Java, but is designed to work with the native protocol of a particular database. IBM makes a JDBC type 4 driver for DB2, which it now calls the Universal JDBC driver. This is actually a unified driver that is capable of working with any database offered by IBM in the DB2 family, including iSeries and z/OS versions of DB2. It even works with Derby—the open source, in-memory database formerly known as Cloudscape.

For many years, the de facto standard when working with JDBC was a type 2 driver. This was a practical trade-off between the design purity of a clientless, all-Java-style type 4 driver and the reality of the performance edge that type 2 drivers had (thanks to their leverage of native libraries, compiled components, and so on). Type 4 drivers are now on the ascendance with the ongoing effects of Moore's law on CPU power and speed, the rise of broadband and fast networks, and the maturity of just-in-time compilation for Java.

As you might expect of a mature development API such as JDBC, the choice of driver type can be made at run time. Typically, JDBC driver choice is dependent on a URL string, and it can be parameterized to give you maximum flexibility in deployment. You'll look at the details of JDBC connection URLs in the first examples that follow. If you're interested in relating directly to the underlying classes, IBM packages the Universal JDBC driver in the class com.ibm.db2.jcc.DB2Driver.

Writing the First Java DB2 Application

Writing Java applications will be familiar to experienced Java developers. I don't plan to take you through a tedious introductory tutorial on Java because it's exhaustively covered in many other books and on various websites. I'll focus instead on ensuring that you have the basic mechanics for DB2 connection management and query processing covered, and then highlight the specific features available with DB2's JDBC implementation.

Before diving in to the first example, it's worth highlighting the minimum Java and JDK versions that are required for using the DB2 Universal JDBC driver and for general compilation of Java programs. At a minimum, you'll need the 1.4.2 version of the JDK to compile Java programs. The IBM full client and server installation actually bundles version 1.5, so that easily meets the requirement. If you want to use new features from the JDBC 4.0 standard, you'll need the Java6 software development kit (SDK). When deploying any applications (instead of compiling or debugging them), it's sufficient to use the equivalent Java run time.

In the first example, in which the main class is JavaDB2ex1, you can see the basic technique for defining a connection object, providing its required connection parameters, and invoking the getConnection method:

```java
import java.sql.*;

public class JavaDB2ex1
{
  public static void main(String[] args)
  {
    try
    {
      // First attempt to load the DB2 JDBC driver
      Class.forName("com.ibm.db2.jcc.DB2Driver");

      // Now make a new connection object, and pass your DB2 details
      Connection myDB2conn = DriverManager.getConnection(
        "jdbc:db2://localhost:50000/sample","db2admin","PasswOrd");

      // Test your connection explicitly using a connection property
      if ( myDB2conn.isClosed())
      {
      System.out.println("No Connection. Check exceptions & stack trace");
      }
      else
      {
        System.out.println("Connected! Your DB2 JDBC code is working");
```

```
      }

      // clean up connection
      myDB2conn.close();
    }
    catch (ClassNotFoundException ex)
    {
      ex.printStackTrace();
    }
    catch (SQLException sql_ex)
    {
      sql_ex.printStackTrace();
    }
  }
}
```

The main objects of note include the connection object, generated by the DriverManager; and the Class.forName invocation, which ensures that the relevant JDBC driver can be found and loaded for the application.

Required CLASSPATH Inclusions or Imports

Before your project builds, you need to ensure that you include the necessary .jar and .zip archives for the basic JDBC and related classes in your project's library build path. If you're using a command-line environment, your CLASSPATH environment variable usually takes care of this. If you source the db2profile script under Linux, or run the db2cmd environment under Windows, it is done automatically. The class files in question are usually common.jar, db2java.zip, db2cc.jar, and db2cc_license_cu.jar. You'll find these libraries in the default java directory of your DB2 installation, which by default is /opt/IBM/db2/V9.5/java under Linux and C:\Program Files\IBM\SQLLIB\java under Windows.

Unless you like typing inordinately long class names, you'll almost certainly want to include the java.sql.* import for your code (as in the JavaDB2ex1 example).

JDBC Connection URL

In the JavaDB2ex1 example, you can see that the connection is specified with the following URL:

jdbc:db2://localhost:50000/sample

This form of URL implicitly causes the loading and use of a JDBC type 4 driver. The general form of the type 4 URL is as follows:

jdbc:db2://hostname:port/database_name

In the JavaDB2ex1 example, the call to the getConnection method also explicitly passes literal user name and password strings. Not the most secure or flexible approach, so I'll tidy that up in the next example.

The alternative JDBC URL available to you for DB2 is the kind that invokes the type 2 driver. In general, the type 2 URL invocation is as follows:

```
jdbc:db2:catalogued_db_name
```

Because the type 2 driver in turn leverages the underlying DB2 client on the machine executing the Java code, the cataloged alias for a database is used. Naturally, there's nothing stopping this alias being identical to the actual database name.

Refactoring the Connection Code

Now that the basics of connections are understood, let's move immediately to turning your DB2 Java development into a robust, secure, and flexible technique. Instead of having to hard code connections and associated credentials into every application you write, you can refactor the code to build a generic connection management class. You want methods that let you create a new connection based on credentials provided and close existing connections cleanly. The following ConnMgr class example is a good starting point to show you how you can begin your own connection management class:

```java
import java.sql.*;

public class ConnMgr
{
  // A method for making new connections
  public static Connection openConnection(
    String username, String password, String connURL)
  {
    Connection myConn=null;

    try
    {
      Class.forName("com.ibm.db2.jcc.DB2Driver");
      myConn = DriverManager.getConnection(connURL, username, password);
    }
    catch (Exception ex)
    {
      ex.printStackTrace();
    }
    return myConn;
  }

  // A method for closing connections
  public static void closeConnection(Connection myConn)
  {
    try
    {
      if ((myConn == null) || (myConn.isClosed()))
      {
        return;
```

```
      }
      myConn.close();
    }
    catch (Exception ex)
    {
      ex.printStackTrace();
    }
  }
}
```

Over time, I'm sure you'll want to add more methods and capabilities to this class. For instance, you might want to add auto-retry capabilities to the openConnection method if it detects timeouts, and you might want to detect and manage transaction states before closing a connection. Thus you can provide helpful return information to callers, letting them know that certain transactions will be automatically rolled back because a connection is closed.

You can now use the ConnMgr class to greatly simplify the first example, as well as benefit from the enhanced security you now have, with no "plain text" user credentials in sight:

```java
import java.sql.*;

public class JavaDB2ex2
{
  public static void main(String[] args)
  {
    try
    {
      Connection myConn = ConnMgr.openConnection(
        args[0], args[1], "jdbc:db2://localhost:50000/sample");
      if (!myConn.isClosed())
      {
        System.out.println("Successful connection");
      }
      ConnMgr.closeConnection(myConn);
    }
    catch (Exception ex)
    {
      ex.printStackTrace();
    }
  }
}
```

In the JavaDB2ex2 example, I'm leveraging the ConnMgr class and I'm also gathering the required user name and password from the command-line arguments passed to the application. If you're still coming to grips with Eclipse, and how you can debug and test with such arguments, choose Run ➤ Debug to switch to the Debug perspective. The Debug dialog box shown in Figure 16-1 appears.

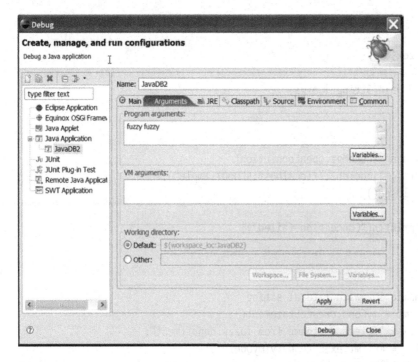

Figure 16-1. *Using command-line arguments to remove hard-coded credentials from the code*

Under the Arguments tab, fill in your desired values in the Program Arguments field (in this case, your user name and password). In the previous JavaDB2ex2 code, there's nothing stopping you from making all the connection parameters dependent on command-line arguments. In this way, you can make the target host, port, and database vary as well. You'll examine other ways of securely coding these values shortly.

Working with Data

An application that simply connects and then disconnects from your database won't set the world on fire. There are two major classes that will help you work with your DB2 data in Java: Statement and ResultSet. You might be familiar with them from Java work on other databases, but let's explore how they work with both dynamic SQL and stored procedures.

The Statement class has several child class variants that cater for different kinds of statement execution. The basic Statement class caters for ad hoc dynamic SQL that typically is used for literal SQL statements (strings that represent your SQL).

The PreparedStatement class is the more robust class, allowing bind parameter markers to be included in the SQL statement and offering a variety of setter methods to set appropriate values for these parameters before execution. It also facilitates statement reuse with different parameters.

The third class is the CallableStatement class, which is used for programmatic constructs such as stored procedures. It also allows bind parameters, which support both inbound and outbound binding, as well as facilitate the handling of multiple result sets.

The following code shows examples of all three types of statements. The ResultSet class' behavior should be obvious from the context. It provides all the usual access methods you'd expect, being able to fetch next, previous, first, last, and other positional elements in results:

```java
import java.sql.*;

public class JavaDB2ex3
{
  public static void main(String[] args)
  {
    try
    {
      Connection myConn = ConnMgr.openConnection(
      args[0], args[1], "jdbc:db2://localhost:50000/sample");
      if (myConn.isClosed())
      {
        System.out.println("Connection failed");
        return;
      }

      //Example dynamic SQL with literal string
      Statement myStmt = myConn.createStatement();
      String myQuery1 = "Select deptname from fuzzy.department";
      ResultSet myRS1 = myStmt.executeQuery(myQuery1);
      while (myRS1.next())
      {
        String deptName = myRS1.getString("deptname");
        System.out.println(deptName);
      }
      System.out.println("End of results\n");

      //Example dynamic SQL with bind parameters
      String myPrepQuery = "Select firstnme, lastname from fuzzy.employee" +
        " where empno < ?";
      //The following String value could be sourced as a program argument,
      //value from a web page, client application, etc.
      String empNo1 = "000100";
      PreparedStatement myPrepStmt = myConn.prepareStatement(myPrepQuery);
      myPrepStmt.setString(1,empNo1);
      ResultSet myRS2 = myPrepStmt.executeQuery();
      while (myRS2.next())
      {
        String firstName = myRS2.getString("firstnme");
        String lastName = myRS2.getString("lastname");
        System.out.println(firstName + " " + lastName);
      }
      System.out.println("End of results\n");

      //Example stored procedure call which returns no result sets
      CallableStatement mySPStmt = myConn.prepareCall(
        "call fuzzy.employee_vote(?, ?)");
```

```
        String empNo2 = "000240";
        mySPStmt.setString(1, empNo2);
        mySPStmt.registerOutParameter(2, java.sql.Types.INTEGER);
        mySPStmt.executeUpdate();
        System.out.println("Employee no " + empNo2 + " currently has "
          + Integer.parseInt(mySPStmt.getString(2)) + " votes.");

        //clean up statements and results
        myRS1.close();
        myRS2.close();
        ConnMgr.closeConnection(myConn);
      }
      catch (SQLException sql_ex)
      {
        sql_ex.printStackTrace();
      }
      catch (Exception ex)
      {
        ex.printStackTrace();
      }
    }
}
```

A few interesting techniques used in the preceding code are worth exploring. First, the String values passed as parameters to the PreparedStatement and CallableStatement classes can just as easily be sourced from a user interface sitting in front of this code or command-line parameters passed to the application (as with connection credentials).

More interestingly, I chose an example stored procedure that doesn't return a result set. Ordinarily, if a result set (or multiple result sets) were returned from the stored procedure, I'd handle them in exactly the same way used for PreparedStatement. Simply iterate through the results of the ResultSet object, and if necessary, move on to the next ResultSet. Because the EMPLOYEE_VOTE stored procedure you wrote in Chapter 8 doesn't return a result set at all, you don't need a ResultSet object to hold its return value. But the executeQuery method of a CallableStatement object always returns one, and if you used executeQuery in your code, a SqlException would be thrown complaining about a stored procedure call that returned no result set. Instead of using executeQuery, use the executeUpdate method, which despite its name, can be used to execute any stored procedure that doesn't return a result set.

The other methods you should become familiar with (or refresh your existing knowledge of) are the setter methods for IN parameters, such as setString and setInt, and the corresponding registerOutParameter method for allocating OUT parameters.

Working with DB2 JDBC Features

In the JavaDB2ex3 class example, each of the statement objects I worked with included a query string, and those query strings used fully qualified objects, specifying both schema and object name. Wouldn't it be great if you could build statements independent of a specific schema in your code and have the schema determined at run time? You can do this by passing around schema names as string parameters and performing string concatenation left, right, and center. Or you can use a Java `Properties` object and benefit from all the DB2-specific goodies that this opens up for you.

The `Properties` object allows you to group together key/value pairs that start out as just text. But when passed to the JDBC API, specific behaviors and characteristics you want for a given database connection can be set in a single step when the JDBC driver creates your instance of a connection. The following example shows how a `Properties` object can handle credentials for you and specify a schema:

```java
import java.sql.*;
import java.util.Properties;

public class JavaDB2ex4
{
  public static void main(String[] args)
  {
    try
    {
      Class.forName("com.ibm.db2.jcc.DB2Driver");

      // Use a Properties object for connection options
      Properties myProps = new Properties();
      myProps.setProperty("user", args[0]);
      myProps.setProperty("password", args[1]);
      String mySchema = "FUZZ";
      myProps.setProperty("currentSchema",mySchema);

      // Now make a new connection object using the Properties object
      Connection myDB2conn = DriverManager.getConnection(
        "jdbc:db2://localhost:50000/sample",myProps);

      // execute a SQL statement using our pre-configured schema
      Statement myStmt = myDB2conn.createStatement();
      String myQuery = "select deptname from department";
      ResultSet myRS = myStmt.executeQuery(myQuery);
      while (myRS.next())
      {
        String deptName = myRS.getString("deptname");
        System.out.println(deptName);
      }
      System.out.println("End of results\n");

      myRS.close();
      myDB2conn.close();
    }
    catch (SQLException sql_ex)
    {
      sql_ex.printStackTrace();
    }
```

```
  catch (Exception ex)
  {
    ex.printStackTrace();
  }
 }
}
```

The approach in the JavaDB2ex4 example is useful, allowing you to programmatically set the schema. This can be useful when developing and deploying code across design, test, and production environments. But one drawback you can immediately see is that you need to know an obscure string name to set the property appropriately. If this doesn't appeal to you, another option is to use the DB2 JDBC-specific configurations to set connection-wide properties. They include db2.jcc.currentSchema to set the current schema, the db2.jcc.DB2BaseDataSource.ROUND_* set of configurations to managing numeric rounding semantics, and db2.jcc.traceLevel and db2.jcc.traceDirectory to assist with diagnostic tracing efforts. Note that the property used to set the default schemata for stored procedures and functions differs from the currentSchema technique used for SQL statements. In these program-construct cases, use the db2.jcc.currentFunctionPath property, which can contain multiple schemata separated by commas. These configuration options, and many more, are available by importing the com.ibm.db2.jcc.* class libraries.

Developing Java Stored Procedures

Creating DB2 stored procedures in Java requires coding two distinct elements. First, you need to write a Java class to implement the business logic (including SQL statements) that you want the procedure to execute. In its simplest form, this class will have a single method, although you can create multiple methods in a single class for mapping to different stored procedures. With the class written, you then require a stored procedure defined in DB2 to reference your Java class.

Writing the Stored Procedure Java Class

Let's start the Java stored procedure examination by writing a simple Java class to record a vote for an employee in the employee of the year system. This is analogous to the preceding EMPLOYEE_VOTE procedures that you wrote in SQL, but you'll be using Java for the heavy lifting. A simple class to insert a vote is as follows:

```java
import java.sql.*;

public class MYJAVASP
{
  public static void my_JAVASP (String inparam) throws SQLException, Exception
  {
    try
    {
      // Obtain the calling context's connection details
      Connection myConn = DriverManager.getConnection("jdbc:default:connection");
```

```
      String myQuery = "INSERT INTO FUZZY.EMP_VOTES VALUES (?, CURRENT DATE)";

      PreparedStatement myStmt = myConn.prepareStatement(myQuery);
      myStmt.setString(1, inparam);
      myStmt.executeUpdate();
    }
    catch (SQLException sql_ex)
    {
      throw sql_ex;
    }
    catch (Exception ex)
    {
      throw ex;
    }
  }
}
```

There are several important features for this class and any similar classes that form the core of a Java stored procedure. First, connection management is assumed to be handled by the calling context. This means that the connection object created in the class references a special default JDBC driver string: `jdbc.default.connection`. This invokes connection inheritance from the caller, and greatly simplifies and streamlines connectivity management for Java stored procedures.

Second, minimal exception handling is managed in the Java class body itself. Strictly speaking, you can undertake more-complex exception handling, but it should be guided by your environment of choice for resolving problems. By throwing exceptions to be caught by the calling context, you can then manage all exceptions in DB2. This does have some inflexibility, but is often preferable to juggling parallel DB2 and Java debugging simultaneously.

Deploying the Java Stored Procedure Class

You need to compile your class into a `.class` file to prepare it for access for the DB2 stored procedure. If you're using an integrated development environment (IDE) such as Data Studio, the auto-build feature does this for you automatically. In other environments (or if you want the practice), you can use the javac command-line compiler to generate the class file:

```
javac MYJAVASP.java
```

The resulting `MYJAVASP.CLASS` file needs to be copied to a location suitable for your DB2 database to find. Your DB2 installation includes a `function` subdirectory designed to house `.class` files and `.jar` archives for Java DB2 stored procedures. This directory is by default `/home/db2inst1/sqllib/function` under Linux and `C:\Program Files\IBM\SQLLIB\FUNCTION` under Windows. If you prefer to house the class files elsewhere, you can use a fully qualified path with the external name parameter, described in the description of the "external name" modifier.

■**Caution** DB2 uses an internal cache of external routines, such as Java stored procedures, for perform-ance reasons. If you find yourself refining or debugging your procedures, you need to ensure that this cache is flushed of any existing .class or .jar files when you change your code. Otherwise you might find your-self believing your new code is in use, when in reality an older cached version is still being run by DB2. Much fun and hilarity will ensue as you try to further debug code that's not actually being used.

Use the SQLJ.REFRESH_CLASSES() procedure to force DB2 to refresh its cached classes from the current definitions provided in the external .class or .jar files. You can invoke it with a simple CALL SQLJ.REFRESH_CLASSES() command from the Command Editor, the DB2 Command Line Processor (CLP), or even Data Studio.

Writing the Stored Procedure

Thanks to the previous tour of stored procedures in Chapter 8, you already know most of what you need to complete your Java DB2 stored procedure. The first—and biggest—difference between traditional SQL-style stored procedures and Java stored procedures is that no logic is included in the body of the procedure. That means that all you need is a definition and to set the relevant options for your procedure; the remainder is covered by the Java class you've already written.

A Java stored procedure declaration for the MYJAVASP stored procedure looks like this:

```
create procedure MYJAVASP (in input char(6))
specific myjavasp
dynamic result sets 0
deterministic
language java
parameter style java
no dbinfo
fenced
threadsafe
modifies sql data
program type sub
external name 'MYJAVASP!my_JAVASP';
```

You'll no doubt have noticed that there are a few new options introduced for a Java stored procedure:

- **parameter style java**: Indicates that Java-style parameter passing will be used. This usually means that parameters are marshaled into arrays for exchange between the stored procedure and the underlying Java. This is essentially transparent to the devel-oper.

- **[no] dbinfo**: dbinfo allows DB2-specific constructs to be passed to the underlying code on calling. no dbinfo is the only supported option for Java stored procedures.

- **[not] fenced [[not] threadsafe]**: Fencing is the concept of allowing or preventing exter-nal code to run in the same process space as the DB2 instance itself. A fenced procedure is spawned in a separate process to the instance (on the other side of a fence, so to speak). Thread safety in this context is identical to typical Java thread safety.

- **program type { main | sub }**: The program type controls whether the argument passing will be using the argv/argc style typical of main methods or as individual parameters to submethods.

- **external name**: The external name is perhaps the most self-evident of the options, specifying the class file and method name for your underlying Java code. Where the routine is part of a package multiple directories deep, use the period to separate directories (for example, 'MYPACK.MYPROCS.MYJAVASP!my_JAVASP').

From those descriptions, you can determine that all these modifiers act to control the programmatic behavior of the Java stored procedure instead of altering its SQL characteristics.

Testing the Java DB2 Stored Procedure

With your Java and DB2 code written, deployed, and debugged, you're ready to execute in anger! Are you ready for the fireworks? The spectacular results? The culmination of all your effort? Calling a Java stored procedure uses exactly the same syntax as a regular stored procedure. You can call the new MYJAVASP procedure as follows, to vote for the employee with empno '200170'.

```
call MYJAVASP('200170')
```

I could have spent some time beautifying the results and formatting them elegantly for presentation here. Instead, I'll give you the raw results and then proceed to a deep explanation. The results are as follows:

```
Return Status = 0
```

That was somewhat of an anticlimax. A return status of zero means exactly what it means in nearly every programming environment: success. To confirm this, let's see whether the vote for employee '200170' is registered in the EMP_VOTES table:

```
db2 => select * from emp_votes where empno = '200170'

EMPNO   TIMEOFVOTE
------  ----------
200170  01/08/2008

  1 record(s) selected.
```

Oh dear. It seems to have worked perfectly. I haven't previously used that empno when registering votes, so there's no sleight of hand here. And really, that's the point. Coding Java DB2 stored procedures is straightforward and doesn't require complicated development processes or deployment techniques. You can always take things further with more-sophisticated Java class packaging in archives, and more elaborate multilevel logic and exception handling. But the key is that you are in complete control of the complexity.

There are some drawbacks to external procedures such as Java stored procedures. At the interface level, because the implementation of a procedure is now totally abstracted from its definition in the DB2 catalog, there are extra steps that must be followed to test your code, and to ensure that changes don't break other unrelated procedures or their supporting classes. Operationally, using Java stored procedures raises the issue of your database server performing non-database-style workloads. You might want to ask whether your Java logic is better placed in a dedicated application server, such as WebSphere or JBoss, to avoid the possibility of competing workloads affecting your performance (or worse, seriously risking the stability of your entire data processing environment). Lastly, you'll find that Java stored procedures enjoy the least coverage in user groups, journals, online articles, and other forums. But maybe that's an excuse for you to become an expert!

Getting Started with DB2 pureQuery for Java

With the release of DB2 9, IBM launched a new object-relational mapping component to ease development of complex Java applications in Eclipse leveraging data in DB2. Named pureQuery, it greatly speeds up development by using a discovery technique to probe all the objects available via a given database connection and then exposing a standard set of Java objects to developers so that they can manipulate their relational data via a mapping layer.

Creating a pureQuery-Enabled Project

A pureQuery project starts life as an ordinary Java project. To get started, open the IBM Data Studio version of Eclipse installed earlier and create a new standard Java project. You can call it anything you like—I called mine Purequeryexample. When the skeleton of the Java project is in place, you'll see that the context menu has a surprise for you, as shown in Figure 16-2.

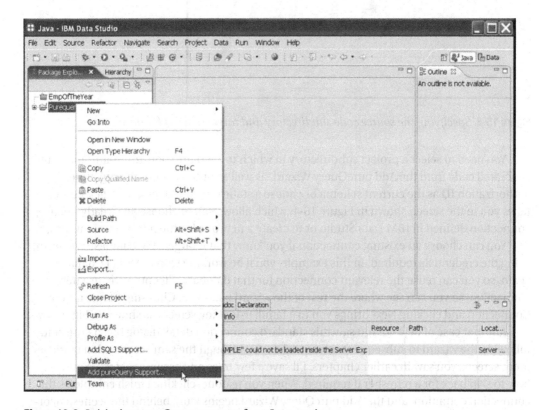

Figure 16-2. *Initiating pureQuery support for a Java project*

Toward the bottom of the menu, the option Add pureQuery Support tempts you to click it. Go ahead and choose that menu option, and the Add pureQuery Wizard kicks into life. The first screen of the Add pureQuery Wizard acts to organize the housekeeping for your project, as shown in Figure 16-3.

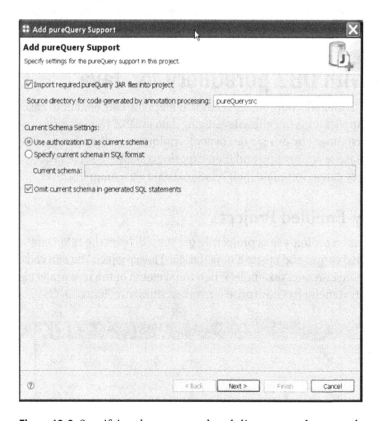

Figure 16-3. *Specifying the source code subdirectory and target schema for pureQuery*

You need to select a project subdirectory in which to keep the soon-to-be-automatically-generated code from the Add pureQuery Wizard, as well as opt to choose the run-time authorization ID as the current schema or choose a static one for the project. Clicking Next takes you to the screen shown in Figure 16-4, which allows you to choose an already existing connection defined in IBM Data Studio or to create a new one for the purposes of this project.

You can choose an existing connection if you know that it targets the database you want, using the credentials required. In this example, you'll be working with the SAMPLE database again, so you can reuse the relevant connection for that database. I'll opt to create a new connection, so you can see where the rest of the wizard takes you. Choosing Create a New Connection and clicking Next brings you to a familiar-looking screen, as shown in Figure 16-5.

Another case of déjà vu! You saw this standard connection detail dialog box before, and following the wizard to subsequent screens takes you through the same connection management screens you saw in earlier chapters. I'll save a few trees and assume that you know how to skip back for a refresher if required. When you're done, clicking Finish completes the connection definition, and the Add pureQuery Wizard begins work behind the scenes, incorporating into your application the many predefined classes and packages that make up the base of pureQuery.

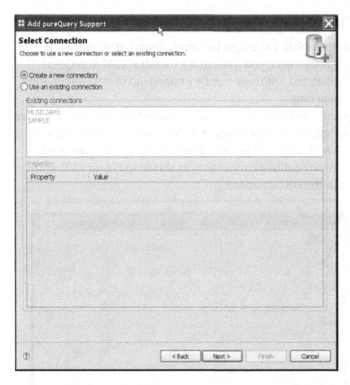

Figure 16-4. *Specifying the source code subdirectory and target schema for pureQuery*

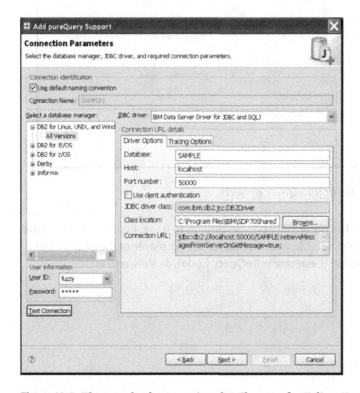

Figure 16-5. *The standard connection detail screen for Eclipse/Data Studio database connections*

Autogenerating pureQuery Java Mapping Classes

Now that your project is pureQuery-enabled, you might be wondering what all the fuss is about. If you browse the classes of your project, you'll see that a wealth of IBM pureQuery and related classes have been included, but nothing's exactly jumped out to start automating things for you. Let's make that happen now.

From your Java project perspective in Eclipse, ensure that you have the Database Explorer view showing; from the Window menu, choose Show View ➤ Other; then from the resulting Show View dialog box, choose Data ➤ Database Explorer. Open the Connections box, and you'll be able to drill down to your newly defined connection, as shown in Figure 16-6, and see the schemas and database objects in the DB2 database.

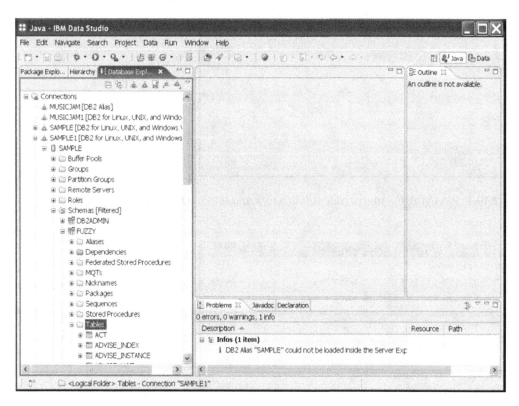

Figure 16-6. *Database Explorer view for pureQuery projects*

Although this view isn't new, the pureQuery powers built in to it are. Right-click any of the objects in a schema, such as the `Prize` table you're using for the employee of the year system, and you'll see a new option available (Generate pureQuery Code), as shown in Figure 16-7.

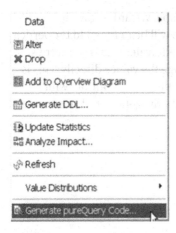

Figure 16-7. *Database Explorer option for generating pureQuery code*

Go ahead and choose the Generate pureQuery Code option. The Generate pureQuery
Code For A Table Wizard springs to life. Figure 16-8 shows the initial wizard screen that allows
you to name the code you're generating, as well as set the scope for what additional components will be automatically coded, such as test cases for annotated and inline methods. For
these introductory purposes, choose the defaults and click Next.

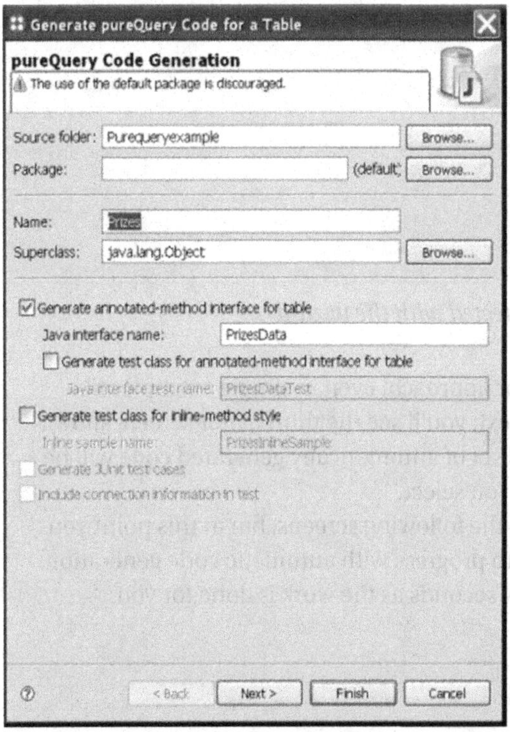

Figure 16-8. *Setting code properties and options for test generation with the Generate pureQuery
Code For A Table Wizard*

The second screen of the Generate pureQuery Code For A Table Wizard, shown in Figure 16-9, allows you to control how the columns of your table will be mapped to properties in the automatically generated classes. You can choose to make equivalent class properties public, meaning that anyone can instantiate an object and change the values directly. This is normally discouraged in contemporary development in favor of the second option, which is to mark the properties as protected and then code accessor methods (getters and setters) to provide access to these values.

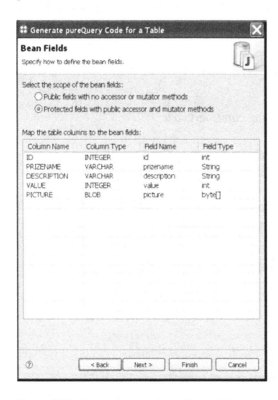

Figure 16-9. *Setting properties to be public or protected with the wizard*

I always prefer the latter protected/accessor approach, even in simple examples like this. It's just a safer coding approach. Choose Next; you'll see the third major screen, shown in Figure 16-10, which controls whether the full set of automatically generated code will be produced for your table or only the subset that you select.

Feel free to explore the options here and in the following screens, but at this point you have specified all you need to allow the wizard to progress with automatic code generation. Click Finish to initiate this and sit back for a few seconds as the work is done for you.

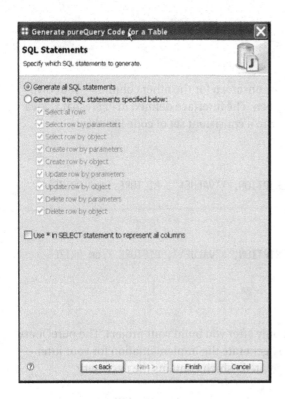

Figure 16-10. *Setting properties to be public or protected with the Generate pureQuery Code For A Table Wizard*

Examining pureQuery Results

The Generate pureQuery Code For A Table Wizard creates two Java files for you: one with a Java class for table getters and setters, and the second with an interface for all the SQL statements you allowed in the final screen of the wizard. For the example of the Prizes table in the employee of the year system, the results are shown in the code that follows.

The Prizes.java file includes the accessors for each column, such as these for the prizename column:

```
...
/**
* Get prizename.
* @return return prizename
*/
public String getPrizename() {
  return prizename;
}

/**
* Set prizename.
* @param String prizename
*/
public void setPrizename(String prizename ) {
```

```
    this.prizename = prizename;
}
...
```

I won't simply reprint here what you can see onscreen for the other columns—your own Java perspective makes far easier reading onscreen. The interface defined in PrizesData.java wrap all the heavy lifting of working with data into a consistent set of code like this:

```
public interface PrizesData {
  // Select all PRIZES
  @Select(sql="select ID, PRIZENAME, DESCRIPTION, \"VALUE\", PICTURE from PRIZES")
  Iterator<Prizes> getPrizes();

  // Select PRIZES by parameters
  @Select(sql="select ID, PRIZENAME, DESCRIPTION, \"VALUE\", PICTURE from PRIZES
    where ID = ?")
  Prizes getPrizes(int id);
...
```

The final piece of the puzzle materializes only after you build your project. The pureQuery extension kicks in at this point to automatically generate the implementation for your interface. In this example, PrizesDataImpl.java is created, which contains the necessary implementation.

So where is all this pureQuery automation heading? In practice, the ability to automatically generate classes, interfaces, and implementations for your object-relational mappings means that you can transition straight from a nominal SQL statement that you want to run against your database to full Java-based object data manipulation, without the need to write all the plumbing yourself! No need to manage connections by hand; worry about the repetitive need to define standard select, insert, update, or delete statements for tables; or map CallableStatements to stored procedures, juggling parameters and result sets.

At its heart, pureQuery is about freeing you from the tedious, laborious, and repetitive work required to build your own object-relational mapping layer. It moves the entire body of work to a sophisticated, automated code generator that understands this task as a well-exercised pattern. In the end, you get to concentrate on your actual unique problems instead of reinventing the wheel every time you need to have your Java code work with a database.

Summary

This chapter covered some of the traditional ways to use Java as a development environment for DB2 database applications. It also cast a spotlight on the new world of the IBM pureQuery tool and has hopefully whetted your appetite in that regard.

In previous chapters I suggested that some material might be served better by a book solely dedicated to its respective topics. When it comes to Java and DB2, a small library could be written. But no amount of reading will substitute for digging in and trying it yourself. I encourage you to tackle the exercises and find areas that you want to know more about. You won't regret it.

■ ■ ■

## CHAPTER 17

Exploring More DB2 Development Options

After your forays into PHP, Ruby, .NET, and Java development with DB2, you might be reaching the point of exhaustion. Would you believe me if I said that there were still dozens of programming languages and environments to cover? In truth there are, but I have to pick up the pace and only lightly touch on programming languages such as Perl, Python, and others to keep this book from blowing out to thousands of pages.

Perl

Larry Wall might not have set out to change the world when he invented Perl in 1987, but Perl certainly has had a global effect. In a few short years following Larry's original post to a usenet group about his solution to all his automation needs, Perl grew to be a ubiquitous part of the fledgling online world, and part of it is Perl's database interface module (DBI).

The DBI acts as a two-layer interface to every database you can imagine, including DB2. Developers work with the DBI application programming interface, making use of common methods and techniques for connection management, statement execution, and so forth; and the DBI interfaces to an underlying database driver, known as a DBD module, which handles the proprietary interface to the target database. Figure 17-1 illustrates how all these layers work together for DB2.

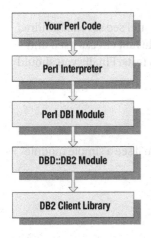

Figure 17-1. *The layers of the Perl DBI and related modules for database access*

Installing the Perl DBI and DBD::DB2 Modules

Your choices for installation are plentiful, regardless of whether you like the old-fashioned hand-compiled approach or the just-get-me-started-in-a-hurry automated installation if you're short of time. Regardless of your preferred approach, the advantage of using such a venerable and robust environment such as Perl is the access to one of the greatest software archives available: the Comprehensive Perl Archive Network (CPAN).

Before Installing

There are a few common-sense prerequisites you'll need to address before proceeding with installing the DBI and DBD::DB2 modules. Naturally, you'll need Perl installed on your system. Because this is part of every Linux distribution I've ever seen, you shouldn't need to source Perl for Linux. Under Windows, the excellent Perl package that ActiveState has made available for decades is available if you like things built for you, or else you can build Perl yourself from source.

You'll also need the DB2 client libraries installed. You'll have them as part of the DB2 server installation if you plan to do your Perl development on your DB2 server or else you can install the DB2 client on a machine of your choice.

Under Linux, you also need to set the DB2_PATH environment variable, with the value of the directory in which you installed DB2. In this case, it's /opt/ibm/db2/V9.5. You might also need to add the DB2_HOME environment variable, which is the default /home/db2inst1/sqllib. Add settings like this to your shell's *rc or relevant profile file. For instance, in bash, add the following to .bash_profile:

```
export DB2_PATH=/opt/ibm/db2/V9.5
export DB2_HOME=/home/db2inst1/sqllib
```

You're then ready to install.

Using Automated Installation

Under Linux, use Perl with the -MCPAN option to install both the DBI and DBD::DB2 modules:

```
$ perl -MCPAN -e 'install DBI'
$ perl -MCPAN -e 'install DBD::DB2'
```

I won't bore you with the output of these commands, but you should see several hundred lines of information scroll past for both packages as the CPAN module first checks itself and then sources the DBI and DBD::DB2 modules, builds them, and runs tests. Finally you should see the following line:

```
(many hundreds of lines not shown for brevity)
/usr/bin/make install  --OK
```

If you already have the latest versions of the modules installed, you'll see a simple module-is-up-to-date message.

Under Windows, the Perl Package Manager (ppm) can be used to achieve the same auto-mated installation. Run ppm at a command line to invoke the graphical installer shown in Figure 17-2.

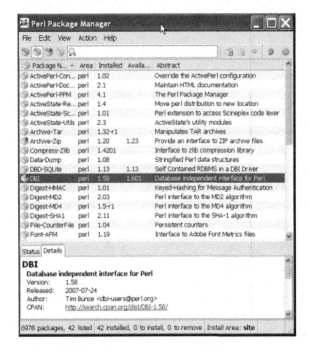

Figure 17-2. *Installing the DBI module using the Perl Package Manager under Windows*

The DBI is probably already installed, but it is worth performing an upgrade if ppm shows that a new version is available. The DBD::DB2 module isn't normally available from the default ppm repository (unlike other DBD modules). Switch the ppm to show all packages available by choosing the View ➤ All Packages menu option. Then choose Edit ➤ Preferences to show the repository configuration for ppm, as shown in Figure 17-3. I added a new repository for DBD::DB2 and pointed it at the server of the kind folks at the Theoretical Physics department at the University of Winnipeg (who host the DBD::DB2 module).

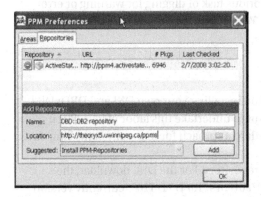

Figure 17-3. *Adding the repository for DBD::DB2 to the Perl Package Manager*

The URL to use is `http://theoryx5.uwinnipeg.ca/ppms`. Once you add this repository, ppm automatically refreshes its package list, and you should be able to scroll through the list of available modules and see the DBD::DB2 module (see Figure 17-4).

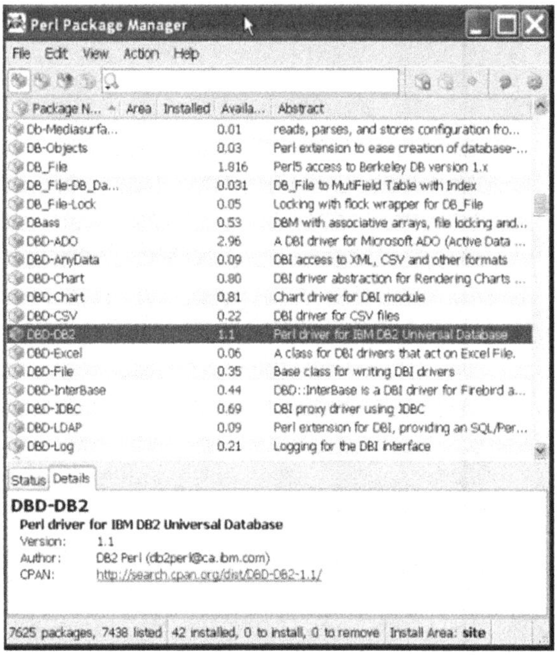

Figure 17-4. *The newly available DBD::DB2 module in the Perl Package Manager*

Mark both the DBI and DBD::DB2 packages for install and then click the green arrow to carry out the installation. If you want to script installation for unattended work or prefer not to use the pretty graphic user interface (GUI), you can execute ppm from the command line to directly install both modules as follows:

```
c:> ppm install DBI
c:> ppm install http://theoryx5.uwinnipeg.ca/ppms/DBD-DB2.ppd
```

The disadvantage of this approach is the laborious task of digging for warning or error messages if there's a problem during installation. With the ppm GUI, they are presented to you front and center.

Compiling from Source

Other than the satisfaction of manually making and installing your own DBI and DBD::DB2 packages *because you can*, you probably don't want to undertake this labor of love. But if you're so inclined, the steps are the absolute standard approach for manually compiling any Perl package.

First, obtain the source code from the CPAN repository. For the DBI, download the latest archive from `http://search.cpan.org/CPAN/authors/id/T/TI/TIMB` (currently version 1.6 in the file `DBI-1.601.tar.gz`). For DBD::DB2, again download the latest archive, this time from `http://www.cpan.org/authors/id/I/IB/IBMTORDB2/` (currently version 1.1 in the file

DBD-DB2-1.1.tar.gz). Note older versions stretching back in time in both directories. By acquiring the latest versions, you ensure that you gain support for the latest DB2 9.5 features.

Unpack your archives into two separate directories (so you don't overwrite files with common names such as the make file). First for the DBI and then DBD::DB2, run the standard make (or nmake under Windows) and install commands:

```
perl Makefile.PL
make
make test
make install
```

Again, after watching many hundreds of lines scroll past, you should see the install return the OK message.

Getting Connected

With the DBI and DBD::DB2 modules installed, you'll actually want to use them to test connecting to DB2. That's usually the best way to ensure that there are no subtle issues with the environment. Let's cut straight to a code example:

```
#!/usr/local/bin/perl
use DBI;
use DBD::DB2;
use DBD::DB2::Constants;

$myDBhandle = DBI->connect("dbi:DB2:sample","fuzzy","fuzzy");
if (defined($myDBhandle))
{
  print "Successful connection to DB2!";
}
else
{
  print "Failed to instantiate connection handle.  Check error trace";
  exit;
}
```

That code is almost self-explanatory, but I'll walk you through the DBI and DBD::DB2 portions. Don't forget to use the correct user name and password for your environment if you copy this example.

PERL HERESY

I should state right now that I abhor terse Perl code. You'll note that my examples include long, descriptive variable names and neat formatting, and they lack the all-too-common pack-everything-on-one-line Perl coding style. If you're a Perl fan, you should try it; you'll be amazed at how much other people appreciate your effort.

The use statements load the modules for this script. DBD::DB2::Constants is explicitly referenced so that a hash function is available without full qualification in the DBI->connect invocation.

The DBI->connect method is called to create a connection handle, through which statements and results can be manipulated. The connect method takes as a minimum three parameters: a DBD module connection string, user name, and password. There are also optional parameters that can be passed, covering both standard DBI options and those parochial to the particular DBD driver being used.

Executing SQL Statements

Once connected, it's natural to then want to actually execute SQL and work with data from the DB2 database. The Perl DBI uses the very familiar concepts of statement handles and result sets to work with data in DB2. To allow DB2 data types to map correctly to Perl (not that Perl has the strongest data typing in the world), you need to include an additional use line in the Perl code to allow easy reference to the data type mappings provided by the DBD::DB2 module:

```
use DBD::DB2 qw($attrib_int $attrib_char $attrib_float $attrib_date $attrib_ts);
```

With this in place, you're now ready to incorporate real SQL into the Perl sample code. In the following example, I select data from the employee of the year system using a prepared SQL statement with bind markers:

```
#!/usr/local/bin/perl
use DBI;
use DBD::DB2;
use DBD::DB2::Constants;
use DBD::DB2 qw($attrib_int $attrib_char $attrib_float $attrib_date $attrib_ts);

$myDBhandle = DBI->connect("dbi:DB2:sample","fuzzy","fuzzy");
if (defined($myDBhandle))
{
  print "Successful connection to DB2!\n";
}
else
{
  print "Failed to instantiate connection handle.  Check error trace";
  exit;
}

$myStmt = "select deptname from department where deptno = ?;";
$myStmtHandle = $myDBhandle->prepare($myStmt);
$myStmtHandle->bind_param(1, "A00");
$myStmtHandle->execute();
while( @arow = $myStmtHandle->fetchrow )
{
  print "@arow\n";
}
```

My results look like this, but naturally yours will differ if you pass a different bind value for deptno or decide to write a more-sophisticated SQL statement:

```
Successful connection to DB2!
SPIFFY COMPUTER SERVICE DIV.
```

In the preceding Perl example, the $myStmt variable simply holds the text of the SQL, using the question mark character as the bind variable placeholder. Note that when drafting your SQL statements for DBI, you'll need to include a semicolon statement terminator for the SQL statement within the quoted string, as well as the normal Perl statement-terminating semi-colon at the end of the line.

You then call the prepare method of the connection, passing the statement and assigning the resulting handle to a variable that then is used to bind desired parameters and actually invoke execution. This statement handle supports various fetch methods such as fetch, which I used in a simple loop to retrieve all the results.

An explanation of some additional options help you stretch this lightning-fast coverage of Perl and the DBI to more examples. If your bind parameter needed to be an integer, this is where you can leverage the additional use call that has imported knowledge of the DBD::DB2 data type mappings. You need to override Perl's default assumption that all variables are strings, and explicitly say "this is an integer." The select statement and binding would look something like this:

```
...
$myStmt = "select fisrtnme, lastname from employee where edlevel = ?;";
$myStmtHandle = $myDBhandle->prepare($myStmt);
$myValue = 7;
$myStmtHandle->bind_param(1, $myValue, SQL_INTEGER);
...
```

You use the explicit type SQL_INTEGER and thus communicate your desires. The method used for bind parameters is different if the parameter is an INOUT or OUT parameter. In these instances, you need to flag to the DBI that the value will change (for instance, a stored proce-dure call such as the employee_vote procedure takes an employee ID as input and returns that ID's current vote count).

```
...
$myStmt = "call fuzzy.employee_vote (?, ?);";
$myStmtHandle = $myDBhandle->prepare($myStmt);
$myEmpno = "000240";
$myCurrVotes = -1;
$max_length = 4;

# bind the IN parameter
$myStmtHandle->bind_param(1, $myEmpno);

# bind the OUT parameter, with the correct method
$myStmtHandle->bind_param_inout(2, $myCurrVotes, $max_length, SQL_INTEGER);
...
```

The `bind_param_inout` method takes an additional mandatory parameter, indicating the maximum length that the OUT parameter will take. This allows Perl to allocate the right amount of storage in advance, thus avoiding data overflows and similar nasty code side-effects.

Going Further with Perl and DB2

There are very few dedicated resources to Perl and DB2 in isolation. You'll find material on the two at the IBM developerWorks site; and a search on Google will return examples, questions, and code snippets that have circulated over the years. There is, however, an excellent book on working with the Perl DBI in general. *Programming the Perl DBI* (O'Reilly, 2000), was written by Tim Bunce and Alligator Descartes (Tim is the author of the DBI module itself). It's getting a little long in the tooth, but all the core concepts and techniques still apply today.

Python

Python has seen explosive growth in use since Guido van Rossum released his creation upon the world. And as with every other programming language, connecting to databases such as DB2 is the first thing you think of when writing applications. IBM has addressed this need for Python through its Open Source Application Enablement Team. This team has released a number of beta versions of Python DBI drivers for DB2, with the current release being version 0.2.0. Don't let that comparatively low version number concern you. The Open Source Application Enablement Team has also played a large part in the release of the PHP and Ruby drivers, and they (along with the Python driver) share many common elements. This means that the Python driver has actually been exercised a great deal more than the 0.2.0 version number might suggest.

The driver has a very imaginative official name, Python driver and DBI wrapper for IBM databases. That's a mouthful and is meant to convey the fact that the driver is good for all IBM databases, including DB2 and others. I'll focus solely on the driver's DB2 capabilities and use the abbreviated name Python DB2 Driver.

Installing the Python DB2 Driver

While the IBM Open Source Application Enablement Team has worked to produce the DB2 driver for Python, you'll find that it isn't hosted directly on the IBM site. Instead the `python.org` website hosts the latest package in the Python Package Index repository at `http://pypi.python.org`. Although the current 0.2.6 driver is available at `http://pypi.python.org/pypi/ibm_db/0.2.6`, you might want to just hit the home page and search for **DB2** from there to find the latest and greatest driver in future. As of this writing, the 0.2.6 DB2 driver requires Python 2.5. If you're using an earlier version of Python, you might want to use the 0.2.0 version.

The site makes available both a Python egg for Windows and Linux (currently named `ibm_db-0.2.6-py2.5-win32.egg` and `ibm_db-0.2.6-py2.5-linux-i686.egg`, respectively. There is also the source distribution: `ibm_db-0.2.6.tar.gz`. Choose the package you prefer and start downloading!

Before You Install

Automated installation of Python eggs requires the easy_install feature of the Python setup-tools package. You can install eggs without this automated assistance, but why would you? If you don't currently have the setuptools package, grab it while you're at the Python Package Index website.

Under Linux, you need to set two environment variables, IBM_DB_DIR and IBM_DB_LIB. IBM_DB_DIR is set to the full path to the DB2 sqllib directory, and the IBM_DB_LIB value is set to the lib subdirectory beneath sqllib. So in my environment, the values would be as follows:

```
$ export IBM_DB_DIR=/home/db2inst1/sqllib
$ export IBM_DB_LIB=/home/db2inst1/sqllib/lib
```

Under Windows, the prerequisites are a little more onerous. Besides the preceding environment variables (in Windows form), you'll need Visual C++ 2003, the Platform SDK and the .NET SDK Version 1.1

Using Automated Installation

The automated installation method for the Python DB2 driver is as simple as invoking the easy_install script with the relevant .egg file downloaded previously. For example, under Linux, the command is as follows:

```
$ easy_install ibm_db-0.2.0-py2.5-linux-i686.egg
```

Under Windows, you need to ensure that the path to easy_install.exe is on your PATH environment variable, or else you'll need to include its full directory and file name. Don't forget to use the relevant .egg file for Windows as well. Regardless of your platform, you should see status information scroll past that includes reassuring details like these:

```
Processing ibm_db-0.2.6-py2.5-win32.egg
creating c:\python25\lib\site-packages\ibm_db-0.2.6-py2.5-win32.egg
Extracting ibm_db-0.2.6-py2.5-win32.egg to c:\python25\lib\site-packages
Adding ibm-db 0.2.6 to easy-install.pth file

Installed c:\python25\lib\site-packages\ibm_db-0.2.6-py2.5-win32.egg
Processing dependencies for ibm-db==0.2.6
Finished processing dependencies for ibm-db==0.2.6
```

That completes the installation tasks.

Building and Installing from Source

In keeping with the elegance and simplicity of all things Python, installing from source is as simple as unpacking the archive to your desired location, following the prerequisites previously listed, and then executing the following commands as root (or someone with permissions to the Python application and modules directories):

```
$ python setup.py build
$ python setup.py install
```

This will take a few minutes to complete because quite a number of test cases are exercised in the build process. When it's done, you're ready to use the Python DB2 driver and associated wrapper.

Getting Connected

It's my pleasure to present to you probably the most straightforward piece of connection code you'll ever see. Connecting to DB2 under Python is as simple as importing the driver and creating a new connection object:

```
#!python
import ibm_db
myConnection = ibm_db.connect("SAMPLE","fuzzy","fuzzy")
```

The connect method takes three parameters: the name of the database from the local catalog, a user name, and a password. You can naturally add whatever exception handling you want to it.

Executing SQL Statements

A very familiar statement and result handle technique is used for Python with DB2. You'll extend the connection example to include statement definition and execution, and also some rudimentary exception testing:

```
#!python
import ibm_db
myConnection = ibm_db.connect("SAMPLE","fuzzy","fuzzy")

if myConnection:
  mySQL = "select firstnme, lastname from fuzzy.employee"
  myStmt = ibm_db.exec_immediate(myConnection, mySQL)
  row = ibm_db. fetch_assoc(myStmt)
  while row:
    print row
    row = ibm_db. fetch_assoc(myStmt)
```

Again, the simplicity is seductive. I must admit I'm much more of a fan of Python than any other scripting language, so the elegance and minimalism appeal to me. Here you can see a connection made, a statement constructed and executed, and results fetched.

Going Further with Python and DB2

Perhaps the one difficulty you'll find with the Python DB2 driver and its associated wrapper is the relative immaturity of supporting documentation, tutorials, and examples. In the next subsection, I give you a flying start using resources you might not realize you have. But for the near future, you'll be best served watching IBM developerWorks like a hawk and lobbying your favorite publisher to commission a work on the topic.

Other Languages

By now you know that this chapter is taking you on a whirlwind ride of other programming languages and development environments that enjoy support for DB2. One of the main factors that make DB2 so popular is the sheer number of languages and environments that work with it. I'll accelerate the whirlwind pace of this chapter and touch very briefly on some languages that might be dear to the hearts of some readers.

Key to this fast and furious coverage is the knowledge that you can leap ahead with material you already have at hand (that I deliberately did not mention until now). When you installed DB2 back in Chapter 2, you almost certainly followed my example of choosing a full installation. At that point, you installed nearly 2000 files of code samples, totaling nearly 25MB in size, which have sat neglected on your hard drive until now! In the /home/db2inst1/sqllib/ samples directory under Linux, or the C:\Program Files\IBM\SQLLIB\samples directory under Windows, you'll find a treasure trove of DB2 samples for a myriad of languages—one of them is sure to be among your favorites.

C and C++

The samples provided for C and C++ are voluminous. Everything from fundamental DB2 CLI programs in ANSI-standard C to Microsoft Visual C++–specific examples, including UI widgets and the latest and greatest managed C++ for the version 2 and later .NET run time.

The examples for C and C++ are scattered across a number of subdirectories, including the c, cpp, cli, and VC directories. Notable among the many samples you'll find there are the inattach.c/inattach.cxx examples, which cover the basics of attaching to an instance and working with the basic DB2 libraries without the baggage of a particular integrated development environment (IDE). For Visual C++ fans, the VarCHAR.dsp and BLOBAccess.dsp projects and related files give a perfect example of connecting to a database and working with Varchar and BLOB data. These examples are easily modified to work with any other data type.

COBOL

I was tempted to say in the previous section on C that it was the most widely used language with DB2, but then I remembered the vast body of work accumulated over the past 20 or more years that uses COBOL. Although I was never a great COBOL programmer, I've heard anecdotes suggesting that 70 percent of the world's data in databases lives in DB2 on mainframes that are manipulated by COBOL programs.

For the COBOL aficionado, there are vanilla COBOL examples with the Windows installation of DB2. There are also examples that use Microfocus COBOL with both the Linux and Windows installations. Microfocus COBOL is one of the more popular incarnations of language variant/development environments. Useful examples to get you started are dbinst.cbl, which covers instance attachment; and client.cbl, which covers typical actions in client connections and related API calls.

Rexx

Rexx is one of the oldest scripting languages, but it took quite a few years to break free of its mainframe roots. You can now get Rexx interpreters for almost any platform and because it was so close to the DB2 world for much of its existence, working with DB2 is a powerful capability of Rexx.

If you've never worked with Rexx and don't think you'd be interested, I encourage you to just take a peek at one of the Rexx samples. You've got to love a language that includes the keyword SAY, used much like `print` or `printf` in other languages. I'm certain that this keyword was put in place by Rexx designers who expect their Rexx and DB2 systems to start talking to them at any time. To get started, try out the `dbauth.cmd` example Rexx file. This file walks you through typical connection and simple administrative commands, which will show you just how quickly you can get a working script.

Visual Basic and Visual Basic.NET

Although VB and VB.NET aren't the same language, they share a lot in common. (Okay, let's not start talking about array offsets, deprecated features, and the like.) Examples for both are included, and there are also examples for legacy Windows APIs such as COM and DCOM, and legacy Microsoft connection APIs such as OLE DB. Two excellent examples are the `dbConn.bas` and `cliExeSQL.bas` files that illustrate connection to DB2, and execution of SQL statements with VB.NET using the ADO libraries.

Other Samples

You'll also find examples for many of the languages already covered in earlier dedicated chapters, including examples for PHP and Java. Also included are examples for other DB2 features, such as extenders, as well as sample pureXML code, sample stored procedures, and even all the data that gets loaded into the SAMPLE database by default.

Summary

This chapter touched briefly on the capabilities of some of the web's favorite languages, such as Perl and Python, and their capabilities when working with DB2. And without writing a book to rival *War and Peace* in size, I also pointed you in the direction of other resources for many of the other languages that I couldn't cover in depth in this book. I hope the last half-dozen chapters have shown you what's possible in the world of application development with DB2. In short, whatever your favorite language might be, DB2 can be your database of choice.

PART 5

■ ■ ■

Ongoing Database Administration with DB2

Part artistry, part science, and a whole heap of knowledge and applied skill, database administration is all about keeping your existing databases humming in perfect order, while planning and executing the work needed for new databases and designs. This section covers the fundamentals of database administration in detail, complementing your existing knowledge of data manipulation and application development. When you're done, you'll wonder why you waited so long to become a DB2 database administrator.

CHAPTER 18

▪▪▪

Database Creation and Configuration

You've used several wizards to create databases in a matter of minutes. Now you'll dive to the lowest level to see exactly how to accomplish database creation (and related configuration and management tasks) using SQL. By using data definition language (DDL) commands, I'll show you that databases can be created in a flash by leveraging intuitive DB2 defaults. I'll also show you how to leverage all the flexibility DB2 has to offer when creating and managing databases.

To appreciate and understand the options as I present them, a quick tour of the fundamental building blocks of DB2 databases is in order. Let's take a quick look at the anatomy of a DB2 database, from the lowest level on disk to the highest conceptual point where users create objects and manipulate data.

Building Blocks of DB2 Databases

When users need to create an index or insert some rows into a table, the last thing they want to do is take control of how those things will be stored—or even where they will be stored. Although that kind of precision control was all the rage in the 1970s, those preferences have gone the same way as paisley flares and disco. Abstracting away these low-level details helps a developer or database administrator concentrate more on the actual data model and less on how spinning platters of rusting metal react under an electrostatic charge.

The first level of abstraction used in DB2 logically separates storage for objects and data into tablespaces. As the name suggests, a *tablespace* provides a space for storing tables, other objects such as indexes, and the data associated with these objects. Tablespaces come in different flavors, which I'll discuss shortly, and a database can have numerous tablespaces. A tablespace belongs entirely to one database; it isn't shared across databases. A user references a tablespace by its logical name or ID number—there's no need to know how or where a tablespace's underlying storage is handled.

Tablespaces deal with the disk level of storage through yet more abstraction. For purposes of using part of the space from a filesystem or a raw device, a tablespace uses the concept of a container. A *container*, which can come in a number of varieties, is the point of indirection between tablespaces and disks at this conceptual level. A tablespace can have more than one container, and containers are used by only one tablespace at a time.

Beneath containers are the disks themselves. Although disks are a very interesting topic, you've reached the level that would properly be handled by another book. You might also be thinking that a page of textual explanation would be greatly assisted by a diagram illustrating a database's building blocks. You're right, and that's what Figure 18-1 is for.

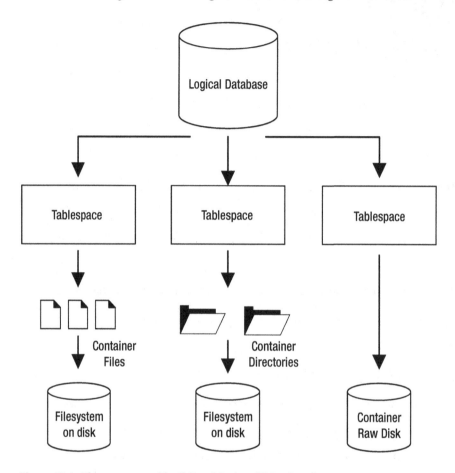

Figure 18-1. *The conceptual building blocks of DB2 database storage*

The figure shows a database with its constituent tablespaces, their containers, and the lowest level of disk. Now that you can picture how these building blocks are built on top of each other, it's time to get busy creating databases!

Creating DB2 Databases

In Chapter 3 you created a database using the DB2 Launchpad, so you're well on the way to moving from beginner to expert in the database-creation stakes. Now it's time to roll your sleeves up and get down-and-dirty with database creation. First, let's explore how easy database creation can be. Three words are all you need to bring a new database to life: create database test1. Seriously, that's it! Here's the proof:

```
db2 => create database test1
DB20000I  The CREATE DATABASE command completed successfully.
```

Every other option, setting, and choice defaults to a predefined value. The defaults include using automatic storage management, choosing UTF-8 as the character set, using the system collation for textual sorting and comparison, and so forth. The only true prerequisites to using this simple approach are to attach to your chosen instance, and you must be a member of the SYSADM or SYSCTRL privilege groups discussed in Chapter 9.

If I were to leave the discussion of database creation at that, you'd be perfectly justified in thinking I hadn't really equipped you for all the possibilities that database creation can throw at you. So I'll build on this statement one step at a time, introducing all the other options that are available.

Specifying an Alias

The first option to consider, and probably the most straightforward, is the alias option. Using an alias allows a database to be cataloged with an alternative name in the database directory. You might use this capability to use some kind of code or naming scheme for the database and present the alias to users as a friendly name by which to know the database. The syntax is very intuitive:

```
db2 => create database test2 alias mynewdb
DB20000I  The CREATE DATABASE command completed successfully.
```

The database now looks like this in the directory:

```
db2 => list database directory

 System Database Directory

 Number of entries in the directory = 15


 ...


 Database 2 entry:

  Database alias                       = MYNEWDB
  Database name                        = TEST2
  Local database directory             = C:
  Database release level               = b.00
  Comment                              =
  Directory entry type                 = Indirect
  Catalog database partition number    = 0
  Alternate server hostname            =
  Alternate server port number         =
```

The next parameters are related to language and text handling, so I'll discuss them together.

Handling Languages and Text in DB2 Databases

A database's *codeset*, *territory*, and *collation* affect the type of textual data that can be accommodated within the database and how it is treated once there. Any one of numerous codesets can be specified for creating your database. You can choose from numeric values that represent common (and not so common) code pages. For instance, 1252 is the typical Western European Latin codeset for Windows, 850 is an earlier incarnation of the Latin codeset popular in the United States, and the list goes on. But there is one important factor with several important implications for your database. That factor is *Unicode*.

The first consideration regarding Unicode is the wider move in the entire IT industry toward *not* being concerned with specific character sets or codesets. Unicode, in its several forms such as UTF-8 and UTF-16, has now been part of the IT landscape for more than a decade, and any of the historical arguments against its use (comparative storage overhead, awareness of other applications, and so on) have long since faded away. The second and more immediate concern for you as a creator of DB2 databases is this: to use DB2 9's formidable new XML technology (pureXML) you must choose the UTF-8 Unicode variant for your database.

A territory is used in conjunction with a codeset to indicate how a given code page should be interpreted and the choice of certain default behaviors, based on the nuances of a language's use within a given country. Territory values are two-character codes from the ISO 3166 standard. Values include US for the United States, FR for France, ES for Spain, and so on.

The third member of the language handling parameters is the collation option, specified with the collate using clause. This option dictates how the text in your database, from your chosen codeset, will be sorted when performing ordering operations such as index creation, case conversion to and from upper- and lowercase, and even aspects of equality comparisons—what characters can be considered identical to others (if any). The collation setting can take one of the following values:

- **IDENTITY**: Using this collation, string values are compared and sorted based on their byte representation. In practice, it means that text in the database is treated in a case-sensitive fashion for those code pages in which "case" is relevant.

- **SYSTEM**: For Unicode databases, this collation is a synonym for IDENTITY. For databases created with a non-Unicode codeset, it instructs DB2 to use the collating rules of the territory nominated for the database.

- **COMPATIBILITY**: This collation instructs DB2 to sort and compare strings based on the original DB2 version 2 rules instead of the enhanced rules introduced and expanded from the time of DB2 UDB version 5. This collation is usually used only when working with legacy applications that expect the older behavior.

- **IDENTITY_16BIT**: This is a Unicode collating sequence for UTF-16. An entire booklet describing its behavior is available from the Unicode consortium, so I won't try to summarize it here. More details are available at the Unicode consortium's website: http://www.unicode.org.

- **UCA400_NO, UCA400_LSK, and UCA400_LTH**: These three collation sequences are all based on the Unicode version 4 algorithm. The first includes implied normalization of some of the more obscure Unicode rules, and the latter two handle specific Slovakian and Thai corrections to earlier Unicode collation approaches. The straightforward examples in this book don't stray into such rarified territory, so if you are interested in these corner cases, consult the Unicode consortium's website for more details: http://www.unicode.org.

- **NLSCHAR**: This collation sequence utilizes special rules based on the national language characteristics of specific codesets and territories. As of DB2 9, this is a valid option only for the Thai codeset, 874. DB2 will return an error if you attempt to use it for any other codeset.

As you can see, there are basically polar opposites available for collations: very broad collation settings governing the entire gamut of text capable of being stored, and very particular variations for quirks associated with specific languages. In practice, the vast majority of databases you create will almost certainly use SYSTEM or IDENTITY collation. Armed with your new knowledge of codesets, territories, and collations, you can extend the scope of your database-creation statement:

```
db2 => create database test3 alias myutfdb using codeset utf-8 territory US
 collate using system
DB20000I  The CREATE DATABASE command completed successfully.
```

Another aspect of database creation mastered. If you're following these examples in your environment and are starting to worry about the sheer number of databases being created, you can relax. You'll deal with tidying up the working databases later in the chapter.

■Note When working with the DB2 Command Line Processor (CLP), by default the carriage return/line feed is considered the statement terminator. In the examples that follow, the text in the book will be formatted to make things more readable. However, when you run the commands, you'll need to ensure that they are typed as one continuous line. The alternative is to start the DB2 CLP with a substitute statement terminator. This can be done by invoking the db2 executable with the –td option, followed by the desired statement terminator character. For example, if I want to use the @ symbol as my statement terminator, I simply run the following:

```
db2 -td@
```

There's no space between the –td and the @ symbol. Within the CLP, I now need to use @ to terminate (and execute) every statement including quit! There's an even shorter variant of this command. If you start the DB2 CLP with just a –t flag, it will implicitly use the semicolon as a terminator:

```
db2 -t
```

After a little while, you'll find that this option becomes second nature. It even provides an extra trick by allowing ;-- as a special terminator in stored procedures, meaning that you can keep things consistent across your code.

Managing Storage for the DB2 Database

Sometimes it's desirable to take close control of how and where DB2 is managing storage for your database. This can include situations in which you're sharing storage with other users or applications, or when you know that the storage environment for the database will change considerably at some point in the short to medium term.

DB2 supports two fundamental types of logical storage for databases, known as tablespaces. I use the term *logical* to indicate that these are notional storage "places" governed by a simple-to-remember name for the tablespace. In using this approach, database administrators, developers, testers, and others who work with the database can refer to and use storage without actually needing to know precise disk layout, storage size, directory/file names, or other low-level details. I'll cover the two tablespace storage types shortly, but first let's explore how tablespaces are used in DB2.

Understanding Tablespace Use in DB2

I'm sure you're thinking, "Tablespaces are spaces for storing tables. I get that bit." And fundamentally, that's it! There are nuances to the way tablespaces are used that are worth understanding, particularly because this area of DB2 has undergone change over the last several releases as IBM ramps up its push into autonomic management. So yes, I'm asking you to understand things that just about take care of themselves.

DB2 supports five different types of tablespaces, each for a specific purpose:

- **System tablespace**: Each database has one, and only one, system tablespace, whose purpose is to store the system tables and other objects that form what is usually referred to as the system catalog. In effect, these are the objects that support all other objects you'll eventually create and use in the database. This tablespace, which is also referred to as the *catalog tablespace*, is named SYSCATSPACE by default.

- **System temporary tablespace**: Again, one tablespace (per page size) that exists in every database to support temporary objects that are automatically created and governed by DB2. An example of such work is managing sorting that overflows the available memory for sort tasks in DB2. By default, the first system temporary tablespace will be called TEMPSPACE1.

- **Regular tablespace**: As the name suggests, a regular tablespace is the common tablespace type used to store regular user objects—tables and indexes. A database must always have at least one regular or large tablespace (see the following bullet), but it can have literally thousands if you so desire. The first regular or large tablespace will be given a default name of USERSPACE1.

- **Large tablespace**: A tablespace designed specifically for supporting LOB-style data. Large tablespaces are equipped to handle bulk data transfer associated with LOBs most efficiently. Interestingly, as the underlying design of these tablespaces has evolved with new versions of DB2, they're also excellent at storing regular tables and indexes, too. Large tablespaces are optional and need to be explicitly created if you decide that one is warranted.

- **User temporary tablespace**: A distinctly different kind of tablespace, not to be confused with the system temporary tablespace type. User temporary tablespaces are used to store user-defined global temporary tables. I'll discuss more about global temporary tables shortly. User temporary tablespaces are optional and again need to be explicitly created if you need to use global temporary tables.

So there are five distinct uses for the tablespaces in your DB2 databases. Every database you create will have at least three tablespaces: the system tablespace, the system temporary tablespace, and the first regular or large tablespace for user objects. These tablespaces and any others you choose to add to your database need to have their storage managed by one of the two storage-management mechanisms available.

Choosing the Right Tablespace Storage Management Type

The two historical tablespace storage types supported by DB2 are the system managed storage tablespace (SMS) and the database managed storage tablespace (DMS).

Occasionally I wish that IBM would dispense with euphemisms such as DMS and use unambiguous terms instead. In this case, I think the phrase "you-managed storage" would be appropriate. When wondering who manages the storage for this tablespace, the answer is obvious: you!

In IBM's inimitable way, it answered my unspoken request, but not as I expected. A special type of DMS tablespace is available, known as an automatic storage DMS tablespace, which gives the best of both worlds. It provides the automatic management you'll find in SMS tablespaces, together with the tunable characteristics for maximum application performance that are the hallmarks of DMS tablespaces. Automatic storage DMS tablespaces are also the default from DB2 9 onward, so unless you deliberately seek out a different behavior, you'll get these benefits without lifting a finger.

By using the automatic storage yes on '*path*' syntax within a database-creation statement, DB2 is instructed to take over all storage-management tasks, including using its autonomic tuning capabilities to ensure that the physical storage is accessed and used in the most efficient fashion. Because this is now the default with DB2 9, you actually need to go out of your way to not use automatic management and start specifying your own storage details. All the previous database-creation work you did has defaulted to automatic storage management. You can also explicitly request automatic storage, as shown in this example:

```
db2 => create database test4 alias myutfdb
 using codeset utf-8 territory US collate using system
 automatic storage yes on '/home/db2inst1'
 catalog tablespace managed by automatic storage
DB20000I  The CREATE DATABASE command completed successfully.
```

You could have repeated the managed by automatic storage clauses for the user (regular) tablespace and temp tablespace, but they will default to this behavior in any case. There are very few details regarding automatic storage that you then need to worry about, other than the base path under which you want the storage to be managed. You'll deal with the few options that are available toward the end of the chapter when you alter databases and tablespaces.

Where automatic storage management is not used, the concept of a storage container is used by DB2 tablespaces to indicate the location on disk allocated for storage. A tablespace container is the level at which DB2 interacts with the underlying physical disk, or filesystem. There are three different types of containers that can be used, each with its own particular advantages and benefits (see Table 18-1).

Table 18-1. *Tablespace Storage Options*

Underlying Storage	SMS or DMS	Features
Raw disk	DMS	Direct I/O with disk—no filesystem interposed
Directory	SMS	Easily managed directory-based storage
File	DMS	Precise file placement, sizing, and addition/change/removal

Using System Managed Storage Tablespaces

SMS tablespaces are designed for ease of management. When created—either at database-creation time or at some later stage—SMS tablespaces use a nominated directory as the container, in which the database will subsequently "grow" tables, indexes, and large objects (LOBs). This simplicity is the key benefit. By using a directory as the container, you maintain the ability—at the operating system level—to manage available storage at the filesystem level, and even redirect the container through the use (some would say *very careful* use) of Linux/UNIX features such as soft links, and Windows features such as directory volume mounting. Another consideration is the method by which space is allocated after the SMS tablespace and its directory container are created. Space is allocated on demand within a directory container, so at the point of creation DB2 checks only to ensure that the directory exists; it doesn't concern itself with how much storage is available at that directory. This can be a blessing or a curse.

Because SMS tablespaces and their directory containers were originally designed with ease of management in mind, several advanced capabilities of DMS tablespaces are lacking in SMS tablespaces. In particular, the capability to split tables, indexes, and LOBs into separate tablespaces is not available. Another limitation is that additional directory containers can't be added easily to an SMS tablespace after creation—storage is expected to grow within the already-nominated directories, and one must go through a rather circuitous backup-and-redirected-restore process to overcome exhausted space.

To use an SMS tablespace at database-creation time, the clause TABLESPACE-TYPE TABLESPACE MANAGED BY SYSTEM USING (CONTAINER-PATH) must be used, along with the directory location for the container. Continuing with sample database-creation statement illustrating this evolving understanding, this statement will create a database specifying various different locations for the SMS tablespaces that are mandatory for database creation:

```
db2 => create database test5 automatic storage no on 'c:\'
 alias testdb5 using codeset utf-8 territory us collate using system pagesize 4096
 catalog tablespace managed by system using ('c:\db2\node0000\test5\cattbs')
 user tablespace managed by system using ('c:\db2\node0000\test5\usertbs')
 temporary tablespace managed by system using ( 'c:\db2\node0000\test5\temptbs')
DB20000I  the CREATE DATABASE command completed successfully.
```

As you can see, that's a rather long statement. But looking closely, you can spot the repeated pattern for each tablespace, making the syntax far easier to remember.

Using Database Managed Storage Tablespaces

DMS tablespaces have been constructed to maximize the capabilities of your underlying storage and to provide fine-grained control over factors that affect the performance of using that storage. DMS tablespaces can use two types of container for storage: files and devices. You'll note that I didn't mention directories. By using files and devices, DMS tablespaces gain benefits such as knowing the exact storage size at the time of creation (although this can be changed later); the ability to spread data over different storage devices by controlling file location or device mount points; and, for devices in particular, the ability to bypass any filesystem cache overhead that might degrade performance.

When using files as DMS tablespace containers, you might choose either absolute path and file names, or a path and file name relative to the database directory. I recommend that you don't use relative paths, even though they are technically fine. The chances for mayhem when humans misinterpret the result of relative path resolution are surprisingly high. DB2 creates any missing paths and files necessary to satisfy your file container specification if you use absolute paths. When using devices, the device must exist at the time of database creation.

The tablespace specification clause used for DMS tablespaces is similar to SMS tablespaces, but it includes more details. Generally, it is of the form TABLESPACE-TYPE TABLESPACE MANAGED BY DATABASE USING ({FILE | DEVICE} CONTAINER-PATH NO-OF-PAGES). This example uses file containers to illustrate the command:

```
db2 => create database test6 automatic storage no on '/home/db2inst1'
 alias testdb5 using codeset utf-8 territory us collate using system pagesize 4096
 catalog tablespace managed by database using
 (FILE '/home/db2inst1/db2inst1/NODE0000/test6/cattbs.001')
 user tablespace managed by database using
 (FILE '/home/db2inst1/db2inst1/NODE0000/test6/usertbs.001' 10240,
 FILE '/home/db2inst1/db2inst1/NODE0000/test6/usertbs.002' 10240,
 FILE '/home/db2inst1/db2inst1/NODE0000/test6/usertbs.003' 10240)
 temporary tablespace managed by database using
 (FILE '/home/db2inst1/db2inst1/NODE0000/test6/temptbs.001' 10240)
 DB20000I  the CREATE DATABASE command completed successfully.
```

Again, a rather long statement, but the same tablespace specification pattern is easily spotted, and this should be starting to seem like second nature with your growing knowledge of database and tablespace creation. Your biggest problem will be not making typing errors. For the user (regular) tablespace, I included three file containers. DB2 uses them in a round-robin fashion as data is added to the tables housed within this tablespace.

Note Notice that I didn't specify a size when specifying the system (catalog) tablespace; that's because the system tablespace is critical to the operation of your database, and it would be churlish to economize on its space, only to run into problems later. I seriously recommend never allocating a fixed size for the system tablespace; instead enable AUTORESIZE to allow for all current and future system catalog tables and other system objects to grow unimpeded. If you attempt to economize on this setting, you'll start to encounter errors and/or warnings during database creation. Common examples are receiving the error SQL1088W warning that after database creation, the core utilities couldn't be bound successfully, and SQL1043C stating that the database services could not create the database because of insufficient storage allocated to the catalog.

Tuning Initial Tablespace Parameters

When creating or altering tablespaces, five performance parameters can be set for each tablespace to communicate to DB2 the relative speed and performance of the underlying storage and caching area in which to buffer data. This in turn helps DB2 make optimization decisions about how to fetch and use data when executing queries. The five parameters are as follows:

- **EXTENTSIZE:** The EXTENTSIZE parameter determines how much data will be added to a container of a tablespace before DB2 moves on to the next container in the tablespace. This can be measured in database pages or in an absolute number of bytes (although that latter option is rarely used in practice). This is the main method for controlling how evenly multiple containers are filled. It also affects the minimum number of storage pages DB2 allocates for new objects and it sets the size of a read that DB2 performs during a scan of a table. Once set during tablespace creation, it cannot be changed.

- **PREFETCHSIZE:** The PREFETCHSIZE parameter governs how much data DB2 will attempt to proactively fetch from a tablespace in anticipation of a query's needs. The goal with prefetching is to already have the data cached in the buffer pool (see BUFFERPOOL in the following bullet) before the query gets to the point where the data is required. This parameter can also be set in database pages or number of bytes. PREFETCHSIZE should always be set as a multiple of EXTENTSIZE, although you can modify it at any time to a different multiple.

- **BUFFERPOOL:** The BUFFERPOOL parameter is DB2's mechanism for caching data from the database in memory. One or more tablespaces can be allocated to a buffer pool. I'll discuss these in more detail shortly. A tablespace's buffer pool can be changed if desired.

- **OVERHEAD:** The OVERHEAD value tells DB2 about the access characteristics of the underlying storage media—disks and even NAS/SAN where these are used. It is a combined estimate of the disk seek, read latency, and I/O controller overhead time. DB2 uses this information, in an advisory instead of a strict fashion, to help optimize queries and estimate the time it will take to actually read data from disk. This is measured in milliseconds. OVERHEAD can be difficult to calculate, especially if you had no direct involvement with the hardware setup of your server. The Control Center wizard for tablespace creation includes a calculation tool to turn figures you would know, such as disk rpm and seek time, into equivalent OVERHEAD and TRANSFERRATE values. You can change the OVERHEAD value at any time.

- **TRANSFERRATE**: The TRANSFERRATE parameter works in conjunction with the OVERHEAD parameter. TRANSFERRATE indicates to DB2 how quickly a page of data can be read into the nominated BUFFERPOOL once it has been found on disk. The optimizer treats this as advisory instead of a strict guaranteed measure. This value is measured in milliseconds. TRANSFERRATE benefits from the calculation tool for OVERHEAD mentioned previously. You can change the TRANSFERRATE parameter at any time.

Introducing Buffer Pools

Expecting a database to constantly read data only from disk to satisfy queries is like expecting you to push your car from home to work and back every day. Although certainly possible, it's not very practical, and there's one key technology that will greatly boost your speed! For cars, this is petrol/gas; for databases, the "vroom!" comes from memory. Specifically, enormous performance benefits come from keeping the most frequently referenced and change data from the database in a cache in memory, from which DB2 can fetch and write at hundreds or thousands of times the speed compared to actual disks.

DB2 calls these caches *buffer pools*, and one or more are present in every database. Every tablespace that you implicitly or explicitly create with your database has a buffer pool associated with it, and it is into this buffer pool that pages from the database are placed both on demand and when prefetching is triggered for user activity. A buffer pool can have multiple tablespaces associated with it. The benefit of having multiple buffer pools might not be immediately apparent. But consider the SAMPLE database. If you were to use only one buffer pool, your employees could quite happily nominate people for employee of the year, vote for them, and so on with only a few kilobytes of data being loaded into the buffer pool and used by DB2. But the first time someone stores a very long description of their reasons for nominating a colleague, DB2 pushes megabytes of data through the buffer pool. This could conceivably "eject" much of the frequently used data out of the system back to disk to accommodate such a comparatively oversized chunk of data. If I introduce a separate tablespace for oversized tables and indexes, and allocate it a separate buffer pool, activity dealing with long nominations doesn't affect how frequently accessed information such as employee data, votes, and other information is cached.

When a database is created via any means, DB2 creates the first buffer pool automatically and calls it IBMDEFAULTBP. It is given a page size to match the page size you specify for your database or it defaults to 4KB, along with the database, if you don't specify an explicit value. Until such time as you create additional buffer pools, all tablespaces are implicitly allocated to the IBMDEFAULTBP buffer pool. Even better, you also automatically gain the benefit of DB2's Self-Tuning Memory Management (STTM). This part of DB2's autonomic management features continually monitor the buffer pool's memory use and the memory used by other parts of DB2, seamlessly reallocating memory to where it's needed most.

You can create new buffer pools with the CREATE BUFFERPOOL command, providing the page size you want this buffer pool to use:

```
db2 => create bufferpool awardbp size 10000 pagesize 4K
DB20000I  The SQL command completed successfully.
```

I'll cover how you then allocate a tablespace to use this buffer pool in the ALTER TABLESPACE section that follows. DB2 checks the current memory allocation and availability to ensure that your available memory can accommodate the size of your new buffer pool, but you should still be prudent about how much memory you allocate with the size parameter. The size parameter is a number of pages, so don't forget to multiply it by your pagesize to determine the true memory required. If you do overallocate, DB2 reports the following warning:

```
SQL20189W  The buffer pool operation (CREATE/ALTER) will not take effect until
the next database startup due to insufficient memory.  SQLSTATE=01657
```

This is usually a transient error, and DB2 allocates the specified buffer pool on the next database restart. It is prudent to double-check that you didn't accidentally create a gargantuan buffer pool by mistake because that might prevent the database from starting at all.

There are several advanced features of buffer pools that go beyond simply specifying size and pagesize. There are also parameters that allow buffer pools to perform caching operations based on groups of database pages called *blocks*. This topic is a little beyond the scope of the introduction, but where you have a scan-intensive workload and would benefit from asynchronously prefetching a lot of data from disk, you should refer to the DB2 Information Center for the BLOCKSIZE and NUMBLOCKPAGES parameters.

Moving Beyond Database, Tablespace, and Buffer Pool Basics

There are additional parameters that can be set for tablespaces that don't involve performance. For regular tablespaces, such as the default user tablespace that every database has, you might specify a DROPPED TABLE RECOVERY option, which allows fine-grained, table-level restoration during recovery operations. I'll talk more about this in Chapter 19 when I discuss backup and recovery.

There are quite a few other options available for database and tablespace creation that go beyond the scope of an introductory book. Two of the features I'll skip at this point are DB2's database-partitioning feature and partition groups, which are features of DB2 that allow for massively scalable databases to operate across multiple database nodes—most commonly, different physical or virtual machines. In many of the previous examples for database creation, you'll notice a directory named NODE0000 appearing in many of the paths used for tablespace containers. DB2 Express-C doesn't support the use of database partition groups, nodes, and so forth. Implicitly, there is only a single node for Express-C, and IBM's default naming for the nodes (regardless of whether partitions and so on are supported) is to start counting from zero—thus the name NODE0000. You are free to use completely different path/directory names when working with your databases and tablespaces.

DB2 rigorously checks directories at database- and tablespace-creation time to ensure that its rules about data placement are followed. For instance, if you try to store the containers for one database in a subdirectory of another's, DB2 reports a container path in use error. Similarly, if you lack permissions to use a directory, DB2 responds with a bad container path error. I stuck with the default placement that DB2's wizards and automatic storage management use to avoid cluttering your disks with DB2 data all over the place.

Creating Databases with Many Options

If you're like me, you'll get a great sense of accomplishment from realizing how sophisticated your knowledge of database (and tablespace) creation has become. You now know how to create databases, identify language-based settings, decide on storage characteristics, and finesse the performance profile of individual tablespaces. You can put this all together to create databases using all these options:

```
db2 => create database test7 automatic storage no on 'c:\'
 alias testdb6 using codeset utf-8 territory us collate using system pagesize 4096
 catalog tablespace managed by system using ('C:\DB2\NODE0000\test7\syscat')
 extentsize 16 prefetchsize 16 overhead 10 transferrate 0.2
 user tablespace managed by database using
 (FILE ' C:\DB2\NODE0000\test7\usertbs\usertbs.001' 102400,
 FILE ' C:\DB2\NODE0000\test7\usertbs\usertbs.002' 102400,
 FILE ' C:\DB2\NODE0000\test7\usertbs\usertbs.003' 102400)
 extentsize 16 prefetchsize 64 overhead 10 transferrate 0.2
 temporary tablespace managed by database using (DEVICE 'F:' 204800)
 extentsize 16 prefetchsize 16 overhead 4 transferrate 0.05

DB20000I  the CREATE DATABASE command completed successfully.
```

That's an 11-line-long, database-creation SQL statement—and you now know what every detail within that statement means! That's a long way from the simple three-word command you used at the start of the chapter to get this topic rolling. Admittedly, the wizard-based approach to creating databases and even tablespaces is probably looking more appealing because there's far less syntax to remember.

Altering Databases

The structural aspects of databases, their tablespaces, and their configuration are controlled through quite a variety of commands. You are already familiar with the graphical and command-line approaches to modifying the database configuration (DBM CFG) parameters. You'll deal with altering tablespaces under the very next heading, so that leaves what can actually be achieved with the ALTER DATABASE command. The short answer is that there is only one purpose to using the ALTER DATABASE command: to provide additional automatic storage management locations for a database. Almost every other aspect of changing databases relates to changing one of the subordinate features or parameters.

To use the ALTER DATABASE command to add automatic storage, the syntax is incredibly straightforward. I created the database test4 earlier in this chapter, providing it the location /home/db2inst1 for storage. Let's assume that you mounted a new disk under /extra/db2space and want to have DB2 manage this automatically instead of resorting to rebuilding the database with normal SMS or DMS tablespaces and containers. The command is the following:

```
db2 => alter database test4 add storage on '/extra/db2space'
DB20000I  The ALTER DATABASE command completed successfully.
```

That's it! You successfully added space to an automatic storage management database. DB2 takes all the necessary steps to use this storage, balance existing objects, calculate performance characteristics, and so on. I starved you of graphical tools in this chapter, which can achieve the same outcomes as the SQL you are learning. Just to put you at ease, this storage allocation can be achieved by selecting your desired database within the Control Center and right-clicking to open the context menu. Choose Manage Storage ➤ Add Automatic Storage to open the graphical dialog box shown in Figure 18-2.

Figure 18-2. *Using the Add Storage dialog box in Control Center*

Working with Tablespaces and Buffer Pools

If you've gone to the effort of selecting SMS tablespaces, or especially DMS tablespaces, you'll eventually want to alter them to manually add storage, indicate changes in underlying disk drive characteristics, and so forth. The CREATE TABLESPACE command exists to add tablespaces to databases after database creation. The ALTER TABLESPACE command is used to alter the storage and performance parameters of an existing tablespace, and the DROP TABLESPACE command is used to drop tablespaces.

To use any of these commands, you first must connect to the database as a user with SYSADM, SYSMAINT, or DBADM privileges. In these examples, I log in to my Windows operating system as the DB2ADMIN user:

```
db2 => connect to sample

    Database Connection Information
```

```
Database server          = DB2/NT 9.5.0
SQL authorization ID     = DB2ADMIN
Local database alias     = SAMPLE
```

Let's add a regular tablespace to explore:

```
db2 => create tablespace extratbs managed by database using
 (FILE 'c:\db2\node0000\sample\extratbs\extratbs.001' 10240K)
DB20000I  The SQL command completed successfully.
```

So far, so good. Let's also create a tablespace especially for large objects to use in the employee of the year system to house data such as award pictures, video clips, and so forth.

```
db2 => create large tablespace awardlobs managed by database using (FILE 'c:\db2
\node0000\sample\awardlobs\awardlobs.001' 1024M)
DB20000I  The SQL command completed successfully.
```

That gives one gigabyte to start with for storing the picture files. If that isn't enough, you can add another one gigabyte of storage using the ALTER TABLESPACE command:

```
db2 => alter tablespace awardlobs add
 (FILE 'c:\db2\node0000\sample\awardlobs.002' 10240K)
DB20000I  The SQL command completed successfully.
```

Of course, you might decide that constantly adding small files is a laborious process. Instead, use the DROP CONTAINER option for ALTER TABLESPACE and then show off its resize capabilities:

```
db2 => alter tablespace awardlobs drop
 (FILE 'c:\db2\node0000\sample\awardlobs.002')
DB20000I  The SQL command completed successfully.
db2 => alter tablespace awardlobs resize (ALL 20480M)
DB20000I  The SQL command completed successfully.
```

Note that dropping a container requires DB2 to redistribute the data housed within that container. If there isn't sufficient collective space in the remaining containers for the tablespace, the ALTER TABLESPACE command fails. Your data is safe. Here I used the resize option for ALTER TABLESPACE to specify the ultimate storage allocation I want for the container instead of using the EXTEND option to specify the extra storage I want allocated. There is also a REDUCE option to lower the storage available to a container. I also used the ALL synonym, which implicitly matches all the containers that exist for a tablespace. This is a handy way to cut down on the amount of typing you need to do.

You can alter the performance parameters using an appropriate command. Here's how you can specify PREFETCHSIZE, OVERHEAD, and TRANSFERRATE for the extratbs tablespace created previously:

```
db2 => alter tablespace extratbs prefetchsize 64 overhead 15 transferrate 0.5
DB20000I  The SQL command completed successfully.
```

You might decide that you no longer want a particular tablespace. Because you haven't created any objects in the extratbs tablespace nor stored any data in those (nonexistent) objects, it is a safe candidate to drop. The command couldn't be easier:

```
db2 => drop tablespace extratbs
DB20000I  The SQL command completed successfully.
```

Any file or directory type containers for the tablespace are removed by DB2. Any device containers are left untouched.

There are quite a few other options for tablespaces that can be explored with the ALTER TABLESPACE command. You can control storage at a higher level using the AUTORESIZE, INCREASESIZE, and MAXSIZE parameters. As discussed earlier, DB2 Express-C doesn't support multinode database partitioning, but for the more advanced editions of DB2 that do, additional parameters that govern the node on which a command is executed are available. You can also create and manage STRIPE SETs, a method of striping data across containers at the DB2 level, instead of relying on operating system and storage facilities such as RAID 0.

One interesting setting is the choice of using filesystem caching on UNIX and Linux systems. When filesystem caching is on, arguments can be made about the inefficiency of using double buffering and other problems. Because LOBs are unbuffered at the DB2 level, filesystem caching is valuable in some circumstances. But for normal table and index data, it can be very inefficient use of memory on a server. This book is probably not the place to conduct this argument, so instead I'll just illustrate turning filesystem caching off so you're comfortable with the procedure:

```
db2 => alter tablespace extratbs no file system caching
DB20000I  The SQL command completed successfully.
```

Once again, very intuitive. If you're familiar with the benefits of raw disk, you've already guessed that using raw containers for your tablespaces implicitly benefits from bypassing the filesystem cache. From now on, any data in the awardlobs tablespace is accessed using direct I/O, bypassing the filesystem cache.

By now, you're probably thinking, "What have I done? I made so many changes to my tablespaces that I can't remember what is stored where, and with what options." To round out your command-line knowledge of tablespaces, you need the LIST TABLESPACES command. In its basic form, it reports the tablespaces present, and their simple details:

```
db2 => list tablespaces


            Tablespaces for Current Database

Tablespace ID                     = 0
Name                              = SYSCATSPACE
Type                              = Database managed space
Contents                          = All permanent data. Regular table space.

State                             = 0x0000
  Detailed explanation:
    Normal

Tablespace ID                     = 1
```

```
Name                              = TEMPSPACE1
Type                              = System managed space
Contents                          = System Temporary data
State                             = 0x0000
  Detailed explanation:
    Normal

Tablespace ID                     = 2
Name                              = USERSPACE1
Type                              = Database managed space
Contents                          = All permanent data. Large table space.
State                             = 0x0000
  Detailed explanation:
    Normal
... (and so on)
```

There is also an extension to the command, LIST TABLESPACES SHOW DETAIL, which goes to town on the relevant information. Here's a snippet:

```
db2 => list tablespaces show detail

          Tablespaces for Current Database

...

Tablespace ID                     = 6
Name                              = AWARDLOBS
Type                              = Database managed space
Contents                          = All permanent data. Large table space.
State                             = 0x0000
  Detailed explanation:
    Normal
Total pages                       = 5120000
Useable pages                     = 5199968
Used pages                        = 96
Free pages                        = 5199872
High water mark (pages)           = 96
Page size (bytes)                 = 4096
Extent size (pages)               = 32
Prefetch size (pages)             = 64
Number of containers              = 1
```

That output includes one useful extra detail: the Tablespace ID. You can incorporate it into the third variant of the LIST TABLESPACES command, which is the LIST TABLESPACE CONTAINERS command:

```
db2 => list tablespace containers for 6

          Tablespace Containers for Tablespace 6
```

```
Container ID            = 0
Name                    = c:\db2\node0000\sample\awardlobs\awardlobs.001
Type                    = File
```

A buffer pool is ready and waiting for the awardlobs tablespace, and you can use another variant of the ALTER TABLESPACE command to associate the two:

```
db2 => alter tablespace awardlobs bufferpool awardbp
DB20000I  The SQL command completed successfully.
```

If you decide that you have under- or overestimated the necessary memory needed for the buffer pool, you can use the ALTER BUFFERPOOL statement to resize the memory settings:

```
db2 => alter bufferpool awardbp immediate size 50000
DB20000I  The SQL command completed successfully.
```

Notice that I included the key term immediate to indicate I want DB2 to start allocating extra memory to this buffer pool as soon as demand dictates instead of having to wait for a database restart or tablespace quiescence. You can force the latter behavior by using the keyword deferred instead of immediate.

All these management and tuning options are naturally available through the Control Center graphical interface, too. Now that you're an expert on SQL techniques, you can appreciate what the Control Center is doing on your behalf (see Figure 18-3).

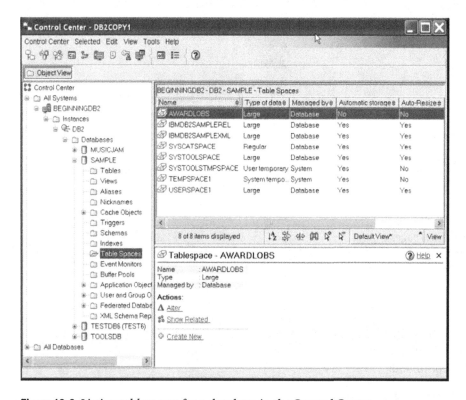

Figure 18-3. *Listing tablespaces for a database in the Control Center*

Each database displays its tablespaces in the dedicated Table Spaces folder. You can right-click any tablespace and manage its available properties in the one dialog box, as shown in Figure 18-4.

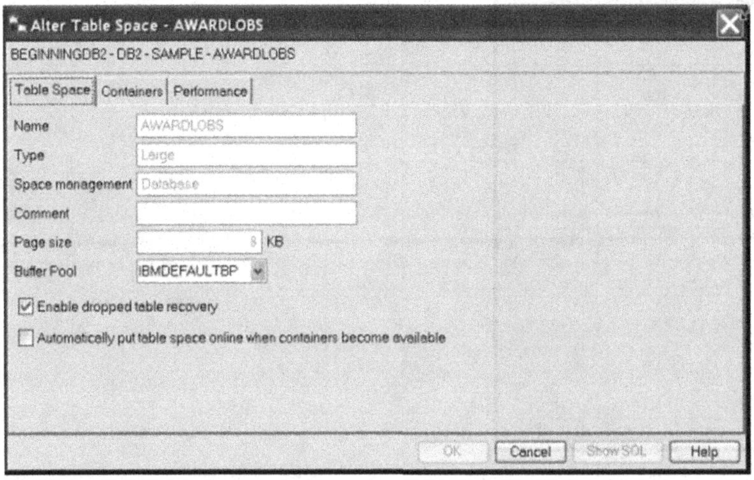

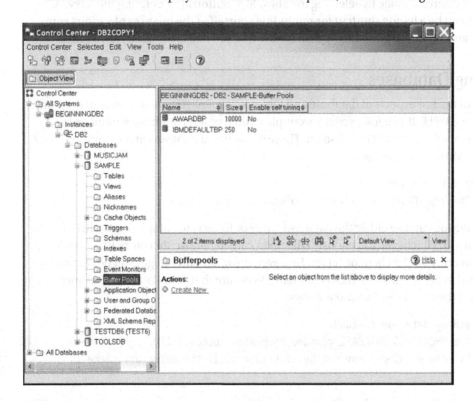

Figure 18-4. *Altering tablespace properties in the Control Center*

Each database also displays the available buffer pools, as shown in Figure 18-5.

Figure 18-5. *Listing buffer pools for a database in the Control Center*

To change a buffer pool, right-clicking and selecting Alter displays the buffer pool management dialog box shown in Figure 18-6.

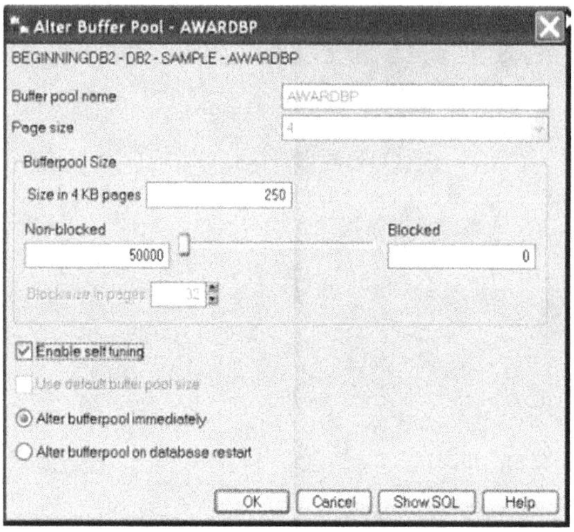

Figure 18-6. *Listing buffer pools for a database in the Control Center*

For all these dialog boxes you can provide a friendly reminder of the right SQL syntax to achieve your desired change by selecting the Show SQL button after entering the relevant details. This can be a handy shortcut for reminding yourself of the nuances of various commands and also for quickly building typical scripts that you can later modify as required.

Dropping Databases

I waited until the last aspects of database and tablespace management to return to the working database, SAMPLE. If you followed the examples, you'll now have a host of other test databases, named test1, test2, and so on. These unwanted databases can be dropped using the DROP DATABASE command:

```
db2 => drop database test3
DB20000I  The DROP DATABASE command completed successfully.
```

Note that you can use either the database name or its alias to complete the DROP DATABASE command. Whichever you choose, DB2 takes care to remove that entry from the database directory on the client or server. However, the other entry might still be cataloged, and you need to use the UNCATALOG command to ensure that your database directory details reflect the real state of your databases:

```
db2 => uncatalog database testdb3
DB20000I  The UNCATALOG DATABASE command completed successfully.
DB21056W  Directory changes may not be effective until the directory cache is
refreshed.
```

The Control Center provides a Drop option on the context menu of every database and database alias.

Summary

Where previously the wizards and graphical user interface (GUI) tools for DB2 did all the work of database creation for you, this chapter's introduction to SQL for DB2 enables you to create, manage, and change databases and related tablespaces and buffer pools at will. You might find that you only rarely need to use the SQL commands that manipulate databases, but you'll be thankful that you're fully versed in the right commands to use to manage tablespace storage, manipulate buffer pools, and set language settings for databases like a pro.

## CHAPTER 19

DB2 Backup and Recovery

The topics of database backups and database recovery are often dealt with in a dry, matter-of-fact way by discussing syntax options, hypothetical scenarios, and notions of clinical execution of a few commands in much the same way you'd pour a glass of water. I tend to deal with these subjects a little more emotionally. The reason for this is clear-cut and best phrased as a question. Exactly how important is your data to you? What would your situation be if you lost your database, whom would it affect, and how would you deal with the loss?

These kinds of questions sound a little trite, but they really get to the heart of the topic of backups and recovery. Endless pages discussing backup options and techniques are cold comfort if you can't actually restore your data, shielding your users from suffering possible impact from disasters of all kinds. If there's one thing you get from this chapter, I hope it is that you should always be concerned with *database recovery*; database backups are merely a tool to achieve the ability to *recover*.

Why You Should Care

This is the part of the book where I scare you with stories of wildly erratic power supplies that seem like a scene from the lab of Dr. Frankenstein, calamitous user actions that smite your data like a falling asteroid, and spontaneous server destruction triggered by marauding Japanese monsters such as Godzilla and Mothra. In reality, the events that lead you to rely on your backups, and make you resort to restoration and recovery, can be as mundane as a poorly constructed data manipulation language (DML) statement or a failed software upgrade. It's at those times when a 700-feet-tall, fire-breathing lizard and your pointy-headed boss seem uncannily similar.

It usually falls to database administrators to perform backup and recovery tasks—although sometimes the responsibility is shared with system administrators and even storage administrators. Regardless of your job, you'll need the right permissions to do the job.

Permissions for Backup and Recovery

To perform any kind of database backup, the person issuing the backup command needs to be a member of the SYSADM, SYSCTRL, or SYSMAINT group for the DB2 instance. Note that once a backup is taken, the files on disk or tapes are treated as normal operating system objects instead of DB2 objects, so your operating system privileges are also important in deciding how secure your backups are after DB2 has created them.

To perform a normal recovery of an existing database in place, the person performing the recover and rollforward commands has to be part of the SYSADM, SYSCTRL, or SYSMAINT group for the DB2 instance. If a new database is being created as part of the restore operation, either SYSADM or SYSCTRL is required.

Understanding DB2 Logging

One of the four capabilities that all relational databases aspire to is assuring durable transactions during normal operation and when things go wrong. (Durability is the *D* in *ACID*.) Like most databases, DB2 builds much of its durability framework on the notion of logging. In essence, whenever a transaction is attempted in DB2, it is first written to the log (sometimes known as write-ahead logging), and only then is it actually performed on the tables, data, and so on. DB2 backup and recovery rely heavily on the existence of the DB2 log files for a database, and on the options set for logging in the system. Understanding them provides the necessary foundation for understanding and using the backup and recovery options.

General Logging Principles

DB2 uses log files as a permanent record of every change made to database objects and their data. These files are normal operating system files, and can be written to a regular file system or raw devices. I recommend against using raw devices, however, because all it takes is a colleague using a clumsy dd command, and there goes your all-important log file. The flow of data and logging when you attempt to execute a transaction, or unit of work as it is known in DB2, is pictured in Figure 19-1.

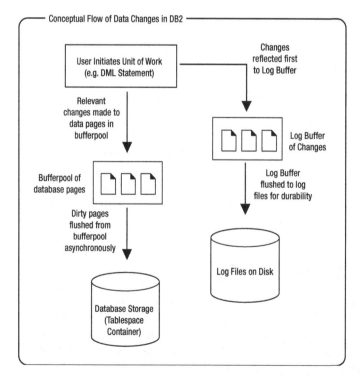

Figure 19-1. *The flow of changes and logging during a unit of work in DB2*

The flow of actions in Figure 19-1 reinforces the fact that logging happens prior to actual data changes being reflected in object pages. Notice the Log Buffer, which has the role of acting as the fast, in-memory location for staging log writes before they're flushed to the log files on disk. The size of this buffer is controlled by a database configuration parameter called LOGBUFSZ. The LOGBUFSZ parameter, which can range from 4 to 4,096 pages in size, indicates the number of pages (at 4KB each) that will be buffered.

Log File Types

DB2 databases use two sets of log files during operation. When a database is activated, either at startup time or when the first connection is made, the database immediately acquires all its primary log files. The database configuration parameters that control how many primary log files to use and their size are LOGPRIMARY and LOGFILSIZ, respectively. LOGPRIMARY indicates how many primary log files to use, and LOGFILSIZ controls their size, measured in 4KB database pages.

Secondary log files act like a standby mechanism, allocated only when a unit of work exhausts all the space configured for primary log files before reaching its commit point. They are allocated one at a time, up to the limit imposed by the LOGSECOND parameter. Once the transaction(s) using the secondary log files commit or roll back, DB2 returns to using primary log files until the next time it needs to overflow logging into the secondary log files again.

You can spot all these parameters easily from your database configuration. (You'll remember this command from way back at the beginning of the book.) In this instance, I'm running it against the SAMPLE database:

```
db2 => get db cfg
...
Log file size (4KB)                    (LOGFILSIZ) = 1000
Number of primary log files            (LOGPRIMARY) = 3
Number of secondary log files          (LOGSECOND) = 2
...
```

Those values are the default for any newly created database. In this instance, SAMPLE is configured for three primary log files, with the option to overflow to two secondary log files for long-running transactions. Each file is 4MB: 1,000 pages, each 4KB in size.

The total space allocated to all log files can't exceed 256GB, so there is a theoretical limit to how far DB2 can go with primary and secondary log files. The naming scheme used is S*nnnnnnn*.log, where *nnnnnnn* is a monotonically increasing number. So starting at S0000001.log, it's possible to generate 10 million log files before the numbering is exhausted. Whether this ever happens is dictated by the type of logging in operation—*circular* or *archive* logging.

Circular Logging

DB2's default logging technique for newly created databases is to use primary log files in rotation, starting at log file 1, moving to log file 2 when log file 1 is exhausted, and so on up to the number of log files indicated by the LOGPRIMARY parameter. Having filled the last log file, DB2 returns to the first log file and continues in a circular fashion. Visualizing this often helps to quickly grasp the concept (you can see the process pictured in Figure 19-2).

Primary Log Files

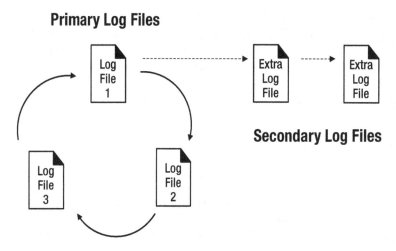

Figure 19-2. *Circular logging for a DB2 database*

If a long-running transaction exhausts all the primary log files before completing, the transaction spills over to the secondary log files, as previously described. You can easily imagine scenarios in which circular logging could be exhausted by particularly large transactions. For instance, common business-level tasks—such as end-of-month processing or large data-importing tasks—could run out of log space before completion. But circular logging does have its place, particularly in environments such as development and testing systems, in which data is often easily replaced; and also with summary and reporting systems, which are typically loaded once and then have only select-style statements run against them (which naturally change nothing and therefore have nothing to log).

There is, however, one significant drawback to circular logging that can tip you in favor of one of the alternatives. Databases in circular logging mode can be restored only from full backups. A circular logged database has no history of log files because they are constantly being overwritten and therefore cannot be restored to an arbitrary point in time, or benefit from incremental or delta backups (discussed shortly). With circular logging, it isn't possible to back up the database while it's online, so you need to deactivate the database, stopping all work, to perform a backup. When those more-flexible backup and recovery options are needed, you should use *archive* logging.

Archive Logging

DB2 archive logging is designed to record every change to your objects and data, and *keep* every change ever logged, for as long as you deem necessary. It does this by never overwriting a log file. Figure 19-3 shows the way DB2 continues to add new log files to your database logs in archive log mode. To carry on with the previous example, if log file 1 fills, DB2 then creates and uses log file 2. When it fills, the database moves on to log file 3, and so on.

Primary Log Files

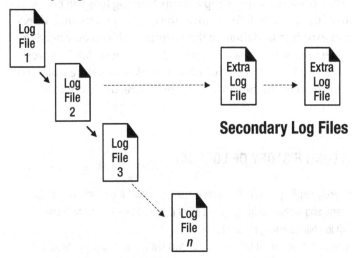

Figure 19-3. *Archive logging for a DB2 database*

Archive logging provides access to the full range of backup and recovery capabilities offered by DB2. I'll cover them in detail shortly, but the essence of archive logging is to retain the log files representing your transactions so you can recover all or part of your database to any arbitrary point in time. To enable archive logging, you must change the value of the LOGARCHMETH1 parameter to one of the following values:

- **LOGRETAIN**: This setting is the most straightforward method for activating archive logging. It indicates to DB2 that log files should be kept and not overwritten. You and the database administrator must manage the archive log files.

- **USEREXIT**: This setting goes one step further than LOGRETAIN. Not only does it ensure that archive logging is in effect, but it also triggers the use of automatic log file archival and retrieval, using a custom utility, or user exit, called db2uext2 in the ${DB2_INSTALL_PATH}/sqllib/adm directory under Linux or the %DB2_INSTALL_PATH%\sqllib\bin directory under Windows.

- **DISK:*path_to_directory***: Using the DISK setting is akin to using USEREXIT, but in this case the DB2 engine itself performs archiving to and retrieval from a nominated location on disk. No custom executable is involved.

- **TSM:*tsm_management_module***: This is a special case of user exit, which relies on IBM's Tivoli Storage Manager software to provide the archival and retrieval functions.

- **VENDOR:*vendor_management_module***: Third parties such as EMC, Veritas, and others provide plug-in modules that mimic the preceding TSM technique.

- **OFF**: This setting is often forgotten in the list of possible values for LOGARCHMETH1. If you want to turn off archive logging and go back to circular logging, OFF is the setting to use.

Those options might seem complicated at first, but in reality you'll probably start using either LOGRETAIN or DISK, which provide for a very simple setup. Your log files will be retained indefinitely; if you choose DISK, DB2 helpfully moves the files to a nominated directory for long-term storage. You can expect to find them in the same place if you ever need to use one of the advanced recovery techniques, such as roll forward recovery, which I'll cover shortly. By enabling archive logging, you have all the information needed to restore a database to an arbitrary point in time and have access to the most sophisticated recovery options DB2 offers.

A LONG HISTORY OF LOGGING

From its very early versions, DB2 has provided for points in its backup code to allow for custom tasks to be run. In particular, when it comes to managing archive logging files, a point in the code—known as a user exit—allows people to write their own log file–handling routines.

A parameter called USEREXIT was historically used to indicate that this feature was to be invoked. With the advent of more automatic management features, IBM introduced the LOGRETAIN parameter to help simplify archive logging where some other task would take care of log files, but where no user exit need be triggered. You can see how these older parameters influenced the new settings that are available.

The two deprecated parameters USEREXIT and LOGRETAIN are still present, and if you try to set either of them, DB2 is smart enough to work out the equivalent setting for LOGARCHMETH1. It then performs an automatic complementary change to that parameter, too.

Activating archive logging is as simple as setting the relevant database configuration parameter:

```
db2 => update db cfg using LOGARCHMETH1 LOGRETAIN
DB20000I  The UPDATE DATABASE CONFIGURATION command completed successfully.
SQL1363W One or more of the parameters submitted for immediate modification
were not changed dynamically. For these configuration parameters, all
applications must disconnect from this database before the changes become
effective.
```

Okay, so maybe not as simple as I made out. Although changing the setting is straightforward, you'll note the informational message that accompanies such a change. Having altered the logging method, DB2 is wise enough to figure out that regardless of what my old logging method was and the new one is, I will almost certainly be in a position in which old and new backups can't be restored contiguously if I encounter a problem in the future. As such, it's forcing me to take a full backup of the database now—before any new work can be done. I'll cover such a backup in the coming pages. If I try to reconnect to the database now, I'll be met with the following:

```
db2 => disconnect sample
DB20000I  The SQL DISCONNECT command completed successfully.
db2 => connect to sample
SQL1116N  A connection to or activation of database "SAMPLE" cannot be made
because of BACKUP PENDING.  SQLSTATE=57019
```

If I'm not the last to disconnect from the database (thus deactivating it), or if the database was activated explicitly with the ACTIVATE DATABASE command, I won't necessarily see this behavior. As the database administrator, if you need to be certain about the state of your databases pre- and post-change to the configuration, LIST ACTIVE DATABASES shows you exactly which databases are activated and deactivated.

Now it's time to bring on the explanation of backups!

Infinite Logging

There is one more permutation of logging that's worth investigating. Even in archive logging mode, the parameters LOGPRIMARY and LOGSECOND can still constrain the maximum size of a transaction, even though you can keep allocating as many log files as your storage can hold. If a transaction exhausts the sum of the log files represented in the two parameters, DB2 halts the transaction. This can even happen at a lower point if either the MAX_LOG or NUM_LOG_SPAN parameter is set. MAX_LOG controls the maximum percentage of log space a single unit of work can consume, and NUM_LOG_SPAN performs a similar constraint based on the maximum number of log files allowed to be used by a single unit of work.

There are times when it's nice not to worry about the minutiae of how much logging is happening and what fine-grained allocation you can offer to your applications and users. If you're blessed with abundant storage, and an efficient régime for log archival and retrieval, you might want to tell DB2 to use only as many log files as required to keep your transactions humming. It is for this scenario that infinite logging was created.

Activate infinite logging by setting the LOGSECOND parameter to -1. You also implicitly activate USEREXIT and archive logging if it was not already set in your database. With infinite logging in place, DB2 uses the primary log files in a typical fashion; if any transaction requires more space, DB2 continues to allocate secondary log files until the unit of work commits or storage is exhausted.

Caution It is tempting to think you should just set infinite logging to free yourself of another housekeeping task. I offer a word of warning here to dent your potential enthusiasm a little. With infinite logging enabled I've seen log storage blow out to consume all available space dozens of times. In almost every case, the culprit wasn't a large *bona fide* transaction; instead, it was due to developer error, typing errors in writing SQL, a unit of work being left uncommitted for a long time, or miscalculated effects of certain business logic. It might sound like a good idea, but remember the old Chinese proverb, "Be careful what you wish for—it might just come true."

Log Housekeeping

To complete the logging foundation for later use in backups and recovery, there are two more details worth knowing. In all the discussions about logging, you'll have noticed that logs are written to disk when the Log Buffer is flushed. And you're probably aware that disks are the one part of a computer guaranteed to fail at the most inopportune time, usually right after you mutter these words: What could possibly go wrong?

DB2 provides a method to mirror your log files, so DB2 writes identical log file information to two separate locations. If the MIRRORLOGPATH parameter is set, your logs are written to both the normal and mirrored directories specified. Naturally, for it to be of any benefit in protecting against disk failure, your path for mirrored log files should point to a completely separate disk drive. Be especially careful if your environment uses RAID or some form of storage array, in which different logical volumes used under your file systems might actually reside in whole, or in part, on the same disk!

Sometimes it's important to make sure that information possibly still being tracked in an active log file (one that hasn't been filled and archived) is securely closed off and processed by the user exit or other archive log-management tools. Typically, this might be before a big upgrade or as part of some quality assurance task. You can manually force DB2 to archive a log on demand by using this command:

```
ARCHIVE LOG FOR DATABASE your_database_name
```

This command forces the Log Buffers to flush and it also forces existing transactions to switch over to a new log file, thus freeing the current log files on disk for archiving.

DB2 Backups

It's time! Time to back up your database. You created it, added objects, changed data, tweaked parameters, and potentially even altered the log parameters if you've followed this chapter. Enough talk. It's time for action. Run to your command line (*don't walk!*) and type the following commands:

```
db2 => attach to db2inst1

   Instance Attachment Information

 Instance server        = DB2/LINUX 9.5.0
 Authorization ID       = DB2INST1
 Local instance alias   = DB2INST1

db2 => backup database sample to /db2backups/sample

Backup successful.  The timestamp for this backup image is : 20080301153901
```

If your instance is named something else (such as DB2 if you're using Windows), be sure to attach to the relevant instance name. Choose a directory that exists on your platform (and doesn't contain any other database files that might confuse you later) and use backslashes again if you're on Windows. The outcome should be very similar to the previous text. When you see the key phrase Backup successful, you know you've achieved your first backup.

Congratulations! Open the champagne, and cue the beach scene from the film *From Here to Eternity*. Well, perhaps I'm taking the celebration too far. You just took your first DB2 backup, so all that remains is to explore the added options that a backup provides. You'll have mastered one half of the goal you set out to achieve at the start of this chapter: the ability to recover from any disaster.

Here the simplest form of the backup statement is used, which conforms to the following structure:

```
Backup database database_name to backup_location
```

The value for *database_name* can be the name of the database or the alias used to catalog it from the location from which you want to perform the backup. The *backup_location* is typically a directory or a device such as a tape drive. Before you explore the backup options further, let's investigate exactly what it is you've backed up.

Anatomy of a Backup

When you create a backup, what is it exactly that is being generated? I'm glad you asked. By issuing the backup command, you instruct DB2 to do the following:

- Take a logical copy of all the tablespaces in a database, and place them in the specified location.

- Copy the catalog information about tablespaces and containers.

- Copy the database configuration information, and log details.

- Copy the Recovery History file contents.

For all these elements, the backup does not simply copy underlying operating system files, which would be both wasteful and difficult. Instead, for configuration and administrative information such as the database configuration and recovery history file, DB2 copies the contents of these files to include in the backup image. For your data, DB2 examines the tablespaces for your database and backs up the used data pages in the tablespaces, as well as the unused pages that share an extent with other used pages. In this way, partially and fully populated extents are backed up, and totally unused ones are skipped in an extent-based logical fashion. DB2 Enterprise edition includes capabilities to compress unused pages to save space. This is understandable when you think about very large, freshly created tablespaces and containers.

Because all the components of a backup are copied logically, you won't find individual configuration files or tablespace container files in your backup location. Instead, you'll find a file such as SAMPLE.0.db2inst1.NODE0000.CATN0000.20080301153901.001. Such a long name deserves a little explanation. The general format is as follows:

```
DBALIAS.TYPEID.INSTANCE.NODE.CATALOGNODE.YYYYMMDDHHMISS.SEQUENCE
```

The date and time information in that file name are fairly self-explanatory, but the other parts could do with a little detail:

- **DBALIAS**: Your database name or cataloged alias.

- **TYPEID**: The type of backup: 0 for full and 3 for tablespace.

- **INSTANCE**: The instance name from which the backup was taken.

- **NODE**: The database node for a partitioned database. In this single-partition world, it is always NODE0000.

- **CATALOGNODE**: The catalog node number for a partitioned database. Again, because you're dealing only with single-partitioned DB2, it always reads CATN0000.

- **SEQUENCE**: The sequence number for backups taken at the current timestamp.

This naming scheme can be useful for keeping track of your backups and it is also used by DB2 at restore time to match the time of your desired backup to the restore job being performed.

Note DB2 on Windows historically used nested subdirectories for each element of a backup image name instead of a single long file name. With the release of DB2 9, IBM switched to the consistent format it used on Linux and UNIX to make it the universal format. You might still encounter older backups taken with earlier versions of DB2 that use the nested folders under Windows, however.

Taking Backups from the Control Center

Given how easy it was to perform a backup from the command line, the Control Center graphical user interface (GUI) has a tough challenge making backups simpler and easier. The good news is that not only are backups easy to take through the Control Center, but the options available for backups are easily controlled as well.

As you'd expect, there's a wizard to drive the backup process available from the context menu of your chosen database, as shown in Figure 19-4.

This wizard is like most others in the Control Center, in that it asks you to choose from a range of possibilities before performing its work. So it's perfectly safe to invoke it now and follow along. The first screen, shown in Figure 19-5, asks you to nominate whether a full database backup or a selection of tablespaces should be attempted.

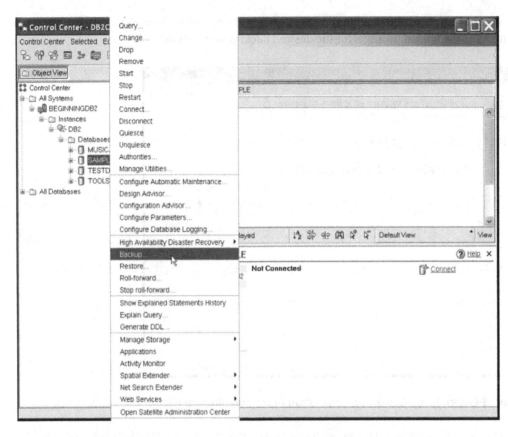

Figure 19-4. *Invoking the DB2 Backup Wizard from the Control Center*

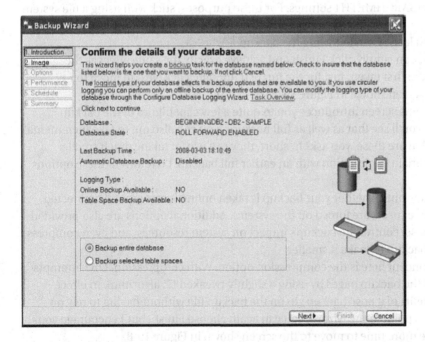

Figure 19-5. *Selecting full or tablespace backup in the DB2 Backup Wizard*

For the current example, opt for a full backup and proceed to the next screen. In Figure 19-6, the wizard prompts for the desired backup destination.

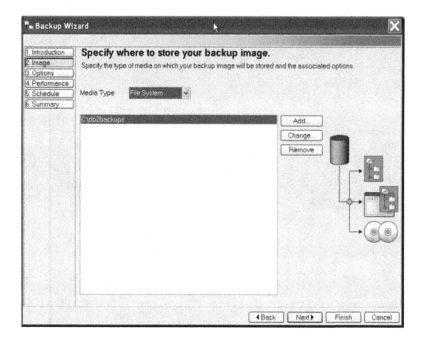

Figure 19-6. *Specifying the backup destination in the DB2 Backup Wizard*

Note the drop-down list for Media Type, in which you can specify a file system for a directory, a tape drive, or one of the advanced tools you first encountered earlier in this chapter in the discussion on LOGARCHMETH1 settings. For these purposes, stick with using a file system for a directory because it provides the most immediate results and gives you something tangible to investigate and learn from following the backup.

At this point you can simply click Finish and achieve exactly the same effect as the command-line backup first taken. Just for the fun of it, though, click Next to move to the backup options screen shown in Figure 19-7.

The backup options screen introduces you to quite a few capabilities of the backup engine. For starters, you'll see that as well as full backups, you can also opt to take incremental or delta backups. What are these, you ask? In short, they're a way of taking much smaller backup slices that work in conjunction with an earlier full backup. I'll return to these options shortly.

You can also determine whether your backup is taken online (users are still connected and working) or offline (users are forced off the system). Additional options are also provided to quiesce the database, control the backup's impact on system resources, and even compress the contents of the backup to make it smaller.

The only new concept here is the compression option. With compression, DB2 attempts to reduce the size of the backup pages by using a slightly tweaked LZ algorithm. In effect, you'll get all the benefits of a post-backup zip on the backup file without having to rely on another utility. At this point in the wizard, you can again choose Finish, but I encourage you to click Next just one more time to move to the screen shown in Figure 19-8.

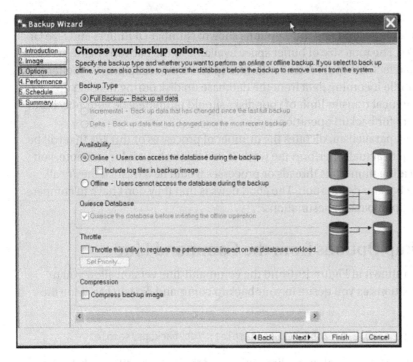

Figure 19-7. *Specifying the backup type and database availability in the DB2 Backup Wizard*

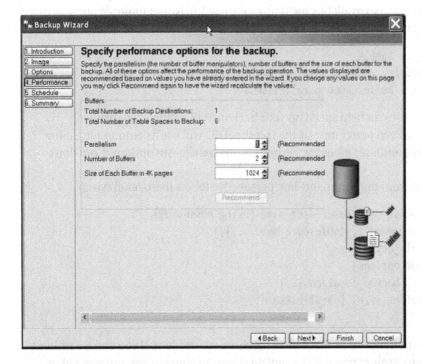

Figure 19-8. *Specifying performance characteristics for a backup in the DB2 Backup Wizard*

The last set of options you can specify for the backup covers specific performance characteristics. Let's start with the second and third options shown: Number Of Buffers and Size Of Each Buffer In 4K Pages. The total size of buffer space available to the backup engine acts as a governing resource. In effect, the more memory (buffer space) the backup has, the better the backup engine can handle incoming data from the database on disk during the backup, meaning that the theoretical transfer limit of your disks should ultimately be your only bottleneck instead of memory for backup operations.

The first parameter, parallelism, dictates the number of processes or threads that will be spawned by the backup to actually perform the work. If you think about it for a minute, you might worry that allocating numerous threads or processes would be a waste if they're all competing for a single backup destination. The good news is that they don't have to compete because you can back up to parallel destinations!

Advanced Backup Options from the Command Line

Both the wizard screen shown in Figure 19-6 and the command-line version allow you to specify as many destinations as you desire in your backup command. So you can issue the following command:

```
db2 => backup database sample to /db2backups/sample1, /db2backups/sample2
```

You'll see two files, one in each of those directories, and their names differ only by the sequence number component at the end of the file (another mystery solved). By adding a parallelism clause, or using the options in the GUI, you can leverage the fact that you might have significant hardware resources available, including multiple CPUs, and multiple physical disk spindles to which you can write backups. For example:

```
db2 => backup database sample
        to /mount1/sample, /mount2/sample, /mount3/sample, /mount4/sample
        with 16 buffers buffer 4096 parallelism 4
```

Options such as these can help speed up your backup to fit within ever-shrinking maintenance windows. Even better news is the fact that DB2 will use its autonomic tuning capabilities to work out optimal values for the buffers and parallelism options if you don't specify them.

The other options from the command-line perspective follow this overall syntax:

```
Backup database database_name [user user_name [using password]]
Tablespace (tablespace_name [, tablespace_name ...] )
[online] [incremental [delta]]
[use advanced_storage_options]
to backup_location [, backup_location ...]
[with n buffers] [buffer size] [parallelism n]
[without prompting]
```

Some of the options included in that syntax block are self-evident. If you choose without prompting, DB2 doesn't prompt you with helpful questions in your backup process. Other options, such as the use of advanced storage options for Tivoli and other systems, are beyond the scope of a beginner's book. There are some important options there that deserve deeper coverage that I've glossed over to this point, however. Let's tackle them in turn.

Tablespace Backups

It sometimes makes sense to back up a portion of the database, but not all of it, because you're sharing a development server or have different schemas at different points of evolution that need to be handled independently. If you use tablespaces to separate the storage of database objects, you can benefit from tablespace backups to target only that data for backup and recovery purposes.

A tablespace backup is very similar to a full DB2 database backup in most other respects. For instance, if you want to back up the USERSPACE1 tablespace from the SAMPLE database, you can use the following command that includes many of the other options already examined:

```
db2 => backup database sample tablespace userspace1
       to /db2backups/sample1, /db2backups/sample2
```

You have to remember some technical considerations when performing tablespace level backups. First, when objects in different tablespaces have referential integrity defined between them, it makes sense to include all the relevant tablespaces in the backup. If you don't, when it comes time to restore your data, you'll find problems with unmet foreign key constraints. Similarly, if you have data, indexes, and LOBs for a given table split across appropriate tablespaces, backing up these tablespaces in unison is also a good idea.

■**Caution** Be careful of the inability of a tablespace-level backup to back up temporary tablespaces. If you think about it, it makes sense because temporary tablespaces never hold permanent meaningful data.

Online and Offline Backups

The examples so far are offline backups, which is DB2's default behavior. But the good news is that DB2 supports online backups, meaning that users need not be interrupted during the processing of a backup. To invoke an online backup, simply include the keyword online in the syntax:

```
db2 => backup database sample online
       to /db2backups/sample1, /db2backups/sample2
       include logs
```

When a backup is taken in online mode, new work performed in the database is recorded in the archive log files until the backup is complete. For this reason, online backups are available only to databases configured with LOGRETAIN- or USEREXIT-style settings (including the options for advanced/third-party user exit libraries and infinite logging).

Incremental and Delta Backups

When it comes to backing up very large and/or very active databases, you might find that the time and resources required to perform a full backup start to affect your system and your users. To aid in these situations, you can use DB2 backup features to take a smaller backup of only the data that's changing in the database.

An *incremental backup* backs up only those pages from the database in which the data has changed since the last full backup. Figure 19-9 shows the logic of how successive incremental backups work following a full backup.

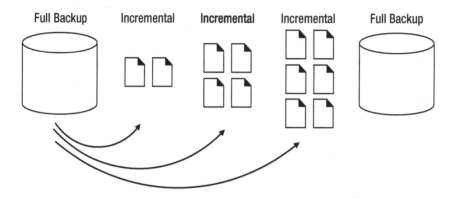

All Changed Pages Since Last Full Backup

Figure 19-9. *The effect of incremental backups in DB2*

A *delta backup* is an even more refined version of an incremental backup. Taking a delta backup captures only those changes reflected in the database since the last backup of any kind: full, incremental, or delta. Figure 19-10 shows how ongoing delta backups capture the changes to your data.

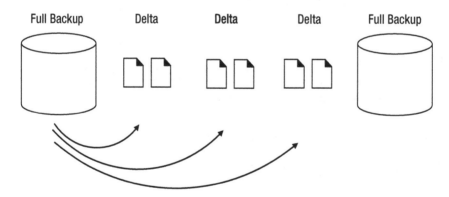

Changed Pages Since Last Full, Incremental or Delta Backup

Figure 19-10. *The effect of delta backups in DB2*

Using incremental or delta backups is as simple as including the relevant keyword in the backup command. For instance, to take a delta backup following the last backup of the SAMPLE database, I use the following syntax:

```
db2 => backup database sample online incremental delta
       to /db2backups/sample1, /db2backups/sample2
```

Database Recovery with DB2

If you ever bought any kind of insurance policy, you know the feeling of having gone to a significant amount of effort in the hopes of never having to call on that effort. Database recovery is very much like that—a lot of work and training in the hopes of never having to do a restore and recovery. That attitude might be a little pessimistic because there are certainly times when knowing how to restore your database is actually easy, painless, and desirable (for example, cloning an existing environment for testing or development, all the way through to building advanced disaster–recovery standby systems).

Knowing why you need to restore a database is really the first step because it guides your choice of commands and the backup images to which you'll need access. So be sure you know what you're trying to achieve before you start. Lost a database to disk corruption? It's likely you want to do a full restore. Developers asking for a self-contained tablespace to look the way it did yesterday? Chances are a tablespace restore suits your needs. Armed with the knowledge of what you need to achieve, you're ready to cover the commands and tools that let you achieve it.

Database Recovery for Free

The first kind of database recovery you should know about is the kind that comes for free with an industrial-strength database such as DB2. When a DB2 instance terminates abnormally, such as from an unprotected power outage or a hardware failure, there's no chance for the instance to roll back incomplete transactions or flush dirty pages to disk. Fortunately, thanks to the logging system already described, DB2 has all the information it needs to recover from such a crash when the database instance is next started. This is known as *crash recovery*, and it happens automatically; you need not lift a finger in most normal circumstances. If crash recovery finds a problem it can't deal with, such as missing log files or tablespace containers (you might have completely lost a disk without knowing it), crash recovery reports the problem to the db2diag.log file, allowing you to resort to one of the other recovery techniques I'll discuss shortly.

Restoring a Database from Backup

Getting started with database recovery is as simple as the backup process you've already mastered. Database backups are restored with the restore command; its most straightforward variant is as follows:

```
Restore database database_name from backup_directory taken at backup_timestamp
```

To restore the very first database backup you did previously, you can run the following statement:

```
db2 => restore database sample from/db2backups/sample taken at 20080301153901
```

You'll immediately be presented with the following warning prompt:

```
SQL2539W  Warning!  Restoring to an existing database that is the same as the
backup image database.  The database files will be deleted.
Do you want to continue ? (y/n)
```

This message frightened the daylights out of me the first time I ran a DB2 restore. Database files will be deleted? I want them restored, not removed! Fortunately, it's only the warning message that leaves a little to be desired. What it means is that the current database files will be deleted and replaced with versions reconstructed from the information found in the backup image. Answer yes, wait a few moments, and you should see the reassuring final notification:

```
DB20000I  The RESTORE DATABASE command completed successfully.
```

If your database were in circular logging mode, your restore process would end because no logs can be rolled forward for databases that are logged in circular fashion. You could connect to your freshly restored database and carry on about your business. But because you switched to archive logging before taking your first backup, if you try to connect now to the database, DB2 prevents you because the recovery isn't yet complete. You'll see a message such as this:

```
db2 => connect to sample
SQL1117N  A connection to or activation of database "SAMPLE" cannot be made
because of ROLL-FORWARD PENDING.  SQLSTATE=57019
```

At this point, you need to tell DB2 how much, if any, rolling forward through log files you want done to complete the database recovery.

Roll Forward Recovery from a Backup

Recovering a database in archive logging mode, including infinite logging, allows you to use all the accumulated log files following a backup to assist in your recovery efforts. The options are to use all, some, or even none of the log files. To instruct DB2 what you want done, you need to use the rollforward command. Its basic syntax looks like this:

```
Rollforward database database_name
{ complete | ( to some_timestamp | end of logs ) [and complete] }
```

Using the rollforward command in practice is the best way to come to grips with its initial options. Let's complete the recovery from the initial restore statement against the SAMPLE database:

```
db2 => rollforward database sample to end of logs and complete

                          Rollforward Status

 Input database alias                   = sample
 Number of nodes have returned status   = 1
```

```
Node number                        = 0
Rollforward status                 = not pending
Next log file to be read           =
Log files processed                = -
Last committed transaction         = 2008-03-04-10.41.00.000000 UTC
```

```
DB20000I  The ROLLFORWARD command completed successfully.
```

That's probably more information than you were expecting from the rollforward command, but its purpose is to give you a full snapshot of how your recovery completed. Most of the information there is self-explanatory, but the one item that is crucial in the example is the Rollforward status = not pending line. Because you instructed DB2 to use all available logs to roll forward by using the to end of logs directive, you don't want the rollforward status to report anything else.

Notice that I included the and complete directive in the command, which instructs DB2 that no further rolling forward will be performed and allows DB2 to perform final housekeeping on the database before making it available for use.

You could also have rolled forward using timestamp information, using a command such as this:

```
Rollforward database sample to 20080304061500
```

In this example, I roll forward to a particular point in time. I have also omitted the completion clause, so the database is still pending further roll forward recovery. I can decide at any time to simply complete rolling forward by issuing a completion command:

```
Rollforward database sample complete
```

Many more recovery and roll forward options are also available (discussed shortly).

Database Recovery Using the Control Center

You learned to recover databases and restore backups by using the recover and rollforward commands from the command line, so you're expecting me to say the GUI approach via the Control Center is just as easy. Clearly, the suspense trick won't work any more because you are absolutely right! Database recovery using the Control Center is easy! Jump all the way back to Figure 19-4. When you right-click a database such as SAMPLE, immediately below the Backup option sit the three amigos of database recovery: the Restore, Rollforward, and Stop Rollforward options.

Go ahead and choose the Restore option for the SAMPLE database; the Restore Database Wizard starts (see Figure 19-11).

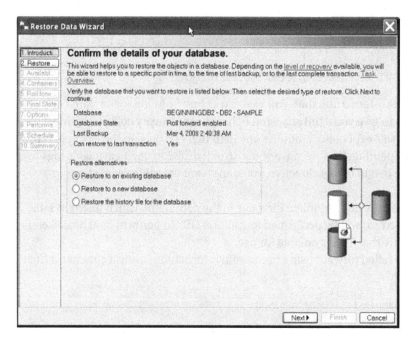

Figure 19-11. *Choosing the type of recovery in the Database Restore Wizard*

Besides the ability to restore to the current database, the wizard shows some of the other restore options I've yet to cover: restoring to a new database and restoring just the database recovery history file. You'll get to those options soon. For now, opt for a database restore to the existing database and choose Next. The wizard progresses to the screen shown in Figure 19-12.

Your choice is to select a full database restore or simply the tablespaces you might want to recover from your backup. Note that your backup image must include the tablespace you want if you propose to restore a given tablespace. Choose a full restore and click Next. Figure 19-13 shows that the wizard performed some kind of magic because it seems to know about all the backups performed.

In truth, it's a little simpler than that. The Restore Data Wizard has read the contents of the recovery history file to determine which backups are available. Choose any backup you like, but be aware that if you've moved backups on disk (to save space or because you sweep backups to tape as part of an off-site backup routine), the wizard won't be aware that the backup image has moved, and you'll quickly run in to an error. Choose your desired backup, and you'll notice that the Finish button is now active. You could do this now to mimic the first restore earlier in the chapter, but the wizard has a few tricks left, so click Next to continue.

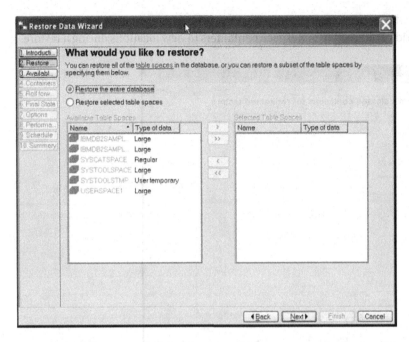

Figure 19-12. *Choosing a full database or tablespace restore in the Database Restore Wizard*

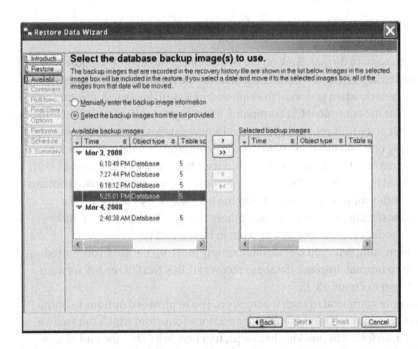

Figure 19-13. *Selecting the backup image to restore in the Database Restore Wizard*

You'll be presented with the screen shown in Figure 19-14, which is a deceptively simple interface into the world of redirecting tablespace containers to new locations during a restore.

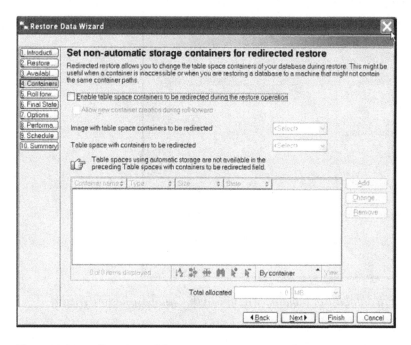

Figure 19-14. *Redirecting tablespace containers with the Database Restore Wizard*

Ask yourself why you want to do that. Back on the first screen of the wizard, suppose that you chose to restore the backup into a new database instead of the existing SAMPLE database. This is a very common scenario when you want to clone or duplicate a database for testing purposes. When the wizard (or the equivalent CLI command) actually gets to the point of restoring your data, where should it place it? If your intent is to seed a new database, instead of restoring (overwriting) your existing one, you hardly want to use the existing tablespace container locations. They're still being used by the original database. But your backup (by default) knows only about these. What's needed is a way to tell the restore operation to place the tablespace containers somewhere else, so both your existing database and the new one being created from a *redirected restore* can coexist without clobbering each other's storage. Presto, you now understand the purpose of the redirected restore option shown in Figure 19-14.

With that explanation complete, you can actually simply move on because you started this restore operation as a normal, in-place database recovery. Click Next to see roll forward recovery options, as shown in Figure 19-15.

This screen looks more complicated than it actually is. You're provided options to nominate a completion point for your roll forward recovery and locations from which the archive log files can be retrieved. To follow in previous footsteps, try choosing either the end of logs option or one of the point in time options, and then click Next.

The next screen of the wizard (not shown) is the Final State, which asks whether the recovery should actually be marked as complete, or the restored database left in roll forward recovery pending state. For this example, choose to complete the recovery. At this point, there are more screens in the wizard that deal with replacing log files and tweaking performance parameters such as buffers and parallelism that are conceptually similar to the same options you learned in the discussion on backups. Feel free to explore the contents of the remaining screens to understand what's offered. When you're happy with the various settings, click Finish to complete your database recovery.

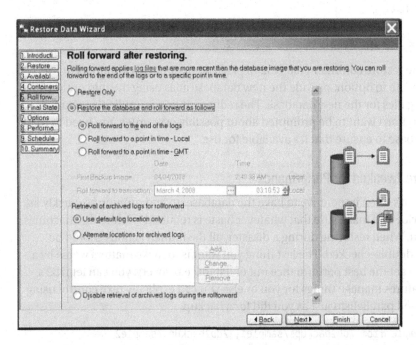

Figure 19-15. *Roll forward recovery options of the Database Restore Wizard*

Advanced Recovery Options from the Command Line

All the advanced recovery features you just witnessed in the Control Center GUI are available through the command line. In fact, there are so many options that I could fill several chapters on restoring databases and still not cover all the conceivable situations you might find yourself in. At that point you'd curse my name and attempt to beat your database into submission using the considerable bulk of this book.

A better approach to the advanced recovery features offered at the command line is to explore a number of the features, such as those I'm about to show you, and then to slowly but surely combine them into more and more complex scenarios that match more and more outlandish disasters that might befall you.

The complete syntax for the recover database command runs for nearly 20 lines. Repeating it here would serve to simply fill space and confuse you. So let's perform a range of common restore and recovery tasks to give you a feel for the options.

Full Database Restore with Redirection

Let's assume that I want to restore one of the SAMPLE database backups to a new database called SAMPLE2. I need to ensure that the tablespace containers are relocated to not jeopardize the current SAMPLE database. I use the following commands:

```
restore database sample from /db2backups/sample
taken at 20080301153901
to /db2/sample2 into sample2 newlogpath /db2/sample2/logs
redirect without prompting.

rollforward database sample2 complete
```

The options in the restore command tell DB2 to place the redirected containers in the directory indicated by the to option, provide the new database alias using the into option, and set the path for the log files for the new database. The redirect option is implicitly included and indicates that you don't want to be prompted about possible overwrites. You need to roll forward the new database to ensure that it's available for use.

Full Database Restore Tweaked for Performance

When disaster strikes, it's often imperative to have the database up and running as quickly as possible. Take my advice and make sure that whatever haste is required is left to the machines and not forced on you. When restoring during a disaster, all the human actions should be measured, calm, and double-checked. The last thing you want is to make matters worse by a misdirected action. To get the best performance out of database recovery, you can let DB2's autonomic tuning features manage things for you or else you can explicitly take control using buffers, buffer sizes, and parallelism just as you did for a backup.

```
restore database sample from /db2backups/sample1, /db2backups/sample2
taken at 20080303195125
with 16 buffers buffer 4096 parallelism 2
```

In this case, you allocate 16 buffers with 4096 pages each and have two threads performing recovery in parallel. Note that parallelism is used only by the restore command, not the rollforward command.

Individual Tablespace Restore with Database Online

One or more tablespaces can be restored in their own right with the restore command. You gain added flexibility with tablespace restores because they can source their backup information from relevant tablespace backups or from full backups. To restore the userspace1 tablespace from the full backup, you can issue a command like this:

```
restore database sample tablespace (userspace1)
from /db2backups/sample1, /db2backups/sample2
online
```

Adding the online clause directs DB2 to keep the rest of the database online and protects the tablespace(s) in question from user activity only until the restore process is complete. Using this technique, it is often possible to restore schemas, sets of tables, and other groups of objects with users even realizing that a restore has taken place.

When restoring tablespaces, you must include an explicit roll forward to account for the fact that your restored tablespace is now at a distinctly different logical point in time compared to the rest of your data. A tablespace roll forward is structured in a very similar way to a database roll forward, so you can use all the same timestamp and completion options with which you are already familiar. To complete the current example, you have to perform this roll forward:

```
rollforward database sample to end of logs and complete
tablespace (userspace1) online
```

Going Further with Advance Recovery Options

You'll almost certainly be getting that dazed look in your eyes after all this recovery work. Instead of bombarding you with more examples and syntax options, I recommend the following approach to learning more about DB2 backups and recovery. Using either good old-fashioned paper or a word processor, start writing down all the major building blocks for your database—everything from the configuration file, to containers, to log files. Next to each one of these, write down what type of backup is required to protect that part of the database. In a third column, note which command(s) you need to run to restore with the least impact on your system.

It won't take long to make a reasonably long list. Then practice each kind of backup and recovery, so you know all the little steps and nuances that are involved. As an added exercise, every time you see some horrendous data loss reported in the press or online, ask whether it is a situation you could have dealt with. If not, add it to you list of known disaster types and see whether you can simulate both the problem and successful recovery. The DB2 documentation online and the Information Center list all the esoteric options for recovery and roll forward that I've not covered in detail.

Summary

Database backup and recovery in DB2 are purposefully designed to be simple by default. The good news is that there is also a wealth of advanced options to help you cope with complex scenarios such as building cloned environments, point-in-time recovery, and even partial restoration of tablespaces while the database is in full use.

If there's one chapter to which you should pay attention (and follow the examples) it is this one. Think back to the start of this chapter, when I said the most important thing you can say about your database is that you have the ability to recover. Backups are important, but if you aren't versed in how to use them, they'll be cold comfort when your database is down and your users are relying on you to get it started again. Practice your recovery techniques and then practice them some more. With luck, you'll never be the star of one of those disasters you read about in the press.

CHAPTER 20

■■■

Sharing Your DB2 Environment

It has probably struck you that installing the entire suite of DB2 9.5 on any given computer just to have access to DB2 databases might not always be the most efficient solution. In fact, the most common scenarios for database access are from client machines that talk to servers hosting a database or from web front ends that talk to middle-tier servers, and those middle-tier servers then handle all database communication. This is classic two-tier and three-tier client-server stuff.

DB2 makes these and other access approaches very easy. For most client-to-server work, a set of libraries is bundled together to form the DB2 Client. It can be installed on nearly any operating system and configured to talk to one or more databases, for some or all users of a given machine.

Other approaches are also available, including "zero-footprint" methods of gaining access to DB2. Some of these approaches, such as JDBC thin drivers, are provided by IBM, and some are provided by third parties.

The installation and setup of these clients can be done from a graphical user interface (GUI) and also the command line or shell (no surprises there), so let's take a look at how installation and configuration is achieved under both Windows and Linux.

DB2 Clients on Linux and Windows

You have several options for installing the DB2 Client on a given machine. The DB2 Express-C edition download you obtained in Chapter 1 incorporates all the major components of the DB2 Client. Its one drawback is that the installer is streamlined to always include the DB2 server components, even when you want only the client. That's not as big an impost as you might expect because by choosing the relevant options to not create an initial instance or any databases, you consume a few megabytes of extra disk space—but otherwise you have exactly what you want.

An alternative is to revisit the IBM DB2 home page and obtain one of the specific DB2 Client installers to deploy the precise components for your client needs and nothing more. Let's examine both approaches so you'll be armed with the knowledge for future installations.

Using the DB2 Express-C Edition Installer

A complete reprise of Chapter 2 will no doubt put you to sleep. Better then to focus on the point of installation where selecting the DB2 Client components is made.

Recall that as you step through the wizard for installing DB2 Express-C edition, you're prompted with the feature selection screen, as shown in Figure 20-1.

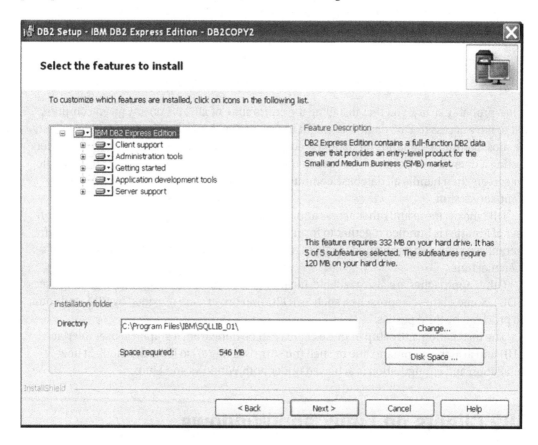

Figure 20-1. *Feature selection from the DB2 Express-C edition installer*

The first subcategory is Client Support. Opening this subcategory shows the components from which you can choose for client connectivity. As you can see in Figure 20-2, the components are Interfaces, Base Client Support, Satellite Synchronization, Spatial Extender Client, DB2 LDAP Support, and XML Extender.

Each of these components is covered in detail in the next section, in which I discuss all the components available in the dedicated DB2 Client installer. Another major difference between that installer and the DB2 Express-C Edition installer is that the scope and categorization of the client components is greatly simplified in the DB2 Express-C edition installer. The Client Support options are quite a reduced set that still gives you all the basic connectivity tools you require, but it assumes that the server management tools and other utilities are first-class installation categories in their own right instead of components of the Client Support category.

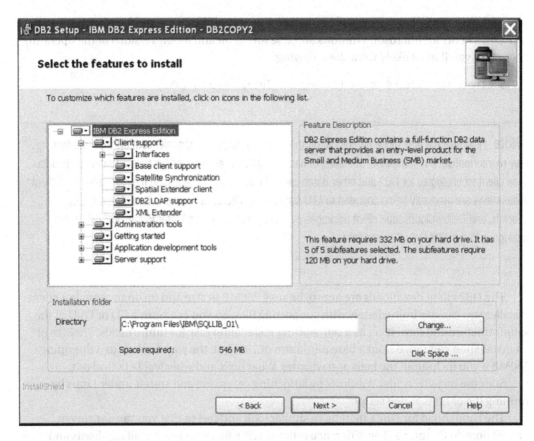

Figure 20-2. *The streamlined set of Client support components packaged in the DB2 Express-C edition installer*

Using the Dedicated DB2 Client Installers

The DB2 Client installers available from the DB2 download page are available for nearly every conceivable operating system. Everything from AIX to zLinux, and all places in between—and each and every one of them is free of charge except where the DB2 Connect gateway to mainframe systems is required. That's not meant to be quite the advertisement I've made it out to be; instead it's a pointer to be sure that you download the client for your particular operating system. At the time of writing, clients for Linux are available for x86, PPC, and mainframe-based Linux. Your dealings with DB2 -C edition to date have meant working with x86-based Linux, so to continue that trend (and I'm guessing you're probably not sitting at a mainframe reading this), the client you'll want is listed as the following:

```
DB2 9 Client for Linux on 32-bit AMD and Intel systems (x86)
```

And don't think that being spoiled for choice is only for Linux users. IBM also makes available DB2 clients for Microsoft Windows suitable for 32-bit and 64-bit versions of the operating system, so you'll most likely want the following:

```
DB2 9 Client for Windows on 32-bit AMD and Intel systems (x86)
```

Note I just love the way those names roll off the tongue. I suppose I can take comfort from the fact they're informative, if nothing else. Speaking of names, IBM has recently been repacking many of its database client technologies for DB2 and other databases into common packages. So the names for DB2 client installations are gradually being changed to *IBM Data Server Client*, as a generic term to cover DB2, Informix, and Derby/Cloudscape client packages owned by IBM. Any time I refer to the *DB2 Client*, it is analogous to the *IBM Data Server Client*.

The DB2 client downloads are approximately 250MB in size and unzip to provide a client installer you can use immediately with supporting files. So you can burn a CD or DVD of the same structure and have it act as a self-starting installation disc for future needs. The size of an installation can range from a bare minimum of 70MB all the way through to a thumping 560MB if you include all the bells and whistles. What bells and whistles? Let's find out.

Start the installer under Windows by launching setup.exe and start it under Linux by running the db2setup shell script.

The Launchpad for DB2 Client has a similar look and feel to that you saw for server installations in Chapter 2. The difference is the specific focus on just installing clients and their components. If you jump straight to the Install A Product tab, you'll see that it states very clearly that this installer "provides a set of graphical and non-graphical tools" for doing all manner of client-based work: administration, connectivity, and development (see Figure 20-3). Click the Install New button, and the installer will commence work.

Many of the screens—such as the welcome and license agreement screens—appear just as they did for a server installation. So instead of describing each in detail, I'll focus on the few that give you overall control of your new client installation.

Be sure to choose Custom as the installation type when prompted because it exposes all the possibilities inherent in the client installation package. You eventually get to screen 6 of the wizard, as shown in Figure 20-4, which allows you to select the features you want to have installed.

As you can see, there are five broad subcategories of components available, each of which collects together related items that are either required or optional.

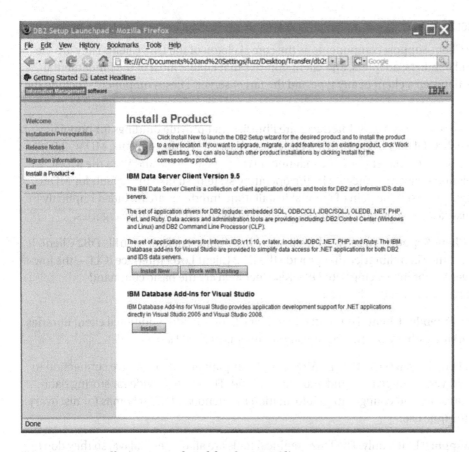

Figure 20-3. *Installation Launchpad for the DB2 Client*

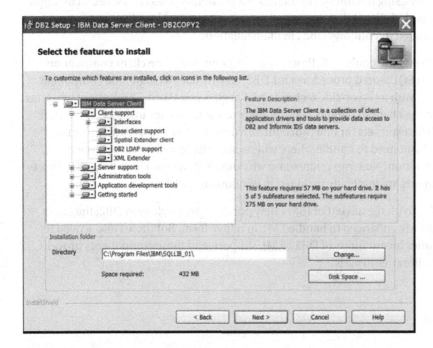

Figure 20-4. *Selecting the features to install for a custom installation of the DB2 Client*

Client Support

Think of the Client Support components as the core skeleton of the DB2 Client. They are the basic protocol handlers, adapters, and client libraries that enable most of the fundamental connectivity between a client of any type and the target server. These components include the following:

- **Interfaces**: Windows only. Interfaces are libraries that provide bindings for popular APIs such as ODBC, OLE DB, SQLJ, and more. Also, for Windows clients, MDAC 2.8 is included for completeness. Note that under Windows XP, 2003, and Vista the MDAC 2.8 installation is always protected by the operating system, so take the default for MDAC and spare yourself the pain of manual installation. Interfaces are included implicitly in a Linux-based installation, so you won't see it in the installation subcategories.

- **Base Client Support**: This is it—the absolute bare-bones, naked, no-frills DB2 Client. It contains the client libraries that provide the DB2 Client Level Interface (CLI)—the lowest level API for interfacing with DB2. Also included are the basic command interpreters you're already using.

- **Spatial Extender Client**: The Spatial Extender Client provides additional client libraries for working with the Spatial Extender components of a DB2 server.

- **DB2 LDAP Support**: The DB2 LDAP Support components enable native connection to LDAP servers through bind and anonymous bind. They also provide for storing database directory and configuration information in extended LDAP schemas for discovery and run-time use.

- **Java Support**: Linux only. The DB2 graphical tools are all written in Java, so they don't work without Java support. You can operate as a client with only the command line or shell tools, or by using the interfaces mentioned previously. This can be useful in "appliance" or embedded clients that don't need or have a graphical interface. Java support is implicitly included in Windows DB2 client installations.

- **SQL Procedures**: Linux only. SQL Procedure components are the client components that assist with SQL stored procedures for DB2. So why does a client-side component help in dealing with a server-side technology? I'm glad you asked. Think about what has to happen on the client to handle truly complex procedures—for instance, those that return multiple result sets for one procedure invocation. A storm of data is heading your way, and you need to handle when, where, and why to collect or separate that flood of information. Now you understand why the client needs a little help. SQL Procedure components are implicitly included in Windows installations.

- **XML Extender**: With the advent of IBM's new pureXML technology in DB2, the client has been similarly enhanced to handle XML in native form. But there's also a need to work with earlier incarnations of DB2's XML support, and these components provide the necessary libraries to assist.

Getting Started

The Getting Started components are centered on helping you use the client tools you're installing (you saw the power of some of the included components in Chapter 3).

First Steps

I have fond memories of creating my first DB2 database. And I bet you do, too, because it probably happened when you were reading Chapter 3! That's right; this is the very same First Steps tool that you already used. If you found it useful, you can understand how other new starters to DB2 will feel, which is why it's offered as part of every DB2 Client installation.

XML Extender Samples

A number of sample programs, stored procedures, and XML files are bundled together in the XML Extender samples to allow you to work with the server-side XML Extender technology for DB2 v8 and earlier. The XML Extender technology is effectively deprecated in favor of the revolutionary pureXML features you explored in Chapter 11, so these examples are maintained only to help those who might find themselves using older versions of DB2.

Administration Tools

Meaningful names always make the job of installing software easier, and there's really no confusion about the term *Administration Tools*. This category includes some of the tools you've used already, such as the Control Center; and others you'll find indispensable for your database administration and client management tasks.

Control Center

No need for an in-depth discussion of what the Control Center is because you've already used it! It's essential for administration, but not necessary for simply enabling access to DB2.

Configuration Assistant

The Configuration Assistant is the primary graphical tool to discover local and remote instances and databases, and to configure the various client options available when working with them. I personally categorize it as part of the Base Client, but IBM makes the distinction based primarily on its GUI interface and the added components it needs to have in order to operate.

Replication Tools

DB2's replication facilities could have an entire book written about them! To avoid such a huge tangent to this current discussion, suffice it to say that DB2 has a good and mature replication technology that's largely configured and run at the servers involved in the replication work. As an administrator, the client Replication Tools allow you to monitor, administer, and report on replication activity.

DB2 Instance Setup Wizard (Linux/UNIX Only)

One small but important difference for Linux and UNIX DB2 clients involves their use of a special client-side instance to manage known databases. I'll discuss this shortly, but for now you can trust me that the DB2 Instance Setup Wizard is the key component that eases the configuration of clients under Linux.

Application Development Tools

The set of tools included in the Application Development Tools set are primarily intended for developers of desktop or web-based applications. If you've ever worked with earlier versions of DB2, you might have heard of different types of DB2 Client with names such as *DB2 Application Development Client*. These packages were essentially subsets of the tools presented in the DB2 client—targeted at specific categories of end user, such as administrator, developer, and so on. A small amount of confusion sometimes cropped up when people worked with DB2 clients that had different names. In DB2 9.5, IBM consolidated all the Client pieces in one installer—with one consistent name—and has kept the categories of components clearly identified so you can pick those elements required for your particular need (in this case, application development).

Base Application Development Tools

If you'll do any form of development, the Base Application Development Tools include the basic building blocks required for you to get started. Included are C/C++ header files, libraries and debug symbols, a precompiler, and other goodies.

IBM Software Development Kit (SDK) for Java

The SDK for Java extends the base development components to include a large set of DB2-specific Java classes, plus the building blocks used by all Java-based graphical tools. It also includes the necessary components for writing Java stored procedures, which are one of the development options discussed in a later chapter.

Server Support (Windows Only)

The Server Support category of tools includes only one component, the Thin Client Code Server:

- **Thin Client Code Server**: The Thin Client Code Server is a special packaging of the DB2 Client components that can leverage Windows support for thin client distributions. This type of setup acts a lot like Network File System (NFS) or network-based installs and hosting under Linux or UNIX—the client code is physically located in only one place, and operating system facilities are then used to make it available and usable by multiple machines.

In a Windows environment, you nominate one machine—a client or a server—to host the Thin Client Code Server. It then acts as the staging point for providing DB2 Client capabilities to appropriately configured Windows clients. These clients get to use the DB2 Client, and therefore connect to and use DB2 databases, without having any locally installed components.

Details on configuring and using Windows thin clients would take you far out of the realms of beginning DB2 (into some very esoteric places in Windows-land), so I'll leave the Thin Client Code Server behind at this point.

The Rest of the DB2 Client Installation

Having mastered the intricacies of the client components (regardless of the installer you used), you'll be pleased to know that the remaining steps are straightforward (and you've done them all before). Under any operating system, after selecting the desired components you'll see the installation wizard prompt you for items identical to those you saw during the server installation:

- **Language files**: You can nominate which languages you want supported by any DB2 Client interfaces.

- **Installation location**: Controls where on disk to place the installation files.

- **DB2 Information Center**: Decides the installation location for the help resources.

Under Windows, the installer asks you to nominate a DB2COPY name to associate with the DB2 Client, just as the server installation did. The purpose is identical—to allow multiple simultaneous installations to exist side by side so that you can use them, upgrade them, and so forth without one affecting another. The Windows installation also asks whether you want to apply operating system security to the installed files. The defaults are perfectly okay for these options.

For Linux installations, the DB2 Client installation asks you to decide whether to create an instance or defer it to a later point. You might need to read that sentence twice. The client installer asks you whether you want to create an instance. It was only a few chapters back where you confidently mastered the art of instance management, and you might now be wondering what on earth I'm talking about. Are instances server-side concepts—the memory and process structures—that manage databases?

Yes, they are. But under Linux, a special kind of lightweight client-side instance is used to solely manage connectivity to remote databases. This lightweight instance is incapable of hosting or managing databases itself; think of it more as part of the glue that gets you from A to B. You can go ahead and elect to create this now, and I'll also show you how to create a DB2 Client instance after the installation is complete.

Deciding Which Components to Install

The previous descriptions of the individual components encapsulated in the DB2 Client installation included a discussion of each item's purpose and how you might use them, but no advice on whether or not you should install them *right now*. There was a definite goal in that approach.

First, now that you know what each component and subcomponent does, you're armed with the information to experiment with different installation options. Have you ever wondered what would be missing without Java support? Well, now you know. Have you ever considered the bare minimum components needed for a run-time environment? You now know that the Base Client is the key.

The second reason not to burden you with a low-level checklist is that the decision about what to install is really a very easy one. Look at the main subcategories that are available: Client Support, Getting Started, Administration Tools, and Application Development Tools. (I'll leave server code for thin client support out of the picture for now.)

You no doubt have a reasonable idea, however rough, about the purpose of a given client installation. If it's only to enable third-party applications to access DB2, Client Support will be enough. If you need to administer databases from a given machine, you'll be thankful to have the Administration Tools. Developing in any language would be a pain without all the great developer wizards and samples available in the Applications Development Tools. And if other people will be learning DB2 from a given client—following in your footsteps—they'll benefit from the Getting Started tools just as much as you have.

There will be times when the desire to perfectly tailor the DB2 Client installation motivates you to delve deeper and select individual subcomponents. A perfect example is provisioning the minimum DB2 client components required for a third-party embedded or read-only system, such as a "live trial" operating system image on a CD or DVD. You now have the information you need to know which component is used for any given purpose, and you can satisfy such an installation quickly and easily.

Configuring the DB2 Client for Your Database

The installation of the client was easy, as you've come to expect. But now that you have the software installed for your DB2 Client, how do you tell it about DB2 instances and databases? Let's look at the wizards available that help you connect the dots, so to speak, and I'll then cover the command-line equivalents.

The DB2 Client Configuration Assistant

The Client Configuration Assistant (CCA) is a boon if you struggle with editing obscure text files or (even worse!) registry settings to connect a client to its sought-after server. The CCA acts as a discovery tool to find your instances and databases, and acts as an ongoing management and maintenance tool to tweak the options available to a given connection.

To start the CCA under Windows, navigate through the Programs menu, and drill down into the menus IBM DB2 ➤ DB2COPY1 (default) ➤ Set-up Tools. You'll see the Configuration Assistant shown at the top of that group. You can also start the Configuration Assistant from the DB2 command line or from a shell under Linux with the db2profile already set, by issuing this command:

```
$ db2ca
```

Up pops both the normal screen for the Configuration Assistant, as well as the wizard that helps you simply and easily discover and configure databases (see Figure 20-5). The wizard starts automatically at this point because it has detected that you have no current databases configured, and it's a pretty good guess that you've invoked the Configuration Assistant to go find one!

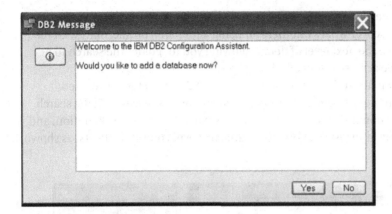

Figure 20-5. *The DB2 Client Configuration Wizard starts on first invocation to help you find databases on your network.*

Probably the most straightforward dialog box you'll ever see. Press Yes to actually start the action, and the first tab of the Add Database Wizard shows its true colors, as seen in Figure 20-6.

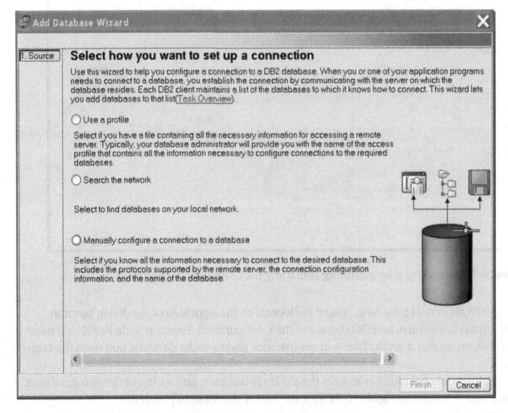

Figure 20-6. *The Add Database Wizard provides options for database discovery, manual configuration, and configuration from an existing profile.*

You're offered the choice of manually configuring a connection to your chosen server, searching the network to discover what's out there, or using a prepared profile. Start with the search option, and you'll see the next level of detail, allowing you to "guide" the search to a given host or let it roam free across your network.

Depending on your own network, firewall settings, and DB2 parameters (discussed shortly), you might or might not be able to discover instances and databases with the search option. To try it out, simply double-click the Other Systems (Search The Network) option, and the search will begin. On my little test network, the search discovers one of my hosts, as shown in Figure 20-7.

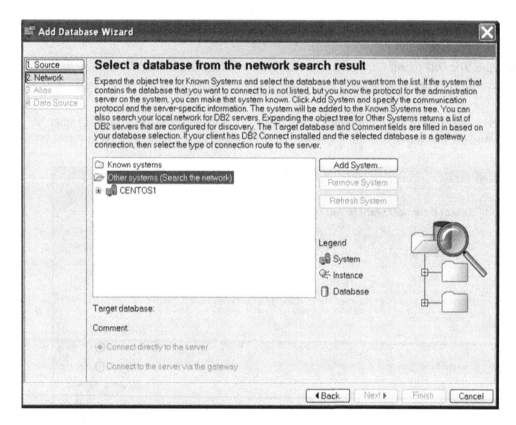

Figure 20-7. *Discovering a host running DB2 using the Configuration Assistant*

CENTOS1 is my Linux host. Notice the legend on the right side of the dialog box that shows System, Instance, and Database. For the Configuration Assistant to do its job you have to drill down further than the host—to the instance and then the database you want the client to use.

Exploring my host further unveils the db2inst1 instance, and within in the two databases SAMPLE and TOOLSDB (see Figure 20-8). Pick the SAMPLE database to proceed.

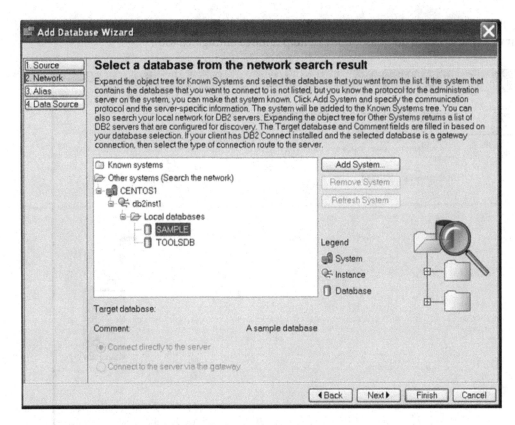

Figure 20-8. *Select your chosen database from those discovered.*

The next screen prompts you to allocate an alias for the database if you want. You can usually keep the database's own name for its alias, but consider situations in which multiple instances are running databases with the same name. In these circumstances, the DB2 Client's design means that each must have a unique alias. This can happen in environments as diverse as full-scale production/test environments, in which testing is a complete clone of production. But it could also happen in more straightforward cases. For example, what if you and your colleagues were working through this book at the same time and wanted to examine each other's SAMPLE database? In this case, you'd need to allocate a different alias to your friend's SAMPLE database so DB2 can differentiate it from your own.

■**Tip** Remember that DB2 clients and database applications using DB2 concern themselves only with the alias, so they are never confused by the underlying instances' names. You might want to adopt the same philosophy so that you always have an unambiguous view of your databases and instances.

Figure 20-9 shows the Alias tab of the wizard, which allows you to provide a comment for your newly discovered database (this can help remove ambiguity, too).

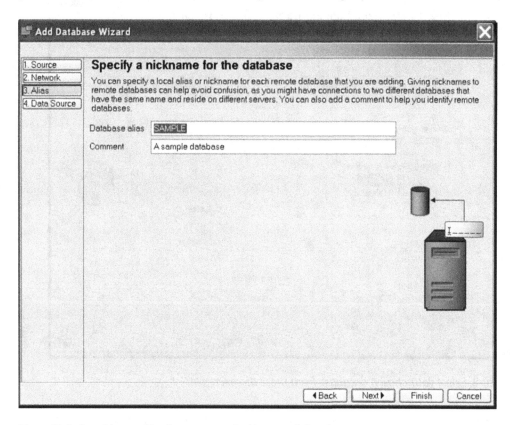

Figure 20-9. *Provide an alias for your newly discovered database.*

Finally, the Configuration Assistant prompts you to allow for an equivalent set of ODBC configuration to be configured. ODBC is the Open Data Base Connectivity standard, a long-time favorite of Microsoft (although ironically based on the CLI standard from which DB2's own protocols come). Thus, working with ODBC is something that comes naturally to all DB2 clients.

If you know that you'll be working with any ODBC-capable applications, you should choose to register this database as an ODBC data source. I normally recommend choosing the As System Data Source option because it makes the configuration available to all users of a machine. The As User Data Source option restricts use of the ODBC data source to only the user performing the configuration, and As File Data Source is restricted to applications that can both access the nominated file and can understand a file data source. Figure 20-10 shows how easy it is to just "click the box" to make this happen.

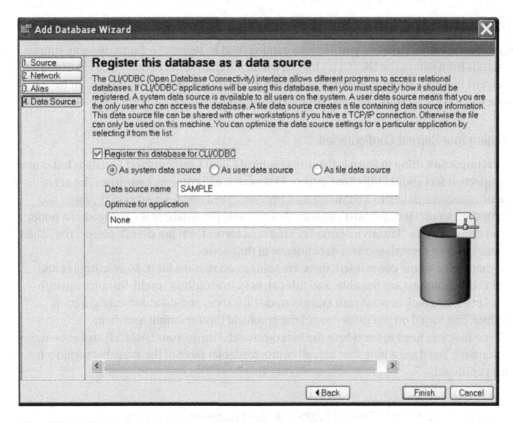

Figure 20-10. *Nominate the database for ODBC registration.*

Click Finish, and the progress dialog box springs to life, followed a few seconds later by the completed database registration appearing in the Configuration Assistant. This process is known as *cataloging a database* in DB2 parlance. Before returning you to the main Configuration Assistant screen, the wizard provides a short summary, as seen in Figure 20-11, and offers you the options of editing the work you've just completed or testing the connection to see whether it's ready for future use.

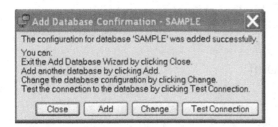

Figure 20-11. *Confirmation of your new database registration, with editing and testing options*

That's all there is to it. You discovered and configured the database, and it's now ready to be used from this client. You can prove this by running the DB2 CLP or the Command Editor and connect from your newly configured client to your server.

Command-Line DB2 Client Configuration

From either Linux or Windows, you can also catalog (that is, register) a database using simple commands from within the DB2 CLP. This is a useful alternative in circumstances in which you haven't installed any of the graphical tools, but can also be useful when you want to include client configuration steps as part of some larger configuration script.

Examining Your Current Configuration

The first important thing to learn is that the graphical Client Configuration Assistant hides one very important fact about DB2 client setup—I know that will come as a surprise. The act of configuring a client to talk to a database on a previously unknown server actually takes two configuration steps. First, the host instance that controls the database is cataloged as a node; you can think of it as a "known instance" of DB2 on a server from the client's perspective. Then the database itself is cataloged as a dependency of that node.

If that seems a little convoluted, there are some good reasons for it. More-complex and abstract configurations are possible, and this can help in multihost, multi-instance environments. Let's take a look at what your current node (instance) and database configuration might look like, based on the earlier use of the graphical Configuration Assistant.

To do this, you need to introduce the list command. Fire up your DB2 CLP, and issue the ? list command. You'll see a long (but actually quite readable) table of the available variants for the list command:

```
db2 => ? list
LIST ACTIVE DATABASES [AT DBPARTITIONNUM db-partition-number | GLOBAL]

LIST APPLICATIONS [FOR DATABASE database-alias]
[AT DBPARTITIONNUM db-partition-number| GLOBAL] [SHOW DETAIL]

LIST COMMAND OPTIONS

LIST DATABASE DIRECTORY [ON drive]

LIST DATABASE PARTITION GROUPS [SHOW DETAIL]

LIST DBPARTITIONNUMS

LIST DCS APPLICATIONS [SHOW DETAIL | EXTENDED]

LIST DCS DIRECTORY

LIST DRDA INDOUBT TRANSACTIONS [WITH PROMPTING]

LIST HISTORY {BACKUP | ROLLFORWARD | REORG |
CREATE TABLESPACE | ALTER TABLESPACE | DROPPED TABLE | LOAD |
RENAME TABLESPACE | ARCHIVE LOG}
{ALL | SINCE timestamp |CONTAINING {schema.object_name | object_name}}
FOR [DATABASE] database-alias
```

```
LIST INDOUBT TRANSACTIONS [WITH PROMPTING]

LIST [ADMIN] NODE DIRECTORY [SHOW DETAIL]

LIST [USER | SYSTEM] ODBC DATA SOURCES

LIST PACKAGES [FOR {USER | ALL | SYSTEM | SCHEMA schema-name}] [SHOW DETAIL]

LIST TABLES [FOR {USER | ALL | SYSTEM | SCHEMA schema-name}] [SHOW DETAIL]

LIST TABLESPACE CONTAINERS FOR tablespace-id [SHOW DETAIL]

LIST TABLESPACES [SHOW DETAIL]

LIST UTILITIES [SHOW DETAIL]
```

The two variants you're interested in are LIST DATABASE DIRECTORY and LIST NODE DIRECTORY. On the client just configured, you see the following:

```
db2 => list node directory

 Node Directory

 Number of entries in the directory = 1

Node 1 entry:

 Node name                        = TCP911A5
 Comment                          =
 Directory entry type             = LOCAL
 Protocol                         = TCPIP
 Hostname                         = centos1
 Service name                     = 50000

db2 => list database directory

 System Database Directory

 Number of entries in the directory = 1

Database 1 entry:

 Database alias                   = SAMPLE
 Database name                    = SAMPLE
 Node name                        = TCP911A5
 Database release level           = b.00
 Comment                          = A sample database
 Directory entry type             = Remote
```

```
Catalog database partition number    = -1
Alternate server hostname            =
Alternate server port number         =
```

Certainly more succinct than looking at the help on the list command, but what is it actually telling you? First, the list node command shows that the Configuration Assistant created a node called TCP911A5 to represent the remote DB2 server, CENTOS1, the service on that server listening at port 50000—that's the instance db2inst1.

Note Before you ask—no, I don't know why it invents such crazy names, although I might call my next dog TCP911A5. It's really only a local handle on some configuration information, so try not to lose too much sleep over that point.

The list database command shows that the local client current knows about one database associated with that strangely named node called SAMPLE. This won't be a huge surprise to you if you've followed the chapter to this point. Databases for a local instance use a special indirect cataloging technique. So the node entry for the local instance usually has no local databases cataloged beneath it (by default).

So now you know how to investigate existing nodes (instances) and their databases. How exactly do you add information about new instances and databases so that your client might use them? You can use the catalog command.

Using the Catalog Command

You can use the by-now familiar ? option to see the capabilities of the catalog command. Among the numerous options are the following:

```
db2 => ? catalog
...

CATALOG DATABASE database-name [AS alias] [ON drive | AT NODE node-name]
[AUTHENTICATION {SERVER | CLIENT | DCS | DCE SERVER PRINCIPAL principalname
| KERBEROS TARGET PRINCIPAL principalname | SERVER_ENCRYPT | DCS_ENCRYPT
| DATA_ENCRYPT | GSSPLUGIN}] [WITH "comment-string"]

...

CATALOG [ADMIN] {TCPIP | TCPIP4 | TCPIP6} NODE node-name REMOTE hostname
[SERVER service-name] [SECURITY {SOCKS}] [REMOTE_INSTANCE instance-name]
[SYSTEM system-name] [OSTYPE os-type] [WITH "comment string"]
```

Even that shortened output contains a bewildering array of options. So let's step through some examples to see what's really meant by all that.

You first want to catalog a new node. If there's only one DB2 instance in your environment and you already had it cataloged as part of the Configuration Assistant section, the following step isn't required. But suppose that you have another DB2 instance out there. There is another instance in my environment that runs on a host called BEGINNINGDB2. The instance is named DB2 on that machine, and I know that it's using port 50000, with an equivalent service name associated with the port called db2c_db2, because those are the defaults used for a DB2 installation on Windows, which is the operating system it's running.

Tip Why wasn't this server discovered by the Configuration Assistant? That secret, which has to do with the concept of *discoverability*, will be revealed in the next section.

Looking at the catalog [admin] node command, I know that I'm cataloging a normal instance, not an administration instance, so I can drop the admin bit. I know I'm using normal TCP/IP; and I know the remote hostname, its service-name, and the name of the remote-instance. So I have almost all the mandatory fields and the important optional fields that will mean I won't have to do further configuration after cataloging the node. The only thing I seem to be missing is something called the node-name for use in the NODE clause.

Remember that silly TCP911A5 name? That's a node name. Remember that such names are invented by the Configuration Assistant, and the fact they were nonsensical names don't matter because they are just a convenient handle on a set of configuration details. Bingo! You can make up any node name you like! It's for your convenience, so you can decide what's meaningful, useful, and/or memorable. There is one constraint to the node-name: it must be eight characters or fewer (yes, old IBM habits die hard).

I'll choose the name **BEGINDB2**. My catalog node command looks like this when I run it:

```
db2 => catalog TCPIP node begindb2 remote beginningdb2
       server db2c_db2 remote_instance db2
DB20000I  The CATALOG TCPIP NODE command completed successfully.
DB21056W  Directory changes may not be effective until the directory cache is
refreshed.
```

Success! Half the job is done. Now all I need to do is catalog a database at that node. If you have only one DB2 instance to work with (and it's already cataloged as discussed), you can resume paying attention.

To catalog a database, at a minimum you need to know the name of the database and the node associated with its instance—local or remote. My remote instance on the node BEGINDB2 is running the TOOLSDB and SAMPLE databases. To save you the ambiguity of having two SAMPLE databases differentiated only by alias, let's pick on the TOOLSDB. The catalog data-base command looks like this when run (yours might list your already-known nodes such as TCP911A5):

```
db2 => catalog database toolsdb at node begindb2
DB20000I  The CATALOG DATABASE command completed successfully.
DB21056W  Directory changes may not be effective until the directory cache is
refreshed.
```

Another success! Or at least you appear to have configured things correctly. To be sure, try to connect to the newly cataloged database. With the current default security settings, you need to provide a user name and password known to the server, such as the user who actually performed the server installation:

```
db2 => connect to toolsdb user db2admin
Enter current password for db2admin:

  Database Connection Information

Database server      = DB2/NT 9.5.0
SQL authorization ID = DB2ADMIN
Local database alias = TOOLSDB
```

Another part of DB2 mastered!

Discoverability Parameters

A point was made in the previous section about the apparent inability of the Configuration Assistant to actually find one of the database instances and its databases. Before you start worrying that the Configuration Assistant might be broken or lacking in capabilities, I should admit that I used DB2's own parameters to hide that server, its instances, and its databases from the wizard.

What made this possible are the discoverability parameters provided by the administration instance, the regular DB2 instance, and the databases hosted by that instance. These parameters are called DISCOVER, DISCOVER_INST, and DISCOVER_DB, respectively. You can set these parameters by using either the Control Center or the DB2 UPDATE DB[M] CFG commands that you learned about in Chapter 4. The values are either Enable or Disable. Even with the value set to Disable, while wizards like the Configuration Assistant won't find you automatically, you can see that you can always catalog a node or database if you know the relevant details.

So while I'm still connected to TOOLSDB, I can change its discoverability (assuming that I'm connected as an appropriately privileged user, which I am). The command is the following:

```
db2 => UPDATE DATABASE CONFIGURATION USING DISCOVER_DB Enable IMMEDIATE
DB20000I  The UPDATE DATABASE CONFIGURATION command completed successfully.
```

Controlling discoverability can be very useful for environments in which you want to provision users with a full set of client tools, but don't want them going mad adding hundreds of nodes and databases to their local catalogs.

Other Connectivity Options

To round out the discussion on client connectivity, I'll briefly highlight the other facilities available to you.

DB2 Runtime Client

The DB2 Runtime Client is a totally streamlined client installation that just provides the base libraries and interface support to allow third-party applications to connect with DB2 and work with databases. No extraneous graphical tools or helpers are included, so this kind of client is best suited for coupling with home-grown or procured applications for which no further development or administration need to be done from the client.

Type 4 JDBC Driver

IBM makes available a Type 4 JDBC driver for DB2, which effectively allows clientless connectivity for JDBC-based applications. Type 4 drivers are implemented purely in Java and rely solely on Java-based technology to connect and communicate with the database server. There are obvious deployment and management benefits—no clients to configure! But Type 4 JDBC drivers also introduce issues of their own, and there is usually healthy discussion among both DB2 and Java professionals about the possible performance and capability impact that adopting Type 4 drivers might imply.

■**Tip** The DB2 download page on the IBM website has the Type 4 driver and documentation if you're interested in exploring it further.

Third-Party Connectivity Options

A thriving industry has grown up around the IBM DB2 software line, and there is some competition in the area of connectivity software, mainly centering on interface bindings such as ODBC, JDBC, OLE DB, and so on. Some vendors provide "wire-line" drivers that can provide connectivity without the need for a local installation of a DB2 Client (in much the same way Type 4 JDBC drivers operate). I've worked with several from DataDirect, HiT Software, and similar vendors; if more-advanced connectivity options are of interest, run a quick Google search to see what else is out there!

Summary

How's that for being connected? You now have a thorough grounding in all the components available for installing DB2 Clients, and have mastered both the graphical and command-line configuration tools. You're in a good position now to actually deploy complete DB2 9.5 Express-C Edition environments, including servers and clients, and get them all working together.

CHAPTER 21

■ ■ ■

Moving Data in Bulk with DB2

You had fun in previous chapters inserting data into DB2 with the ever-useful insert state-ment. Combined with some of the programming tricks you know, it would be easy to come up with an application that could run insert statements on reasonably large volumes of data. Maybe thousands, tens of thousands, or even hundreds of thousands of rows could be han-dled in reasonable time. But what if you had to get millions of rows of data into your databases? And what if millions turned to billions one day?

DB2 comes fully equipped with a range of data import and export utilities designed to tackle everything from a single row of information to terabyte-sized parcels of data. Each tool has a role to play, but there is also a common foundation that maximizes the flexibility you have when it comes to shifting data in bulk. Best of all, the bulk data movement utilities are designed to be *fast*. They're faster than any other method for moving lots of data into, out of, and between your databases.

File Formats for Moving Data

For a variety of historic and practical reasons, DB2 supports a number of different file formats for the export, import, and load utilities. The text-based formats are mostly self-explanatory, but there are a few tricks with the more-advanced formats that will make your life easier.

ASCII Format

ASCII format (abbreviated as ASC in import/export commands) is exactly what you think it is: data represented as human-readable text using ASCII encoding. It has the advantage that you can open an ASC file with any text editor and browse your data. The disadvantage is that not all your data is necessarily encodable in ASCII. Think about all the wonderful Unicode XML information you might be working with—you'll see limitations right away.

Delimited Format

Delimited format (abbreviated as DEL in import/export commands) is remarkably similar to ASCII format, with the addition of delimiters to help manipulate column and row boundaries, and provides a definitive end-of-file marker. These delimiters help avoid conflicts when mov-ing files from UNIX or Linux to Windows, and vice versa. Again, you can open a delimited format file with your favorite text editor. Delimited files utilize the parochial end-of-line and end-of-file markers for the platforms on which they're used. So on Windows the two-character combination of CR+LF is used for the end-of-line marker; on Linux and UNIX the single LF is used. When transferring delimited files between operating systems, ensure that you choose text as the transfer mode. This choice helps the transfer tool (such as FTP) make the necessary modifications on the fly to preserve the right format in conjunction with your target system. Don't transfer DEL files in binary mode.

Lotus 1-2-3 Worksheet Format

Worksheet format (abbreviated as WSF) is compatible with the spreadsheet format of Lotus 1-2-3. As such, it is a useful format for exchanging data with people such as financial analysts, data miners, and others who use spreadsheet applications as their graphical user interface (GUI) of choice when working with data. Worksheet format stores all numeric information in little-endian format. To prevent file transfer utilities from "helpfully" switching the byte order of your numbers, always transfer WSF files in binary mode when using applications such as FTP or SCP.

Worksheet format is very useful for database-to-spreadsheet transfers, and vice versa. I recommend against using it for DB2-to-DB2 transfer because it does have limitations, and there is an even better format available for that purpose.

Integration Exchange Format

I saved the best format until last. Integration Exchange Format (IXF) is designed to be the general-purpose, multiplatform, bonus-feature data transfer format for DB2. IXF format is designed to be the format of choice for DB2-to-DB2 transfers of information. It handles truly enormous file sizes with in-built support for multipart files. IXF also handles numeric representation on big-endian and little-endian architectures. It uses a little-endian format for numeric values, and all DB2 utilities understand how to translate little-endian numbers to the required format for a target architecture.

Perhaps the best feature of IXF files is that they can include more than just the data being exported or imported. The data definition language (DDL) for the table can be included in the IXF file, meaning that the transfer of data becomes fully self-contained. When importing the information at the target, all the metadata required to reconstruct the target table is present.

Exporting Data

The export utility is the general-purpose tool used to extract information in bulk from a DB2 database. It works by accepting your instructions regarding the desired output format and the SQL select statement to run to generate your exported data. To use the export utility, the general authorities SYSADM or DBADM give you carte blanche. Or for the mere mortals among your users, the CONTROL or SELECT privilege must be held on the source table or view. The general form of the export syntax takes this form:

```
export to export-file-name
of export-file-format
[LOB-handling options]
[XML-handling options]
[Modifiers for export file(s)]
[Messages message-file]
Select-or-xquery-statement
```

Thankfully, that's as complex as it gets, and even the options for handling LOBs and XML are very straightforward.

Performing a Simple Export

Let's dive in to an example to see the possibilities and results. I want to extract all the data for the employees in the SAMPLE database. To read the output file, I choose the DEL format. The export command therefore looks like the one in the following example:

```
db2 => connect to sample

  Database Connection Information

 Database server        = DB2/NT 9.5.0
 SQL authorization ID   = FUZZY
 Local database alias   = SAMPLE


db2 => export to employee_ex1.del of del select * from employee
SQL3104N  The Export utility is beginning to export data to file
"employee_ex1.del".

SQL3105N  The Export utility has finished exporting "42" rows.

Number of rows exported: 42
```

The burning question is this: what exactly did that command produce? Let's take a look at the output file to answer that question. Use your favorite utility or text editor to examine the contents of the employee_ex1.del file. I'm using the more command because it's universal, and I have truncated the output to better fit on this page. When you view the file, you see all the columns and rows:

```
$ more employee_ex1.del

"000010","CHRISTINE","I","HAAS","A00","3978",19950101,"PRES    ",18,"F", ...
"000020","MICHAEL","L","THOMPSON","B01","3476",20031010,"MANAGER ",18,"M", ...
"000030","SALLY","A","KWAN","C01","4738",20050405,"MANAGER ",20,"F", ...
"000050","JOHN","B","GEYER","E01","6789",19790817,"MANAGER ",16,"M", ...
"000060","IRVING","F","STERN","D11","6423",20030914,"MANAGER ",16,"M", ...
...
```

No surprises here. I asked for all the information from the employee table—and I got it.

Exporting LOBs

If the SQL statement passed to the export utility includes large objects, DB2 follows a simple set of rules to handle the LOB output. By default, the export utility places the first 32KB of a LOB in the export file used for the regular data, specific in the to clause. If your LOBs are longer than 32KB, they're truncated by default. Because that might cause a little frustration if you're expecting to get all the LOB data, there are options to instruct DB2 to export the full LOB data in a manageable way.

The first option is to provide the export utility with a directory into which to extract the full LOB information. The export then generates one or more LOB export files using the naming scheme *export-file-name.nnn*.lob, where *nnn* is a simple incrementing number to differentiate multiple target files that might be needed to store all your LOB data. For example:

```
db2 => export to empresume_ex2.del
 of del
 lobs to c:\export\lobs
 select * from emp_resume


SQL3104N  The Export utility is beginning to export data to file
"empresume_ex2.del".

SQL3105N  The Export utility has finished exporting "8" rows.

Number of rows exported: 8
```

Examining the directory c:\export\lobs shows that I have the file empresume_ex2.del. 001.lob. All well and good, and because this example is targeting CLOB data, you can actually open that file and see the text of the employees' resumes. If the information were photos, video, or other binary LOB data, you'd see the usual chaotic random assortment of text, control characters, and special symbols you get when trying to read binary data in text mode. Thankfully, DB2's import tools, such as import and load utilities, understand this.

An interesting thing has happened to the main export file, empresume_ex2.del. Examining its contents shows you that the export utility has played a few tricks in the spot where the LOB data would have been if I had exported that data inline. The following example shows the exported data:

```
C:> more empresume_ex2.del


"000130","ascii","empresume_ex2.del.001.lob.0.1313/", ...
"000130","html","empresume_ex2.del.001.lob.1313.2512/", ...
"000140","ascii","empresume_ex2.del.001.lob.3825.1316/", ...
"000140","html","empresume_ex2.del.001.lob.5141.2537/", ...
"000150","ascii","empresume_ex2.del.001.lob.7678.1363/", ...
"000150","html","empresume_ex2.del.001.lob.9041.2564/", ...
"000190","ascii","empresume_ex2.del.001.lob.11605.1292/", ...
"000190","html","empresume.del.001.lob.12897.2499/", ...
```

Where the source table held LOB information, the export utility has replaced it with a placeholder of the form *export-file-name.offset.length/*. That format should be reasonably self-explanatory, in that each LOB is present in the given file, starting at the offset position and continuing for *length* bytes. This is known as the LOB Location Specifier (LLS). If you prefer a different name for the files containing the LOB data, you can add the lobfile *lobfile-name* option, like this:

```
export to empresume_ex3.del
 of del
 lobs to c:\export\lobs
 lobfile remumes.lob
 select * from emp_resume
```

The first of the modifier parameters to be aware of is lobsinfile, which ensures that LOB information is created in its own dedicated subdirectory if your query statement includes LOBs, but you don't want to (or forget to) specify lobs to or lobfile parameters. Choosing either lobs to or lobfile implicitly triggers the lobsinfile behavior. There is also a lobsinsepfiles option to force each lob into its own file. If you specify none of these parameters, LOB data is placed in files in the same directory as your base data export file.

Exporting XML Objects

Exporting data that includes XML is conceptually very similar to exports that include LOBs. The names of the parameters differ, but you'll spot the obvious pattern. If you want to export data that includes XML from the products table and control its destination, use the export command with the xml to and xmlfile options. Just for fun, I'll also use the xmlinsepfiles modifier, too, and switch to working with the IXF file format in the following example:

```
db2 => export to products_ex4.ixf of ixf
 XML TO c:\export\xml XMLFILE productdescriptions
 modified by xmlinsepfiles xmlsaveschema
 select * from product
SQL3104N  The Export utility is beginning to export data to file
"products_ex4.ixf ".

SQL27984W  The export command completed successfully. Some recreate
information has not been saved to the PC/IXF file during Export. This file
will not be supported in Import CREATE mode. Reason code="2".

SQL3105N  The Export utility has finished exporting "4" rows.

Number of rows exported: 4
```

A quick glance at the c:\export and c:\export\xml directories shows exactly what I was hoping for, but what's that warning all about? I'll get to that in a moment. The products_ex4.ixf holds the non-XML data, and there are four XML files in the c:\export\xml directory, one for each XML product description. There's one extra option that I snuck in to the syntax in that example. The xmlsaveschema option is not strictly a modifier—it should always follow all other modifiers specified. Its purpose is to instruct the export command to include the XML schemata of exported XML objects so they can be reimported along with the XML data.

In this particular example, the warning SQL27984W from the export utility informs you that XML column definitions can't be saved for use in re-creating the table. As long as you're aware of it if you later import or load the data, that's fine. If you prefer not to be inundated onscreen with this and other warnings and errors, you can use the messages clause, as in the following example:

```
db2 => export to products_ex4.ixf of ixf
 XML TO c:\export\xml XMLFILE productdescriptions
 modified by xmlinsepfiles xmlsaveschema
 messages exportmessages.txt
 select * from product

Number of rows exported: 4
```

With that, all information is sent to the nominated file instead of echoed to the screen. Only the number of rows exported is repeated there (it is also in the messages file). This is a handy option when you want to perform many exports and have a central place to view all information. The export utility always appends to this file, so your message history isn't lost.

■**Tip** When I defined the export utility earlier in this chapter, I mentioned that it exports the results of queries, not the contents of tables. Think about that for a minute, and you'll realize that the possibilities stretch way beyond simply what's stored in your database, all the way to what can be calculated, inferred, or constructed in a query. That means you're free to use literals, functions, or any other part of a SQL or XQuery statement to generate your data for export.

Exporting via the Control Center

By now you've come to expect nothing less than full support for DB2 features through both the CLP and the Control Center. And export is no slouch in this regard. Figure 21-1 shows how to invoke the export utility from the context menu of your desired table.

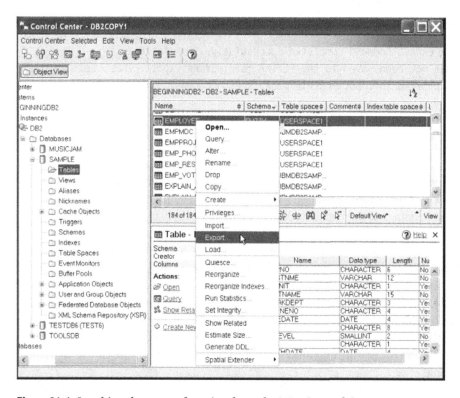

Figure 21-1. *Invoking the export function from the DB2 Control Center*

Once invoked, a simple multitabbed dialog box is used to allow you to choose export options equivalent to those you're already familiar with from the command line. Figure 21-2 shows the Target tab of the Export Table dialog box.

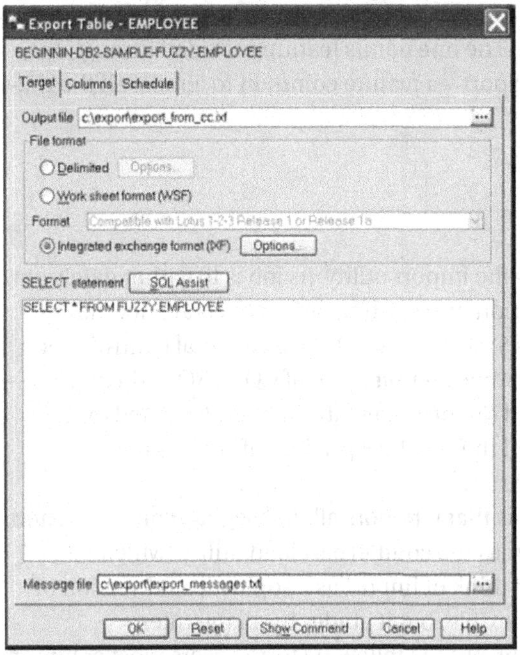

Figure 21-2. *Nominating export and message files and formats for export*

Here you can nominate your chosen output file, select the export file format to use, name your messages file if you elect to use one, and finally modify the SQL statement in any way you see fit to generate your export data. Figure 21-3 introduces the Columns tab, in which you can specify which columns from the table you want to export graphically, as well as identify LOB and XML options equivalent to those used from the CLP.

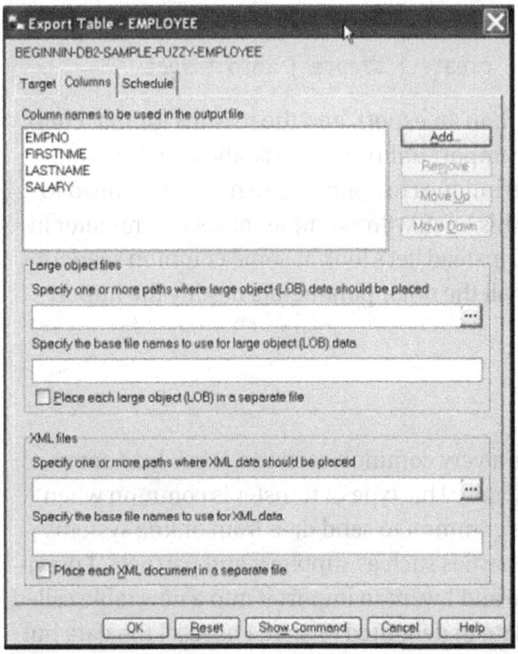

Figure 21-3. *Nominating columns, LOBs, and XML for export*

The operation of the export tool from the Control Center is identical to the CLP, so the choice is really a matter of personal preference. The one bonus feature provided through the Control Center is the ability to schedule your export—a feature common to almost all the wizards in the Control Center.

Importing Data

The natural complement to the export utility is the import utility. Its job is to gather data from specified external files and import the information into existing tables, or create new tables as part of an IXF-based import. The authorities SYSADM and DBADM give you total control over import operations. If you lack those privileges, some combination of CONTROL, SELECT, UPDATE, INSERT, and/or DELETE must be held on the target table or view (dictated by options I'll shortly discuss). You might also need the CREATEAB privilege if your import will create a table as part of its actions.

One important aspect of the import utility is that it honors all the logging, constraint, and trigger logic associated with a given table, whereas the counterpart load utility (which I'll cover shortly) does not. In this respect, you can think of import as a sophisticated version of the insert statement. It's fast, convenient, and flexible, but it abides by all the rules.

The scope of the import syntax is quite wide, but the following form covers most common use cases:

```
import from import-file of file-type
[lobs from directory]
[xml from directory]
[method options]
[xml options]
[concurrency control]
[restart and commit options]
[warnings and message options]
{insert | insert_update | replace | replace_create | create } into target
```

This syntax is considerably more complex than an export, and the reasons for that complexity are fairly clear. Because the target of the import utility is your database, with all the sophistication and complexity it implies, the techniques to control data movement need to be equally sophisticated. I could fill the rest of this book with examples of each parameter in action, but that would put you quickly to sleep. Instead, let's look at some common scenarios and then give you a working knowledge of how all the other parameters modify the import utility's behavior.

Performing a Simple Import

To get started with the import utility, let's tackle a very common scenario. You'll load some of the data you previously exported into a new table. This type of transfer is common when sharing data in unconnected environments. It's common to send data from online systems to data warehouses, and even to external third parties such as suppliers and partners. I previously exported the data from the employee table and I want to import it into a new table called promotion_candidate. Because I exported the data in delimited format, I have all the data but no DDL with which to create the table. So first, I'll connect to the SAMPLE database and create the destination table in the next example:

```
db2 => connect to sample

   Database Connection Information

 Database server          = DB2/NT 9.5.0
 SQL authorization ID     = FUZZY
 Local database alias     = SAMPLE

db2 => create table promotion_candidate like employee
DB20000I  The SQL command completed successfully.
```

I now have an empty table named promotion_candidate that's ready to accept data from an import. I can now run the import utility. In this case, I'll instruct it to insert the data from the source file into the new table. The command is as follows, which is formatted for readability:

```
db2 => import from c:\export\employee_ex1.del
 of del
 insert into promotion_candidate

SQL3109N  The utility is beginning to load data from file
"c:\export\employee_ex1.del".

SQL3110N  The utility has completed processing.  "42" rows were read from the
input file.

SQL3221W  ...Begin COMMIT WORK. Input Record Count = "42".

SQL3222W  ...COMMIT of any database changes was successful.

SQL3149N  "42" rows were processed from the input file.  "42" rows were
successfully inserted into the table.  "0" rows were rejected.

Number of rows read         = 42
Number of rows skipped      = 0
Number of rows inserted     = 42
Number of rows updated      = 0
Number of rows rejected     = 0
Number of rows committed    = 42
```

Hooray! A successful import. But what is achieved? There's a weighty amount of output for a supposedly simple task. That output can be tackled in three sections. The last part, in which you're told number of rows read, skipped, and so forth, is the statistical summary of the import utility. This is useful as a snapshot covering the many previous lines of detail the import utility can report.

In the employees/promotion candidates example, you're importing only 42 rows of data. There are numerous DB2 information and warning codes in the output, and the import was a simple one that succeeded without issues. As the number of rows you're importing reaches into the thousands or millions, the chances for problems multiply, and having such a summary gives you a quick way to identify the overall outcome of your import task.

Take a look at the various information and warning codes in the output; you'll see they are all thankfully very self-informative. You're informed that the import is beginning, that 42 rows were then read, and a commit for the unit of work was attempted and succeeded. You also see the final total of inserted and rejected rows. In this example, you used the insert option of the import command. But there are five major options that you can see in the syntax diagram, each with different consequences. Table 21-1 describes how these options determine what happens to new data, what happens to existing data, and what to do if the target table does not exist.

Table 21-1. *Major DB2 Import Options that Determine Import Behavior*

Option	Behavior
insert	Data from the source import file is inserted into the target table.
insert_update	Data from the source import file is inserted into the target table. Where new and existing rows have matching primary keys, the existing row is updated with the new data from the import file.
replace	The target table is first truncated to remove all existing information. Then data from the source import file is inserted.
replace_create	If the target table already exists in the database, it is truncated per the replace behavior. If it does not exist, it is first created per the create behavior. Note that this option is deprecated and *might not be present* in DB2 versions after 9.5.
create	Attempts to first create the target table before inserting the data from the source import file. Note that this option is deprecated and *might not be present* in DB2 versions after 9.5.

You can already see how your knowledge of these options can be narrowed down. The latter two options, replace_create and create, have been deprecated. It's useful to know that they exist and how they work, so any current DB2 environments that you work with don't surprise you. In the future, however, you should concentrate on the insert, insert_update, and replace options and keep an eye on how the import options evolve in future DB2 releases.

Dealing with Import Warnings and Errors

You saw the basic insert option in action, so it's time to illustrate its similarities to and differences from insert_update. You created a `promotion_candidate` table using the create table ... like ... syntax. This has given you the table structure necessary to import employee data, but lacks any indexes or constraints. So if you ran the import again, you'd get all the same data inserted into the target table and effectively duplicate the data. Although you might need to do that in some circumstances, assume that you're interested only in the information about each candidate once. You can enforce uniqueness based on the empno value because you know this is unique in the source data set:

```
alter table promotion_candidate add constraint promo_pk primary key(empno)
```

If I run exactly the same import, I would expect the primary key constraint to be evaluated as part of the import utility's work, and based on the duplicates I know I'd be attempting to generate, the data should be rejected. Learning how import fails and why is one of the best ways to become educated about its nuances. So go ahead and try to repeat the import. I'll log any messages to a file, using the messages clause because I have an inkling that there will be a lot of information to read. Following is my attempt to import the same data twice:

```
db2 => import from c:\export\employee_ex1.del of del
 messages promo_insert_ex2.txt
 insert into promotion_candidate

Number of rows read         = 42
Number of rows skipped      = 0
Number of rows inserted     = 0
Number of rows updated      = 0
Number of rows rejected     = 42
Number of rows committed    = 42

SQL3107W  There is at least one warning message in the message file.
```

I wasn't expecting success, and it's instructive to take a look at the messages file, promo_insert_ex2.txt, to see exactly what went wrong and what information gets reported about the problem or problems that caused 42 rows to be rejected. Following is a summary of the contents of that file:

```
SQL3109N  The utility is beginning to load data from file
"c:\export\employee_ex1.del".

SQL3148W  A row from the input file was not inserted into the table.  SQLCODE
"-803" was returned.

SQL0803N  One or more values in the INSERT statement, UPDATE statement, or
foreign key update caused by a DELETE statement are not valid because the
primary key, unique constraint or unique index identified by "1" constrains
table "FUZZY.PROMOTION_CANDIDATE" from having duplicate values for the index
key.  SQLSTATE=23505

SQL3185W  The previous error occurred while processing data from row "1" of
the input file.

... Another 41 instances of these 3 messages, for nearly 500 lines ...

SQL3110N  The utility has completed processing.  "42" rows were read from the
input file.

SQL3221W  ...Begin COMMIT WORK. Input Record Count = "42".

SQL3222W  ...COMMIT of any database changes was successful.
```

```
SQL3149N  "42" rows were processed from the input file.  "0" rows were
successfully inserted into the table.  "42" rows were rejected.
```

My messages file is 518 lines long, but I don't print the whole thing here. I showed the first set of messages regarding the attempt to insert the first row of data, and you'll be pleased to know that the pattern repeats for the other 41 rows. In essence, you're given the overall warning, SQL3148W, that the row was not inserted, with a SQLCODE -803. You're then shown SQLCODE in detail as SQL0803N. Lo and behold, a primary key violation was detected. The third message, SQL3185W, tells you that the previous message (the SQL0803N primary key violation) occurred while processing row 1 from the input file. Although you would have guessed the result, knowing in advance the volume and quality of the information presented in the messages file is a great help. Think of how many other systems or tools you've used that happily tell you an error has occurred, but not where to find it! The beauty of the import utility is that it gives you an overall status, exact problem, and exact row details for every warning or error encountered.

Importing a Mix of New and Updated Data

Now that you know how to interpret messages from the import utility, you'll naturally want to address them to make your import a success. I hypothesize that you're loading employee details that are being changed or refreshed over time, and you want both changed and unchanged data in the source import file inserted into the target table without having to do awkward queries or multistep processes to detect and handle these automatically. You've already guessed that insert_update is the answer to these desires. I copied my employee_ex1.del file to employee_ex3.del and changed a few job titles to reflect the updates that might have happened.

I'll also introduce several of the other options available with import, so you can start expanding your repertoire when it comes to loading data. First, I assume that other people are working with the promotion_candidate table and want to continue working while my import progresses. To this end, I use the allow write access concurrency control option, which lets any other connection perform inserts, updates, and deletes on the promotion_candidate while the import progresses. Because I know that others might be updating the very rows I could be changing with my import, I use the notimeout option to indicate that I'm willing to wait indefinitely for the transactions to commit on rows I want to change instead of implicitly timing out and having to deal with the consequences.

You learned in the previous exercise that things can go wrong, so I want to stop the import if too many warnings or errors are being generated. I use the warning option warningcount *n* to achieve this, choosing a value of 10. If the number of warnings or errors exceeds ten, the import stops. So my command and results look as follows:

```
db2 => import from c:\export\employee_ex3.del of del
allow write access warningcount 10 notimeout
messages promo_insert_ex3.txt
insert_update into promotion_candidate

Number of rows read       = 42
Number of rows skipped    = 0
Number of rows inserted   = 0
Number of rows updated    = 42
```

```
Number of rows rejected      = 0
Number of rows committed     = 42
```

My import succeeded, but look closely at how many updates the utility reports that it made. Not just the five or six lines that I changed in the employee_ex3.del file, but all 42 rows were updated. This is an important consequence of using the import_update option. If the primary key found in the source import file matches one found in the target table, an update occurs, even if the result is to change the row's data to the same values it currently has. This has consequences for the time taken for your import and the resources consumed by it, so you might want to avoid reimporting data carte blanche.

Performing More-Complex Imports

Sometimes an import task requires the work be split into smaller sets of data, or even scenarios in which a failure or a change in requirements means that you need to restart an import from a given point. In these circumstances, the import options restartcount, skipcount, and rowcount can be very useful. The restartcount and skipcount options are equivalent operations, and only one or the other is permitted in an import invocation. The rowcount option acts as a counter, telling the import utility to import only a certain number of rows. If used alone, this row count is measured from the beginning of the import source data file. If the import includes both the rowcount and restartcount/skipcount options, the count of rows to be imported is calculated from the first row after the restartcount/skipcount value.

In the export examples, you created the file products_ex4.ixf based on exporting the information from the product table. Let's reimport this file, but break the process into two steps to simulate a failure or to show how to perform some interstep processing. Here's the two-step process:

```
db2 => import from c:\export\products_ex4.ixf of ixf
 xml from c:\export\xml xmlparse preserve whitespace
 rowcount 2
 warningcount 50 notimeout
 replace into product

SQL3150N  The H record in the PC/IXF file has product "DB2    02.00", date
"20080314", and time "222002".

SQL3153N  The T record in the PC/IXF file has name "products_ex4.ixf",
qualifier "", and source "              ".

SQL3109N  The utility is beginning to load data from file
"c:\export\products_ex4.ixf".

SQL3503W  The utility has loaded "2" rows which equals the total count
specified by the user.

SQL3181W  The end of the file was reached before the expected ending record
was found.
```

```
SQL3110N  The utility has completed processing.  "2" rows were read from the
input file.

SQL3221W  ...Begin COMMIT WORK. Input Record Count = "2".

SQL3222W  ...COMMIT of any database changes was successful.

SQL3149N  "2" rows were processed from the input file.  "2" rows were
successfully inserted into the table.  "0" rows were rejected.


Number of rows read         = 2
Number of rows skipped      = 0
Number of rows inserted     = 2
Number of rows updated      = 0
Number of rows rejected     = 0
Number of rows committed    = 2
```

You can now perform the second half of the import, telling the import utility to skip the first two rows of source data, as well as using the insert_update option to ensure that the data loaded in the first run is not removed:

```
db2 => import from c:\export\products_ex4.ixf of ixf
 xml from c:\export\xml xmlparse preserve whitespace
 skipcount 2
 warningcount 50 notimeout
 insert_update into product

SQL3150N  The H record in the PC/IXF file has product "DB2     02.00", date
"20080314", and time "222002".

SQL3153N  The T record in the PC/IXF file has name "products_ex4.ixf",
qualifier "", and source "                ".

SQL3109N  The utility is beginning to load data from file
"c:\export\products_ex4.ixf".

SQL3110N  The utility has completed processing.  "4" rows were read from the
input file.

SQL3221W  ...Begin COMMIT WORK. Input Record Count = "4".

SQL3222W  ...COMMIT of any database changes was successful.

SQL3149N  "4" rows were processed from the input file.  "2" rows were
successfully inserted into the table.  "0" rows were rejected.


Number of rows read         = 4
Number of rows skipped      = 2
```

```
Number of rows inserted    = 2
Number of rows updated     = 0
Number of rows rejected    = 0
Number of rows committed   = 4
```

Success again, and the product table is now reloaded with all the originally exported information. In both runs of the import utility, I snuck in a new option regarding the handling of XML: xmlparse preserve whitespace. This is one of a number of XML options you have available to help with parsing and validating XML source data. Table 21-2 lists these XML options.

Table 21-2. *XML Parsing and Validation Options for the Import Utility*

Option	Behavior
Xmlparse {strip | preserve} whitespace	This option controls how the import utility treats whitespace—either as significant and therefore to be retained, or insignificant and therefore to be removed.
xml validate using {xds [options] | schema [options] | schemalocation hints}	The xml validate ... options control whether a schema will be used to validate the XML and from where that schema will be sourced at import time.

Graphical Import Using the Control Center

Figure 21-1 showed that there was an import option immediately above the export option in the context menu for a table. By now it should be second nature to assume that there's a graphical equivalent for any command-line tool in DB2, and the import utility certainly follows that rule. Because its behavior matches the command-line version very closely, I'll focus only on those areas in which there are differences. Invoke the graphical import on a table such as emp_resume, and you should see the File tab of the Import Table dialog box (see Figure 21-4).

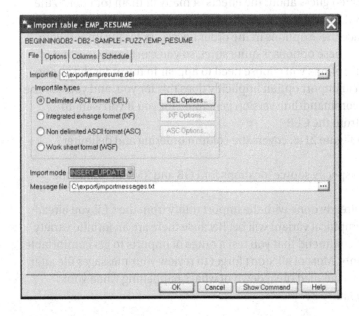

Figure 21-4. *The first tab of the import function in the DB2 Control Center*

Note that the deprecated options replace_create and create are not available in the Import Mode selection list. That should reinforce the idea that you should be focusing on the three supported methods. The other options on source file and type, related options based on that type, and messages file, are per the command-line variant of the import utility. Moving to the Options tab, you see the dialog box change (see Figure 21-5).

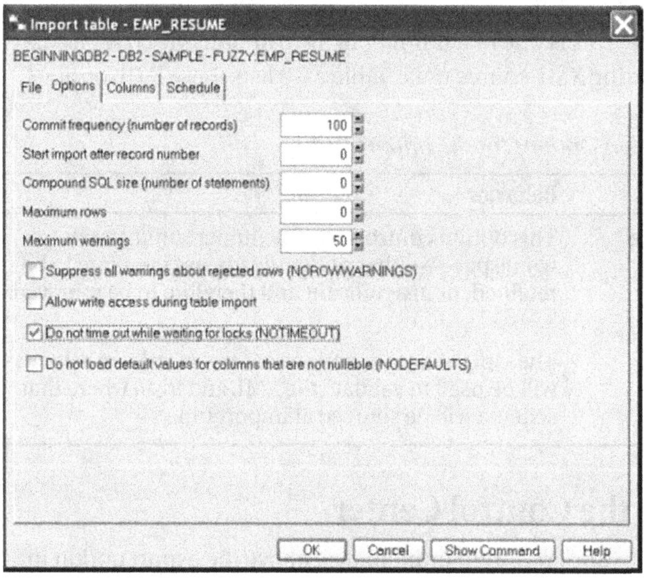

Figure 21-5. *The Options tab of the import function in the DB2 Control Center*

The Options tab presents all the concurrency, commit control, warning control, and similar options in one tab. Although I haven't introduced each of these options with its own example, you can make an educated guess about the effects of many of them (or refer to the 36 pages of online help in the IBM Information Center to learn more). One very useful feature of this tab is that it helps you place these options in the order necessary for the import command. As it stands, the parsing of these options is quite strict, so you can't freely mix and match them in just any order; all options you choose need to appear in the order the import utility expects. Using the graphical import option implicitly does this for you, and you can use the Show SQL option to get the command-line version generated for you if you want to include it in scripts to run later from the CLP.

The Columns tab, shown in Figure 21-6, covers the column ordering and delimiter options for your import.

In the Columns tab you also specify source locations for LOB and XML data, and the modifiers to use on them.

Thanks to the work you've already done with the import utility from the CLP, you already know what the behavior of the graphical variant will be. Because there are an infinite variety of import scenarios, I strongly recommend that you test a range of imports to get comfortable with their quirks and requirements. Most of all, don't forget to review your messages file after each import because it gives you a detailed breakdown of what's happening when your imports succeed *and* when they fail.

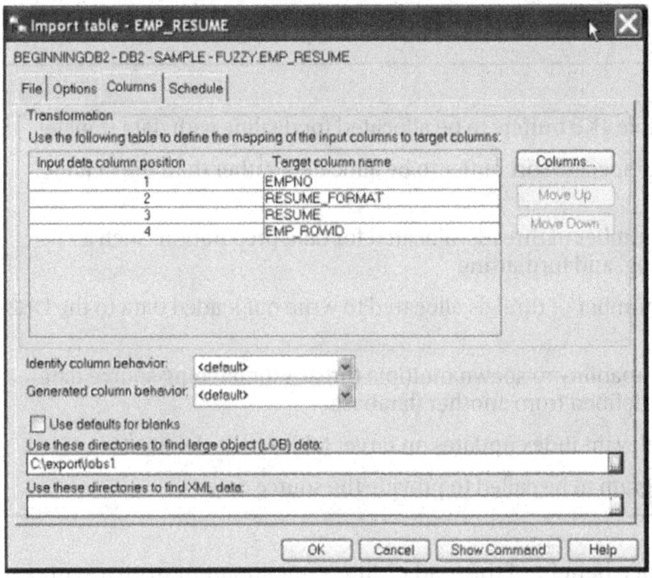

Figure 21-6. *The Columns tab of the import function in the DB2 Control Center*

Loading Data with the Load Utility

The load utility is a little bit like the supercharged, street-racer version of the import utility. It supports the full range of capabilities of the import command, but has many more options to control the speed and efficiency of a given load process. But with added speed comes a cost. To provide this breakneck capability to load data, the load utility sacrifices several important checks and defers several others. The load utility only minimally logs its actions and completely ignores table triggers. It defers the changes to indexes and the checks for referential integrity, potentially masking problems until late in the load process. Although the load utility provides ways to deal with problems in these circumstances, you are left with some house-keeping tasks after using the load utility, which I'll cover as we explore load's features.

The syntax for the load utility is *vast*. Trying to represent it here would span multiple pages and leave you thinking that it was misplaced in a beginner's book. To better describe its capabilities, Table 21-3 has a breakdown of some of the features made available by the load utility to enable higher performance than import can give.

Even with only that subset of options highlighted, you can already see some of the power available to the load utility and its associated complexity. The fetch_parallelism and sourceuserexit options suggest that the load utility can acquire its data from sources other than just files on disk. The options are even more diverse than those parameters suggest. The load utility can work directly with connections to other databases, files on disk, applications and APIs, and even pipes.

Table 21-3. *Sample Performance Optimization Options for the Load Utility*

Option	Behavior
data buffer	Enables multiple 4KB buffers to be allocated for dealing with data transfer
sort buffer sortheap	Enables a load-specific sort buffer to be allocated, rather than the default
cpu_parallelism	Controls the number of threads allocated for data preparation, such as reading, parsing, and formatting
disk_parallelism	Controls the number of threads allocated to write out loaded data to the DB2 containers
fetch_parallelism	Controls the capability to spawn multiple threads for fetching source data from a cursor defined from another database
indexing mode	Enables the relevant index updates on target tables to be deferred
sourceuserexit	Enables a program to be called to provide the source data

Perhaps the biggest performance benefit of the load utility is not apparent from a syntax diagram or list of parameters. The load utility performs its work directly with the underlying storage for the DB2 database, bypassing much of the relational engine of DB2 and some of the rules and controls it would normally impose on an insert, update, or delete statement; or on an import command. I reload the data for the product table so you can see the markers of this behavior in the load utilities output messages. Following is the load command and its output:

```
db2 => load from c:\export\products_ex4.ixf of ixf
 xml from c:\export\xml
 replace into product
SQL3109N  The utility is beginning to load data from file
"c:\export\products_ex4.ixf".

SQL3500W  The utility is beginning the "LOAD" phase at time "03/18/2008
21:39:21.885950".

SQL3150N  The H record in the PC/IXF file has product "DB2     02.00", date
"20080314", and time "222002".

SQL3050W  Conversions on the data will be made between the IXF file code page
"1252" and the application code page "1208".

SQL3153N  The T record in the PC/IXF file has name "products_ex4.ixf",
qualifier "", and source "              ".

SQL3519W  Begin Load Consistency Point. Input record count = "0".

SQL3520W  Load Consistency Point was successful.

SQL3110N  The utility has completed processing.  "4" rows were read from the
input file.
```

```
SQL3519W  Begin Load Consistency Point. Input record count = "4".

SQL3520W  Load Consistency Point was successful.

SQL3515W  The utility has finished the "LOAD" phase at time "03/18/2008
21:39:22.568833".

SQL3500W  The utility is beginning the "BUILD" phase at time "03/18/2008
21:39:22.571556".

SQL3213I  The indexing mode is "REBUILD".

SQL3515W  The utility has finished the "BUILD" phase at time "03/18/2008
21:39:23.036854".

Number of rows read        = 4
Number of rows skipped     = 0
Number of rows loaded      = 4
Number of rows rejected    = 0
Number of rows deleted     = 0
Number of rows committed   = 4
```

All that effort to load only four rows! There's a lesson here: the trade-offs of using the load utility instead of the import utility are outweighed only when you're loading substantial amounts of data. There are marker messages used in every load to signal the transition between the three key phases: loading the data, building necessary ancillary structures (such as updating indexes), and deleting data. Note the SQL3500W and SQL3515W messages that mark the beginning and end of the load phase in the preceding output. They are used again on the build phase. You always want to see these two messages bracketing work in the load output. Failure to finish a phase usually means that something catastrophic has happened, and you should see errors and warnings to that effect.

Finally, notice the pairs of SQL3519W and SQL3520W messages marking the beginning and end of a load consistency point. DB2 uses them to indicate that it might have played fast and loose with the normal rules of consistency to load your data in the fastest possible time, but that it will make sure that data passes muster via a commit. You should always see these two messages in tandem. If the SQL3520W message doesn't appear, there's a problem committing the load. You'll see a stream of further warnings and errors to follow up on.

One consequence of the capability of the load command to perform high-performance data movement is the need to revisit internal housekeeping tasks that might have been skipped, index rebuilds, and other internal checks. If this happens, a table's underlying tablespace is placed in check pending status, and the tables that were the target of a load need to have their integrity reviewed and status cleared using the set integrity command. The syntax involves quite a few options, but the most common is to use the all immediate checked variant to process all outstanding integrity checks and tasks against a table:

```
db2 => set integrity for product all immediate checked
DB20000I  The SQL command completed successfully.
```

The immediate unchecked option simply removes the check pending flag from the table and doesn't run any necessary checks. This option can be useful when you really understand its consequences, but the scope for disaster is wide, and you might find that it's a false economy to load and bypass checking if the resultant set of data is unusable.

The load utility presents an enormous number of options for data movement, but I have space to discuss only a small subset. One of the best ways to explore both the capabilities I covered and those I didn't mention is to invoke it the utility from the Control Center. You can see how the options are grouped and the equivalent load command that's generated using the Show SQL option. Mastering the load utility is not something that you'll achieve in one attempt, so use this, along with the DB2 documentation in the Information Center, to build up your experience and know-how with the load utility.

Other Data-Movement Tools

The export, import, and load utilities of DB2 are very data-centric and have been honed over the years to move data with flexibility and power. But there's more to a DB2 database than the data—although data will always be its most valuable part. IBM recognized some time ago that database developers and administrators often need to copy the definition of database objects in a form like the DDL required to re-create them, as well as all of the data from a database in logical form (instead of as a backup).

For these reasons (and others), IBM developed the db2look and db2move utilities. The db2look utility can extract the definition of database objects, tablespaces, and even the statistics used by the optimizer for use in creating the same objects and supporting data in other databases. The db2move utility acts like a set of export or import tasks running in parallel against all tables in a database.

I'll explore more of the capabilities of these tools in the next chapter when I discuss why you might need to move on to editions of DB2 with other capabilities and how best to go about orchestrating such a move.

Summary

You've now experienced the tools that DB2 offers for serious data movement. The export and import utilities have a variety of uses for both manipulating and sharing data within your environment, and also sharing with other parties such as different projects, other developers, and even external customers and suppliers. The load utility is the Formula 1 variant of import, used for maximum performance when moving data into a DB2 database. Whether you prefer the nuts-and-bolts approach to data movement via the CLP or the graphical approach to guide you, you are now equipped to start serious data movement in bulk with the full power of DB2 behind you.

CHAPTER 22

■ ■ ■

Working with Design

If design is so important, why am I dedicating only a small chapter to it toward the end of the book? Well, this is a DB2 book, not a dissertation on the fundamentals of database design. Many of you already have knowledge of normalization, entity modeling, object-relational mapping, and other design concepts; and some of you probably don't care. So instead of derailing this book with a tangent into a different problem space, let's look at designing the database layer of the Employee of the Year application that you've been gradually building, and how you can leverage (and learn about) DB2's features in the process. For those interested in more design topics in depth, I'll include references to websites and other books that I've found invaluable over the years.

I trust that my readership isn't so small that you all work in exactly the same field on exactly the same systems. If that were the case, I could choose a system common to your working lives on which to base examples. It's much better to have fun while learning than to simply repeat your day-to-day business activities, such as a social networking website such as Orkut, MySpace, Facebook, Friends Reunited, LinkedIn, and the like. But that might alienate other readers who have no time for the latest web fads or (worse) one of those quaint artifacts of recent history by the time this book has reached your hands. So instead you'll compromise on your socially oriented system to help find the number one employee in your fictitious company for the last year.

With your headline idea of the Employee of the Year system now sketched out, at least in technological terms, it's time to think seriously about how design decisions you've made along the way are going to affect your website in future, and how you'll best leverage what DB2 has to offer. By following some of the basic tenets of good database design, you'll also avoid some of the problems I alluded to earlier. You want your DB2 database to be a great platform from which your system can grow to be used year after year. If it's really successful, it's something that can be packaged and offered to thousands or even millions of organizations—and all the cacophonous celebrations they can create for their star employees instead of a hastily constructed bit-bucket, which serves your purposes now, but starts to buckle at the first sign of popularity.

There are countless books, websites, and presentations that cover numerous different design philosophies, techniques, and methods. Although they all have their pluses and minuses, one thing they mostly have in common is a roadmap to follow to ensure that you make good design decisions. In no particular order, these resources include Joe Celko's corpus of excellent books and articles on SQL; Clare Churcher's *Beginning Database Design*; and the many articles of prolific authors such as Craig Mullins, Steven Feuerstein, and others. I'll outline a straightforward design from beginning to end for the Employee of the Year DB2 system, recapping the steps you've taken throughout the book.

I'll draw on several of these invaluable sources, and even the works of the original database pioneers I mentioned in Chapter 1. A great recent example is *Database in Depth*, by Chris Date, published by O'Reilly. Many of you will be familiar with these and other design texts, so I'll try to keep focused on the overlap between good design and illustrating how you have used DB2's great and useful features, and how you can use them for the basis of good design.

Database Design Overview

It's always good to know where you're going on any journey, including a database design one, so here's the map of what you'll do to build your system:

1. **Develop a statement of need or purpose.** This is the guiding requirement that governs your design steps. It will be familiar to many of you who have worked on software projects.

2. **Identify users and use cases.** Who is (or might be) eligible for employee of the year, what might others like to do to recognize it, and what do you want to do with the information collected?

3. **Analyze use cases to find basic data requirements.** With some idea of who will use the site, and why, each use case reveals details about data that needs to be recorded and tracked in the system.

4. **Find relationships in the data.** Your use cases explicitly state some of the relationships that exist in the data, but when building a solid database design, make sure that any subtle or not-so-obvious relationships are highlighted. This helps make your design resilient to change and growth.

5. **Develop a logical data model to suit your needs.** With use cases and a range of data describing your new system, you can model it using general database concepts such as entities, attributes, and other building blocks.

6. **Translate your logical model into a physical DB2 database design.** This is where the rubber hits the road. All your modeling helps you translate your data and process needs into tables, functions, stored procedures, and other facets of a DB2 system.

7. **Review your model.** Does your model meet your needs? This is the litmus test of whether your design stands up as a good solution to your originally stated need or requirement. Did you build what you said you'd build?

Now you're armed with the knowledge of what was already covered in previous chapters and where you're going in this chapter. You'll certainly be using the DB2 Control Center and DB2 CLP, with which you are now familiar. After your sojourn in design, you'll also need the IBM Data Studio and the great facilities it provides for database design and development. You'll get to exercise many of the special features of SQL provided by DB2 that you've come to know and love.

You've used a range of programming languages and integrated development environments (IDEs) that really shine when working with DB2 to illustrate concepts and explore the capabilities of those tools. At the completion of your design review, you might want to consider what languages and environments you like best, and think about redeveloping some of the examples you've already used to suit your preference.

Statement of Requirements

You have the design map outlined in the previous section, so you know where to begin—with the statement of what it is you're trying to build, and the problems or opportunities it's designed to address. This statement needs to encapsulate what you want to achieve with the Employee of the Year system, and either imply what you'll leave out or specifically state what you're not going to do. Following is the statement of what you'll design and build over the next few chapters.

Employee of the Year will be a socially orientated networking website. It will allow visitors to the site to

- *Register their votes for employees.*

- *List employee achievements.*

- *View voting standings.*

- *View prize categories and prizes.*

- *Find results of vote counts and how prizes were awarded.*

At this time, the Employee of the Year system won't attempt to

- *Provide a live testimonial service for employees.*

- *Manage the awards ceremony itself—it will simply record the results of that ceremony.*

This is a very straightforward description, and those of you who've designed database systems before might be thinking, is that all? It's certainly enough for these purposes to show off the database design with DB2 and its related development tools. It's also a succinct list that you can reference later (and ask questions such as "Can I do what I said I'd do?") and equally make certain that you didn't get sidetracked doing things you weren't meant to do.

In that small description, you can already see descriptions of some of the components of the database you've built to support the site. In that respect, you performed your work out of order, and I wouldn't normally encourage that approach in the real world. But starting a book on DB2 without actually getting your hands dirty would have been equally wrong, so forgive this reversal of the recommended practice. Now that you know about DB2's capabilities in more depth, you should be able to follow a "design first, build later" philosophy for your future work.

You need to gather information about why people want a given employee to win the award, store reasons in text (and even image files to handle pictures of prizes). Staff members need to see some of each other's information to match their votes to the right person.

What you need to do now is crystallize what you know about your proposed system into use cases that reflect the various function desires explored throughout the book.

Identification of Users and Use Cases

The last decade has seen many different modeling techniques come and go, but one enduring part of many of them is the use of the Unified Modeling Language (UML) as a diagramming and description standard. One of its key modeling techniques is to employ the use case to describe a single scenario in which a person or other system interacts with the software being designed, and a brief story is told indicating how the experience should unfold, the outcomes to be achieved, and so on. My choice of the story metaphor is intentional because in use case modeling, the people using your system are usually called actors. Besides a description, a simple stick-figure notation supplements the model to communicate visually the interactions that are expected.

I don't want to get sidetracked in the minutiae of UML, so I'll make the following use case discussion as straightforward as possible.

Having found the Employee of the Year site, staff members will want to do a number of things to register their desired votes, illustrated in the use case diagram shown in Figure 22-1.

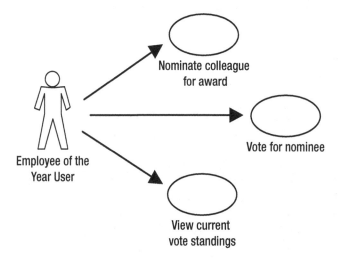

Figure 22-1. *The basic use cases for a user of Employee of the Year*

These use cases cover some of the basic relationship aspects of using your proposed Employee of the Year system, in which a user wants to do something to benefit, or interact with, other staff members. You know that your DB2 database needs to cater for these uses, but you also know that there are more use cases pertaining to how you've built up capabilities you've already seen, see award details, run mini-support campaigns to get extra votes, and so on. Some of these "power" use cases are shown in Figure 22-2, and I'm sure you can think of several more for your model.

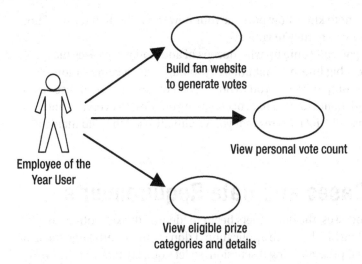

Figure 22-2. *Use cases for more-powerful personal activities on the Employee of the Year system*

With some simple use case descriptions, you're covering a huge variety of actions supported by the system. So in the preceding cases, view prizes and categories will cover quite a range of searching and comparison—but much of those details can be covered with simple SQL statements and stored procedures, and you cheated by building them first.

As the designer, developer, owner, and operator of Employee of the Year system, you'll probably have some particular requirements. Some possible use cases are shown in Figure 22-3, covering reporting and maintenance of the site.

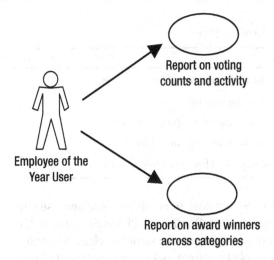

Figure 22-3. *Use cases for the owner of the Employee of the Year system*

No surprises there—you want to know how popular your new site is, both in terms of how many people have voted and for whom they're voting!

Given more time, I'm sure you can come up with dozens of additional use cases that might actually make you the next big Internet millionaire (you might run a competition called Employee Idol, and have companies pay you to do it). But I digress. The eight use cases described here are more than adequate for you to proceed with your design overview and collect some of the extremely useful DB2 features that you've already used to build many of your system's features.

Analysis of Use Cases and Data Requirements

At this point in most design processes, the developers begin to identify the key entities, or classes, that will form the building blocks of the application. I don't want to turn large tracts of this book into an object-oriented programming discussion, so let's quickly pick out the obvious candidates from your use cases, and follow them through the database design process.

The clearest example of a class in your early use cases is the employee. That is, someone who's working for your fictional company and uses the site's facilities to nominate and vote for others, or drum up support for themselves. A class model would include a thorough analysis of the functional requirements of the class and come up with methods supporting it such as constructors, comparators, various getter and setter methods for the attributes, and so on. You want to focus more on the database–level entity and data requirements, to support those and other functions outlined in your use cases. You know some of the attributes you will want to model about employees. Table 22-1 illustrates some of the details that should be obvious about employees that your system will likely need to manage.

Table 22-1. *Analysis of a Staff Member for Employee of the Year*

Employee Attribute	Description
Name	What are the given name and surname of the employee?
Employee Role	What job or position does the employee hold?
Department	Where in the organization does the employee work?
Qualifications	What skills or education does the employee have?
Date Joined	How long has the person worked for the organization?

You might be thinking that you don't really need to model an employee table because one already existed in the SAMPLE database when it was created. But this is still a useful exercise for two reasons. One, you get to try out how your model compares with someone else's; and two, you might find yourself in future being given control of a system that has no documentation, including data models. A little practice lets you design what *should be* present, and compare it with what *is* present. Another example of a prototype class can be gleaned from the description of your second group of use cases. You know that staff members will be vying for prizes in your awards, and people will be naturally curious about what's offered in various categories. You can start modeling it using the detail shown in Table 22-2. You actually created a prizes table in Chapter 14 on Ruby, but you want to think about it without Ruby or SQL syntax at this stage.

Table 22-2. *Analysis of a Prize*

Prize Attribute	Description
Prize Name	Name of the prize
Prize Description	If it's not obvious from the name, a description of the prize
Prize Value	What the prize is worth
Picture	Image or picture of the prize

You can already see some of the recurring themes and the relationships that exist between your entities—some of which you've already used, and others of which you'll explore shortly. At this point, you can also see that some items you might nominally list as attributes are first-class entities (or classes) in their own right, and you need to model them accordingly. So a prize's category isn't an attribute of a given prize, but instead a related entity that you want to know about in far more detail, as shown in Table 22-3.

Table 22-3. *Analysis of an Award Category*

Category Attribute	Description
Name	Name given to the category; for example, Best Intern or Salesperson of the Year
Eligibility Criteria	Some categories are restricted to certain employees
Description	Purpose of this award category
Previous Winners	Other staff who won this prize

In a full-scale design process, you could take this analysis much further. You would also work in tandem with the class designs being developed to ensure appropriate object-relational mappings. But because you want to complete your design and relate it back to the work you accomplished in previous chapters, let's pause here to study what you already have done.

Finding Relationships in the Data

You might have heard of the modeling concept of normalization. I'll skip the academic description and stick to a very straightforward discussion. Key to a good data model, and classes and other programming constructs built on top of it, is asking this question: Does an attribute really relate only to the object it is associated with and nothing else?

Let's use an example of employees using your site and the award categories for which they might be nominated. In your initial sketch of your design, you highlighted that employees are indeed the main entities you'll work with at a data and code level, and you listed the award categories available as a second entity. *Categories* implies more than one, so think about just including a list or subset of categories for a given employee. But you might need to work with a given award category even if no one qualified for it. In order to do that you also need to manage award categories as first-class beings in the data and code, which was outlined previously. But that means you shouldn't keep a textual list of award categories as an attribute of an employee because it would require double-entry of data and include attributes that are really one step removed from the employee. You really want to relate staff members to the categories for which they are eligible.

For those new to the idea, what I really want to say is best illustrated in the diagram shown at Figure 22-4.

Figure 22-4. *Modeling the relationship between an employee and award category*

The notation on that diagram is a common way of recording the strength of the relationship between two entities. By using 0..*n*, I'm indicating that when you read the relationship at one side, you'll find anywhere from 0 to *n* related entities at the other end. In this example, you're saying that a staff member can qualify for zero or more award categories, and a given award category can be open to zero or more staff members.

Note Why should you allow award categories if no employees are eligible for them? This allows you to be more flexible in the use cases you can handle. For instance, you might introduce a new category in anticipation of hiring new types of staff!

If you drank as much coffee as I did today, you'll also be thinking, "Hey, not only is that easy, but I can see many other relationships in that little model." And of course, you are right. Another example is the relationship between a staff member and a nomination for one of their peers. When one employee wants to vote for another to win the award for a given category, it's a nomination. To illustrate, Figure 22-5 shows the relationship between the two.

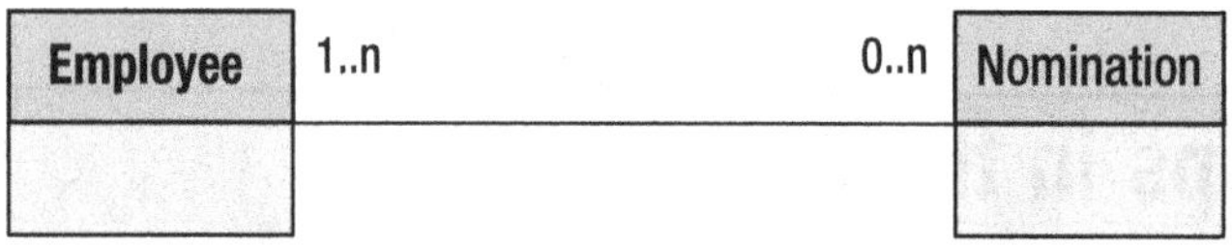

Employee	1..n	0..n	Nomination

Figure 22-5. *Modeling the relationship between an employee and a nomination*

In this relationship, I used 1..*n* notation, meaning that at least one employee is required as part of the relationship for a nomination. When you think about it, there aren't too many ways to nominate *nobody* for something. Some might argue that you need at least two employees to qualify: one to make the nomination and one to be the nominee. So you'll consider that as you iterate through the modeling steps.

You can continue in this vein, examining the relationships that are immediately apparent and those that are discernable only after some thinking, until you come up with an idea for how all the information you'll collect and use interrelates. At that point, you're most of the way toward having a logical data model constructed.

Building the Logical Data Model

Don't let the term *logical data model* put you off. A quick "sanity check" should allay any fears you might have that I've left the realm of normal systems design and have entered some strange world known only to database experts.

What you're designing is logical because you stepped through the use cases, basic data requirements, and their relationships, and come up with a basic design that captures what makes sense, and excluded what doesn't. You highlighted the data that describes all the elements that make up your design, although you haven't done so right down to the level of lengths, units, dimensions, and similar minutiae (but you'll get there soon). Your data design mimics and supports what you're proposing your system will present to users of all shapes and descriptions, meaning that it models your real-world requirements well.

In a full design process, you would iterate through use cases, analyses, relationship probing, and so on several times to continuously improve the model. Because you don't want to spend the rest of the book on more and more refined examples of the same thing, you'll work with your existing model together with the examples you've developed throughout the book. If you put together the pieces from your use cases and analysis, you can see that your logical model is already well formed. Figure 22-6 shows those entities you already investigated and those that should be immediately recognizable from this chapter's discussion.

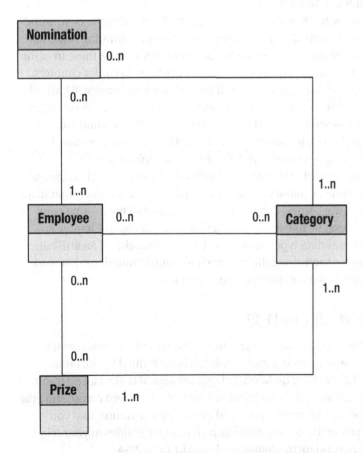

Figure 22-6. *The prototype logical data model for the Employee of the Year system*

At this stage, each entity or class-like object that you're modeling can be described with attributes in a generic fashion. I suggest that nominations have a date, but I haven't specified how you'll record such a date. The same lack of detail exists for all the other attributes. You might be tempted to think it obvious and assume a particular date format, character set for names, or what have you. But this is where the distinction between the logical model and its next step—the physical model—sits. Only when you translate your logical model to the physical model will you include information about the information—often called *metadata*—that governs the low-level characteristics of your database.

Translating a Logical Model to a Physical Model

You're nearly at the end of your rapid tour of design. To map your logical model to your physical model—which describes exactly what you need to build in your DB2 database—you need to know how DB2 supports such a mapping (and what on earth *mapping* really means).

The idea of mapping your model into a physical database will be very familiar to many of you. There are no big secrets, so let's jump straight to the heart of the matter. The entities you modeled and their attributes translate directly to underlying tables in the database, or (when relationships exist between your entities) you can introduce an intermediary table that allows you to track the relationships at the data level.

With the processes that have been identified, such as nominating a colleague or winning an award, you can translate these actions into one or more pieces of programming logic that will use your tables. Normally, decisions would be made about whether to code these in at the application layer, using a language such as Java or C++ that was explored in earlier chapters, or to encapsulate this logic at the database layer in stored procedures and functions. I mixed the implementation approach in this book to give you as wide an exposure as possible to the possibilities of DB2, so you could experience building the logic in the database and application tiers. In practice, you'd probably opt for some database-level logic and application-level logic in one (or possibly two) languages to suit your desired style of deployment.

One last piece of background is needed before you sketch the physical model. At the end of the discussion on the logical model, I stated that you need to decide the low-level metadata that describes your information—the names, dates, numbers, text, and so forth—that comprise your entities. If that sounds exactly like the DB2 data types introduced in Chapter 7, you're right! The physical model uses data types to control the data "domain" of an attribute, and gives you all the benefits you've seen along the way, such as built-in functions that work with data types, conversion between data of different types, and more.

Building the Physical Model in DB2

The award categories, nominations, prizes, and other entities from a logical model need a physical representation. In DB2, as in other databases, this job is performed by the table, which you explored in depth in Chapter 7. The Award Categories logical entity can be translated into a physical table representation by thinking about each attribute and considering the actual data it will contain. But before doing this, you need to consider attributes that you listed in the logical model that you realized were relationships to other entities in your relationship review. Flag them for appropriate modeling, as shown in Table 22-4.

Table 22-4. *Dealing with Attributes in the Move to a Physical Data Model*

Category Attribute	Simple Attribute or Relationship	Result
Category Name	Simple attribute	Keep as attribute
Eligibility Criteria	Simple attribute	Keep as attribute
Previous Winners	Relationship	Model as related attribute

When moving to the physical model, you also need to consider the concept of key attributes—those values that can be used to uniquely identify your award categories in this case—and whether any of those keys can be considered your preference for becoming the primary key, or main unique identifier, for the physical model. For your awards, neither names, criteria, nor any of the relationship-based information help you uniquely identify an award. Even Name, which might help, isn't unique over time if award names change to reflect sponsors, changing criteria, or other factors.

You're left with a very common physical modeling requirement. You need to introduce an attribute that you'll assign to every instance of your entity to uniquely identify them. This approach is often termed *adding a surrogate or synthetic key* because the attribute doesn't have any intrinsic meaning, and its only purpose is to act as a key identifier for the sake of uniqueness. I'll choose the name AwardID, which will be a simple unique number added as an attribute to the award categories.

Where a name or description is concerned, you need to consider whether it's best to keep these attributes as single blocks of text, or break them up according to social or application rules. In this case, it has already been dealt with for an employee's name in the SAMPLE database. This is common with people's names, which normally consist of a first name or common name, and a family name or surname (and possibly many others). Because you're not running a national identity database, you can be satisfied with what is already provided.

Where attributes have been identified as describing a relationship to another entity, you'll perform a common modeling approach in which these relationship details will be split out into a separate table, usually called an intersection or relationship table. For your awards categories, it will use your new AwardID value, along with the unique identifier of the related employee, to store the details of relationships. This means that your physical model is now firm enough to start thinking about data types; Table 22-5 shows the candidate types to consider.

Table 22-5. *Considering Data Types in the Move to a Physical Data Model*

Attribute	Nature of Attribute	Possible Data Types
CategoryID	Unique identifier	SMALLINT, INTEGER, or BIGINT
CategoryName	Textual	CHAR, VARCHAR, GRAPHIC, or similar
Eligibility	Textual	CHAR, VARCHAR, GRAPHIC, or similar

That should look very familiar from Chapter 7. At this point, you can think about more detail for your data type candidates, such as whether fixed or variable length is important, how long or large your data types might be, and whether any of the values can be left empty—or Null—in your model.

WHAT DOES IT MEAN TO BE NULL?

Relational databases, including DB2, are all modeled on three-valued logic. In straightforward terms, that means that any two attributes fall into one of three categories. For example, you could say that two attributes are equal, or that they are not equal, or that their equivalence is unknown. It is this third option, the unknown quantity, which best embodies the idea of Null. A Null value is not equal to anything else, nor is it greater than or less than anything else—even another Null value! Adding a Null to the end of some text will result in nothing, and dividing a number by Null doesn't bear thinking about. A Null also doesn't impact aggregates such as MIN, MAX, or AVERAGE. So although Null can be very handy, with its power come certain side effects.

Some theorists argue that using Nulls is a sign that a data model is flawed and hasn't been sufficiently normalized. You might have strong feelings one way or the other or be like me: pragmatic enough to use them when they fill a well-defined need but with full knowledge of their characteristics.

Your model has extracted the relationship between the employee and award category, so to complete the description you need to illustrate what happens here. Your intersection table, which I'll call AwardWinner, will take the form shown in Table 22-6.

Table 22-6. *Physical Design of an Intersection Table*

Attribute	Nature of Attribute	Possible Data Types
AwardID	Unique identifier	SMALLINT, INTEGER, or BIGINT
EmpNo	Unique identifier	CHAR(6)
DateWon	Date of yearly award	DATE or TIMESTAMP
TotalVotes	Number of nominations	SMALLINT, INTEGER, or BIGINT
Picture	Image of the award presentation	BLOB

The use of the primary key identifiers from the two related tables is the standard way to construct such an intersection table. Note that I've been specific about the data type of the EmpNo field to make sure it matches that already provided by the same field in the Employee table in the standard SAMPLE database. This ensures that DB2 doesn't need to perform data type conversions when you compare these values in joins and other queries, and generally is a good performance rule of thumb. The third, fourth, and fifth fields are attributes of the relationship, and so meet your earlier stated goal of ensuring attributes related to this specific intersection entity: an employee receiving a reward.

From here you can make other sensible decisions based on what you know from your use cases. For instance, I probably don't need to track trillions of possible identifiers for awards, so of the options of SMALLINT, INTEGER, and BIGINT to record this attribute, INTEGER suffices. You could also look at the value of every possible item that can be awarded as a prize and decide that you don't need to track the value down to the cent, and so choose INTEGER instead of DECIMAL. If you follow this process, you'll end up with a model similar to the one shown in Table 22-7.

Table 22-7. *Physical Model for the Prize Table*

Attribute	Data type	Nullability
PrizeID	INTEGER	Not Null
PrizeName	VARCHAR(255)	Not Null
Description	VARCHAR(255)	Nulls allowed
PrizeValue	INTEGER	Nulls allowed
Picture	BLOB	Nulls allowed

You should recognize that physical design as the one you developed in Chapter 14. You need not be so exhaustive in describing the other logical to physical mappings. You'll remember working with your nomination table, and its physical design looks like Table 22-8 when modeled all the way to specific data types, synthetic keys, and so forth.

Table 22-8. *Physical Model for the Nomination Table*

Attribute	Data type	Nullability
NominationID	INTEGER	Not Null
Nominee	CHAR(6)	Not Null
Nominator	CHAR(6)	Not Null
Reason	VARCHAR(250)	Nulls allowed
NomDate	DATE	Not Null

This leaves you with your remaining relationship data. The complete physical model is pictured in Figure 22-7. Here, your entities use intersection tables to model many-to-many relationships, and you've constructed the model to be useful in perpetuity by ensuring that all temporal instances of entities have relevant dates as attributes. You can, in theory, use this design well into the future without having to worry about anything more than a few date criteria in your site's SQL statements.

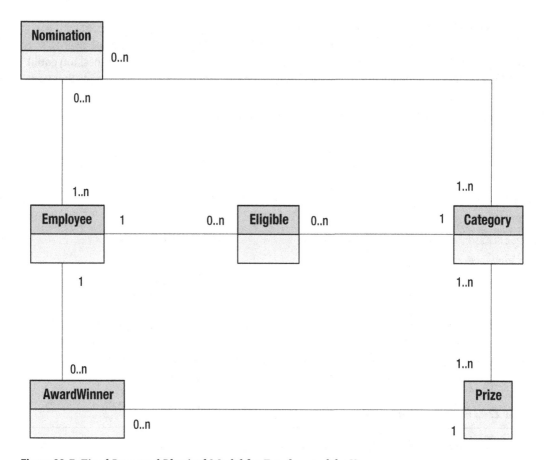

Figure 22-7. *Final Proposed Physical Model for Employee of the Year*

Model Review

Much of this application, use case, and logical and physical modeling is familiar to anyone who's worked with other databases and applications. But for those of you who haven't, you can now look back and see how the design you outlined supports the goals you stated way back at the start of the chapter (and indeed the exercises and examples you've used along the way to learn DB2 features). You have the structures to record information about Employee of the Year users—their nominations, awards, and more. By simply tracing where data would be stored and from where it would be read, you can see how other functions, such as reporting and organizing an awards ceremony, can be supported. In the end, the model is only as good as the utility it provides the users—both end users and developers.

Summary

An entire chapter devoted to modeling might have seemed a diversion from learning more about DB2, but you're now set to make top-quality databases and systems with your newfound DB2 knowledge. If your design differs from mine, that's perfectly valid. In many design and development scenarios, there's no single correct model for the database. Instead, judge your models by the fullness with which they let you easily and intuitively build your applications.

CHAPTER 23

■■■

Moving Up to More Advanced DB2

This chapter introduces a range of features in DB2 that can really *shift* your data. Although you already know about the import, export, and load utilities for simple data movement, DB2 offers a range of more advanced features to extract data, maintain copies for other purposes (such as disaster recovery), replicate your data in truly remarkable ways, compress data for storage and performance efficiency, and much more. I'll give you a brief tour of some of these technologies and leave you with enough knowledge of the basics to decide where to spend your attention learning more.

Using the db2look and db2move Utilities

The db2move and db2look utilities are almost partners in crime—or partners in data movement, at least. Each of these utilities offers movement options that go beyond the traditional import, export, and load tools with which you are now familiar. I'm introducing them in tandem because they are often used together to move both data and metadata between DB2 systems.

Using db2look

The db2look utility is designed to extract the data definition language (DDL) of database objects, so that they can be re-created elsewhere. It is also capable of generating update commands to configure the database manager, the db2 registry, and the statistics that the system catalog holds on a database object. The ability to generate DDL is obviously useful, but you might be wondering about the usefulness of other features. Imagine being able to mimic the configuration of a huge production database with billions of rows of data and a meticulously configured database. db2look allows you to capture those configuration settings and statistics, and make a much smaller test or development database appear exactly the same—without the need for all that data. I'll cover the importance of statistics for the optimizer in the next chapter, but this feature of db2look becomes invaluable in performance-tuning work.

db2look is invoked as a utility from the command line, and in its most simple form it takes a set of parameters to tell it which table, schema, and database to target for extraction. Let's say you want to capture the DDL for the nomination table for your employee of the year work.

A simple db2look invocation requires you to nominate the database, schema, and table. It looks like this:

```
$ db2look -d SAMPLE -z fuzzy -t nomination -e

... many lines of header and other details ...


--------------------------------------------------
-- DDL Statements for table "FUZZY   "."NOMINATION"
--------------------------------------------------


CREATE TABLE "FUZZY   "."NOMINATION"  (
                  "NOMINATIONID" INTEGER NOT NULL ,
                  "EMPNO" CHAR(6) NOT NULL ,
                  "REASON" VARCHAR(250) )
                DATA CAPTURE CHANGES
                IN "IBMDB2SAMPLEREL" ;

-- DDL Statements for indexes on Table "FUZZY   "."NOMINATION"

CREATE INDEX "FUZZY   "."NOM_EMPNO" ON "FUZZY   "."NOMINATION"
                ("EMPNO" ASC)
                ALLOW REVERSE SCANS;

COMMIT WORK;
CONNECT RESET;
TERMINATE;
```

You asked for DDL, and that's exactly what you received. You now have the create table statement for the nomination table, as well as the associated index creation DDL. db2look has more sophisticated features. The -tw option allows you to use wildcards to match multiple table names.

The -e option used previously instructs db2look to extract DDL. Without it, you extract statistical information from the table(s) and associated indexes, which covers measurements such as data distribution, storage and page counts, and so forth:

```
$ db2look -d SAMPLE -z fuzzy -t nomination
...
--******************************************
TABLE NOMINATION
--******************************************

--

          CREATOR       FUZZY
          CARD          89873
          NPAGES        322
          FPAGES        322
          OVERFLOW      0
          ACTIVE_BLOCKS 0

--

          COLUMNS
```

```
--
                    NAME     NOMINATIONID
                    COLNO    0
                    TYPE     BIGINT
                    LENGTH   8
                    NULLS    N
                    COLCARD  5632
                    NUMNULLS 0
...
--
           INDICES
--
                    INDEX_NAME     NOM_EMPNO
                    INDEX_CREATOR  FUZZY
                    NLEAF          99
                    NLEVELS        2
                    FULLKEYCARD    42
                    FIRSTKEYCARD   42
...
```

I edited the statistical information returned to just that brief summary, so you can imagine how much detail would be output for all the tables for one database. db2look has numerous options you can learn about by invoking the utility with the -h option. The most useful are the following:

- **-d** *database-name*: Database name

- **-u** *name*: Creator ID for target objects

- **-z** *name*: Schema name

- **-t** *table-name*: Individual table name

- **-tw** *wildcard-string*: Wildcard string to match with table names

- **-v** *view-name*: View name

- **-o** *file-name*: Output to file

- **-e**: Extract DDL, not statistics

- **-m**: Mimic mode

Using db2look creates a command file suitable for running directly against another database instead of just printing human readable values to screen.

Using db2move

Where db2look moves information about tables between systems, db2move is its counterpart in moving the data contents. You might assume that it's what the export and import (or load) utilities are for. Well, you're right, but remember that they deal with one table at a time. db2move is the "multiplying" factor that you can use to target entire schemas and sets of tables, and the data contained in them, for moving between databases.

Instead of acting as yet another import/export tool, db2move acts as a wrapper utility around the existing DB2 data movement tools, invoking export, import, or load multiple times for the tables from which you want data moved.

You have plenty of experience with export, import, and load now, so there's no need to rehash those utilities. Instead, focus on the options specific to db2move that will be of use to you. The general format for db2move syntax is as follows:

```
db2move database-name {export | import | load} {object rules} [options]
```

Much of that syntax, such as the database and choice of data movement option, is self-explanatory. The object rules identify which tables, schemas, and so forth to target. If you want to export the existing employee and nomination tables, you can invoke db2move as follows:

```
$ db2move sample export -tc fuzzy -tn employee,nomination

Application code page not determined, using ANSI codepage 1252
*****   DB2MOVE   *****
Action:  EXPORT
Start time:  Mon Apr 07 05:12:12 2008

All creator names matching:  FUZZY;
All table names matching:  EMPLOYEE; NOMINATION;
Connecting to database SAMPLE ... successful!  Server : DB2 Common Server V9.5.0

EXPORT:     42 rows from table "FUZZY   "."EMPLOYEE"
EXPORT:  89873 rows from table "FUZZY   "."NOMINATION"

Disconnecting from database ... successful!
```

In the example, the -tc option is used to list the table creators, and -tn is used to list the desired tables. You can specify more than one option (and even specify wildcards) for each of those switches.

■**Tip** Make sure that there are no spaces before or after the commas in the list of table names or creators with those options.

You might be thinking that the output is nice, *but where is the data*? Good question. The good news is that it's right there in the directory from which you invoked the db2move utility. You should see a file named db2move.lst, which acts as a master directory for all the files created by a single use of db2move, and whose contents will be the platform-independent description of all the related data files and message files for your use of db2move. In this case, the db2move.lst file has the following contents:

```
!"FUZZY   "."EMPLOYEE"!tab1.ixf!tab1.msg!
!"FUZZY   "."NOMINATION"!tab2.ixf!tab2.msg!
```

You don't normally need to read it, but it's comforting to see that it's referring to the files `tab1.ixf`, `tab1.msg`, `tab2.ixf`, and `tab2.msg` for the two tables. Lo and behold, they are right there in the directory; they contain the data in IXF format, and related messages from the export in the message file.

`db2move` has a number of useful command-line options. The following subset is the most immediately useful, which you should commit to memory:

- **-tc** *creator(s)*   List of table creators to match

- **-tn** *table-name(s)*   List of tables to match

- **-sn** *schema(ta)*   List of schemata to match

- **-ts** *tablespace(s)*   List of tablespaces to match

- **-l** *path*   LOB path to use for import, export, or load

- **-u** *username*   User name to use for `db2move` connection

- **-p** *password*   Associated password for the user name

Using db2look from the Control Center

Those of you who have come to appreciate the graphical interface to nearly every DB2 feature will be pleased to know that `db2look` is available from the Control Center. Note that IBM went for a slightly different name on the context menu of a table to invoke it. Instead of calling it `db2look`, you'll see that there is an option called Generate DDL on the context menu of every table, which launches the Generate DDL dialog box shown in Figure 23-1.

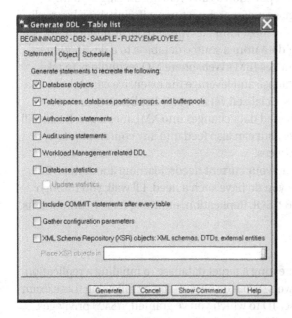

Figure 23-1. *Generate DDL dialog box for a table in the DB2 Control Center*

The options on the Statement tab are akin to the command-line switches you just learned for db2look. If you click the Show Command button in the dialog box, you'll see that the Generate DDL user interface is simply calling db2look under the hood.

Unfortunately for those of you who like the Control Center, there's no graphical equivalent of db2move at the moment (although export, import, and load all have a GUI).

DB2 Replication

Anyone who has worked with databases for any length of time quickly discovers that part of their value comes from the ability to share the data they hold. Sometimes that means sharing *all* the data and tracking changes in real time. Database replication is one of the central techniques used to copy data in DB2 *en masse* and to maintain those copies in real time. At this point, it's prudent to highlight that although the DB2 replication features are active in the DB2 Express-C edition, they are not licensed for use in that edition. To legally use them, you have to purchase at least the yearly support option for Express-C or one of the higher editions of DB2 mentioned in Chapter 1. Nevertheless, it's good to know what the technology is about before you invest in it.

DB2 has a long and glorious track record of supporting replication technologies; it now boasts the most advanced replication technology set on the market today. Key to DB2's approach to replication is its universal approach to what replication means. Although other database systems treat replication as simply copying the data from one database to another, IBM realized that the ultimate outcome of replication varies from use to use. For example, you might want some or all of your data replicated to another database, but you actually want to feed that data through a bus or queue approach. Or maybe you're really interested in the *changes* in the data and might prefer to treat replication as an event-messaging system.

DB2's replication capabilities span all these major architectures, offering three key replication functions. SQL Replication, which is the most familiar type of replication for many readers, enables DB2 to transmit changes of data from a source database to a destination database via staging tables. Q Replication utilizes IBM's Websphere MQ technology to take responsibility for replication outside the database and leverage the extensive capabilities of a message-queuing system. This extends to a specialized version of Q Replication known as Event Publishing, which transforms all replicated data changes into XML messages. It can still be used to ultimately target replica databases, but can also feed into any contemporary system that understands XML—such as web services!

If such sweeping notions take you beyond your current needs, learning about the DB2 replication tools now prepares you for when you do have such a need. I'll walk you through the most common replication setup with DB2, SQL Replication, outlining its key components.

Preparing for Replication

Much of the work you're about to do, from creating a target database to building a replication definition, requires SYSADM and/or DBADM powers. You'll be best served by following these examples as your instance owner or by using a user ID to which you've granted SYSADM privileges.

You'll build a scenario in which you copy data from the existing SAMPLE database to another database to exercise the powers of replication. To do that, you have to actually create another database to be that target. If you still have other databases available after the various exercises in Chapter 18, you can use one of them as your replication target, or you can create a new database to be your target. I created a database called REPLICA to be the target of my replication.

You need to create (or already have) a target table that will receive the replicated data. (I'll use the nomination table from the SAMPLE database as my example source table. I want a quick and easy way to create an identical nomination table in the REPLICA database.) Fortunately, having just learned about the db2look capabilities to generate DDL, you know exactly how to easily set up this table.

Configuring Replication via the Replication Center

About now I'd normally make an attempt at humor or suspense to lead up to the revelation of a wizard for replication. But DB2 has even more in store for you when it comes to creating and managing your replication needs. There is an entire Replication Center dedicated to running lots of wizards and letting you view and control your replication from a central console.

Launching the Replication Center

To launch the Replication Center, use the db2rc command under Linux. Under Windows, browse to the General Administration Tools start menu folder under the DB2 installation and choose Replication Center. You should see the normal splash window for any DB2 Java-based product. The Replication Center Launchpad displays (see Figure 23-2), which is intended to let you jump straight in to replication.

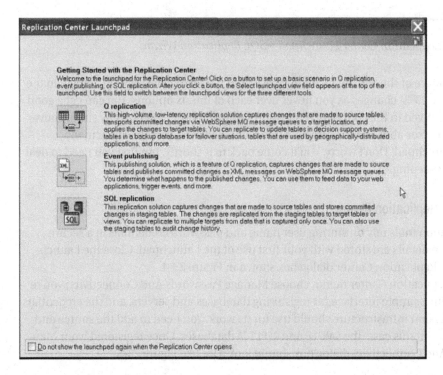

Figure 23-2. *DB2 Replication Center Launchpad*

You'll explore SQL Replication because it is the most database-centric of the replication technologies that DB2 offers and because it has the fewest external dependencies. Click the

SQL Replication button; the Launchpad switches to the six-step wizard shown in Figure 23-3, which will take you through configuring all aspects of your replication.

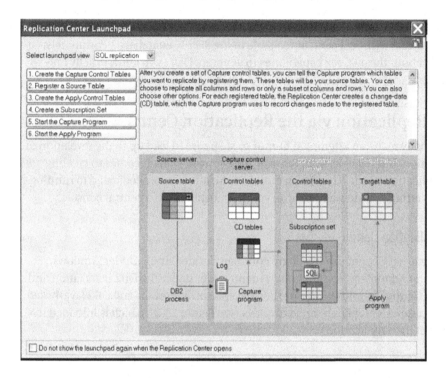

Figure 23-3. *DB2 Replication Center Launchpad—SQL Replication Wizard*

One nice feature of the SQL Replication view is that the textual description (shown in the top right of Figure 23-3) changes as you hover over each of the six options. You can get a good feel for what's involved in the complete replication setup and how data flows by simply hovering your mouse cursor above each button. At this point, however, you need to actually abandon the Launchpad! Don't worry, you'll come back to it shortly, but first you need to deal with some housekeeping.

Configuring the Replication Center

The DB2 replication tools rely on storing user name and password credentials in a secure repository, but no details are stored with your first use of the Launchpad. Close the Launchpad; you see the Replication Center dialog box shown in Figure 23-4.

From the Replication Center menu, choose Manage Passwords And Connectivity; you're be presented with a simple interface for registering databases and servers, and the credentials that DB2's replication infrastructure should use for its work. You need to add the source and target databases—in this case, the SAMPLE and REPLICA databases. Once registered, your Manage Passwords And Connectivity dialog box should look a lot like Figure 23-5.

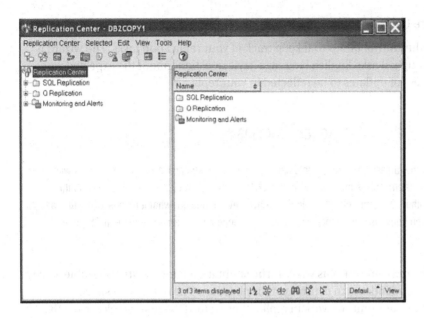

Figure 23-4. *DB2 Replication Center*

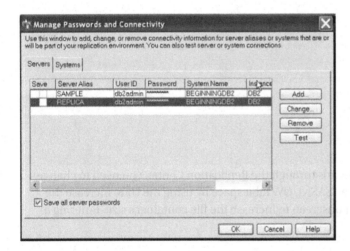

Figure 23-5. *Managing passwords and connectivity with DB2 Replication Center*

I spared you endless screenshots of wizards that will be very much self-explanatory, but be sure to use the Test button to ensure that you entered credentials correctly. With the authentication details in place, you're now ready to run each of the replication wizards. Again, to spare you dozens of pages of screenshots, I'll highlight the tips, tricks, and pitfalls to be aware of when running each of the six wizards.

Creating the Capture Control Tables

This wizard creates the control tables that keep track of your replication tasks. The wizard is very easy to step through; it asks English language–style questions about the expected workload and the timeliness of updates to be reflected in your replica.

WHO (OR WHAT) IS ASN?

You're about to see many tablespace names, table names, information screens, and error messages with the term *ASN* embedded in them. This is an historic throwback to IBM's early replication technology and the terminology that went with it. The term ASN is so old that I have never found out what it means, even after all these years. So now you know its provenance and have a challenge if you want to beat me at DB2 trivia.

I found only one problem with this wizard. The script it prepares creates two tablespaces and numerous tables and indexes to control your replication. One of the tablespaces, TSASNUOW, is used to track units of work in replication. In the first general release of DB2 9.5, the file container for the tablespace defaults to a size too low to allow the subsequent scripts to run successfully. You'll see this SQL as part of the set of commands it proposes to run:

```
...
CREATE  TABLESPACE TSASNUOW
 IN NODEGROUP IBMCATGROUP
 MANAGED BY DATABASE
 USING
(
 FILE 'TSASNUOW' 1M
);
...
```

To successfully run the commands through the Replication Center, you need to change the size of the file container for the TSASNUOW tablespace by using the UI to increase the container size or editing the script onscreen to increase the file container's size. Entering a value of **10M** works well:

```
...
CREATE  TABLESPACE TSASNUOW
 IN NODEGROUP IBMCATGROUP
 MANAGED BY DATABASE
 USING
(
 FILE 'TSASNUOW' 10M
);
...
```

With that change in place, you can run the wizard to completion. Note you can also copy and paste the entire script into the Command Editor, DB2 CLP, and so on. Make the same change and manually take control of the Capture control table-creation process. Another useful change to consider is switching this tablespace to automatic storage as you now know that feature saves you most of the worries associated with low-level tablespace management. The tables created are used by the Capture program, which is one-half of the application pair that does the hard work of managing your DB2 replication.

Registering a Source Table

This wizard allows you to find the tables you want to provide the data that will be replicated. The table registration wizard provides a great graphical way to find the tables (and even columns) you want to replicate. The only gotcha is the search logic it uses. Figure 23-6 shows the Add Registerable Tables dialog box. The key to finding what you want, without having to scroll through every object in the database, is to realize that the Values fields accept SQL-style values.

Figure 23-6. *Adding desired tables to your replication with DB2 Replication Center*

In my example, because I'm using the like operator I need to use the percentage symbol to get SQL-style wildcard behavior when I click the Retrieve button. If you're wondering why you can't get the search to work properly, just think about what the SQL syntax would look like for an equivalent search, and you won't go wrong.

With your possible tables found, selecting one presents it in the Register Tables dialog box, which allows you to modify and refine the data from your chosen table, which will be copied to your replica.

Creating the Apply Control Tables

The Apply program is the partner process of the Control program mentioned previously. They act in tandem to do the actual shuttling of data between the source and target systems. Just like Capture, Apply needs to know where to keep its working data and the tablespace in which to house this information. It can technically be any database you like, but it's common to use the target database and have the Apply program's tablespace TSASNAA and associated tables created there.

The wizard for creating the Apply control tables doesn't have any quirks that I've experienced, and running it is almost identical to the Capture control tables process.

Creating a Subscription Set

A *subscription set* is a set of rules that tells the DB2 Apply program how to transform data gathered from the Capture program for applying to your replica tables. My recommendation for your first foray into DB2 replication is to create a subscription set that simply copies the data without transformation from source to target. So I'll simply point the Apply program to map the NOMINATION table and its rows straight from the captured data in the SAMPLE database to the REPLICA database.

Starting the Capture Process

At this point, you're ready to start capturing changes. Starting the Capture process throws up a simple dialog box, shown in Figure 23-7, whose sole purpose is to have you nominate the schema in which the Capture control tables exist for this instance of Capture.

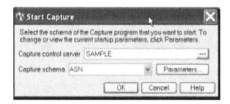

Figure 23-7. *Starting the Capture process and nominating its related schema*

Because you'll most likely have created only one set of Capture control tables, you'll almost certainly be using the example ASN schema. Click OK; you'll then see a large dialog box that lists the connection credentials and the command-line equivalent of starting the Capture process:

```
asncap capture_server=SAMPLE
```

It's as simple as that to get your replication Capture started. The proof of success will come when you have the complementary Apply process running and start changing data in the source NOMINATION table.

Start the Apply Process

All that's left to do now is start the Apply process on the target, meaning that changes from the NOMINATION table in the SAMPLE database filter through and are applied to the same table in the REPLICA database. Again, the dialog box is very similar to the Capture process starting dialog box, and again you're taken to a second dialog box to confirm connection credentials and actually run the command that starts the Apply process. With it running, you have successfully configured a complete replication environment.

Testing Replication in Action

After all the hard work getting replication set up—even an example as simple as this one—the testing is remarkably simple. Does the act of changing data in the NOMINATION table of the SAMPLE database result in the same change in the REPLICA database? Let's test it by adding a new nomination using any of the many techniques you've developed in the book. You can choose straight SQL, a web page, a stored procedure, or any other technique you might have developed along the way. Here's my example:

```
db2 => connect to sample

   Database Connection Information

 Database server        = DB2/NT 9.5.0
 SQL authorization ID   = FUZZY
 Local database alias   = SAMPLE

db2 => select empno, firstnme, lastname from employee where empno = '200340'

EMPNO  FIRSTNME     LASTNAME
------ ------------ ----------------
200340 ROY          ALONZO

   1 record(s) selected.

db2 => select * from nomination where empno = '200340'

NOMINATIONID        EMPNO  REASON
----------- ------ --------------------------------

   0 record(s) selected.
```

At this point, Roy Alonzo has no nominations for employee of the year. Let's go ahead and insert a nomination for him:

```
db2 => insert into nomination  values (123456, '200340', 'Replication Test')
DB20000I  The SQL command completed successfully.
```

So you now there's a nomination for Roy Alonzo, empno 200340. It's time to see whether replication has done what I claimed it can do:

```
db2 => connect to replica

   Database Connection Information

 Database server        = DB2/NT 9.5.0
 SQL authorization ID   = FUZZY
 Local database alias   = REPLICA

db2 => select * from nomination where empno = '200340'

NOMINATIONID        EMPNO  REASON
-------------------- ------ --------------------------------
            123456 200340 Replication Test

   1 record(s) selected.
```

A resounding success! Okay, it's only one row of data in a fairly contrived example, but you can extrapolate from here to sophisticated possibilities. DB2 replication is such a deep topic that there are DB2 database administrators who specialize in nothing but designing, implementing, and managing replication. If you like the technology you've seen, there's certainly a long way you can go.

Data Row Compression

You wouldn't be reading a book on databases without realizing that data storage is exploding in almost every business and human endeavor. Whether you're designing a system to manage employee of the year awards, or something as large as a data warehouse or online trading system, you'll no doubt expect the data you're storing to grow in size and keep growing! But what do you do when the sheer size of data starts to overwhelm your storage capabilities—or when you keep storing the same data over and over again?

Using DB2 *Data Row Compression* is what you do! IBM's revolutionary technology takes the concept of data compression into the database and arguably executes it better than any other database on the market. Using techniques I'll shortly cover, DB2 can compress all manner of data in your tables in a fashion *completely transparent* to your applications and users. If I offered you free disk space without any impact on your customers, you'd probably jump at the chance.

Many of you are very happy about the fact that Data Row Compression saves you storage space and you're content with that as the key benefit. But think for a minute about what consequences it might have in other areas—you'll start to see that a whole raft of benefits come your way through one elegant tool:

- **I/O efficiency**: Because data is compressed on the page level, you effectively need to call fewer pages into the buffer pool to retrieve the same data from disk, thus putting less load on your I/O infrastructure.

- **Memory efficiency**: Because you need fewer pages to store the data, you consume less buffer pool memory when those pages are loaded into memory with the same data, freeing up that memory for other tasks or use outside the buffer pool (such as sort heaps or utility working areas).

- **Backup efficiency**: One of the biggest headaches database administrators suffer is the increasing time needed to back up every larger database. Because Data Row Compression results in few pages in the database, backups are smaller and faster.

- **CPU utilization**: This is perhaps a benefit to some, but a drawback for others. Pages need to be decompressed when accessed by a query, thus taking a little CPU that might not normally be used. But so many systems have spare CPU capacity—contrasting with limited memory and few I/O access paths—that sacrificing CPU effort for all the other benefits is a very valuable trade-off.

Data Row Compression Design

DB2's Data Row Compression is implemented by using a dictionary of compression values for a given table. These dictionaries act as a reference between the stored compressed data and the equivalent uncompressed data for that table. Each table's dictionary is stored in hidden objects within the database to prevent accidental damage to the dictionary, such as an administrator inadvertently dropping a dictionary. Dictionaries are very small; even for the largest and most complex compression scenarios, a table's compression dictionary totals in the kilobyte range.

Data Row Compression is another technology that you can play with in the Express-C edition, but production use "in anger" requires an appropriate license (in this case, a DB2 Enterprise edition license or equivalent).

The Data Row Compression subsystem includes algorithms to ensure that efforts such as building dictionaries and managing compression statistics in the system catalog are not performed when compression doesn't save any space. The actual compression is performed using the widely used Lempel Ziv algorithm, which is used in tools such as gzip, WinZip, and other common compression utilities.

Where DB2 gets smart is in considering not just individual columns of your table for compression but also sets of columns. For example, consider the employee table. By now, you are familiar with its data, such as the following:

EMPNO	FIRSTNME	LASTNAME	WORKDEPT	JOB	...
000010	CHRISTINE	HAAS	A00	PRES	...
000020	MICHAEL	THOMPSON	B01	MANAGER	...
000030	SALLY	KWAN	C01	MANAGER	...
000050	JOHN	GEYER	E01	MANAGER	...
000060	IRVING	STERN	D11	MANAGER	...
000070	EVA	PULASKI	D21	MANAGER	...
000090	EILEEN	HENDERSON	E11	MANAGER	...
000100	THEODORE	SPENSER	E21	MANAGER	...
000110	VINCENZO	LUCCHESSI	A00	SALESREP	...
000120	SEAN	O'CONNELL	A00	CLERK	...
000130	DELORES	QUINTANA	C01	ANALYST	...
000140	HEATHER	NICHOLLS	C01	ANALYST	...
000150	BRUCE	ADAMSON	D11	DESIGNER	...
000160	ELIZABETH	PIANKA	D11	DESIGNER	...
000170	MASATOSHI	YOSHIMURA	D11	DESIGNER	...
000180	MARILYN	SCOUTTEN	D11	DESIGNER	...
000190	JAMES	WALKER	D11	DESIGNER	...

...

Typical compression techniques look at columns such as JOB and see that there are repeated instance of values such as MANAGER, DESIGNER, and so on. DB2 Data Row Compression handles this kind of compression with ease. But Data Row Compression has a greater sophistication as well. The values for WORKDEPT and JOB repeat in sets, so D11 DESIGNER and C01 ANALYST repeat. Data Row Compression can compress these values as a set with one mapped value in the corresponding compression dictionary. This is both very clever and very efficient.

Estimating Compression Savings

Knowing the theory and algorithms behind compression is useful, but before subjecting your database to the process, wouldn't you like to know whether it is worth learning? With Data Row Compression, you don't need to guess the outcome nor estimate possible savings on the back of a napkin.

The inspect command includes an option to estimate the space to be saved by activating compression on a table and having DB2 create the associated dictionary. In its most basic and common form, the syntax looks like this:

```
inspect rowcompestimate table name table-name schema schema-name
 results keep file-name
```

This syntax instructs inspect to collect a comprehensive set of details and record them in a file in the db2dump directory. For example, you can run this on the employee table:

```
db2 => inspect rowcompestimate table name employee schema fuzzy
 results keep empcompress
DB20000I  The INSPECT command completed successfully.
```

The output file is not directly readable; you need to format it with the db2inspf utility to then generate a useful report as a text file:

```
$ db2inspf empcompress empcompress.report
```

You can now read the output with your favorite text editor. My example looks like this:

```
DATABASE: SAMPLE
VERSION : SQL09050
2008-04-06-07.21.29.359000


Action: ROWCOMPESTIMATE TABLE
Schema name: FUZZY
Table name: EMPLOYEE
Tablespace ID: 2  Object ID: 6
Result file name: empcompress


    Table phase start (ID Signed: 6, Unsigned: 6; Tablespace ID: 2) : FUZZY.EMPLOYEE

      Data phase start. Object: 6  Tablespace: 2
      Row compression estimate results:
      Percentage of pages saved from compression: 46
      Percentage of bytes saved from compression: 46
      Compression dictionary size: 13312 bytes.
      Expansion dictionary size: 10224 bytes.
      Data phase end.
    Table phase end.
Processing has completed. 2008-04-06-07.21.29.750000
```

You can see that even for a small table such as employee, you'll still save about 46 pages (184KB) of storage by compression. You can also see that the total size of the associated dictionaries will be 23KB, meaning that even for a trivially small table, it can be worth compressing.

Compressing a Table

Now that you're satisfied that compression will do you some good, you can instruct DB2 to perform the necessary compression steps. This is a two-part process, in which you first enable a table for compression and then actually reorganize the storage to implement compression.

To enable (or disable) compression, use the compress {yes | no } clause of the create table or alter table statement. In the current example, to enable compression on the existing employee table, it's as simple as running the relevant alter table command:

```
db2 => alter table employee compress yes
```

Upon successful completion, the table is ready for compression. If you ever need to determine which tables have compression, you can inspect the COMPRESSION column of the sysibm.systables table. It either reports N for no compression, V for individual value compression enabled, R for row compression enabled, or B for both possible compression types. You can see that row compression is now enabled for the employee table, as follows:

```
db2 => select name, compression from sysibm.systables
          where name = 'EMPLOYEE' and creator = 'FUZZY'


NAME                                 COMPRESSION
------------------------------------ -----------
EMPLOYEE                                  R
```

You're now ready to actually perform the compression work against the data in the underlying table. For this, you use the reorg command, which is a very powerful utility allowing the physical data and associated indexes of a table to be manipulated at the storage level. DB2 v9.5 can begin compilation of the compression dictionary without a reorg, but can work only with new values. The reorganization is required to ensure that all old values are also considered for compression. (You'll deal more with reorg in Chapter 24.) Let's explore the compression aspects of its use.

When you reorganize a table with the compression attribute set, the reorg utility implicitly follows the compression algorithms for Data Row Compression. There is no need to explicitly instruct it to perform compression. There is one option available that affects the behavior of compression, however, and it's concerned with whether an existing compression dictionary is preserved during reorganization or whether a new dictionary is generated. Typically, you need to balance the time it takes to generate a dictionary with whether your data has substantially changed and would benefit from a fresh dictionary. The two options you have when performing the reorganization are keepdictionary and resetdictionary.

The reorg command's syntax is prodigious, and I won't distract you with a multipage syntax diagram here. The specific invocation for these compression options can be as simple as this:

```
db2 => reorg table employee resetdictionary
DB20000I  The REORG command completed successfully.
```

Limitations

One last word on Data Row Compression is in order. As you might have experienced in other technical areas when using compression, it is very good for shrinking some types of data and not particularly good at other types. Text data types (and to a lesser extent numeric information) typically compresses very well using the Lempel Ziv algorithm, and you should see regular benefits from using Data Row Compression on this kind of data in DB2.

Binary data such as BLOBs tends to have fewer benefits, particularly when you're storing image or video format data that has been created using schemes that embed compression. Like most compression technologies, you gain no advantage trying to compress already-compressed data. To test this, try compressing a .gif image file. The .gif format has Lempel Ziv compression as part of its makeup, so you'll see no benefit. IBM recognizes that any effort to do this leads to disappointment, so it has declared that Data Row Compression is simply not applicable for indexes, long objects, LOBs, and XML. You also can't mix Data Row Compression with replication.

Finally, you might have noticed one other minor limitation with Data Row Compression: there's currently no GUI to manage compression, so you have to be comfortable with the DB2 CLP to manage compression for now.

Summary

I tried to give you a quick flavor of some of the more advanced data-management features that DB2 has to offer. Each of the sections in this chapter should be treated as an entree to a larger topic that deserves much more attention, but you now have a working knowledge of replication, data compression, and different data and metadata movement techniques. You can now start thinking about how these tools might assist in your next DB2 project.

CHAPTER 24

■ ■ ■

Monitoring and Tuning DB2 Performance

You've now made it to the last chapter, and what a chapter it promises to be! Performance tuning is a huge topic, not only because everyone has performance problems but also because they all have a particular task or process that they want to run faster. It might mean more happy users, it might mean beating the opposition to a goal, and it might mean more money—but no matter what the motivation, performance tuning is a hot issue for most database users.

DB2 provides a wealth of performance-tuning and management tools right out of the box. There's also a range of additional tools that can be downloaded for free or licensed (in addition to your DB2 software). I'll introduce you to the DB2 performance-tuning tools available in *every* edition of DB2, so you'll be equipped to tackle performance issues no matter what edition you use. I'll also introduce the autonomic tuning features of DB2 that do most of the work so you can do more interesting things.

Starting with a Sensible Approach to Tuning

There are almost as many tools and utilities to help with monitoring and tuning a database environment as there are theories about how such monitoring and tuning should be done. Without diverting this chapter to a long-winded discussion about theory versus practice, business outcomes versus the endless quest for speed, and "compulsive tuning disorder," it's worth providing some perspective on contemporary monitoring and performance tuning. I will be brief, but hopefully I'll provoke some thought on the matter.

For much of the history of databases (and for IT in general), a lot of performance tuning was carried out with the notion that the way to approach monitoring and tuning was to tweak the system in an endless quest to get a better metric—any metric!—out of it. Often, such observations and modifications were done to get notional improvement in measures such as buffer hit ratios, disk I/O, or other areas. Equally as often, the actual end users were never asked about what their real problems were and were expected to try to translate phrases like "We now get 0.8 Bogo-mips more" into a tangible benefit for them. Thankfully, system monitoring and performance tuning have moved on to a more enlightened era, in which two complementary techniques are generally considered best practice.

First, know your system. To be precise, know your system and how it operates normally by forming a baseline of what normality really means. What do important numbers such as user connections, response times, and disk and memory usage look like when things are normal? This is often referred to as a *benchmarking exercise* and it's done easily using DB2's powerful tools. The second area that complements the idea of a known baseline is to tune what matters to the business and then stop! That's right. Actually ask the people affected by system behavior what should be improved, and stop tuning once it's improved! If your users don't have a problem, you can more productively use your time elsewhere on new designs, feature improvements to existing systems, learning new features from books like this one, and so on.

You might find this notion of ceasing to tune a system after users are happy with it strange. It might even be anathema to some of you. I perfectly understand if you don't believe me. But don't discount the idea just yet. As for my first premise, I think you'll find the notion of benchmarking a system less contentious. Configuring your DB2 database for typical operation is the logical first step of monitoring and tuning, so that all future work starts from a known baseline. To help, DB2 offers the Configuration Advisor to quickly deploy a full set of database and database manager configuration options for you.

Proactive Tuning with the Configuration Advisor

Let's walk through the Configuration Advisor, focusing on the more complex of the 11 dialog boxes. If you're not currently connected as a user with SYSADM authority, I recommend that you reconnect to the Control Center as a user with that authority because the changes to be made can affect both database and instance configuration. From the SAMPLE database context menu, choose the Configuration Advisor option. The Configuration Advisor starts and shows its first dialog box, the Introduction dialog box (not shown here), which confirms the host, instance, and database name for which Configuration Advisor will perform its analysis and advice. Assuming that you chose your desired database, click Next. You see the Server dialog box, as shown in Figure 24-1.

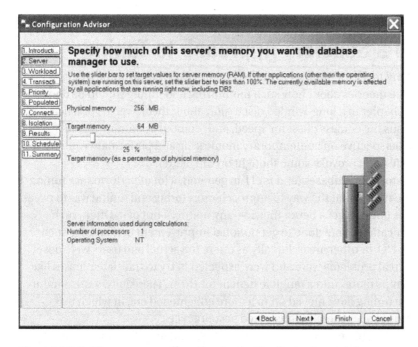

Figure 24-1. *Setting memory allocation in the Configuration Advisor*

The Server dialog box is concerned with the amount of memory the database manager (that is, your instance of DB2) will take from the total memory available. As the description reads in the dialog box, DB2 shares your host with any other processes running, as well as the operating system, so ensuring that nothing is starved of memory is the usual concern. You'll revisit memory allocation in some detail shortly, so for no, it's safe to retain the suggested value shown in the dialog box.

The Server dialog box of the wizard is a very simple interface, and clicking Next brings you to an even simpler dialog box called Workload. This dialog box is so simple that I haven't shown it here to save paper. It gives you three options to choose from to guide DB2 in optimizing its behavior for your workload. Your choice here simply dictates whether the subsequent Transactions dialog box will be included in the wizard. The three options are as follows:

- Queries (Data Warehousing)

- Mixed

- Transactions (Order Entry)

Other literature would use the phrases *decision support*, *mixed*, and *online transaction processing* to mean pretty much the same thing. If you choose Queries, you won't see the Transaction dialog box as the next dialog box in the wizard. I suggest that you choose Mixed because it's most appropriate for the current SAMPLE database. Click Next to see the Transactions dialog box, in which you specify your transactions (see Figure 24-2).

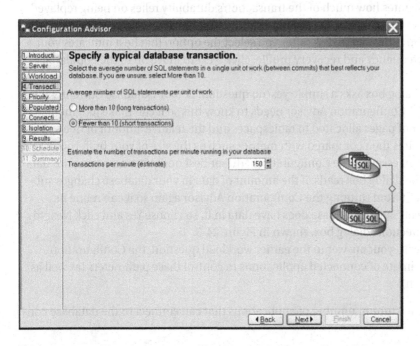

Figure 24-2. *Profiling a transaction load in the Configuration Advisor*

In effect, the Transactions dialog box asks how many transactions run against your database per minute and how complex each is by counting constituent statements. Estimating complexity is usually a moderately straightforward task. Look at the stored procedures, application code, dynamic SQL in units of work, and so forth. Are they big, small, or somewhere in between? Armed with that information, you can then estimate frequency. You'll look at some monitoring later in the chapter to help refine this value, but from a business or end user perspective, you should be able to take a guess at how many transactions are happening. For instance, in the Employee of the Year system, you can see by looking at the nominations and voting tables how often transactions are happening.

The Transactions dialog box takes your answers and uses the values to contribute to its calculation of several database parameters, including LOCKLIST for the memory available for lock management, and log management parameters such as LOGFILSIZ and LOGBUFSZ. It also affects more obvious parameters such as MAXAPPLS and related parameters that control the maximum number of applications that can be serviced by the DB2 database. When you're done, click Next to move on to the Priority dialog box.

The Priority dialog box is simple enough not to show here. It hosts one question about database administration priority, which is actually a little ambiguous, but you might guess what it's really asking from the three options it provides:

- Faster Transaction Performance (Slower Recovery)

- Both

- Faster Database Recovery (Slower Transactions)

It mostly affects one parameter for DB2: the SOFTMAX parameter, which is the guiding number of transaction logs that DB2 ideally needs to recover in the event of a crash. In effect, the priority choice dictates how much of the transaction's durability relies on being replayed from a log file in the event of failure. On the flip side, it determines how often DB2 checkpoints where log information is flushed to disk. After you select the option that best indicates your desired checkpoint frequency and recovery profile, click Next to move on to the Populated dialog box.

The Populated dialog box asks a simple yes/no question: Is Your Database Currently Populated With Data? The Configuration Advisor needs to know this so it can make judgments based on the number of pages allocated to tablespaces and the relative amount of free space in those tablespaces. It is then compared with metrics such as the size of your bufferpools and other memory areas. In essence, the Configuration Advisor best optimizes a system with data already present. As the dialog box reads, if the amount of data in your database changes substantially, you'll benefit from running the Configuration Advisor again so it can refine its recommendations. The SAMPLE database does have data in it, so choose Yes and click Next to continue to the Connections dialog box, shown in Figure 24-3.

In conjunction with your answer to the earlier workload question, the Configuration Advisor uses your estimate of connected applications to control these parameters (as well as many more not shown):

- MAXAPPLS: The maximum number of applications that can connect to the database concurrently

- MAXLOCKS: The maximum lock count that one application can hold, expressed as a percentage of total locks, before escalation from row to table locks occurs

- APPLHEAPSZ: The amount of private memory allocated to an application (or its agents if the INTRA_PARALLEL operation is enabled)

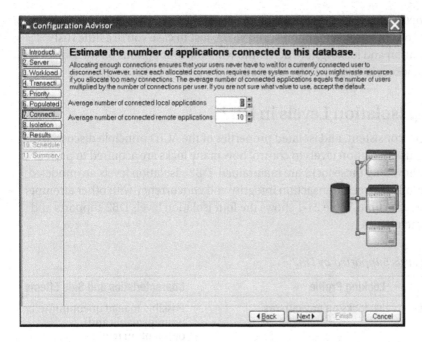

Figure 24-3. *Setting connection estimates in Configuration Advisor*

With the average number of connections estimated, it's time to click Next to move on to the Isolation dialog box, shown in Figure 24-4.

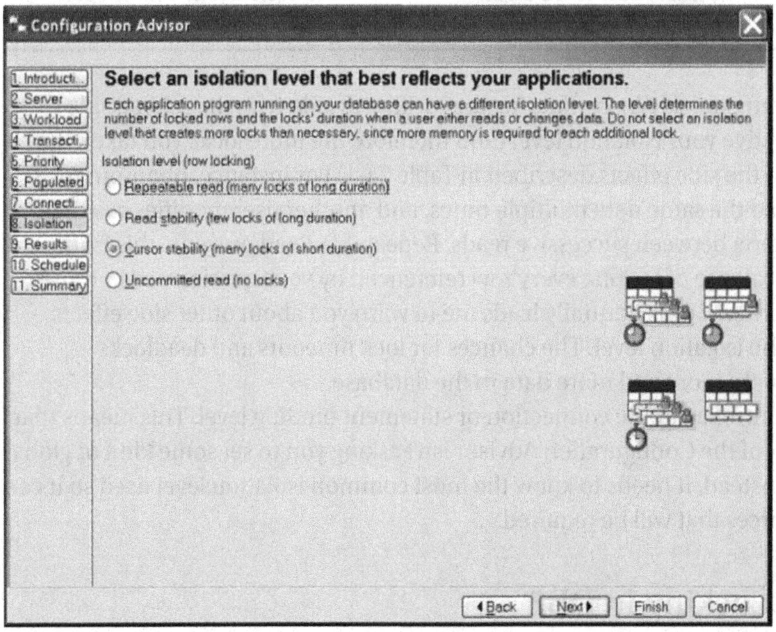

Figure 24-4. *Choosing a default isolation level in the Configuration Advisor*

Locking and concurrency control are common to all databases, and even non–database development has notions of locks, semaphores, and so on. Just in case you're a little rusty when it comes to isolation and locking, let's delve into what the four options on the Isolation page mean and how locking is subsequently affected.

Understanding Isolation Levels in DB2

To support the atomic, consistent, and isolated properties of the ACID principle discussed in earlier chapters, DB2 uses isolation levels to control how many locks are acquired to protect a unit of work, and for how long these locks are maintained. DB2's isolation levels are modeled on well-known trade-offs between transaction integrity and concurrency with other attempts to modify data at the same time. Table 24-1 shows the four isolation levels DB2 supports and their associated characteristics.

Table 24-1. *Isolation Levels Supported by DB2*

Isolation Level	Locking Profile	Characteristics and Side Effects
UNCOMMITED READ	No locks on any cursors	Possible to read uncommitted, nonrepeatable and/ or phantom rows
CURSOR STABILITY	At least share lock on current row of each cursor	Possible to read nonrepeatable reads and/or phantom rows
READ STABILITY	At least share locks on all qualifying rows	Possible to read phantom rows
REPEATABLE READ	At least share locks on all referenced rows	No concurrent side effects

You get the idea pretty quickly by comparing the locking profile with the related side effects. The more restrictive your isolation level (and therefore the more locks you take), the less likely you are to see the side effects described in Table 24-1. For instance, phantom rows can occur when you read the same data multiple times, and another user modifies existing data to match your criteria between successive reads. Repeatable Read prevents this from happening, but at the expense of locking every row referenced by your queries—even those that don't match your criteria! This naturally leads me to warn you about other side effects you'll see as you raise the isolation level. The chances for lock timeouts and deadlocks increase as your code locks more and more data in the database.

Isolation level is controlled at the connection or statement binding level. This means that the Isolation dialog box of the Configuration Advisor isn't asking you to set some kind of global setting for all actions. Instead, it needs to know the most common isolation level used so it can judge the locking resources that will be required.

Understanding Locking in DB2

Locks are the mechanism by which all data concurrency is managed. Although locks are also used in some specific cases for bufferpools and tablespaces, most often you'll be concerned with locking data in tables, either at the row or table level.

■Note A healthy, normally functioning database predominantly sees row-level locks acquired because well-written transactions typically need to lock only a minimal set of rows. It's quite rare to see locks escalate—usually it has to do with some restrictive maintenance task.

Table 24-2 shows the lock types used by DB2 on rows (and even tables, although locking at this level is quite rare) and their effect on the owner of the lock (and other users concurrently trying to access the locked data).

Table 24-2. *Lock Types Supported for Tables by DB2*

Lock Type	Code	Access Notes
Intent None	IN	Owner can read underlying committed and uncommitted data, but not update it. Others can read and update the data.
Intent Share	IS	Owner can read underlying committed data, but not update it. Others can read and update the data.
Next Key Share	NS	NS locks apply to rows only. The owner and others can read the locked row(s), but no changes can be made.
Share	S	The owner and others can read the locked data, but no changes can be made.
Intent Exclusive	IX	The owner and others can read and change the locked data.
Share with Intent Exclusive	SIX	Owner can read and update the data. Others can read but not update the data.
Update	U	Owner can update the data. Others can read but not update the data.
Next Key Weak Exclusive	NW	Used in special cases on rows for inserts into indexes. Owner can read but not update the data.
Exclusive	X	Only the owner can typically read and update the data. Others must set isolation to read uncommitted to see data.
Weak Exclusive	W	Another special case for some row inserts.
Super Exclusive	Z	Special lock used to prevent access to an entire table or index during DDL operations.

The compatibility of different locks is usually a matter of common sense. For instance, locks that use the word *share* in their name typically mean that others with similar share intentions can access the data (although not always update it). Similarly, the phrase *exclusive* denotes that data is locked exclusively. Other lock types would be incompatible and therefore cause users to wait before they can be acquired after the exclusive-style locks are released. There are some subtle cases that might arise that involve quite complex lock compatibility decisions. For these cases, it's best to refer to the DB2 Information Center because it has many pages that cover every conceivable unusual scenario.

So the type of lock, the number of locks, and the duration of locks all affect the resource consumption for lock lists within DB2. These are in turn are largely dictated by the isolation levels already discussed, together with settings at the table level that specify whether table-level or row-level locking is the default. In combination, all these factors affect the decisions the Configuration Advisor makes about optimal parameter settings.

Using DB2's Optimistic Locking Features

To round out this discussion of locks, I'll talk about a common dilemma in development. Should you be optimistic in your locking and just assume that DB2's great column-and-row-level locking will spare you from contention issues? Or should you be pessimistic and use some form of explicit locking, with all the nasty side effects it entails? The good news is that you can have the best of both worlds by using DB2's new features for optimistic locking. The normal optimistic-locking techniques are employed at the application level and usually rely on storing an additional timestamp, which you include in your update criteria to ensure that no one else has tampered with the row in question you want to change. The alternative is to use a "last change wins" approach that lets the multiple applications change data at will and live with the consequences of false positives for updates. DB2 has introduced some excellent features that give you built-in database support for these types of optimistic locking without any of the nasty side effects.

First are the row identifier functions RID_BIT and RID. Using the row identifier ensures that only the same "generation" of a given row is updated—that is, no one else has updated the row in the time between the user selecting it and later attempting an update.

Another feature supported is ROW CHANGE TOKEN, which is a calculated BIGINT value derived from all the data in the row that effectively translates to that row's state at a given point in time. Using the ROW CHANGE TOKEN allows you to reference a given row at a constant relative point in its sequence of changes.

The third new feature formalizes the timestamp technique already mentioned. The ROW CHANGE TIMESTAMP feature uses a generated timestamp column to ensure the success of optimistic updates and prevent false positives. Another great feature of such timestamps is that they are portable across to mainframe DB2. You can read more about these new optimistic locking functions in the DB2 Information Center.

Continuing with the Configuration Advisor

I recommend Cursor Stability as your best option for isolation level in the current SAMPLE database because this is the default for most DB2 client access technologies. With that selected, you can click Next to move on to the Results dialog box. The appearance of the Results dialog box can take a few seconds (even a minute or longer) as the Configuration Adviser gathers information from DB2 about your data, existing configuration, and other metrics. When it does appear, you'll see your specific results (see Figure 24-5).

All the questions you answered have contributed to the Configuration Advisor's decisions regarding configuration change suggestions. Right now you should scroll through the full list of suggested values and look at how many have the option (AUTOMATIC) included in them, either confirming the existing automatic setting or activating it for the first time. In this case, 15 parameters largely related to memory heaps are set to (AUTOMATIC). You'll explore more about what that means in a moment.

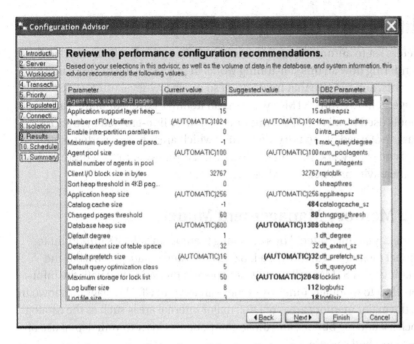

Figure 24-5. *The Results dialog box of the Configuration Advisor, showing suggested changes*

If you jump to the Summary tab, you see the full list of UPDATE DATABASE CONFIGURA-TION, UPDATE DATABASE MANAGER CONFIGURATION, and even ALTER BUFFERPOOL and other commands that implement all the Configuration Advisor's suggested settings. A sample appears as follows:

```
UPDATE DATABASE CONFIGURATION FOR SAMPLE USING APPLHEAPSZ 256 AUTOMATIC;
...
UPDATE DATABASE CONFIGURATION FOR SAMPLE USING LOGBUFSZ 112 ;
UPDATE DATABASE CONFIGURATION FOR SAMPLE USING LOGFILSIZ 18 ;
UPDATE DATABASE CONFIGURATION FOR SAMPLE USING LOGSECOND 2 ;
UPDATE DATABASE CONFIGURATION FOR SAMPLE USING MAXAPPLS 40 AUTOMATIC
 MAXLOCKS 60 AUTOMATIC;
...
NUM_POOLAGENTS 100 AUTOMATIC;
UPDATE DATABASE MANAGER CONFIGURATION USING NUM_INITAGENTS 0 ;
...
CONNECT TO SAMPLE;
ALTER BUFFERPOOL AWARDBP  SIZE 10000 ;
ALTER BUFFERPOOL IBMDEFAULTBP  SIZE 2500 ;
...
CONNECT RESET;
```

You can execute these changes immediately, save the script for later manual execution, or use the Scheduling tab to have the changes applied at a predetermined time. Of most interest are the various parameters that have had automatic management enabled. In doing so, this facilitates one of DB2's greatest performance management features: self-tuning memory!

Understanding Self-Tuning Memory in DB2

With so many parameters set to automatic management (thanks to the Configuration Advisor), you might be wondering how all this self-tuning works in practice. One of DB2's most sophisticated components, and the one that frees you of so much low-level tuning, is Self-Tuning Memory Management (STMM). STMM works as an iterative governor of the various memory heaps and pools used by all the DB2 components. It uses fine-grained metrics to determine which areas are starved of memory, determine which areas have a surfeit of memory going to waste, and can even work intimately with the operating system to acquire and release memory from the environment as workload demands vary.

Traditional DB2 Memory Management Model

To fully appreciate all the capabilities offered by self-tuning memory in DB2, it's important to understand the traditional memory structures of a DB2 instance and database. This has the dual benefit of illuminating what STMM will manage for you and preparing you with the information you need if you elect to manually tune any of these areas yourself. The diagram shown in Figure 24-6 highlights the major memory areas of DB2: major internal areas such as the catalog and package cache, lock list and log buffers, and those components closer to your actual use of the data, such as bufferpools and sort areas.

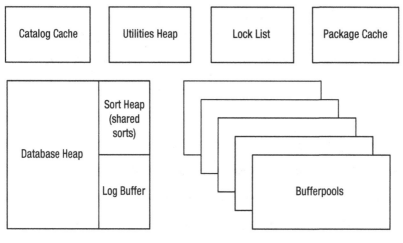

Database Shared Memory

Figure 24-6. *The major memory areas of a DB2 database*

Each of these areas is controlled by a database configuration parameter, and each parameter has the option of manual or automatic management. The parameters and related areas are as follows:

- `catalogcache_sz`: The number of pages taken from the database heap for caching catalog information. By default, 4 times the MAXAPPLS parameter, but it can be set between 8 and 500,000 4KB pages.

- `pckcachesz`: The number of pages used to cache static and dynamic SQL and XQuery statements. By default, automatic, but can be set to -1 to then be calculated as 8 times MAXAPPLS, or a value between 1 and 64,000 pages.

- `util_heap_sz`: The number of pages of memory available to the BACKUP, RESTORE, and LOAD commands. Defaults to 5,000, but can be set between 16 and 524,288 pages.

- `locklist`: The number of pages available for all locks acquired in the database. Defaults to automatic, but can be set between 4 and 524,288 pages.

- `dbheap`: The catch-all area for control information and other miscellaneous memory allocation. Defaults to 300, 600, or 1,200 depending on platform; and can be set between 32 and 524,288 pages.

- `logbufsz`: The number of pages allocated to log buffer from the `dbheap`. Defaults to 8 pages, and can be set between 4 and 65,535 pages.

- `sheapthresh_shr`: The number of pages at which the threshold for shared sort throttling kicks in. This helps control excessive memory saturation by sorting. Defaults to automatic, and can set between 250 and 524,288 pages (or 2 billion on 64-bit platforms).

- `bufferpool-name`: Bufferpools can be allocated to varying page size and total memory to your database.

Traditionally, the best way to manage all those values was to use the Configuration Advisor to generate an appropriate working set for the database's workload and (where necessary) fine-tune to control for any atypical behavior in the environment. This worked well for reasonably constant workloads or somewhat static environments in which the data changed, but the business logic didn't change. But you might need to run systems that operate in a fast-paced online transaction mode for some part of the day and then participate in bulk operations such as data import or export, or business intelligence activities at another point of the day and periodically be subject to heavy reporting loads. When your system has such diverse workloads, you can either spend all your effort constantly changing parameters manually, or you can use a system such as DB2, which brings STMM to the table and completely automates such varied tuning for you. Each of the previous parameters has the option to be set to automatic, freeing you of the need to manually adjust them as your workloads vary.

Activating STMM Mode

There are two key parameters that govern the operation of self-tuning memory in DB2: `SELF_TUNING_MEM` and `DATABASE_MEMORY`. Together, they determine to what extent automatic memory tuning will occur, if at all.

The `DATABASE_MEMORY` parameter governs the total memory available for the database's shared memory region. Under Windows and AIX, it can be set to automatic, which enables the full STMM capabilities to be used in conjunction with the operating system's own memory management. In essence, an automatic `DATABASE_MEMORY` parameter means that DB2 can trade memory back and forth with the operating system as workload demands. On platforms in which this is not supported, the bulk of the automatic memory management features still operate within the amount of memory allocated or computed for this parameter.

The `SELF_TUNING_MEM` parameter is concerned only with the internal memory constructs illustrated in Figure 24-6. When `SELF_TUNING_MEM` is set to ON, it instructs DB2 to allow the exchange of unused allocated memory from one heap to another, more needy heap. For instance, unused bufferpool space for tablespaces that might have not been accessed in some time could be reallocated to the lock list or sort heap to benefit other work. The `SELF_TUNING_MEM` parameter takes one of two values: ON or OFF. However, you might see it report itself with an additional comment when set to ON. A GET DB CFG command might show the following:

```
db2 => get db cfg
...
Self tuning memory                         (SELF_TUNING_MEM) = ON (Inactive)
...
```

When SELF_TUNING_MEM reports itself ON but Inactive, either zero (or one) parameters capable of automatic memory management have been so configured. In essence, the Inactive comment lets you know that you have fewer than two memory parameters configured for automatic management, so there are no candidates between which memory could be exchanged. The obvious solution is to configure more of your parameters to be managed automatically. For example, you can set pckcachesz and locklist to automatic through the Control Center or via a simple CLP command:

```
db2 => update db cfg using pckcachesz automatic immediate
DB20000I  The UPDATE DATABASE CONFIGURATION command completed successfully.
db2 => update db cfg using locklist automatic immediate
SQL5146W  "MAXLOCKS" must be set to "AUTOMATIC" when "LOCKLIST" is
"AUTOMATIC".  "MAXLOCKS" has been set to "AUTOMATIC".
```

Note that automating the behavior of some parameters, such as locklist, can implicitly switch other related parameters to automatic as well, such as maxlocks in this case. You might also see the value ON report with an Active comment. This means that STMM is currently actively altering the memory allocation between constituent heaps, so that other values in the same database configuration report might be changing even as you read them.

Self-Tuning Memory Management Mechanics

STMM follows a few elegant rules to ensure that its behavior doesn't cause performance or other problems. Internally it uses its own tuning clock to wake itself up and then assess what tuning, if any, is required. The first thing that STMM checks is whether any heap under automatic control is under stress. That is, does any heap need more memory? If no heaps need more memory, the STMM takes note of this event and assesses whether it was also the result in immediate previous instances of its memory check. In this way, the STMM can actually slow down its internal polling interval, so it tunes itself to measure the system less frequently. Such advanced self-control isn't perfect, of course. It's still possible that a given set of queries that wildly fluctuate in their demands for memory could leave STMM playing catch-up, trying to balance competing memory needs. Such workloads are not common, but you're most likely to encounter this scenario if your system goes from near-idle to near-maximum memory demand in a short period of time, such as the starting point in heavy reporting workloads.

If STMM determines that memory heaps need more memory, it evaluates whether memory can be acquired from the operating system. It uses both the DATABASE_MEMORY parameter and the amount of available memory reported by the operating system to determine what's possible. If it can, it requests more memory from the operating system and allocates it to the needy memory heaps. If DATABASE_MEMORY is set to COMPUTED, or the operating system indicates there is no free memory to donate to DB2 for STMM to distribute, STMM then seeks to identify other heaps in the database shared memory that have memory to spare.

After heap memory needs are addressed, or if STMM determines that there is no more it can do to address memory requirements, STMM goes back to sleep, ready to act the next time its internal clock wakes it up.

Using the Memory Visualizer

All this memory tuning, both automatic and manual, can leave you wondering where all your memory has been allocated at any one point in time. You might also like to see the effects of STMM against your real databases because you might realize that the optimal distribution of memory between the various database heaps was not as you envisaged. Although you can use the Control Center or the DB2 CLP to call up the current memory heap parameter settings and see their individual values, you are left having to do your own arithmetic and comparisons when using those tools.

DB2 includes an excellent utility to help you graphically present memory allocation and use within your DB2 system: the Memory Visualizer. The Memory Visualizer is available via the program shortcut in the Monitoring Tools folder under Windows or via the db2cc -mv command under Linux. When launched, it asks you to nominate an instance to which the Visualizer should connect; the main interface then launches. Figure 24-7 shows the Memory Visualizer interface.

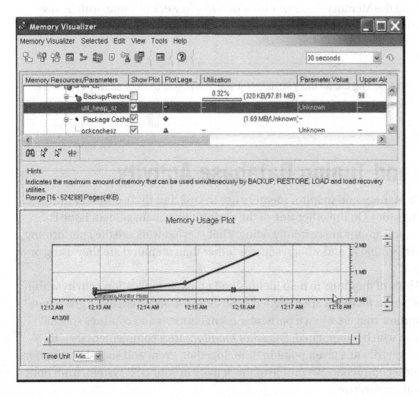

Figure 24-7. *The Memory Visualizer utility for DB2*

The upper half of the Memory Visualizer shows a scrolling list of every memory heap that can be allocated at every level in the DB2 instance being interrogated. Each parameter shows its current value, relevant utilization metrics, and alerting thresholds for the Health Center (which I'll discuss shortly).

The lower half of the dialog box shows the Memory Usage Plot, which is a fantastic device that enables you to *see* where your memory has gone. This is particularly useful when STMM has reallocated memory, and you need a quick summary of where your memory is now. It can help you plan for upcoming changes in your workload because you can tell whether larger loads (bufferpools), complex sorting and aggregates (sort heaps), or other changes will align well with current memory allocation or likely demand a different one. This feature is particularly useful when you know that no extra memory will be available. You can then predict whether overall memory contention will be a performance factor and plan accordingly.

The Memory Visualizer's other great advantage is its capability to plot memory consumption over time. As shown in Figure 24-7, you can watch how the allocation of memory changes as the time and workload progress. This can be particularly useful when modeling how the varied online transaction, batch, reporting, and other workloads affect the system over the course of the day. There's a small drop-down list in the bottom left of the dialog box that allows you to specify minutes, hours, or days as the x-axis (you can see a refresh frequency drop-down list in the upper right). By choosing a useful time frame and refresh frequency, you can learn a lot from running the Memory Visualizer for a period of a week or more; watch how your memory needs fluctuate throughout the period.

▪**Caution** Be careful about closing the Memory Visualizer if you're trying to capture activity over a long period of time because it doesn't offer an option to save or persist its output.

Monitoring and Tuning Database Activity

You now know how to manage and monitor memory use in DB2, but that's only half the monitoring and tuning story. On the other side of the performance management issue is the business of what applications are currently doing. That is, what work are they performing, how often are they performing it, and what resources (other than memory) are they using or abusing in the process?

DB2 offers two kinds of monitors to help identify and manage application activity within a given database. DB2 *event monitors* are designed to observe the occurrence of a given type of event. An event monitor triggers when a particular event happens and captures specific details of the context in which it happened. *Snapshot monitors* are a complementary—they gather defined system metrics at a given point in time. Together, event and snapshot monitors can be used to provide a comprehensive profile of the activity in your DB2 system, from both a resource and temporal perspective.

Activating Monitor Switches

The underlying control mechanism used by both event and snapshot monitors is the *monitor switch*. As its name suggests, throwing one of these switches tells DB2 to start exposing or collecting the underlying information for the related switch. I used the term *exposing or collecting* because the underlying monitoring information is always present within the DB2 engine for all but a few of the switches. It just takes a flick of the appropriate switch to make it available to external observers. Table 24-3 lists the monitor switches available in DB2 and denotes the purpose of each one.

Table 24-3. *Monitor Switches for Event and Snapshot Monitoring in DB2*

Switch Name	Purpose
BUFFERPOOL	Usage metrics on bufferpools
LOCK	Information on the number of locks and deadlocks
SORT	Sort metrics, including details on sorts that overflow sortheaps to disk
STATEMENT	Details of SQL run and running
TABLE	I/O metrics on tables
TIMESTAMP	Generic timing information used by other monitors
UOW	Unit of work (transaction) timing and related metrics

To throw the switch to expose the relevant metrics, you must issue the UPDATE MONITOR SWITCHES command with the appropriate switch of your choice. The syntax is very simple:

```
update monitor switches using switch-name {on | off} [switch-name {on | off} ...]
```

To collect information for a single switch, simply turn it "on." You can also turn on multiple switches in one command:

```
db2 => update monitor switches using statement on lock on uow on
DB20000I  The UPDATE MONITOR SWITCHES command completed successfully.
```

Simply throwing the monitor switch is not enough to complete the task of gathering your monitor data. It instructs DB2 to expose that information when asked, but additional steps need to be taken for your event or snapshot monitors (discussed shortly). When your work with the monitor switches is complete, simply reissue the UPDATE MONITOR SWITCHES command with the off option. After you're comfortable with the operation of the switches, you'll find yourself relaxed with idea of leaving the monitor switches activated by default. They consume vanishingly small amounts of CPU on modern hardware, and the minor impost pays for itself the first time an unexpected performance issue occurs.

Using DB2 Event Monitors

Event monitors are designed to record the activities in the database that fall within the realm of the switches listed previously. Each event monitor is designed to track activity over time, giving you some historical perspective on one area of your DB2 database's operation during regular processing. The event monitors don't match the switches exactly (nor do snapshot monitors, which are covered next). Instead, they sit one level higher to show you conceptual actions or parts of DB2 processing. Table 24-4 lists the event monitors and their purposes:

Table 24-4. *Event Monitors for Historic Profiling in DB2*

Event Monitor Name	Purpose
BUFFERPOOLS	Track bufferpool activity
CONNECTIONS	Track attempted and successful connections and disconnections
DATABASE	Track database-related data at the last application disconnection
DEADLOCKS	Track deadlocks with optional details and values
STATEMENTS	Track SQL statements with optional details
TABLES	Track actions against a given table
TABLESPACES	Track tablespace-level activity
TRANSACTIONS	Track commit and rollback activity

The general syntax for creating an event monitor is as follows:

```
create event monitor monitor-name
for event-to-monitor
write to {table | pipe | file } details
[ { MANUALSTART | AUTOSTART } ]
[ further event conditions ]
[ further table options ]
[ further file options ]
[ further workload manager options ]
```

I tried to simplify a complex set of syntax so that you can concentrate on getting a working event monitor. You might name your monitor anything you like, although reusing an existing name effectively overwrites that monitor definition with the new settings. The event to monitor can be one of the types already discussed, and the most simple output option is to write to a file or table. In the example that follows, I don't use further event conditions, but they are useful as you become more adept at working with monitors because they allow you to effectively filter the event information before it is recorded, discarding unwanted or unrelated data. With the exception of the DEADLOCKS monitor configured with detail collection, all event monitors by default are set to MANUALSTART. This means that after definition, they're not running and need to be started using this command:

```
set event monitor monitor-name state=1
```

This starts the monitor, and data starts flowing to your write to destination. You can choose to set any monitor to AUTOSTART, which activates the monitor as soon as the first application connection happens to the database after instance start. I'll create one of the most useful monitors for tuning purposes: targeting STATEMENTS. This event type, along with snapshot monitoring, is extremely useful for finding out what SQL runs most frequently, what runs for the longest time, and which statements are the biggest resource hogs. This is often the key to isolating what's causing your users grief.

```
db2 => connect to sample

   Database Connection Information

 Database server        = DB2/NT 9.5.0
 SQL authorization ID    = FUZZY
 Local database alias    = SAMPLE


db2 => update monitor switches using statement on
DB20000I  The UPDATE MONITOR SWITCHES command completed successfully.
db2 => create event monitor empofyear for statements write to file 'c:\eventmon'
DB20000I  The SQL command completed successfully.
db2 => set event monitor empofyear state=1
DB20000I  The SQL command completed successfully.
```

My statement event monitor is now active and will track any matching events. Go ahead and do the same on your system. From another DB2 CLP or Command Editor dialog box try executing a few SQL statements against the Employee of the Year system, execute a few of the stored procedures to add votes or nominations, and do pretty much anything else that takes your fancy. When you're done, you need to stop the event monitor by setting its state to zero:

```
db2 => set event monitor empofyear state=0
DB20000I  The SQL command completed successfully.
db2 => terminate
DB20000I  The TERMINATE command completed successfully.
```

You deactivated your empofyear event monitor on statements, but its definition persists if you want to reactivate it. If you check the c:\eventmon directory, you should see a number of .evt files representing each event (in this case, SQL Statement) that was captured by the event monitor, and one file named db2event.ctl. The latter file is the control file that organizes the information in the event files.

Just for kicks, try opening one of the event files with a text editor. You see pages of absolute gibberish because it has captured low-level information straight out of DB2, including memory dumps, binary representations of access paths, and more raw data that isn't readable to the human eye. DB2 provides a very useful formatting utility to use with event data: db2evmon. A simple invocation to db2evmon, telling it which database and event monitor generated the source event files and control file in the current directory, and directing its output to another text file, looks like this:

```
c:\eventmon> db2evmon -db SAMPLE -evm empofyear > empofyear_statement_events.txt
```

Now take a deep breath, exhale slowly, and tell yourself that too much detail is never enough. I say this because even with the most simple of event monitors, you'll collect *lots* of data. In my example, I executed only three or four select and insert statements, and my empofyear_statement_events.txt file is 2.8MB in size—with 84,500 lines! That's one hefty report. This prolific behavior is a useful contrast with monitor switches, which are generally safe to leave running. The overhead for an event monitor is, by comparison, quite large, especially for the statement event monitor, so you should think twice about leaving this event monitor running for extended periods. Having shocked you with those metrics, don't panic. The file is actually easily digestible.

First, because I didn't specify any event monitor conditions, I gathered event data for every SQL statement that ran while my monitor was active. That data includes all the internal SQL that DB2 uses to manage itself, as well as the SQL it uses to parse and execute your commands. So in this example, there are hundreds of references to statements against the system catalog, such as the view SYSCAT.TABLES.

The report also includes header information to give you important summary details. In my report, the header is as follows:

```
--------------------------------------------------------------------------
                           EVENT LOG HEADER
  Event Monitor name: EMPOFYEAR
  Server Product ID: SQL09050
  Version of event monitor data: 9
  Byte order: LITTLE ENDIAN
  Number of nodes in db2 instance: 1
  Codepage of database: 1208
  Territory code of database: 1
  Server instance name: DB2
--------------------------------------------------------------------------


--------------------------------------------------------------------------
  Database Name: SAMPLE
  Database Path: C:\DB2\NODE0000\SQL00002\
  First connection timestamp: 04/14/2008 21:51:37.643715
  Event Monitor Start time:   04/14/2008 22:13:14.102791
--------------------------------------------------------------------------
... lots of statement details for thousands of lines ...
```

That header gives you platform information such as DB2 version, database details, time window for the event capture, and so on. It does leave 84,000+ other lines to consider, but there's a convenient repeating pattern. Because I asked for statements to be monitored, I have a detailed account of every statement in the monitor time frame, in 50-line blocks of detail for a given statement. I searched for the word *nomination* in my report to find one of the statements I actually executed. Here's what the report looks like, with some key information in bold:

```
1670) Statement Event ...
  Appl Handle: 119
  Appl Id: *LOCAL.DB2.080415051406
  Appl Seq number: 00001

  Record is the result of a flush: FALSE
  -------------------------------------------
  Type     : Dynamic
  Operation: Describe
  Section  : 201
  Creator  : NULLID
  Package  : SQLC2G11
```

```
Consistency Token   : AAAAANBX
Package Version ID  :
Cursor    : SQLCUR201
Cursor was blocking: FALSE
```

Text   : select nominationid from nomination where nomdate < current date

```
-------------------------------------------
Start Time: 04/14/2008 22:14:12.416802
Stop Time:  04/14/2008 22:14:12.872888
```

Elapsed Execution Time: 0.052746 seconds

```
Number of Agents created: 1
User CPU: 0.015625 seconds
System CPU: 0.031250 seconds
Statistic fabrication time (milliseconds): 0
Synchronous runstats time  (milliseconds): 0
Fetch Count: 1210
Sorts: 0
Total sort time: 0
Sort overflows: 0
```

Rows read: 1210

```
Rows written: 0
Internal rows deleted: 0
Internal rows updated: 0
Internal rows inserted: 0
Bufferpool data logical reads: 0
Bufferpool data physical reads: 0
Bufferpool temporary data logical reads: 0
Bufferpool temporary data physical reads: 0
Bufferpool index logical reads: 0
Bufferpool index physical reads: 0
Bufferpool temporary index logical reads: 0
Bufferpool temporary index physical reads: 0
Bufferpool xda logical page reads: 0
Bufferpool xda physical page reads: 0
Bufferpool temporary xda logical page reads: 0
Bufferpool temporary xda physical page reads: 0
SQLCA:
  sqlcode: 0
  sqlstate: 00000
```

That's a hefty chunk of data to digest, but look at the salient points formatted in bold. You know that this is a dynamic statement, and the text of the SQL is select max(nominationid) from nomination. That immediately gives options for tuning. If this is a common statement that's repeated in the event monitor report, it's a great candidate for turning into a stored procedure or function, so it's parsed and has an execution plan bound and ready to use without the dynamic overhead.

It took 0.052746 seconds to execute the phase of the command, which doesn't include the overhead of preparing the statement, nor opening the cursor prior to results being returned. Around one-twentieth of a second isn't bad, but if it were five seconds or five minutes, it would be a possible culprit for user-facing performance problems. It read 1210 rows to return the result, which isn't necessarily bad. But if a statement reads 1.21 million rows to return one trivial answer, you have a problem. But you can also spot it and then do something about it.

The event monitor report gives you enormous detail. You can parse and summarize the text file, but you also have the ability to send event monitor output to a table. You can connect the dots from there. Want to know the slowest statement issued against your database? Query the table. Want the count of the number of times a tricky statement is executed? Count them in the table. Who abuses your disk I/O the most? I think you get the idea.

No matter what output method you prefer, you now know that problem statements can't hide! The sheepish look on developers' faces when you ask them why they execute the same statement 4,500 times to return one HTML page is priceless. And they usually learn to write better SQL as a result.

Using DB2 Snapshot Monitors

Where event monitors gather activity information over time, a snapshot monitor acts like a still camera, taking an image of how DB2 looks at an exact moment. Even better, you can use successive snapshots taken at regular intervals to build up a picture of your database over time, akin to using time-lapse photography to get a sense of activity over a long period of time. Snapshot monitors exist to cover the facets of DB2, and the most commonly used snapshots are shown in Table 24-5.

Table 24-5. *Some Useful Snapshot Monitors for Instantaneous Profiling in DB2*

Snapshot Monitor Name	Data Captured
DATABASE MANAGER	The state of the instance at a point in time
ALL DATABASES	The states of all databases in a given instance
ALL APPLICATIONS	The current profile of all connected applications
ALL BUFFERPOOLS	Bufferpool usage characteristics
LOCKS	Locking information
DYNAMIC SQL	Track SQL statements with optional details
TABLES	Track actions against a given table
TABLESPACES	Track tablespace-level activity
TRANSACTIONS	Track commit and rollback activity

There are more esoteric snapshot monitors available, but mastering just those shown in the table is a sign that you've moved well beyond being a DB2 novice. To illustrate their utility, I'll walk you through taking a snapshot of the locks held in a database—perhaps the most common snapshot used, especially when you suspect that blocking conditions exist in your database that are frustrating users and slowing down performance.

As with event monitors, snapshot monitors source their underlying data from the database switches. To take a snapshot of the lock situation in my database, I have to throw the lock switch:

```
db2 => update monitor switches using lock on
DB20000I  The UPDATE MONITOR SWITCHES command completed successfully.
```

With that switch activated, I can now issue the GET SNAPSHOT command to show the snapshot information I want to see. The general syntax of the GET SNAPSHOT command is as follows:

```
get snapshot for snapshot-name [snapshot options]
```

This is a rare occasion of a simple syntax. Even the options for those snapshots that have them are simple, usually being an application or agent ID for those snapshots that target individual application behavior, such as the following lock example.

To illustrate lock snapshot, I started two DB2 CLP sessions: one connected to the SAMPLE database as my usual user, FUZZY, and the other connected as DB2ADMIN. I started the DB2 CLP with the +c option, which explicitly turns off autocommit behavior. A list applications command shows the current connections:

```
db2 => list applications
```

Auth Id	Application Name	Appl. Handle	Application Id	DB Name	# of Agents
FUZZY	db2bp.exe	58	*LOCAL.DB2.080416041054	SAMPLE	1
DB2ADMIN	db2bp.exe	77	*LOCAL.DB2.080416041618	SAMPLE	1

I can identify my FUZZY session as having application handle number 58. In that DB2 CLP session, I can issue a bunch of statements, such as updates, inserts, or even LOCK TABLE, so that some locks are placed on rows of the nomination table—or even the whole table. I can now issue the get snapshot command to look at the locks held by the application with an agent handle of 58:

```
db2 => get snapshot for locks for application agentid 58

            Application Lock Snapshot

Snapshot timestamp                        = 04/15/2008 21:44:07.810454

Application handle                        = 58
Application ID                            = *LOCAL.DB2.080416041054
Sequence number                          = 00016
Application name                          = db2bp.exe
CONNECT Authorization ID                  = FUZZY
Application status                        = UOW Waiting
Status change time                        = Not Collected
Application code page                     = 1252
Locks held                                = 2
Total wait time (ms)                      = Not Collected
```

```
List Of Locks
 Lock Name                      = 0x53514C4332473131D6BAC2F841
 Lock Attributes                = 0x00000000
 Release Flags                  = 0x40000000
 Lock Count                     = 1
 Hold Count                     = 0
 Lock Object Name               = 0
 Object Type                    = Internal Plan Lock
 Mode                           = S

 Lock Name                      = 0x03000F00000000000000000054
 Lock Attributes                = 0x00000002
 Release Flags                  = 0x40000000
 Lock Count                     = 1
 Hold Count                     = 0
 Lock Object Name               = 15
 Object Type                    = Table
 Tablespace Name                = IBMDB2SAMPLEREL
 Table Schema                   = FUZZY
 Table Name                     = NOMINATION
 Mode                           = X
```

Buried in all that information is the detail you're looking for. My DB2 CLP session connected as FUZZY has a lock count of 1 on the nomination table in exclusive mode. Some options, such as Status Change Time, require other monitor switches to be active at the same time. This information is also available via a table-typed function: SNAP_GET_LOCK. This means that you can use SQL statements to access and manipulate lock snapshot information. A similar table-typed function exists for each of the other snapshot types:

```
db2 => select agent_id, lock_object_type, tabname, lock_mode, lock_status
            from table(snap_get_lock('',-1)) as locksnapshot

AGENT_ID LOCK_OBJECT_TYPE   TABNAME     LOCK_MODE LOCK_STATUS
-------- ------------------ ----------- --------- -----------
...
      58 TABLE_LOCK         NOMINATION          X        GRNT
...
```

I selected a subset of the columns available, but you can choose any or all columns from the function to examine. You can see the exclusive lock on the nomination table, meaning that this function is telling you the same thing as the GET SNAPSHOT command. There is a useful DESCRIBE statement you can run to examine all the information available via the SNAP_GET_LOCK table-typed function:

```
describe output select * from table(snap_get_lock('',-1)) as locksnapshot
```

Even better, there are now views that act in place of these table-typed functions.
sysibmadm.snaplock and its related views give the same information. So the statements
can now read like this:

```
db2 => select agent_id, lock_object_type, tabname, lock_mode, lock_status
          from sysibmadm.snaplock
```

Tuning the DB2 Optimizer with RUNSTATS

Like most contemporary relational databases, DB2 uses a query optimizer whose job it is to
make informed decisions about how to execute queries efficiently *and quickly*. At the heart of
the optimizer is a cost model that attempts to weigh the relative expense of executing a given
SQL statement in the many ways it can be satisfied. Chapter 12 introduced the Visual Explain
tool to illustrate the effect of index choice on executing queries. That was your very first introduction to tuning, and as well as highlighting the benefit of appropriate indexes, it also left the
question open as to *how* DB2 decided the index was the best choice by which to access the
underlying table data. The answer to that question is *statistics*.

DB2 keeps statistics about all your tables and indexes in the system catalog to enable the
optimizer to make better choices about the cost of accessing data and answering queries. These
statistics include data characteristics such as the number of rows of data in a table, the number
of pages consumed to store that data, the selectivity and cardinality of an index, what columns
the index might cover, and even details of skewed distribution of data if so instructed.

Automated RUNSTATS in DB2

DB2 offers automatic statistics collection as one of the key features of its autonomic management framework. In essence, this means that you can leave the "what, when, and how" of
statistics collection to DB2 in most common scenarios. Even better, this automatic behavior is
on by default, meaning there's little you need to do in order to benefit. You might, however,
like to know the mechanisms used to activate and control automatic RUNSTATS tasks, so let's
dive in to the mechanics.

Automated statistics generation is a feature of the wider automatic table maintenance
available in DB2. And automatic table maintenance is itself a component of the large automatic database maintenance régime. This nested relationship is important because it is
modeled as three cascading parameters in the database: AUTO_MAINT, AUTO_TBL_MAINT, and
AUTO_RUNSTATS. You can see them in the Control Center, or via the DB2 CLP:

```
db2 => get db cfg
...
Automatic maintenance                    (AUTO_MAINT) = ON
  Automatic database backup         (AUTO_DB_BACKUP) = OFF
  Automatic table maintenance       (AUTO_TBL_MAINT) = ON
    Automatic runstats              (AUTO_RUNSTATS) = ON
...
```

The nesting of those labels using spaces is meant to convey the dependent nature of the parameters. So now you know how easy it is to check whether automatic statistics generation is enabled. But what exactly is it doing, and when? To determine this, let's examine the GUI tool for managing automatic RUNSTATS. Each database has an option named Configure Automatic Maintenance in its context menu, and you should choose that option now to invoke the wizard of the same name. You see an introductory dialog box (not shown) that describes how automatic maintenance works, including a reminder that DB2 runs automatic maintenance only when a relevant maintenance window is available and the need for such maintenance has been triggered (for example, the need for RUNSTATS when a table undergoes DDL alteration or large-scale change in data volume).

If you jump to the Timing tab (see Figure 24-8), you see the definition for automatic maintenance windows, in which automated RUNSTATS and other work can run.

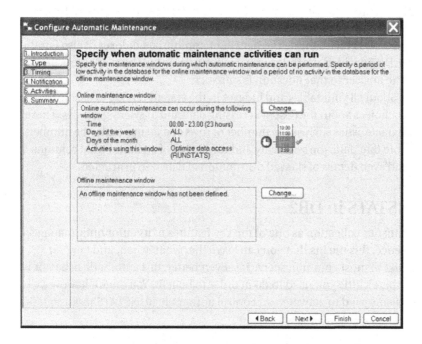

Figure 24-8. *The Timing tab controlling automated RUNSTATS*

Because you understand how time works, I won't give you a tedious description of how to nominate time periods in which maintenance can occur. The default is to allow automated maintenance, including RUNSTATS, at all times. To change this window, click the Change button and configure the dates and times you want nominated as change windows.

Jump to the Activities tab, shown in Figure 24-9, and you'll see a simple list of the categories of maintenance that can be automated. Besides RUNSTATS, you also see BACKUP and REORG.

This is a fairly tame dialog box and almost didn't need a screen shot of its own. I'm sure you would have worked it out without me stating the obvious. But what's important is the Configure Settings button hidden in the lower-right corner. This is the entry point to fine-grained control over exactly which objects have statistics generated when automatic RUNSTATS is in operation. Click the Configure Settings button, and the dialog box shown in Figure 24-10 appears.

Using the selection options provided, you can match schemata, tables, and other sets of objects for multiple users in the database. You can also configure exactly the subset of object for which you want statistics automatically generated. This is very useful when you know that there are certain objects that won't benefit from statistics being regenerated frequently or for those objects for which you want to manually control statistics generation. Examples of such objects include static tables and staging tables that are emptied and reloaded daily.

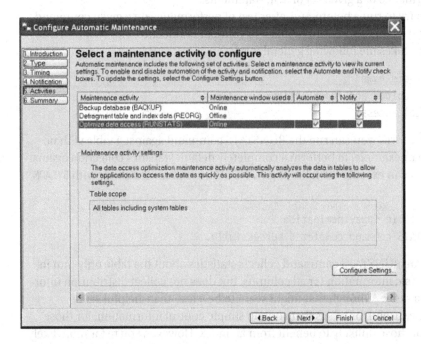

Figure 24-9. *The Timing tab controlling automated RUNSTATS*

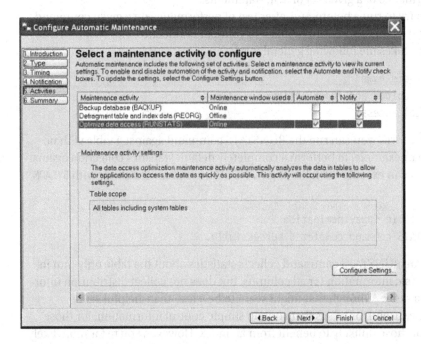

Figure 24-10. *Configuring which objects are targeted by automated RUNSTATS*

Manually Running the RUNSTATS Command

There are times when you'll prefer to use the RUNSTATS command manually, including situations in which you work with very large databases and can't risk even the best estimate that the automated RUNSTATS engine might use for its choice of execution time. You also want to use the manual command for explicit testing of different statistics-collection options and how they affect the performance of a given set of SQL statements.

It's frustrating to try to run a before-and-after test of performance on a given command if you can't control the changes you want to make to your data's statistics. The syntax of the RUNSTATS command takes the following general form:

```
runstats on table table-name
[with distribution, column and index options]
[allow {read | write} access]
```

In its most simple form, you can run the RUNSTATS command against a table with no other options at all. For example, to perform a completely default statistics collection against the nomination table, I can execute the following RUNSTATS command as a user with SYSADM authority:

```
db2 => runstats on table fuzzy.nomination
DB20000I  The RUNSTATS command completed successfully.
```

That version of the RUNSTATS command collects statistics about the table only (not its indexes). It collects basic information for all columns, but does not collect distribution information to detect data skew. Although that might seem to be a less-than-helpful set of statistics, it can be very useful for tables that contain simple control information, for those that are small, and for those unlikely to benefit from an index. However, you're far more likely to have more interesting tables complete with skewed data, several indexes, and other factors that are vital for the optimizer to know. You can collect a range of statistics about the columns' data distribution and index information for any indexes that are in place, but specifying distribution, column, and index options for the RUNSTATS command.

For the nomination table, the nominationid column is a monotonically increasing value, so it will never be skewed. But empno is subject to the fickle nature of people voting for their peers, so it might well have an atypical distribution. The reason column can also be skewed because many people might leave it blank, meaning that there might be a disproportionate number of null values for that column. You can instruct RUNSTATS to model the distribution of both fields, so the optimizer is aware of such a skew:

```
db2 => runstats on table fuzzy.nomination
       with distribution on columns (empno, reason)
DB20000I  The RUNSTATS command completed successfully.
```

Of course, there's a bunch of functionality you've built that accesses the information in the nomination table via an index on empno. You can have RUNSTATS collect a wealth of information about the indexes on the table as well, such as index "height," number of pages at the leaf level, and more. Gathering this index-related information is controlled using the indexes clause. Most often, RUNSTATS should gather statistics about all indexes on a table, which can be shown by example on the nomination table:

```
db2 => runstats on table fuzzy.nomination
        with distribution on columns (empno, reason)
        and detailed indexes all
DB20000I  The RUNSTATS command completed successfully.
```

Finally, you need to be concerned with concurrency when using RUNSTATS. Because RUNSTATS must actively retrieve and work with the data in your system, you might need to consider restricting the changes that other users can make simultaneously, so that your statistics are consistent and not immediately out of date—thanks to changes being made concurrently. Allowing people read access while you generate statistics can be controlled with the ALLOW clause, as follows:

```
db2 => runstats on table fuzzy.nomination
        with distribution on columns (empno, reason)
        and detailed indexes all
        allow read access
DB20000I  The RUNSTATS command completed successfully.
```

Using the REORGCHK and REORG Utilities

There are several physical data-storage issues that can affect database performance in a handful of circumstances. Some major factors to be aware of are how sparsely or densely packed your data is in the pages of the tablespace containers; and whether the data on disk is organized, or *clustered*, to be in the same physical order as the logical order represented by one of your indexes. Clustering the data in a table to match a given index typically benefits all the data access that uses that index. For instance, if a range of values needs to be read for a given table, DB2 prefetch can read contiguous or near-contiguous data on disk, thanks to the data being laid out in accordance with the relevant index.

Whether you want to reorganize your data for space consumption or clustering reasons, you need a technique to let you know whether there are benefits to be had from such work. This is where the reorganization check utility, REORGCHK, comes in handy.

Working with REORGCHK

The REORGCHK utility uses existing database statistics or generates fresh statistics to then prepare a report gauging the relative need or desirability for reorganizing a table or tables. The general form of the REORGCHK command is as follows:

```
reorgchk [ { update | current } statistics ]
[ on { schema | table } details ]
```

The simplest form of the command is to use REORGCHK with no modifiers. It performs a check on all the objects in the currently connected schema and triggers the update statistics option, which performs a RUNSTATS on those objects prior to the REORGCHK. If you have SYSADM or DBADM authority (or CONTROL privilege on a table), you can REORGCHK objects not owned by you.

A more complete example shows the launch of REORGCHK with current statistics and explicitly targets a particular schema. This example targets my tables in the FUZZY schema. I heavily edited the output to show just a few lines, plus the important descriptive information (the REORGCHK report might run for quite a few pages):

```
db2 => reorgchk current statistics on schema fuzzy

Table statistics:

F1: 100 * OVERFLOW / CARD < 5
F2: 100 * (Effective Space Utilization of Data Pages) > 70
F3: 100 * (Required Pages / Total Pages) > 80


SCHEMA.NAME                    CARD    OV    NP    FP ACTBLK    TSIZE  F1  F2  F3 REORG
--------------------------------------------------------------------------------------
...
Table: FUZZY.CUSTOMER             6     0     1     1      -      648   0   - 100 ---
Table: FUZZY.DEPARTMENT          14     0     1     1      -      840   0   - 100 ---
Table: FUZZY.EMPLOYEE            42     0     1     1      -     3696   0   - 100 ---
...
Table: FUZZY.NOMINATION       87682     0   322   322      -  2542778   0  97 100 ---
Table: FUZZY.ORG                  -     -     -     -      -        -   -   -   - ---
Table: FUZZY.PRIZES               -     -     -     -      -        -   -   -   - ---
Table: FUZZY.PRODUCT              4     0     1     1      -      748   0   - 100 ---
...


Index statistics:

F4: CLUSTERRATIO or normalized CLUSTERFACTOR > 80
F5: 100 * (Space used on leaf pages / Space available on non-empty leaf pages) >
    MIN(50, (100 - PCTFREE))
F6: (100 - PCTFREE) * (Amount of space available in an index with one less level /
    Amount of space required for all keys) < 100
F7: 100 * (Number of pseudo-deleted RIDs / Total number of RIDs) < 20
F8: 100 * (Number of pseudo-empty leaf pages / Total number of leaf pages) < 20
SCHEMA.NAME                INDCARD LEAF ELEAF LVLS NDEL KEYS LEAF_RECSIZE NLEAF...
AGE_OVERHEAD NLEAF_PAGE_OVERHEAD  F4   F5   F6   F7   F8 REORG
--------------------------------------------------------------------------------------
-----------------------------------------------------------
...
Table: FUZZY.AWARD_RESULT
Index: FUZZY.AWARD_RESULT_PAIRS    1     1     0    1     0    1           19    14
         694                     800 100     -    -     0    0 -----
...
Table: FUZZY.NOMINATION
Index: FUZZY.NOM_EMPNO         89873    99     0    2     0   42            6     6
        1174                   1174  85    91    -    0    0 -----
...
```

I won't pretend that REORGCHK generates aesthetically pleasing output. But the report is very useful. The report is split into two sections, based on table metrics and then index metrics. Each of the metrics—such as F1, F2, and so on—is explained briefly in the output. So F3 measures the ratio of minimum required pages to store the current data in a table to the actual number of pages used. The definition suggests that this should be above 70 percent (that is, no more than 30 percent free space should exist). When one of the formulae has its threshold exceeded, the REORG column shows an asterisk in the position related to the formula. So if the nomination table has hundreds of additional free pages allocated for storage, the npages value can be something like 700, and the REORGCHK line looks like this:

```
Table: FUZZY.NOMINATION   87682     0   700    322     -   2542778   0  97 100 --*
```

The asterisk in the third position for the table means that the F3 formula's threshold has been exceeded, and therefore the nomination table should be considered for reorganization. In this case, it's pretty obvious that you can free up space and avoid unnecessary scanning of empty pages by releasing the free space back to the tablespace container.

Working with REORG

Thanks to REORGCHK, you know of a table that could hypothetically benefit from reorganizing its data. Such reorganization is the job of the REORG utility. The REORG command has quite a number of permutations and options that would have a syntax diagram that spills over an entire page. You'll look at two of the main options for table and index reorganization, and then add a few of the common modifiers to give you a good grounding in its use. To reorganize the nomination table, you can run the REORG utility in its basic form:

```
db2 => reorg table fuzzy.nomination
DB20000I  The REORG command completed successfully.
```

That REORG invocation reorganizes the data in the pages, but usually means that other users of the table will have only read access, no specific clustering will be performed, and the reorganization will be performed in one go (with no restart control). REORG provides options to address all these areas, so let's add them to see what a more comprehensive REORG would look like:

```
db2 => reorg table fuzzy.nomination index nom_empno inplace allow write access start
DB20000I  The REORG command completed successfully.
DB21024I  This command is asynchronous and may not be effective immediately.
```

The new and improved REORG command reorganizes the data to free excessive unused pages, clusters the data by the order of the nom_empno index, and allows other users to have full write access to the table during the process. The default start option was explicitly chosen because near-identical commands replacing start with pause, stop, or resume can be issued. Because you're allowing full write access, DB2 also warns you that normal users take priority over the REORG command, and it operates asynchronously until it completes (or until you stop it). It's also possible that if this table resides in a DMS tablespace, the additional space required to perform the reorganization will exhaust the allocated space. For these cases, you can employ the USE clause with a system temporary tablespace to instruct DB2 to use the temporary tablespace as the working area and guarantee that no additional space will be required in the original tablespace.

There are times when your tables report no problems from REORGCHK, but one or more indexes do. In these cases, you don't necessarily want to reorganize the underlying data because that might take excessive time. Instead, you just want to target the indexes. REORG has options to do just that:

```
db2 => reorg indexes all for table nomination allow read access cleanup only
DB20000I  The REORG command completed successfully.
```

Here, you allow only read access on the table and indexes while the reorganization takes place and also use the index-specific cleanup only option to flush only unused pages from the index instead of completely rebuilding it from scratch. You can achieve such a rebuild by omitting that option.

To finish the reorganization work, I'll put your mind at ease by confirming that reorganization for tables and indexes is available in graphical form from the Control Center. Each table has a Reorganize and Reorganize Indexes option in the context menu. This launches a simple dialog box to control reorganization (see Figure 24-11).

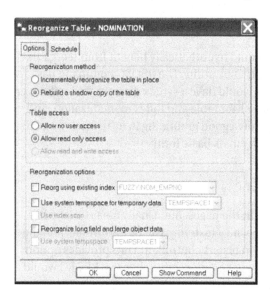

Figure 24-11. *The graphical interface for REORG*

You can explore the options in the GUI and click the Show Command button to explore the equivalent command-line version. The Incrementally Reorganize The Table In Place option has an equivalent option from the command line called the INPLACE option. This option allows users to continue writing to a table that is undergoing REORG and can be invaluable when dealing with very large tables that take considerable time to execute the REORG command.

Summary

You've now finished a marathon chapter on monitoring and performance tuning for your DB2 environment. Again, each topic raised in this chapter can be taken further, and I encourage you to work on slowly but surely extending your knowledge of each tool and utility presented because together they form a formidable arsenal in any database administrator's repertoire.

This also completes the last chapter of this book, and I think you'll agree that you've come a long way from the first actions of clicking a link to download the DB2 software. I hope you've enjoyed reading *Beginning DB2: From Novice to Professional* as much as I enjoyed writing it—and that your interest in DB2 only grows from here!

Index

You Need the Companion eBook